HEART OF A WARRIOR
THE TRUE SAGA OF SWEET BREEZE & WILLIAM WELLS

by
JOE KROM

Eel River Traders
Publishers
10610 18th Rd.
Argos, Indiana 46501
www.eelrivertraders.com

Permission requests: info@eelrivertraders.com

Library of Congress Control Number: 2008908914

ISBN-10:   0-615-22568-3
ISBN-13: 978-0-615-22568-5

Published by Eel River Traders, Argos, IN

Cover design and cover art by Ryan Fish
Maps by Ryan Fish

Printed in the United States of America
Printed and distributed by Evangel Press
2000 Evangel Way
Nappanee, IN 46550
800-253-9315
www.EvangelAuthorServices.com

TABLE OF CONTENTS

CHAPTER 1
The Lake

The first rays of the sun had revealed a wisp of fog hovering above the lake, promising a break from the oppressing heat. It was not to be. The sun rose and the heat rose with it. By midday the sun parched the earth. Turtles lay on their logs and their rocks as still as the air. Frogs crouched with their backs in the water with only heads exposed. All was quiet as the animals of the forest melted into the brush, not one bird sang his song. Near the opposite shore of the lake, mallards dipped to the bottom to feed, generating ripples that spread across the placid water.

A sharp crash sent turtles darting like arrows into the cool water. Only a cloud of sand and mud remained where frogs had been. The reverberation sent ducks thundering, squawking as they beat their wings to take flight, their wingtips whipping the lake to turmoil. The whole world had been awakened by some sudden disturbance.

She, "I once saw a fox fighting a stag elk."

He, "Oh," he played along with her game, "how did it play out?"

"The fox circled the elk; the elk put his nose to the earth and his tines to the fox. They went around such that they could have started a tornado."

"Did you get caught up in the tornado?"

"No, but they worked their way down the bank and right into the lake. The elk was lunging, the fox dancing aside."

"That must have been a sight."

"Indeed, but those beasts did not make such a commotion as you charging into the lake as you did!"

He pushed through the water to her. She made a feint to the side while holding her birch bark bucket high overhead to protect its delicate cargo from his splashing. He grabbed her around the waist and swooped his free hand behind her knees, freeing her feet from the sand. She was disappointed to see her bucket of cattail pollen fall and scatter upon the now boiling surface. She was not disappointed with the speed and grace

1

of his strength as he transported her to the beach and laid her upon the hide. She had carefully laid out the deer hide and had prepared mussel-shell receptacles for tiny grains of gathered pollen to dry in the sun. The calmness of the air and the bright sun presented a perfect presence for preparing spices and medicines. Now the hide was in disarray, and the shells held sand and grass. As she looked directly into the sun overhead, she put aside her plans for the day. Cattail pollen was plentiful anyway.

She thought on how gently he had placed her here, taking care to position her on her side to protect her bulging belly. It was a joy to be his wife. She made a vow to herself to provide him with all his needs. How she yearned that the new life that would emerge from her would be a boy, the strong boy that he deserved. But for now, she would rest beside him in the full of the day.

He ran his finger over her arm from her elbow up the sleeve of her tunic. How could she have gooseflesh on such a day as this? This lake certainly remained cooler than most, but her arm had barely been splashed. Would she be upset that he caused her doeskin to get wet? That meant extra work to soften it. He chuckled aloud at his own thoughts; she had not once complained in his presence. She always went about her daily tasks with cheer, even amusement.

He pushed her wet skirt up and wiped the dampness from her thigh with his palm. He was amazed at his own fascination with the touch of her skin, its color and shadow, its smoothness and shape, its firmness and tenderness. He was glad that the water had not washed away the smell of her skin, a scent filled with mystery. Why was this so alluring? Had he not admired the beauty of the elk, the deer, the bear, and especially the panther? Had he not studied their elegant movements? What marvelous creatures he had beheld in the forest. Neither man nor woman had revealed this same beauty before she had drawn close to him.

He pondered this attraction while gazing at the tiny pools of lingering moisture on the back of her leg. Was he perplexed by her natural beauty, or was it her charm? Perhaps it was her way of moving. She did have a special way of walking, kneeling, and stoking a fire. Most of all he was surprised by his own tenderness towards her. The warmness of the sun was driving away the coolness he had enjoyed from the dip in the lake. His thoughts meshed together in his half-conscious state. No line of thought could survive to a conclusion.

He felt a twitch of her muscle. She made a slight gasp. Before he could fully focus on the meaning of it she said softly, but with a start, "Pottawatomie!"

He followed her gaze up the slope to where they were. A band of Pottawatomie warriors were surveying them, hardly a stone's throw away. Instincts put him on his feet immediately. Stepping in front of his young wife he stood erect. She rose slowly and stepped back to where fish were smoking over the fire. She began to methodically make motions of tending to her chores.

"I am Metea, chief of the Pottawatomie beyond the Tippecanoe!" The voice was loud, firm and solid. "Who is it that makes his camp on this lake of the Pottawatomie?"

He spoke in his own tongue, his face stern and his eyes piercing. Metea quickly sized up the little scene. A white man, darkly tanned, lean and strong though average height for his race, stood totally naked before him. His fiery red hair revealed that he was not a Frenchman; perhaps he was a Canadian trapper or a deserter from the English army. His slim, obviously pregnant companion was of one of the tribes. Her tribal attachment was not revealed by her unadorned doeskin nor by her uncombed hair hanging to her waist.

The hillside on this south side of the lake was open grasses, save for one huge walnut tree. Between the tree and the lake were three small structures in a miniature vale. Two were domed wigwams with the lower part fashioned from reeds and bark, the top covered with white canvas. The third had stone walls plastered with mud, the roof made of logs and bark. Behind these was a spring that had been improved with stone to retain a reservoir, a trickle descending to the lake. Beyond the spring was a patch of tobacco. Behind this developed the natural pattern of the forest, first were blackberry brambles, then sumac leading into a dense stand of mixed hardwood trees.

The lake was pristine, sparkling as a jewel in the bright sun. A natural bowl of hills formed a wide rim with no apparent inlet other than a few tiny springs, not bubbling eruptions, but mere seeps. Fingers of prairie broke through the wooded rim of the lake. The sod was thick with brown grasses, shorter than on the meadows from which this band had emerged. Near the pond, the sod gave way to sandy gravel that could be seen well into the depths of the lake. No other encampments were to be seen.

Metea's eyes quickly darted around the landscape and back to the persons before him, assessing every hint of evidence. They were alone, these two. He was obviously bare of weapons, actually bare of every-thing. A manicured rifle rested against a ramada of sticks used for tan-ning skins; shotbag, horn, and a sheathed knife hung alongside.

The cooking apparatus was iron. Iron and copper utensils mingled with those of gourd, bark, and wood. The one abnormal element to Metea's eye was the unnatural cleanliness and organization of the layout. He concluded by the workmanship of the huts that the girl was Miami. The man must certainly have once been in the English military. Metea looked deep into the man's eyes. He expected to detect signs of fear, but there was none to be found.

The red-haired man was looking directly back into Metea's eyes. He was not looking around for weapons or escape. He was not surveying the leader's companions. His gaze was pure and deep.

"I am the one known as Wild Carrot," the man said.

The words were firm and deliberate, no quaking in the voice, no quivering in the stance.

He continued loudly, "I am warrior of Little Turtle. I have taken coup upon Pottawatomie warriors. I was at the side of Little Turtle when we slew the Virginian invaders at Pumpkinheads."

Metea uncharacteristically broke his stoic stare and let his mouth curl a bit at the name of the battle. He knew why the defeat of the Virginians and the American regulars at the head of the Maumee was known as Pumpkinheads. In the aftermath, the enemy's heads lay in the autumn fields as do ripe pumpkins.

He lightly smiled in admiration of the courage of this man with long red hair. The position of the Pottawatomie was superior in all ways. They were on the upslope and six in number, plus the boy. They were mount-ed; Wild Carrot's feet were planted upon the earth. They had arms aplenty, though only one brandished his rifle aloft and another had secured an arrow from his quiver; Wild Carrot's lay eight strides away. They were overdressed for the occasion with full regalia of their status; he was without clothes or adornment, save the small medicine bag that hung about his neck.

Metea knew that the bravado of the man was neither lying nor brag-ging. Only a Miami warrior would stand unnerved while naked before a potential foe. Nakedness was the natural state of the Miami male. Wearing at most a breechcloth during the warm season, most warriors would discard even that for battle. Metea tried to picture him prepared for battle with hair shaved and plucked save for a blackened queue, his

4

body painted in the Miami black and red, weapon belt around his waist, tomahawk raised.

"It is true," said a comrade with three feathers that point downward on the left side of his head. He nudged his horse nearer the chief, "I have seen this man in battle."

Metea immediately shifted his eyes, his stare halting the companion, who backed off and returned to his place.

Wild Carrot knew instinctively that to leap for his weapons was to invite a brutal death for himself and death or captivity for his bride. This was no time to be agitated that he let himself get into this fix. Together, the two of them had drilled for this very situation: on the beach without weapons, trapped by man or beast. He would stand his ground and face the foe without either defiance or submissiveness. She would calmly ignore the intruder and go to the drying racks where a shield and spear were disguised as part of the apparatus. With his code words, "Fish, bring some fish," she was to raise the shield and walk backwards to the light canoe hidden in the rushes. He would rush past her and launch the canoe. The spear was more to make the enemy hesitate than to serve as an actual defense. It would be a risky escape at best. They would need a few furious strokes to be relatively safe with the shield held high in the rear of the vessel. Having cleared the shore, they could easily reach the cache of weapons and food on the opposite side before anyone or anything could round the lake.

Wild Carrot need not glance at his weapons or his wife. These Pottawatomie were not renegade bandits. Their dress and manner displayed that they were noble men of their tribe. The order of the day was to stand his ground unequivocally. While all Pottawatomie were unpredictable, he knew that they would respect bravery and despise cowardice. The Miami nation had called a truce with the Pottawatomie to drive out the Virginian invaders from across the Ohio River. However, the Pottawatomie villages were loosely aligned, unlike the Miami nation. Pottawatomie chiefs and warrior bands were not bound to a national agenda.

His wife made busy turning fish on the smoke rack. She kept her eyes low, neither on her husband nor on the intruders. Her mind was reaching to send thoughts to Wild Carrot, though she dare not speak. "Tell them! Tell them that I am Sweet Breeze, daughter of the great chief Little Turtle! Tell them that the full power of the Miami, the Wea, and the Piankashaw will be upon them if we are harmed."

Wild Carrot continued in his bold manner, "You said that this is a Pottawatomie lake. You are mistaken. These waters flow southward to the Eel River," his right hand motioned in the direction of the small outlet.

A chief of the Pottawatomie would know that the Eel drainage was considered Miami habitat during the truce. Many nearby lakes and ponds to the north and west did drain towards Pottawatomie villages along the Tippecanoe River.

Metea was not interested in a squabble over a hunting camp on one of the hundreds of lakes in the region. Larger matters weighed on his mind. He surmised that he now knew this red-haired Miami warrior.

The Pottawatomie chief tested him, "What is your village, Miami warrior?"

The reply, "I am the son of Porcupine, village chief of Eel Town."

Now satisfied, Metea turned to his companions and motioned with his right hand. Focusing back towards Wild Carrot, Metea raised his right hand to his chin, palm down, and announced, "We will parley, you and I."

This said, he dismounted with the ease of a great horseman. The others then dismounted and handed their reins to the boy. Three of the warriors were serving as seconds to the chiefs. Two of these watched with weapons in hand as the third gathered a fancy blanket. Running forward, he caught up to Metea and spread the blanket where indicated under the walnut tree.

Wild Carrot kept stiffness to his posture as he took his place upon the blanket opposite the man that was much younger than he had first supposed. The attending warrior trotted up the slope to the place where the small band was now reclining. He brought back a gourd of water and a pouch of nuts which he laid upon a scarf beside the chief. Sweet Breeze observed this and brought a bowl of tea and a bowl of miniature cakes to her man. She took as many steps behind Wild Carrot as the attendant had taken behind Metea before sitting in the grass.

Sun and shadows danced through the boughs, at times glistening on silver drooping in four loops from each ear of the Pottawatomie. Five feathers protruded upright in a fan shape on the rear of his head. All hair had been plucked from the front half of his small head. Lines of tattooing that began on his forehead continued down his neck, disappearing behind a loose linen blouse of blue. A heavy silver ring hung under his nose. A small bronze gorget, engraved in the English way, hung from his neck by a leather thong. A second necklace of multicolored glass beads complemented it. His medicine bag was tucked inside the blouse. A sash of wide red cloth was knotted about his waist; the weapon belt had been removed. Buckskin leggings were unadorned, but the moccasins had fine quillwork of many colors. The apparel stated that he held status among his people.

Metea drank and ate silently while looking out over the waters. Since they were sitting upon Metea's blanket, it was his place to speak first. He had offered no tobacco, therefore it was to be an informal parley. Wild Carrot set his bowls aside and brushed dried grass from his feet.

Finally, Metea spoke, "I see that it is as dry in your country as it is in ours."

"The grass cries for rain. The beans have been poor, yet the corn thrives. The creeks run at a trickle making trapping difficult."

"You have chosen your camp well. The spring flows, the lake shines, the cool air stays below the hills." Metea gestured with a sweeping wave.

Yes, he knew that he had chosen well. Yet he wondered how these travelers had happened this way. He had been careful to make no trail to the lake. The small stream from the outlet was choked with brush. Corn patches were scattered out of view of the little lake valley. He had chosen for utility, beauty, and secrecy. He took the mention of "your country" and "your camp" to be a retreat from Metea's opening demand.

Metea was anxious to hear a first-hand account about the battle at the three rivers. He had heard stories of the great victory and was disappointed that he had been denied doing battle with the Americans.

He inquired in as casual a voice as he could muster, "Tell me about Pumpkinheads."

Wild Carrot nodded and began his discourse in the Pottawatomie tongue, "This was a great battle, actually two battles. Not like the raids across the Ohio into the lands of Kentucky. It was greater than the defeat of LaBalme, even comparable to the defeat of General Braddock and General Washington at the Forks of the Ohio."

The name "Washington" was always "General Washington" to him though Washington was far from being a general during the French and Indian War. He loved the stories told in the council house about the great victory over the English. Little Turtle, as a youth, had gone with his father and other Miami to join with the French in protecting Fort Duquesne from the English invaders. Little Turtle's assignment was to hold the horses during the battle. This seemingly meager task was a special honor among young men of the tribe, allowing travel with the warriors and chiefs and access to the battlefields. From high on a bluff, Little Turtle could clearly view the redcoats routed and driven back upon themselves in total disarray. Washington's later fame in driving the English from the colonies during the American Revolution added weight to the telling of the Fort Duquesne victory.

It was during the War of American Revolution that Little Turtle's status as a war chief was elevated by his defeat of LaBalme. Colonel Augustin de LaBalme, inspired by George Rogers Clark's success on the frontier, recruited a company of French settlers in the Illinois lands. His objective was the British post of Detroit. Whether his was the American cause or his personal desire to establish a renewed French domain was indiscernible. Carrying the American banner, he ascended the Wabash River and sacked the Miami towns at Kekionga. Needing supplies, he detoured towards DeRicherville's trading post on the Eel River. Little Turtle's sister, Talking Bird, operated the post in the absence of her long-gone husband.

Little Turtle determined to avenge the attack on Kekionga and to protect the lightly fortified post of DeRicherville. Three hundred Miami warriors pinned the invaders in a meadow on a bluff overlooking the Eel River. A hatchet deep in the skull of LaBalme ended his days far from the palaces of his native land. Had he been a better diplomat and less of a soldier, his plan may have born fruit. Did not the tribes always search for peace where possible? Did not generations of Miami welcome the French, encouraging their trade and giving their daughters in marriage? The Miami of Little Turtle suffered only minor casualties in the affair, elevating the village chief to be elected war chief of the Miami nation.

Metea nodded in acknowledgement at the mention of these two famous battles of recent times. Sweet Breeze, straining to hear, recalled her father telling these stories. She visualized each in her mind, tracing the routes and events as described during her childhood. As she traveled with her father, he would stop at a landmark and say, "Remember this place. This is where …", then describe in detail events important to him and to his nation. How she revered these landmarks; how she treasured these stories!

Wild Carrot saw Metea's eagerness to listen. He continued, "Ten winters had passed from the defeat of LaBalme to this greatest of battles in the lands of the Wabash tribes. It was the greatest of battles from the Ohio to the grand lakes called Erie, Huron, and Michigan."

The hook was set. Now began the saga, "In the year past, at the time of the dogwood blossoms, an ambassador by name of Antoine Gamelin, who is well known to us as is his brother Pierre of Vincennes, arrived at Kekionga. He visited each of the six villages that make up the community along the St. Joseph, the St. Marys, and the Maumee rivers. He toured the ruins of old French Town. He inspected the dilapidated English fort. He was received at the Kekionga great council house. He brought meager gifts of tobacco, rum, and copper bells. He brought writing on paper from the commander of the Americans at Vincennes."

"I, being the interpreter for Little Turtle and for all the Miami, studied the paper and confirmed Gamelin's words. General Washington and General Knox in the east had directed the Vincennes post to seek peace with the tribes of the Wabash country. The Americans asked for an end to raids in the lands of Kentucky and on the Virginians along the Ohio. The Americans offered to control the Virginians and establish courts of justice. They would establish trade reaching from Kekionga along the Wabash, Ohio, and the great river Mississippi to New Orleans. The chiefs in council realized that the Wabash route would be preferred and would generate revenue at the Miami portage. All agreed, however, that trade with the English at Detroit was good and Spanish trade on the Mississippi could be obtained across the plains of the Illinois country. It was determined to refuse the peace offer. Chief LeGris instructed Gamelin that if he returned to the council before winter with a paper from General Washington stating that the Ohio River would be a line between his country and the lands of the tribes, that settlers on the north side would be relocated to the south, and that no new settlers or armies would appear on the north, then the chiefs would go to Vincennes for council."

Metea knew these things, but also knew that a good storyteller need prepare the soil for the story to grow. Sweet Breeze smiled profusely at the mention of her man standing within the midst of the council house speaking for each side. She knew only a few words of the Pottawatomie, but she knew the story well. She could fill in around the names of the characters and places. She was constantly amazed at his ability to understand papers from either the English or the French. He could calculate their numbers and also put the marks on paper. He could effortlessly speak with people from more tribes than anyone else she knew. She was limited to her Miami and French. She could communicate with the Delaware, and had picked up some phrases of other tongues from the many visitors to her town.

9

"Alexander McKee and Simon Girty appeared at Kekionga wearing the uniform of the English soldiers. They brought medals and many gifts. McKee said that Gamelin would not return. The English spies in the east had heard General Washington's council declare war against the Miami. The Americans would send an army from Vincennes up the Wabash to punish the Miami for waging war on the Virginians. If the Miami did not sue for peace, we would be pushed into the waters of the great lakes to the north. General Washington wanted to make his camp where Kekionga now stands. He would quench our hallowed council fire and thrust his sword in the ground of its ashes."

The smile was gone from the face of Sweet Breeze. She set her teeth at the retelling of this greatest of insults. This was not only an insult to her people, but to their cousins the Wea and the Piankashaw. Even the Delaware, who in ancient times had left the Miami camp and migrated east, revered the Kekionga council fire. Her mind turned to seeing the wretched Delaware refugees being welcomed back at Kekionga. Many settled in the surrounding Miami villages and towns. Others were allowed to form new villages on the White River to the south.

"Shawnee and Miami scouting parties, intent on pillaging river boats, reported regular troops traveling down the Ohio. Piankashaw spies from the village of Crooked Legs confirmed troops and supplies had been moved up the Wabash to Vincennes. Major Hamtramck was improving the fortifications of Fort Knox at Vincennes. Worst of all, light cannon were included in the cargo. A small force of troops was also drilling at Fort Washington near where the Great Miami River empties into the Ohio at its north bend. Girty said the Shawnee had frequently raided the village of Cincinnati a short distance from the fort. The garrison was constantly harassed and was powerless to move into the field.

"McKee and Girty came a second time, joined by a man named Elliott. They brought with them soldiers with boats carrying quality guns, lead, flints, and powder along with many gifts. They vowed to supply all tribes who would stop the Americans on the lower Wabash. Girty said that a man by the name of Scott had been made a general of the Virginians and would bring many horsemen to support Hamtramck's Vincennes garrison. Girty charged all of the tribes of the Wabash to rendezvous at Ouiatenon. This was done in the time of the red sumac, as the Pottawatomie know."

Metea signaled for more water as dry air was pushing over the brink of the hill. The entourage up the hill was preparing a gambling game.

The boy was wondering if he should take the horses to the lake, but was afraid to move or ask. Sweet Breeze leaned as close as she dared. Wild Carrot sipped his tea and shifted his weight.

"I was with Porcupine and Old Wolf and their warriors from Eel Town. We camped upstream from Ouiatenon on the same side as the old French town, opposite the Wea village. In two days we were joined by the warriors from Turtle Town and their great chief. Waters were good for travel."

Metea's nod indicated that he had participated and remembered the good flow of the rivers.

"Miami and Delaware continually arrived from the Eel, the Mississinewa, the Salamonie. Kekionga warriors arrived with the English guns and two canoes with McKee and English soldiers. Pottawatomie from the Tippecanoe and overland from the north country camped below the town. When the Piankashaw and Kickapoo entered the Wea villages, a grand council was held. Many calumets were exchanged in the long house."

Metea had visited Vincennes often and knew Major John Francis Hamtramck well. He knew him as a fine military man and a good representative of General Washington. His thoughts were that the officer had done well working for justice for the tribes. This man was not controlled by the despised Virginians. Metea had not been privy to the business of the head chiefs. He was thinking more about the feasting, the racing and wrestling, and the Wea women of the Ouiatenon villages.

Sweet Breeze observed that the chief's second sat without expression, without movement. She rose and took Wild Carrot's cup for refill and drank a refreshing gulp in the process. She reclined a stride closer upon returning.

"The Americans and Virginians began the invasion, though with hardly more than three hundred men in arms. They moved slowly from Vincennes with boats and horses loaded with supplies. It required ten days' march up the Wabash for them to reach the Vermillion River, one day's march from the lower Wea towns. This was also one day's march from the trap set by the many tribes at the great bend of the Wabash. One day's march and each of the soldiers would find three tomahawks sunk into his body. At the Vermillion, the Virginians argued among themselves. The march stalled and Hamtramck turned about. The Virginians went their own way back to the Kentucky lands. Since the Piankashaw chiefs had moved their families and belongings up the

Vermillion, Hamtramck went to his fort with no prize."

Now Metea agonized anew at the confusion that followed the collapse of the trap. How many of the bands swarmed about the retreating Americans, trying to set a new trap. How they had hung about the fort hoping for a chance to destroy this cowardly enemy. He quickly put his disgust behind him, for now the tale would be beyond his knowledge. Wild Carrot observed the Pottawatomie chief was now uncharacteristically looking down at the blanket, ignoring his surroundings, leaning to the words being spoken.

"Little Turtle left the pursuit to be carried by the Wea as he determined to fall back to Eel Town for a council of all Miami chiefs. Black Loon and fifty warriors continued up the Wabash to support the few with Pecan protecting the three rivers villages. Canoes had just been unloaded at Porcupine's village when runners brought word from Black Loon. That party had encountered three Delaware who had rushed down from the Mississinewa to find Little Turtle. The message was that the Americans from Fort Washington on the Ohio were on the move up the Great Miami River. There were many soldiers under General Harmar, and a great many mounted Virginians. The number must be well over one thousand in all. They had pushed far north into the forests and had not been stopped by the Shawnee and Wyandot tribes. The message could not be more shocking! There was not time to verify the report. Little Turtle immediately sent half of his force across the neck to the Wabash to join Black Loon. He led the remainder of us up the Eel to his town. We raced ahead on foot with materials to follow by canoe. We reached Turtle Town during the night to hear terrible reports."

That had been the most terrible day and night in the life of Sweet Breeze. Women and children were pouring into Turtle Town from the three rivers villages. Stories spread about a monstrous army with long swords, with rifles and cannon, and a thousand horses coming from the south. Panic had sent some family members in this direction and some in that. English traders had beaten a hasty retreat to the Elk Heart villages to the north. Old men stayed behind to torch the three major villages, even the council house, should the army appear. They would burn everything to deny the invaders substance and booty. With the warriors gone, how could even Turtle Town be protected? Families were preparing to move to their winter hunting camps on the many lakes to the north.

Her mother had directed Sweet Breeze to rally neighbors to stay and begin cooking as much food as possible. Refugees would be hungry and those proceeding farther north would need two days' provisions. When Little Turtle arrived home, as her mother Tulip Leaf knew that he surely would, he would need to fill his stomach before preparing the defense. Her mother then went about consoling hysteric travelers and locating shelter. Sweet Breeze wanted to be firm like her mother, but felt her nerves failing. Twice she had to slip away to empty the contents from her stomach. The world she knew had suddenly collapsed. She had wanted to leave everything and begin walking north. She had begun to cry uncontrollably just as Wild Carrot came over the bank from the river leading a handful of warriors. Then another group arrived, and soon Little Turtle with his escort. The men grabbed food and held a quick discussion short of the town long house.

"The great war chief set up a war camp on the site of LaBalme's dying field. Runners were sent to find the position of the enemy and to establish contact with Black Loon, and any Delaware or Shawnee camps. An advance camp was placed midway down the portage to the St. Marys and one on the trail to the Elk Heart lands. At sunrise runners were returning with reconnaissance. The enemy was of even greater numbers than had been told by the Delaware messengers, perhaps one thousand five hundred in number. Many Virginians were already across the Maumee poking through the burning buildings. The American regulars and the majority of Virginians were making camp a bit to the south from whence they came.

"Black Loon was moving into position to block the portage to the Wabash. From here he could harass the enemy from the west, or move north to support Little Turtle. Shawnee and Delaware warriors were being concentrated to the east on the Maumee. The enemy was too strong to be attacked directly, so a network of scouts was to observe their movements and report to the main camp. The day passed with no troop movements. The enemy was content to loot what remained of Kekionga and began methodically destroying the ripened corn standing in the fields. Pockets of the volunteers from the Kentucky lands were digging for 'Indian treasure' among the ruins.

"At the high sun of the second day a company of Virginians, numbering over three hundred, set out in the direction of Turtle Town, into the Miami strength. Our forces were keen to defend Turtle Town. To allow the enemy any successful excursions from their base would be to invite complete devastation. Warriors who had anticipated meeting the

13

invaders far down the Wabash were now confronted in the midst of their home lands. Each warrior inspected his weapons once again while thinking about his mother, sisters, wife and children who were trusting in his protection. This foray must not merely be stopped, but hacked to pieces. However, the enemy did not march directly up the portage, but meandered to the left and the right. They proceeded slowly, so slowly. When the sun became low in the sky, these men broke up and fell back to their comrades. Our hearts cried out, 'Come! Fight! Visit the fury of a Miami warrior!' But we were denied. Only a few scouts of Black Loon skirmished and killed three with a loss of two."

Metea could easily relate to the anticipation of overwhelming an enemy bent on destruction, only to have the opportunity vanish. In the forest it was common to have wild game evade well-laid traps. To have these arrogant murderers escape again was hard to bear. These same thoughts were clouding the head of the chief's assistant, now enthralled with the tale. Sweet Breeze lowered her eyes so that the others would not see them swelling with water.

"A great war dance was held that night on the dying field of LaBalme. The chiefs lit a council fire on a bluff of the Eel upstream from the trading post. The calumet of the Miami was brought. The passing of the calumet was very somber. Each chief smoked and had his say. Little Turtle then declared the battle plan. The one Delaware village chief knew the words of the Miami, and I translated for two lower chiefs of the Shawnee."

Wild Carrot paused long enough to gain the desired suspense. He said, "I will tell you what was heard at the battle council." He looked up to the tree limbs and assumed a low husky voice as he spoke the words of Little Turtle.

"Do not anticipate support from our allies to the north or the west as these are engaging the Americans at Vincennes. In the east we have had no word from the English soldiers, nor from Blue Jacket of the Shawnee. A camp of two hundred on the plains of the Maumee consists of Shawnee and braves from the Erie lands and Canada. They anchor a great arc of camps that reach north and west across the St. Joseph to this place. The arc continues to the south, reaching the St. Marys at the beaver ponds of the portage to the Wabash. Delaware scouts are patrolling the south branch of the Wabash, the Salamonie, and the Mississinewa. They have reported to Black Loon that there are no soldiers in that area. Our braves are eager for battle, well armed and well fed.

14

"The army of the enemy holds two soldiers opposed to each one of our warriors. If more soldiers appear from the south, we must not allow them to join the enemy camp on the Maumee. Upon learning of more soldiers approaching, Black Loon's forces will strike the marching soldiers while the remainder makes a direct attack on the main camp.

"The soldiers must not be allowed to construct a log fort. It appears that they will not, as no cannon have yet been seen. However, at the first indication of felling of great trees a signal will be given. Runners will notify all villages to evacuate far to the north. My forces will consolidate with those of Black Loon. We will make a surprise attack on the enemy camp from the south! I will name chiefs to engage the Americans while the militia is driven against the Maumee. Separated from the regulars and with the river at their backs, the volunteers will surely panic and scatter. Individuals and bands must be hunted to their death. Chiefs must not allow warriors to stop the pursuit to gather booty. All plunder will be distributed in ceremony at a later time. Reunited forces will then drive the diminished American army back to their fort on the Ohio.

"The American General Harmar has come a long distance to this land. If no fort is built to hold the ground, then the army will need to fall back whence they came for want of supplies. To retreat without doing battle would be a dishonor to the General. To find our strength he will probe to the north, then towards the Wabash. We will trap and smash each excursion, frustrating him while sapping his strength and unnerving his men. In his fury he will strike out unwisely. It is then that the Miami will press their weight upon him! Our warriors are taut and poised to strike, but our chiefs must hold them in the camps until the trap is set."

The storyteller raised his hands and clapped them overhead. Relaxing, he took a moment to soothe his throat with some tea.

"You have heard what Little Turtle told the chiefs. The stars were bright as the calumet of the Miami was passed once more under the sycamores. Not one stood to speak; each only nodded in acquiescence to the battle plan after he had drawn the tobacco smoke. A look of resolve was passed around the circle along with the pipe."

The chief on the blanket with Wild Carrot was now himself nodding. Metea knew that Pottawatomie warriors would not be restrained with a hated enemy camped in their homelands. He glanced at the two chiefs up the hill who were intent on their game. One of their assistants and the boy were now taking the horses down to the beach. Two packhorses that had been tied in the timber were being led forward by the other chief's second. At the crest of the hill he slid off some packs of furs and let them plop to the ground.

It was not a habit of Wild Carrot to share with a potential enemy how Little Turtle and the Miami chiefs made war strategy. However, these were indeed unusual times. The Miami and Pottawatomie would need to rally mutual support against the ruthless Americans who were certain to push north again soon. Perhaps one day this visitor would stand and speak in council with his fellow chiefs persuading them to follow the great chief Little Turtle.

"Scouts brought word at the first light of the sun that an armed company was preparing to cross to the north side of the Maumee. They numbered over two hundred, of which soldiers in uniform numbered thirty. It was soon discovered that the invaders were headed north on the trading trail that proceeds to the Elk Heart lands. Little Turtle acted quickly, placing two camps on each side of the trail and four under his direction blocking the crossing at the Eel. The soldiers were under a different leader than the day before. They marched more quickly and orderly and did not wander about. At the bottomlands on the southern approach to the river Eel the trail was narrow; the soldiers then marched in single file. We had positioned a smoldering campfire at the base of the bluff on the northern bank. Around this we had placed a few blankets with some fine clothes; I placed necklaces of silver to hang from the branches. The soldiers in the advance saw these things and rushed to claim their 'Indian treasure.' Others pushed forward to investigate the merriment. As their commander shouted for order, our rifles roared. Virginians and soldiers fell as though a Frenchman was cutting his wheat. The volunteers broke and ran to swamp and timber, leaving packs and weapons behind. The regulars stood and fought bravely on the trail, keeping a steady fire until their ranks were too thin to hold. Organized resistance gave way to chaos. We overran their position and hunted down stragglers. A hundred of the invaders now decorate that bank of the Eel with their bones."

Metea allowed himself a whoop of joy at the victory. His second was startled at the sudden shout and instinctively jumped to his feet. Saving face, he brushed off the back of his breechcloth then stepped forward to swoop up the gourd from the blanket. He innocently trotted up the hill. The boy had just returned from taking a quick dip in the lake. Hearing the whoop, he dove under a horse then stood on the far side of it, peering under its neck. The feathered warrior with the boy reprimanded him for seeking safety rather than quickly securing the horses. The boy's case was not helped by the fact that he began shivering, the lake had been much colder than anticipated. The gambling on the hillside continued without interruption. Metea vowed to himself that when he reached Turtle Town, he would have someone show him the place where these bones lay.

Hiding his smile as best he could, Wild Carrot continued the story, "The following day there was no action from the enemy camp. Were they waiting for reinforcement? Were they expecting cannon to arrive? Did they think that Hamtramck would successfully push up the Wabash to join them? Did they think that the tribes of the forests would bring battle to them where they were in their strength? With the first light of the second day, our eyes beheld the soldiers striking camp and retreating through the meadows. What cowards! A general with no honor is this Harmar! He had boasted all along the Ohio from Fort Pitt to the Illinois settlements how he was going to punish the Wabash tribes. We had only cut his little finger and he cowered like a puppy. He abandoned the corpses of those he had sent out to die.

"The retreating army's new camp was in disarray that night. I went with our spies to penetrate it. We heard much clamoring from the officers and men. We heard that the following day before dawn, Colonel Hardin of the militia, who had led the soldiers to defeat on the Eel, would return to Kekionga to avenge the lives of those lost with the lives of the Miami who were sure to wander back into the destroyed villages. The general would provide one hundred regulars in uniform and three hundred Virginians. All of this was known by the great chief Little Turtle before there was any red in the eastern sky. The war chief positioned the warriors under Black Loon on the north bank of the Maumee along with the Shawnee and their allies. Chief Richardville was given seven camps of warriors to defend the north bank of the St. Marys. The remainder Little Turtle held on the east bank of the St. Joseph under his direction.

"The attackers came swiftly with the American regulars charging directly to the Maumee, bound for the plaza of the council house in the heart of Kekionga. The braves with Black Loon fought frantically, surprising the Americans during their crossing of the river. The waters ran red with the blood of the attackers. Bodies of soldiers and horses cluttered the Maumee from shore to shore. The few remaining Americans broke off the attack and pulled back.

"Meanwhile, the mounted militia swept widely to the east and to the west intent upon looping behind any resistance. LeGris defended the eastern wing with our braves and the warriors from Detroit, but could not hold. His force had many losses and was pushed back behind Black Loon towards the St. Joseph. To the west the horsemen had swung well wide of Richardville's location. Richardville moved us northward between Bonnecamp Creek and the St. Joseph. That was where I saw Colonel Hardin again raising his sword against the Miami. We fought valiantly to hold the western side of the St. Joseph. We could hear the firing to the east drawing closer. Some who had been with Black Loon crossed over to support us. The Virginians were pressing on both sides of the St. Joseph as does a blacksmith's vice. This was the moment when Little Turtle charged with the forces that he had held to the north. The Virginians who were between the Maumee and the St. Joseph were slaughtered. This was where the heads of the enemy fell to join the pumpkins in the fields of Kekionga. A small group of the enemy fled past me from behind to join their countrymen engaging us. When Hardin learned of the rout, he withdrew his men and fled.

"Many Virginians ran past the army and were chased through the forest as far as the Ohio. General Harmar was harassed for many days by the Shawnee and Canadian tribes. He abandoned more than two hundred fallen soldiers on the fields of Kekionga. He lost more on the retreat to his Fort Washington. I think that General Washington will want to have his name stricken from the fort at Cincinnati. This is the story of the battle of the Pumpkinheads."

After the appropriate silence had elapsed, Metea mused, "You have spoken well. Had the Pottawatomie known about the battle and retreat we would have rushed though the forest and kept the rabbits from reaching their hole. We would have piled their bodies in a great heap and burned them to ashes to be blown with the winds across the forests of the tribes." Once more he swept his eyes around the bowl of the lake, "The Creator has provided well for you."

The Pottawatomie chief's eyes rested momentarily on Sweet Breeze. They then turned upward to his companions, "We have been called by special summons from Chief Five Medals of the Elk Heart. The council will be at the town of Little Turtle because Kekionga has been abandoned these days since the great battle. It will be our first assembly with Little Turtle; it is a great honor for us. I will tell the War Chief of the Miami that your camp prospers."

Sensing that the heat of the day had now waned, he stood and shouted to his entourage, "The horses are rested. We shall move on!"

Turning to the now standing red-haired man he declared, "Before snow fills the air the Americans will come again to the confluence of the rivers. The English have come to us in their red coats telling us that their spies know of a great council of the Americans in the east. Washington stands in this council and calls these lands his own." Raising his hand over his head he traced a circle in the air. "Washington wants to drive our villages north beyond the river Chicago or west beyond the great river. He is sending a second army to build a fort on the portage where we cross from the Wabash to the Maumee. You and I and all of the tribes must join as one to bury the Americans below the soil that they are seeking."

Wild Carrot detected the urgency and excitement in Metea's voice at his anticipation of sitting with the great chiefs Five Medals and Little Turtle. The warrior who had fought by the side of Little Turtle did not disclose that he already knew about the American intentions. He personally had carried this same message to his father at Eel Town. He knew that Porcupine had distributed it to the west. Little Turtle was continually holding councils in his village of Turtle Town on the river Eel. The parley with these young chiefs would be one among many in preparation for a grand council to be held among many nations. As the troop in their splendid attire disappeared behind the crest, he could hear them joking about the nakedness of the red-haired Miami.

CHAPTER 2
Eel Town

She was mesmerized by the miniature whirlpools becoming smaller and smaller until finally disappearing within the stream. Each rhythmic stroke created a new family of the swirls. They followed one another along a curve drawn by some unseen force. She now realized where she had seen this pattern. A leaf on a mature corn stalk traced in the air the same curve that these disturbances traced in the water. What connection could there possibly be between corn that grows from a seed in the ground and Wild Carrot powering his paddle? Tiny dimples now spread across the water's surface indicating yet another shower was approaching.

The sun had not made an appearance for several days. The first rains had been hot and steamy, the moisture drunk by the earth. Booming lightning storms producing soaking torrents followed. The corn leaves that had rolled tightly about their stalks reached out widely to receive the life-giving nourishment. Twice Sweet Breeze had to chase down the tarpaulin that the winds had lifted from her wigwam. One night a crack of lightning had sent a huge limb from the walnut tree crashing to the ground. It shook the whole earth. She wondered if the water in these whirlpools could have earlier formed the trickles that made minute cascades tumbling down the hillside during the storms. These waters would have flowed through the small brook at the outlet of the lake, then over the beaver dams to join the creek. The creek meandered to the south while being fed by brook after brook until it fed life into this river at Squirrel's Village. Here this river would carry them to their relatives at Eel Town. The waters would continue on without them past the homes of her ancestral cousins until joining the waters of the mighty Ohio. Beyond this she knew only by stories about the great river and mysterious lands.

She loved this beautiful little river that joined her to her closest relatives. The placid stretches of the Eel were interspersed with short runs of rapid water tumbling over and around gleaming rocks. But now, this stream that had always made her feel so safe was an artery of war.

At Squirrel's Village that morning, she had listened to old man Bull Nose recount the vast number of canoes and horses that had passed up and down since the new moon. He likened the movement of people to ants in an orchard during the season of ripened fruit. Each passing group brought rumors of the war. Late in the spring, a wave of Wea refugees had vastly increased the numbers in his village. He lamented that his little town was now nearly empty, his friends were scattered in all directions. A handful of warriors had gone far south to raid the American war camp. Others moved with their wives to Eel Town to join the battle forces gathering there. These men were known to be relocating guns and powder, and nearly the entire town, to the Forks of the Wabash where a grand war camp was being formed. The majority bonded with their friends in a battle group at Turtle Town. The elderly and children were scattered among the winter hunting camps in the lakes region.

Bull Nose declared to her that he and a few others would stay to keep watch at the village, assisting travelers as they were able. He provided her and Wild Carrot with this log canoe for their passage to Eel Town. He promised to guard their horses with his life. Any Americans coming his way would be met by his arrows.

While passing a familiar narrows she recognized the camping spot on the north shore. In times past, her family would camp here when traveling to visit her aunt. Nights here were spent in eager anticipation. Ahead lay treats from her aunt, perhaps fine moccasins or a necklace. There would be games with cousins, and she was sure to see that fine red-haired boy. She imagined the wonderful goods which filled the French traders' log buildings. She could even smell the smoke filling the entire valley from a hundred cook fires. War parties of many nations from the north resupplied themselves here before continuing to the Kentucky lands. Storytelling and dances filled the nights.

Her husband hailed a clutch of men gathered upon a sandbar at the trailing end of a small island. He steered alongside and lightly lodged the nose of the canoe in the sand. It seemed to her that he knew everyone in each camp and hamlet. He was expected to stop for a visit. She grew accustomed to the routine. First the exchange of compliments followed by the men pointing at her belly and making a comment they considered funny. The talk turned to news about fishing, hunting, war, and perhaps some family matters. After an offer of food they would shove off for their next jaunt.

Sweet Breeze was tired of hearing the continual talk of war. Perhaps it was the life growing within her belly that made her weary. These short delays would make arrival at their destination later and later. She began to wonder if they would make it before nightfall. She thought about her mother, perhaps at this same island, perhaps while carrying unnamed Sweet Breeze within her womb, patiently awaiting Little Turtle to resume a trip downstream. But it was his way as a leader of men to build personal relations. She understood that leaders must seek the mood and desires of the populace.

At the next stop, war talk turned to the terrible late spring raid against the Wea towns. Wild Carrot recalled how he had returned with Little Turtle from Detroit, where they were assured by the English officers that the Americans would bring no action from Vincennes. The chiefs had turned their attention to plundering the supplies bound for Fort Washington. Suddenly, five hundred mounted Virginians charged from the forests onto the fields at Ouiatenon. The surprised townspeople could affect no organized resistance. The raiders wielded devastation from Tippecanoe Town above to the Kickapoo towns below. Thirty braves died in battle. The Virginians disappeared into the forest taking sixty women and children as captives. Scouting parties could not find a trace of their families, their fate remains unknown.

Before the defeat of General Josiah Harmar's army in the fall of the past year, and now the raid on the Wabash this spring, it was believed that the dense forests would be impenetrable by any enemy from the south. Now these men all agreed that it was best to take the fight to the enemy on the Ohio. All of the tribes should join as one army and overpower the land-grabbers.

As the visit grew longer, Sweet Breeze thought that she may as well get out and stretch her legs. Getting in or out of a canoe in her condition was not an easy task. This sandy bar with the surrounding shallows seemed a place for disembarking. Instead of kneeling in her routine paddling position, on this trip she had being lying with her back to the bow. This arrangement eased the pressure on her abdomen. It also gave her an unaccustomed view of the river banks. By the time she decided in favor of the stretch, Wild Carrot was pushing off and the canoe caught the current.

He smiled to his wife in acknowledgement of her patience at the diplomacy that was constantly interrupting their harmony. He knew that she was used to sharing her father and uncles with the Miami nation. Yet, it bothered him to be gone so often and then to not be more attentive when they were together. He leaned more stiffly into his paddle and decided to forego any additional meetings if possible. Even in the mist, with her head wrapped in a red and black shawl, her face was radiant. It reminded him of their wedding day. Though the sun had been bright that day, the wind whipped great mounds of snow sending swirls of crystals through the air. Sweet Breeze appeared with only her face peering from a blue shawl. After the brief ceremony, they stayed five days in the log house at Little Turtle's compound without venturing outside. Blizzard upon blizzard blasted the entire area that year. None of the elders had seen such cold. But the two of them stayed warm together.

He laughed aloud, "I was just thinking, perhaps we should name this baby 'Long Icicle.'"

"I prefer 'Snow From The Roof Falls Down Upon Daddy's Head,'" came the prompt reply.

The contest was on for the most outrageous name.

After the name game played out he thought about her name. How appropriate it was. She moved gracefully as if carried by a soft wind. She walked effortlessly as if floating above the ground. Her voice was like that of songbirds carried on air from the far side of a meadow. He pictured her picking berries with a breeze caressing her hair. After the coming war he would find a way to protect her from the hard life of a squaw that made the women old and stiff.

Sweet Breeze had grown a bit more serious, "Have you thought about what you will say to Small Cloud?"

"Yes, I know," was his reply.

The truth was he had been trying to avoid thinking about this. The purpose of this mission was to bring Primrose back to the safety of the lake. She had injured her back and would not be accompanying her husband Porcupine to the war camp. Little Turtle had been alarmed that the raid had reached up to Tippecanoe Town and knew that Eel Town was the next major village upstream, though a ways off the main river route. The Great Chief of the Miami could not give his full attention to war business with his sister so vulnerable. How Wild Carrot loved and respected this woman! It was she who had protected him during his trials, who had saved him from the fire, and had adopted him to replace her own lost son. She was kind to all and generous to those in need. Now it was his duty to protect her.

Small Cloud was with Porcupine's family. The Wea woman had moved there after escaping the spring raid. Of course, she and her child would be welcomed to the lake camp. The women could harvest crops and gather acorns to help feed the army. With the severe winter, the destruction of the past year's crop at Kekionga, and the trampling of the Wea fields in the spring, food would surely be scarce soon.

Small Cloud had deceitfully wooed Wild Carrot in his youth. She had lain with him only to have a child that carried his blood. She had done none of the duties expected of a wife of a warrior. Before the child was born he sent her away, returning her to Ouiatenon. Though he had passed through several times journeying to Vincennes, he did not inquire about her. During the campaign down the Wabash prior to Pumpkinheads, he spent many days in the area. He located her and went off twice between council sessions to visit Small Cloud and his son. He had only wanted to see the child, but she was constantly making demands of him. He realized that he had no desires for her, and resolved that their paths would never cross again.

The canoe of Wild Carrot and Sweet Breeze was now passing the mouth of a large creek from the north; it would not be long before they were drying themselves before Porcupine's fire. The cold mist was mixing with fog, neither falling nor rising.

"I hope Primrose has prepared her river mussel stew. She knows it is my favorite. She always welcomes me with it when she knows that I am coming," she wistfully said.

"Do not expect too much with all of the commotion of so many moving to the war camp," was his reply. "I will gladly settle for an arm-load of corn that is sure to be at its best now."

He was sitting erect, carefully scanning the banks in the dwindling light. Something was amiss. There had been no fire at the creek mouth. He had seen no camps for quite some time. The rains may have kept some in the town, but surely not all. The old men would not be proceeding up the Wabash with the warriors. Why were they not here fishing? Perhaps they were occupied transporting supplies across the neck of land between the rivers. Wild Carrot loved this river carrying him back to the home of his youth. He knew the bends, the small islands, the rocks jutting here and there. Yet, he had not anticipated the utter darkness that was descending.

The smell of smoke began to mix heavily with the fog. It was not the sweet smell of the hardwood cook fires, but the pungent odor of burning refuse. Wild Carrot quickened the pace of his strokes. Sweet Breeze craned to look ahead for the glow of the town's fires. All was dark and silent. An odd feeling crept over her; things were not quite what they should be. She turned to her husband with a puzzled look on her face. She saw his keen concentration as he motioned for silence. A few more strokes and he turned the canoe to the right bank. He nosed it into the brush-choked outlet of a brook as she lay flat on the bottom of the vessel.

He simply said, "Stay."

She grabbed a tree root jutting from the soil to hold the canoe as he lifted out and disappeared. Her ears followed him scrambling up the little bank.

He was trying to move quickly and silently, but he was slipping here and there on the wet clay of the slope. The unusual darkness was hiding roots and vines that seemed to snatch out to grab his ankles. Reaching the flat ground trodden bare by foot-traffic, he knew the first buildings of the upper Eel Town were only a few steps away. Rushing cautiously forward he ran square into the smoldering upright logs of a French-style building. Feeling with his hands, he found spots that were quite warm. Moving around the building, his eyes finally began to make sense of the weird blackened forms. Now he could see red and white and orange within the interior. The roof had fallen in and mixed with the contents of the home, all reduced to faint embers. Finding his way along, he found what had been twig and bark wigwams, one after another, now just heaps of gray ash. He crouched, leaning back solidly to a tree, listening attentively. He peered intently into the smoke and fog, trying to see past the veil. Only an occasional crackling pop and soft flame of a burning stick catching the faint breeze was revealed. His nostrils had become deadened to the thick smell of smoke.

He moved silently on past wigwam heaps. Finding another shell of a log building he again crouched and listened. His back was warmed by the timbers. He heard slight movements along one side of the building. Was it a combatant, a survivor, a dog or prowling animal? The creature was moving with stealth. A form rounded the building between the corner and a tree. He met it with the point of his knife leveled to strike. Sweet Breeze gasped, rocked back a half-step, and dove to the ground beside the tree. Mud splattered; her left hand poked hard against a stick on the ground. He did not grab her.

With a voice as calmly as he could gather he called softly but firmly, "It is I. It is I. Come."

She turned to see him tucking his tomahawk into his belt and shifting his knife to the other hand. He lifted her and directed her to a rock where they sat blending into the black wall as much as they could. Here they sat for a long while listening for any sign of activity.

He turned to her, "This is how it is when trailing a panther. If he is out there, he has all of the advantages."

He used some soot to blacken his face and arms, then hers. He found her arm to be cold and began rubbing it.

"Over here," her voice was not much more than a whimper as she tugged him to follow.

She led him by the hand though he would rather have it free to fend off potential attackers. Dodging debris that littered the ground, she led him between two log structures and pointed. A woman's body had been hacked deeply on the right neck and shoulder. Her left arm had been severed. The lifeless child at her side had been run through at the abdomen.

"Virginians," he muttered.

She nodded. Stepping back from between the buildings he realized that they were at the row of trading posts. He poked about, hoping to discover some weapons they could use. Finding nothing, they moved to the edge of the town and circled towards the big spring on the hillside. This was his hometown where he had grown from adolescence to adulthood. Having gained his bearings, he could maneuver well even in this wretched darkness. They crossed another mutilated body on their trek. This woman had nearly made it to the cornfields before being overtaken by the enemy.

They paused at the spring. A swig of refreshing water was in order. Wild Carrot was keeping his vigilance while trying to organize a plan.

Sweet Breeze handed him a sword. "It was lying over there," she said.

He looked at her strange find in amazement, then handed her his knife. She took a drink and lay on the soft grass. Closing her eyes, she hoped this dreadful episode would be gone when she opened them.

"It appears that the townspeople had nearly all moved out before the attack," Wild Carrot said. He instructed his wife on the likely sequence of events. "A powerful force of horsemen swept through, likely early in the day, quickly overpowering the few defenders. This completed, they then chased down those fleeing. Next was the pillaging of trade goods and our homes. Then came the hunt for survivors and the stripping of necklaces and rings from the bodies."

He took another drink. "I would guess that they followed the typical pattern of plunderers. They would gather together all the food and rum of the town to have a great feast." He omitted the part about assaulting captured women. "They would make a great fire from what they could not eat or carry. Into the fire they would throw captured weapons that they did not want. They would take this fire to the long house and make a ceremony of torching it. Then the men would run in frenzy to each hut and building, shouting with joy as it burst into flame. Crops would be trampled while the town burned."

Normally he would not let his voice reveal his sadness as he had done now. "I do not know from which direction they came, nor which way they went. They left this day somewhat after midday."

Chokingly she pleaded, "Take me to the home of my aunt Primrose."

"Yes," was the soft reply. "We must proceed cautiously."

He directed them forward across the hillside to find the creek that bisected the town. They stepped around a corpse of an old woman who had sought the refuge of the trees at the stream. Neither of them recognized her. They followed the bed of the narrow stream down to the river then crossed to the lower town. The upright logs of the compound of homes were mostly standing. The scene was the same as the one before, except here were signs of resistance. Sweet Breeze picked up a cloth hoping to recognize it. But neither it, nor anything else, was recognizable. She let it drop to join the other mud-trampled artifacts.

She leaned on her husband, "It is too much for me! I cannot bear it!"

He moved her out to the cottonwoods lining the river. He placed a bench against a tree that spread from three huge trunks and sat her down. He moved several strides downstream and stepped out onto the gravel at the water's edge.

"Come out!" His rage overcame him. "Come out! It is Wild Carrot calling!"

The darkness swallowed up his wail. He repeated his challenge to each of the four directions.

He walked out over the rocks and heaved the sword into the current with a yell. He staggered on downstream to where a finger of limestone reached from the depths of the river up into the town. This is where he had expected to land their canoe and be welcomed by his mother. His wife would have unbundled her handcrafted gifts. He would have carried an engraved silver cross up the stone path to the plaza beside the council house. Here the courtesy of the exchange of gifts would have erupted into gaiety and hugging.

This was the place where wave upon wave of raiding parties had set off. They returned with goods and trophies from the Kentucky lands. Prisoners were traded to be slaves if they were brave, to be tortured to death if they were not. Tales were told in the council house about the conquests. Raids and battles terrified the settlers even as far as the palisades of Boone's fort. Flatboats on the Ohio yielded up their treasure. Farms and settlements had been set ablaze across the frontier.

Now the smell of death was here. The war had come to the town that he loved. He noticed that the stench was again in his nostrils, stronger than before. He turned with a queried look up the path. There was a tall smoldering pile on the plaza. A closer look revealed a revolting sight. The charred bodies of five old warriors were creating wisps of steam with each intermittent raindrop. They had been heaped upon broken canoes and covered with lance shafts and bows. The whole had created a bonfire so hot that there was no chance to identify any of the men. Surely he knew many of this home guard. They would have fought valiantly, delaying the chargers, allowing many townspeople to escape. He let out an uncontrollable howl.

He walked to the center of the remains of the council house. Grabbing a singed buffalo hide he fanned what was left of the council fire. Finding a glow, he went to his knees and blew until there was a pocket of red. Gathering sticks and boards from the destroyed buildings, he renewed the flame and piled it high. Satisfied that it would hold for another day, he returned to the disgusting mass of defiled warriors.

Crying to the dark void above he raised his voice to the Creator of All Things, "Each sunrise I have declared how good you are to me! Now you have brought this into my life! How can it be?"

He tore off his blouse and went down upon all fours. He rocked back and forth and moaned loudly. Crawling forward he took some wet ashes into his hand. These he smeared upon his chest, repeating it over and over. Some remaining on his finger he put it to his mouth. He tasted the bitter charcoal and swallowed. He raised his tomahawk high overhead and held it there a long while.

An oath in the Miami tongue rang out to the trees, "The Americans will taste my bitterness!"

Sweet Breeze wanted to rush to her husband, but dared not. A hazy form was moving near the creek. It was getting closer, moving from ruin to ruin, studying each site. She leaned tightly against the tree while clutching the knife. Her oversized belly ached at the strain. It must be one of the invaders scavenging for treasure. She inched her way up to climb between two of the trunks.

She was coaching herself, "Fight like a bobcat, scream like a panther. Sink the knife into the intruder's throat before he can react."

She heard mumbling; it was very close by. It was not clear, but it was a voice in her native tongue. She peeked to see a woman walking about aimlessly towards the river.

She steeled her nerves and called cautiously, "Woman."

The woman stopped and turned but did not see who was calling.

"Woman", she called again, "I will help you."

The woman sat down in the sand and began sobbing. Sweet Breeze stepped down from the tree and hid the knife behind her once-beautiful skirt.

Walking half the distance she spoke reassuringly, "I am Sweet Breeze, daughter of Little Turtle, wife of Wild Carrot. Primrose is my aunt. I will help you."

The woman reached out with one hand in recognition, but did not try to get up.

Sweet Breeze stepped forward, "Give me your other hand."

This served to comfort the old woman, but also reassured Sweet Breeze that both hands were empty of weapons.

"I will help you," she repeated.

She called to her husband. She crouched in the sand studying the figure before her. No, she did not recognize the face.

"She is harmless," she told him as he approached. "She needs our help."

The three sat quietly in the sand listening to the hushed sound of the river ripples. When Sweet Breeze turned her gaze to her man, she was astounded at his strangeness. He was in as much of a daze as this poor woman.

While wondering at his graveness, she inquired of the stranger, "What is your name, woman?"

"I am the wife of Old Wolf of this village," the woman spoke haltingly. "I cannot find the body of my husband."

"Do you know that he is here?"

"Yes," she said. "I saw him fall."

"Are there others with you? Have you seen anyone else walking in the darkness?"

"I have seen nary a soul."

"Are there soldiers remaining here?"

"They thundered into the village, killed the men and many families, destroyed everything, then left with their prisoners."

"Prisoners? They took people from the town with them?"

"Yes, they came from over there," pointing directly at the opposite bank of the Eel to the trail across the neck to the Wabash, "and left that way with the prisoners." She pointed across the village to the north and west.

"How many prisoners?"

"There are thirty-five women and children. I was with them," she said. She went over the count again in her mind. "Now thirty-four," she corrected.

"You escaped from them?"

"I did not escape. They sent me back!" the woman said forcefully.

Sweet Breeze nudged her husband. Did he comprehend this? Here was a person who could tell about the events of this fateful day. She had always been able to see his thoughts in his face; now there was nothing.

Deciding to press on, she queried, "Did many escape the battle?"

"I do not know. I was here when the horsemen came splashing across the river. We had no warning, no alarm. I nearly went under the horses hooves. There was much gunfire. All the young warriors were gone. My husband and a handful of his friends tried to protect us, but they could not. It did not last long. Surely some escaped to the brush, but I do not know. I was here."

"Why did the soldiers send you back?"

The woman was preparing to answer when she became aware that the man's hair was red and he had light skin under his arms. She jerked back.

Sweet Breeze held her and reminded her, "This is my husband. He will not harm you. He will help us both. He was adopted into your village in his youth. Wild Carrot. Do you remember? Now he is a warrior of Little Turtle. The son of Primrose and Porcupine. Do you remember?"

The woman did not acknowledge this, but settled back down. She squinted at the blackened face of the pregnant girl who asked again, "Why did the soldiers send you back?"

The woman recounted the events of the long day, "The women and children who were not killed in the assault were herded together at the hillside meadow. The children were held in a group separated from the women. Before the raid, most of the mothers had gone to the war camp with their husbands. Only the sick and the older grandmothers were here. The raiders would not allow us to comfort the children or find them water. We waited there while the village was ravaged. We were strong; we did not wail; we did not curse the guards." She was looking straight ahead at nothing in particular. "The guards kept asking us where the warriors were, where were all of the people? It is a large town, there should be many people. We all told them that it was root harvest time. We told them that everyone was at the swamps to the north gathering roots. It was five days' journey to the north and they would not return for many days. They beat some of us, but we kept repeating the story." She paused and gave a haunting laugh. "We would have died in the meadow holding to our story. They asked why the trail to the Wabash was so worn. We told them that many English soldiers had visited, but left when they heard that our chiefs would not come for many days. It was a good story, but they would not have it. We told them that the soldiers wanted to fortify the Wabash at the bluffs opposite the pudding rock. Their interpreter knew this place and began to accept the story.

"I recognized this interpreter; I had seen him before. He was a Frenchman, a voyager who had been with Gamelin, the younger, when he came with the peace offer to our chiefs. I remember also he had been with Gamelin, the elder, when he came to trade. If I had found a stick I would have poked it deep into his eyes. The women kept encouraging each other though we were told not to talk. We would choose an honorable death as the men did. We would send them far to the north looking for our warriors."

Her spirits were now rising. She trained her eyes on those of Sweet Breeze and then those of Wild Carrot.

Wild Carrot stood and paced, then asked the woman, "How many horsemen were there? Where are they now?"

"There were many, a horde" she replied. "There were more than the warriors from here and all of the neighboring villages. They put the prisoners, more than sixty counting the children, on their extra horses, one or two to a horse. Each was led by a mounted enemy. Only a few of the enemy were so occupied, there were so many. We rode swiftly to the west."

"Did any of the enemy stay behind?"

"I do not know, but I would think that they did not. We rode hard for some while. At the second creek all stopped and the prisoners were rounded together. We were given water. The leader of the horde wore a fine uniform. He berated the interpreter. They approached us and selected me to come forward.

"The leader ranted and raved," the woman continued. "The interpreter told me that I was to return to the village with a message for our cowardly chiefs and warriors who had gone into hiding. I was to remember the leader's name and take it to the village for all to know. 'General Wilkinson' was the name. I had to say it to him many times until he was satisfied. I was to carry the message that General Wilkinson was the man who destroyed our village. It was he who was taking captives with him. It will be he who will return one day to hang our chiefs from the sycamores. One of the guards beat my legs with a stick and pushed me back up the trail towards my home." She spat upon the sand and stomped on the blob. "They threw stones until I entered the trees. I circled back and watched from the brambles. They crossed the creek and headed in the direction of the Tippecanoe, the prisoners now walking."

Wild Carrot continued the questioning. "Was Porcupine here?" he asked.

"No, Chief Porcupine and Chief Charley have been gone many days. They went first to prepare the camp at the Forks of the Wabash. The other chiefs followed; none were here. Only some older men of the guard remained."

"What about Primrose? Was she with Porcupine?"

Wild Carrot and Sweet Breeze both braced to hear that Primrose was either safely residing in the new camp, or had been killed in the devastation around them. He was afraid of what the answer might be.

She looked directly to him, "She is with the prisoners. It is the strength of Primrose that is the hope of the women who have been led away."

Sweet Breeze jumped to her husband and clutched his arm. They exchanged startled looks. They did not know what to make of it that she was with the pack of wolves that had swept through their town. What would become of her? His look told her not to expect mercy. Surely Primrose would remain bold. However, bravery in an enemy was not honored by the Americans as it was among the noble tribes.

They turned toward the river, their backs to the old woman.

Sweet Breeze confided, "The woman is greatly alarmed, but her answers ring true."

"Yes, the signs tell the same as she has spoken," he confirmed. "It has been a terrible day for her and for the Miami people. It is a great puzzle about the invaders taking prisoners. She says that they went to the Tippecanoe, but we do not know this. They could be anywhere! If no one escaped, then the alarm has not been spread. Last autumn at Kekionga they came back to attack stragglers. We were ready to battle them then."

He was trying to sort out his duty. It surprised him that he did not have an immediate plan of action. This was a sign of weakness that he did not like. Should he rescue his mother as she had rescued him from certain death? Should he track the enemy and determine their direction? He had no runners to return messages while continuing to scout the enemy. Should he take the short trail to the Wabash? He knew that there were always three young men posted on Big Boat Island by the medicine rocks. They were eternally present to watch the traffic on the Wabash and communicate with the town. One could pass the alarm while he took two with him in the pursuit. But the charge came from that direction; surely they succumbed to the overwhelming force. There was no safe place to leave his wife while he sallied about. The enemy was still largely unknown, unpredictable. He must be decisive. His first duty was to his wife, then to Little Turtle, finally to the Miami people. His mother and father would agree; they had taught him this.

"We must leave here quickly," he told her. "We will take the woman and return to Squirrel's Village. Bull Nose will escort you to our lake camp. I will proceed to Turtle Town and will tell your father the story of this place so he will hear and understand the truth. I will send others to join you. I will remain with him through the coming great battle."

Her eyes were wide as she took in the full meaning of his words. She was distressed that she could be of no help to him. How she had been glad to carry this child, but now she would only be a burden in a war camp. She would go to the lake and welcome those who sought refuge. She would be strong for her people.

He was speaking quickly, "Lighter canoes are hidden across the river. I will bring one to where we landed." He was holding her close to him, "Get what we need from Bull Nose's canoe. The men will still be at the hunting camp upstream. I will instruct them to pass the alarm and to pursue the soldiers carrying the captives."

"Will you now help me find the body of Old Wolf?" the woman was asking, "I have not searched the lower village."

Wild Carrot moved to her and lifted her up. He took a slow breath

34

and tried to speak reassuringly, "Old Wolf was known to all as an honored warrior. The story of the deeds of your husband in the defense of Eel Town will be told across the land. Come with us now. Sweet Breeze will care for you. I will send braves to honor the dead of this place."

He led the widow of Old Wolf along the water's edge. He had to ask, "Did Primrose have family with her?"

"Yes, they, too, are captives," she recounted, "The Wea girl and her child."

CHAPTER 3
Maumee

The Maumee River was filled to its banks, the waters boiling and flowing swiftly. Combining the currents of the St. Marys and the St. Joseph at Kekionga, it rushed through the flatlands to deposit its waters into the grand lake called Erie. Cornfields formed an unbroken ribbon of green on both low banks from the confluence eastwardly to where the great river was joined from the south by the Auglaize. It was to this second merging of the waters that the English traders had relocated after the Battle of Pumpkinheads. The ancient town at this scene of rare beauty had welcomed French voyagers, trappers, and missionary priests. It was here that the legendary great chief Pontiac had grown as a boy. The French had long since moved on to the Wabash and beyond, some even past the great river of the west.

The mixed waters of the Maumee and the Auglaize moved powerfully below bluffs pressing close on each side before spreading into a swampy bay forming the west end of the grand lake Erie. On the lake mighty ships of the English ruled the waters. The sight of these vessels inspired wonder, awe, and fear. How ably they were served by their seamen. The salutes from their cannon bellowed and rolled, shaking earth and man alike. The mighty guns of the fleet had never seen a challenge.

There were often two or three ships moored at the north bank of the Maumee just below the great island that marked the lower rapids of the Maumee. Here the ships could penetrate no further into the forested lands. Red-clad soldiers camped on the high bluff while stevedores labored below. Boats and log canoes rode the waters from the west carrying bales of pelts and leather. Others were laden with the white corn of the Miami, esteemed by all who ate it. Smaller vessels were paddled and poled, tugged and pulled upstream bearing treasures for the west. Cloth, beads, thread, fancy combs, iron and copper utensils, traps, fishhooks, scissors, knives, salt, mirrors, and materials of war and of daily life were hauled westward on the Maumee. Bundles, crates, and kegs would be unloaded at the landing in Kekionga or a bit further up the St. Marys at the portage to the Wabash. A few items would end their journey at Kekionga with the majority to be scattered to the setting sun.

English traders maintained a pier along the steep western slope by the mouth of the Auglaize. The escape from the American march on Kekionga the previous fall had been close. This new location provided a quick escape if the Americans again came calling. From here they could scurry down to the landing at the lower rapids. They could quickly load on a waiting ship with their goods and sail for Detroit in a day's time. There they would wait leisurely in comfort for actions of the war to be played out. For now, local trade was brisk at their little fortified compound. The entire area was filled with camps of the tribes.

The great chief Blue Jacket had moved his Shawnee followers to the opposite bank of the Auglaize, close by to the south. This tribe had inflicted great defeats on the Virginians. Legends of the battle at Point Pleasant on the Ohio and the defeat of Boone at Big Blue Licks near the cane fields were repeated far and wide. Their constant raids sent frightened settlers fleeing east beyond the mountains. Then came the reversals. Counter-raids by Butler and Clark penetrated deep into their homelands. Villages were decimated. Unfortunate events cost the lives of many warriors and war chiefs. Forays by bands of Pennsylvanians brought more destruction. The Shawnee were pushed farther and farther from their lovely Ohio River until the nation split. Fully half migrated to the Spanish lands beyond the great river Mississippi.

Tribes had come to the region from Upper Canada and the Michigan lands. Ottawa, Wyandot, and Chippewa came with entire villages. Groups of warriors from the east attached themselves to these camps. Woodland Pottawatomie and Plains Pottawatomie settled in further upstream. Newly arrived Muncee Delaware mingled into their brothers' villages near the Miami settlements. Little Turtle had concentrated his people on the plains of the Maumee to the east of their usual site. Thus the greater part of the Maumee was a conglomerate of new and renewed villages, a metropolis for the traders. Well-worn footpaths and copious light canoes constantly carried visitors between camps. Herds of horses grazed the pockets of grasslands.

Situated on the south plain of the lower rapids were well-established Ottawa villages. Near these villages McKee maintained his royal trading post. He conducted business of the crown under the auspices of the

Governor of Upper Canada. He regularly frequented Detroit. He routinely granted licenses to trappers and traders and doled out gifts to the many tribes. Rather stingy in the past, the British were now shipping vast quantities of goods and munitions. Though this side of the great lakes had technically been ceded to the United States government by treaty, it continued to be treated as part of the province of Upper Canada. The expressed reason was that the United States authorities had not fulfilled their obligations of the treaty to provide reparations to displaced Tories. Tactically, the British presence was a buffer between the American presence on the Ohio River and the crown's Canadian lands. Detroit, also unfortunately situated on the wrong side of the treaty line, remained the British base of operations. For now, they would retain the western trade and hold the native allies to their side.

It was to his post that McKee summoned the head chiefs of the many tribes. He had long been accustomed to the ritual. A chief would appear with a guard and other men. After receiving a token gift from the chief, McKee would present him with coin, a medallion, or fine trade item. The chief would pledge his loyalty to the king, this being attested to by the offering of tobacco smoke to the Creator. Before the pipe was finished, a lieutenant would hand the chief's second a document sealed with wax and tied with a fancy ribbon. The paper was exchanged at the storehouse for gifts presented to the tribe. When the chief's man returned to indicate that the gifts were obtained as prescribed, a toast of rum was lifted. News and small talk would be interspersed with requests for more gifts until the chief was satisfied or gave up and returned from whence he came.

During these hottest days of late summer, McKee had conducted a series of more urgent councils. He continually cajoled the chiefs to be prepared, to gather more men. The Americans were bent on war. They were keeping no secrets. The British spies were constantly sending reports on their plans. The "council of the thirteen fires" in the east had granted President Washington an immense army. The army was to be lead by General St. Clair, a veteran officer of the War of Revolution. He was now Governor of the Northwest Territory.

The objective was to establish a fort at the three rivers where Harmar had suffered defeat. This fort would fulfill a long-held dream of George Washington: to subjugate these lands and mark it off for settlers to make their farms. All summer the Americans had been building their army at Cincinnati. Fort Washington at Cincinnati could not begin to hold all the supplies. The army built new forges, carpenter sheds, and warehouses. The fort could not even hold all of the soldiers who were arriving on boat after boat.

McKee's latest council was in its third day under a canopy of canvas, flags whipping in the wind. Two officers and a scribe sat at a table, soldiers of the guard in single rank behind them. A company of uniformed men formed a red square in the pasturelands between the buildings and the river. Squads of tribesmen hovered at the river's edge. Each of the head chiefs had his turn to speak; McKee now stood before them. Despite the heat, he wore his fine uniform and hat, medals decorating his chest, gleaming sword at his side. McKee opened with a directive from the King of England. Wild Carrot interpreted the speech to Little Turtle, just as he had interpreted Little Turtle's words to the Englishman, except this time he was seated and spoke softly.

His eyes focused on the orator. He boldly proclaimed, "My children, you have spoken well and I have listened to your words. Our King upon his throne across the great sea has directed me here to watch over you. He sends gifts in honor of his friendship. I have heard each of you declare your nation strong and prepared for the war to come. I know that you are strong and that your warriors will fight well. The American army is strong, too, and is gaining in strength as we speak. Each of you has followed the warpath to harass the soldiers and those who bring them supplies. You have seen with your own eyes that their preparation is earnest. Now I have news that arrived today."

The chiefs looked about; McKee's speeches always brought news from his superiors or from his spies.

McKee declared, "American cannon have arrived at Fort Washington."

With this said, he brought a six-pound ball from a bench and let it thump onto the table. He let the full implication sink in for a moment.

"They have six cannon that will fire six-pound balls and more with lesser caliber." He paused again, and then said, "You have seen the effect of our six-pounders at Detroit." He waited for the murmurs and gestures by the audience to subside. "This verifies that the Americans do intend to build a fort at the head of this river to cut off your trade and drive you from your lands. This has been their intent from the beginning. It also indicates that they will soon move out of their fortifications and begin the invasion."

McKee turned to the table and drank deeply from a pint of rum.

Banging it down, he instructed his men to have rum distributed to all gathered. He paced the grounds while the serving was accomplished. He allowed some time for the chiefs to exchange comments.

McKee continued, "The Americans will be led by a single man, General St. Clair. He is a capable commander and will maneuver his army to his purpose. You cannot defeat him by charging one nation at a time. You must combine your warriors to fight as one great force! Form under one chief. Let the officers of my king lead you! They are trained to fight this war!"

Wild Carrot finished the translation and raised his eyebrows to his chief and mentor. He thought that this fellow red-head had made a good speech, but if he expected rousing support from the chiefs, he was surely disappointed. Perhaps Simon Girty should have delivered it. That man always aroused the lesser chiefs to passion as he moved from camp-fire to campfire. But Girty lacked the authority to stand in such an important council. Each head chief remained quiet, neither looking up nor down, left nor right.

After an embarrassing silence McKee again turned to them, some-what less forcefully, "There is more news. A Virginia officer of the militia by the name of Wilkinson is claiming a great victory over the Eel River Miami. His five hundred mounted riflemen from the Kentucky lands headed directly to the town from St. Clair's camps, destroying the main town and taking prisoners. He then struck Tippecanoe Town and Ouiatenon where he had been before with General Scott. Taking addi-tional prisoners, he returned to the Ohio at the falls with the loss of only two of his men. This man Wilkinson will be an officer with St. Clair. His Virginians will accompany the American army. You cannot deny that every Virginian covets your lands north of the Ohio River. The American government, by inviting them to accompany their invasion force, is endorsing their ambitions."

Wild Carrot bit his lip at this telling. Little Turtle wrapped his thoughts in the hard shell of a walnut.

* * *

Feasting could be heard in the distance as Wild Carrot stood upon the bank of the Maumee surrounded by goldenrod. The low sun reflect-ed brightly on the turbulence of the rapids. He was fuming at the thought of the Virginia raider calling the assault on his home a great vic-

41

tory over the Miami. Crushing a pocket of old men and burning an empty town, then dashing off with the helpless was good fortune, but no victory to tout. Had he come but a few days earlier, the braggart would have battled an equal number of hardened warriors. That would have been a great battle! Perhaps such a great loss could have been inflicted as to force St. Clair to cancel the invasion. In the coming battle he would seek out this hollow officer of the Americans; he would cut out his heart and stick it to a tree. He kicked a stick into the current and watched it float into the distance.

He did not hear Little Turtle approach from behind. The chief of the Miami nation said, "Do not be bitter at the name of Wilkinson. It was a bold stroke by their general. We must learn from it. Do not seek personal revenge. What is to come is important to all of our people, not just to you, not just to my family. I am depending on you to lead your riflemen at the coming battle. Come. Eat. We will return to our camp during the night." They strode together towards the feast. Little Turtle continued, "McKee's remarks were meant to be an arrow to pierce my honor. Everyone knows that he favors Blue Jacket."

Wild Carrot did not eat.

* * *

The council had broken up without a response to McKee's proposal. Three days later, five of the highest chiefs were meeting late into the night. Buckongahelas of the Delaware was the host. His guests were Blue Jacket of the Shawnee, Turkey Foot of the Ottawa, Five Medals heading both the forest and the plains Pottawatomie, and Little Turtle. Only their interpreters and closest advisors were permitted inside the longhouse. Trusted guards were posted outside, forming two rings. The chiefs had the highest regard for one another. Each had established himself as the war chief of his nation, proving himself in battle and in council. Their familiarity and mutual respect allowed for a somewhat less formal decorum.

Buckongahelas decided it was time to get to the serious business. "The English plan is correct in that we need to have one chief over all of the tribes," he said. "You all know this to be true. That leader sits within this lodge today."

There was no dissent. Wild Carrot was afraid to search their eyes. Each leader spoke in turn while remaining seated.

Little Turtle spoke, Wild Carrot interpreted into Pottawatomie and then into Shawnee. "The plan is flawed in having us follow the English officers in battle. I will not have my warriors follow them. They make their plans on what their spies have heard in the east. In the autumn past they had us go down the Wabash to meet the enemy coming from Vincennes when the main army was actually coming another way. My people lost brave warriors driving them back. Now Kekionga sits empty while their blood soaks the ground. The English did not know that the Virginian Scott would pass around Vincennes and strike the lower Wabash towns, or that Wilkinson would dart for Eel Town."

Five Medals was next to address the gathering. "The English give us guns, and balls, and powder only when it serves their interests. They are not like the French who came to live with our fathers and grandfathers. Many people of my tribe and yours," gesturing to all with a swoop of his hand, "carry the blood of the French within them. The English only come when they have their business, then depart."

Blue Jacket spoke in turn, "The Shawnee have held hands with English soldiers in many battles. We have seen them fight well. They plan well and bring good materials to make war. They brought cannon from their ships through our lands even to beyond the river Ohio. You know about the battle where we defeated Boone at Big Blue Licks. They labored hard for these cannon."

Each man knew the others. Though neither voice nor expression revealed emotion, they understood the passion that was behind the carefully chosen words.

Turkey Foot made his case. "My people have held hands with the red coats longer than the Shawnee. What Blue Jacket says is true, their soldiers and officers are good warriors. However, there are always much fewer soldiers than they promise. Their officers hold their papers with plans for battle in their hands too long when events turn against them. They do not fight as we do; they become rigid and hold their plans tighter. What Five Medals says is true. The English come among us with gifts and pretend to be our brothers. They do not hear our complaints. It is their agenda that is held high in council. When they have accomplished their task they withdraw. Now they know that we hate the Americans as they do. They supply us because we strike their enemy and ours."

The circle had gone round to Buckongahelas. He said to his fellow chiefs, "You have each been to Montreal as I have. I have seen many ships that come from the great sea. I have seen many cannon and how the English officers maneuver their men. Their army is powerful. When I turn towards my home I see their garrisons at Niagara, but they are not as strong there. When I reach Detroit I see their large town with many fine houses and shops, but their army is not strong at that place. When I ascend the Maumee I see a small post where the king's troops could be put into a basket and carried away. At Kekionga the French had a strong fort, but the English have only a hut. I reach my home and speak to my villagers who have never seen a soldier in a red coat." His words were soft yet full of power. "The English will surely fight the Americans again in many places, but at this place this is our war."

He stepped to the fire and stoked it. He stood while declaring, "We will hold council again in three days at the longhouse of Little Turtle. There we will decide whether we will be led by the English or by one of us. In another three days we will gather at the longhouse of Five Medals to choose a chief to lead all nations. The Chief of All Nations will hold war council. He will select a place to light a new fire."

"So be it," was the reply from Blue Jacket.

The others concurred. Usually there would be the offering of tobacco at such important talks. But this remained an informal council. If a formal pact had been secured, each great chief would be bound to instruct his village chiefs and hold council over it.

Little Turtle spoke, first in Miami, then interpreting his own words in Shawnee, followed by Pottawatomie. He would speak these languages only in the most intimate settings. In public or formal council he always insisted on an interpreter of his choosing. "We will meet next not at my council house, but at French Town at Kekionga," he said. "I invite each of you to bring along two trusted war chiefs. You all know my friend and interpreter, Wild Carrot. You will soon know him as a war chief."

Little Turtle and the others gazed upon him approvingly. Wild Carrot felt blood rushing to his head and a tightness gripping his chest. He had been in the center of councils large and small, important and insignificant, from Vincennes to Green Bay, from Niagara to the great river. He had translated for Frenchmen and English, Americans and Virginians, tribesmen from nearby and far away. He once sat in line with three frustrated interpreters between a Sioux chief with a great head of feathers and the Miami Pecan. Eyes had often turned to him for his words. Now they were turned upon him for his character. He forced panic from his head down into his chest, then further to his gut where he contained it

44

as he heard his name repeated in three languages.

Little Turtle continued, "He was adopted by Chief Porcupine, who is well known among you, where he proved himself in his village. Together we have hunted turkeys in the forest and buffalo on the wide plains of the Illinois country." Leaving out the skirmishes with the Pottawatomie and others he continued his praise, "He fought at my side against the Americans, also at the side of Chief Richardville. For these battles he was honored with two feathers and presented with the finest rifle captured on the field of battle. The Miami council made him a war chief."

Another flush came to Wild Carrot momentarily at the shame of not wearing his feathers. In fact, the only time he wore them after the ceremony was when he approached the great chief to permit Sweet Breeze to become his wife. It seems his marrying the chief's daughter was not included in the accolades.

Little Turtle pronounced, "He understands not only the words of the Americans, but also their thoughts. The Miami have entrusted him to lead many warriors in the coming battle. In three days I will show you his work."

The chiefs were close by smiling and making approving comments that Wild Carrot did not hear clearly; he was using all of his strength to keep his bowels from passing a monstrous amount of gas.

Yes, these men knew him. He had been to their fires and feasts, in their towns and their camps. Two of the chiefs had offered him maidens, which he declined. Tirelessly serving his chief, he never expressed his own thoughts or ambitions in their presence. Five Medals knew him well. Having become closest friends with Little Turtle, Five Medals had confided more than war talk with him. Together, they shared details that they expressed to no other person. Wild Carrot squared his shoulders, stretched his neck a bit, and mustered a look of optimistic confidence as he surveyed the faces of the elders. The glow of red embers softly lit each face that expressed approval and a hint of wonder. Five Medals was smiling profusely; he looked as if the embers were glowing from deep inside his eyes.

In one motion, Little Turtle got up, threw back the canvas from the opening, and sprang outside. The surrounding guard stirred to alert status as Little Turtle's clutch of guards scurried to fall in behind the great chief. Wild Carrot took a moment to excuse himself and hustled to catch up.

Little Turtle was launching his canoe as he called out, "Be at my wigwam at first light!"

Wild Carrot stood upon the little beach gathering his thoughts. In the distance he heard shouting and the muffled beating of dance drums. These sounds were overpowered by the echoing in his head, "In three days I will show you his work."

* * *

Wild Carrot was shaking off the effects of a listless night as his mother-in-law handed him a carved wooden plate. Eggs for breakfast! He wondered where she obtained them. These eggs were mixed with onions and seasoned with salt and her secret herbs. Tulip Leaf could make tree bark taste good. He was glad that Sweet Breeze had inherited these secrets and had surpassed her mother with her tea blend. Piles of flat corn cakes with beans and maple syrup were served with venison steaks, English sausages, and rabbit. What was not consumed at this largest meal of the day would go into the stew pot and be kept simmering for anyone who came by. He gave his mother-in-law an affectionate touch before perching on a log where he savored his meal.

Tulip Leaf did not allow any war talk at breakfast. Nor was there talk about family that was absent from her compound. Conversation was about hunts, food, and household matters. The light of the fire was giving way to the rays of the sun while she was describing the quillwork on a new buckskin tunic she was making. She described but did not show it, keeping it from the men for a future unveiling. It would be ready in three or four days. The past two nights had been cool, and soon the days would be cool also. She needed to finish this ceremonial garb and a pair of moccasins with matching pattern before she could turn her attention to clothing for the fall and winter.

As the orb began to appear in the east, the men finished the last bites of their meal. Each went to his place of morning prayer. Facing the sun until it broke well clear of the horizon, the men each raised their praises to the Creator in a low, slow chant. Thanking him for his protection during the time since the last sunrise, they asked for protection during this new day. If not, then they asked for an honorable death, death in battle, if possible. They thanked him for the game, saying that they had honored the animals they had taken and had wasted not. Some vowed to strike down the enemies of their people, or to avenge the death of a friend or relative. Some supplicated to have the game come to their path or snare. Little Turtle always asked to be increased in his wisdom since man could not discern by himself, but only by what was revealed to him by the Creator.

Wild Carrot's prayers were somewhat odd. Though it was unkind to pay attention to prayers other than one's own, others noticed. His were a higher pitched sing-song. He knew it too. Words of praise bubbled up from deep within him. His mind did not recognize them as hymns of Charles Wesley that he had heard in his childhood. Different too was that he prayed for others. Always the name of Sweet Breeze was included; today he lifted up the names of Porcupine and Primrose.

He returned to the fire to find it burning low and creating a great deal of smoke. He stoked it and added two small logs just as Little Turtle emerged from his wigwam with his leather travel bag. Sweet Breeze's father held Tulip Leaf until she sighed, "Be gone."

Little Turtle picked up a buckskin food bag. Striding to the riverbank, he motioned to Wild Carrot. "Come with me," he said.

Stroking his paddle in rhythm with the man behind him, Wild Carrot speculated about the trip. The size of the bag indicated two or three days. Trails from Kekionga radiated in all directions. It would be impossible to guess with any certainty the destination until they struck the trail. At these times he spoke to himself as though he was narrating to Sweet Breeze. It was as though she was there sharing the experience with him, or that her mind would follow his silent words wherever she was. The sun was bright behind them as a cool breeze blew from the north. It was a fine day to be on the river. Or perhaps being on the river made it a fine day. There was nothing like paddling to work out the kinks and clear the head.

As they approached the joining of the rivers, Little Turtle indicated to the left. Apparently they were to stop at French Landing and go up to the log cabin where Wild Carrot had set up his headquarters for the training camp. As they neared the little wharf the canoe was directed to the opposite bank and soon entered the mouth of Bonnecamp Creek where they beached. Two canoes of the great chief's personal guard pulled in beside them. These men began pointing and exchanging stories about the past year's war as the two chiefs climbed the gentle grassy slope and sat upon a small ledge of protruding rock.

Little Turtle stacked three rocks and reached into his pouch. He placed a large pinch of tobacco on top of the rocks. He looked across the waters as he spoke to the husband of his daughter. The river made a large sweeping bend away from them. They could hear the popping of guns around the bend to the right at the warrior training grounds. Inside the loop was a grassy field where the cattle of the Frenchmen once pastured. Directly opposite them to the south were the old log buildings of French Town. To their backs were reminders of the Battle of Pumpkinheads. What remained of fallen enemy corpses lay strewn about.

"Near this place is where the Creator protected you from the sword of the invaders. Hold this place in your head and keep it sacred in your heart," the elder chief shared.

The younger chief was unsure whether it was an illustration of words or if his father-in-law actually knew. He had never told anyone, not even Sweet Breeze with whom he shared his deepest thoughts. During the Battle of Pumpkinheads a horseman had swung a heavy sword that was certain to find its mark. A small branch had fallen from a limb above and had entangled itself with the blade. Branch and sticks had smashed against Wild Carrot's neck. He had grabbed the assailant's wrist and pulled him from the saddle, sinking his tomahawk in the man's spine as he thudded to the ground. The battle had continued to rage without notice of the fateful incident. It was late that day before Wild Carrot had contemplated this experience. Had the branch been dropped by a bullet or by intervention of the Creator of All Things? This he had continued to ponder for nearly a year.

"All of my life I have prepared for this time. I have been preparing you also," the great chief spoke as mentor to student. "My sister and Porcupine saw promise in you and adopted you in your youth. I witnessed your games of running and riding and wrestling. You were quick to learn our language. I had you come with me on my journeys to the four directions so that you could learn about the many tribes, how they lived, where they were located, how they spoke. You learned rapidly. I provided you with the documents of the French and the English and you understood their words and their meaning. You have done great service to your chief and your nation with your interpreting. You have been with me in more councils than any chief, so you understand my thinking. You provide wise advice when I request."

Wild Carrot's mind was swimming with visions of the events. He was beginning to understand that his many adventures were not just happenstance.

"Now you must be a war chief and lead these men into battle," the wise man said while lifting a stick in the direction of the popping sounds. "You have done well with them. Keep drilling them with their rifles; do not spare the powder. Put away any personal vengeance from your heart; seek only to avenge our nation which has been defiled."

He spoke about the enemy destroying the Kekionga council house. The whole nation still mourned the loss of their treasured historical and sacred artifacts. These were not taken by the invaders, but were lost accidentally in a fire while they were in exile to be kept safe from the invaders.

Now Little Turtle turned to the business at hand, "I will tell Withered Hand that you have access to the stores. How much powder can you spare?"

Calculating that the battle would surely come before the new moon, and how much would be required for continued training and for the battle, and some to cache, he reached his figure. Wild Carrot said, "There are ten kegs more than will be required. Two from the Americans are bad and cannot be used with guns. They are marked with blue dots. These are in addition to the ten."

"That is good! It is more than I expected!" The elder man uncharacteristically poked the air with his fist. "I am going to the Forks of the Wabash. My people there must not feel forgotten. I will take four kegs to Chief Charley as a gift. I will take eight of your men with me, They will be back in two days."

"There will be rejoicing at such a gift."

"Tomorrow, have your men take four kegs to LeGris in my camp. Have them take one to Buckongahelas and one to Five Medals. When my friends the head chiefs arrive for the private council," Little Turtle pointed towards the wharf with his stick, "we will meet them with ceremony. You will demonstrate the skills of your men and the power of their guns. Make a big spectacle of it! Remember how the officers at Niagara strutted their men in great squares on the field with the beating of drums and the calling of trumpets. They flew their flags and fired their cannon in grand display. In my youth I saw displays by the French in Montreal that lasted the entire day." The stick was waving in the air. Little Turtle continued, "After the demonstration take the men away. Keep them training with their weapons. Stay close enough that the firing of the guns can be heard. Stay with your men, you do not need to attend the council. At the council I will remind my friends that it is General Washington who directs this army, not the field general. It is General

Washington who threw off the English and chased them into the seas. This was in the east where the English were strong with men and ships and cannon. The chiefs will be brief in deciding against following an English command.

"Three days following will be the second council, where the war chief of all nations will be elected. You will be there. The following day you will take Tulip Leaf to the lake. Sleep there two nights. My wife will visit Sweet Breeze and decide whether to stay or return. I will send four young men to carry blankets, canvas, and salt. Leave two of the men behind and return with two. You decide which are to stay."

Wild Carrot was trying to take this all in. How should he reply? He suddenly realized that Little Turtle was gone. Quickly returning, the great chief stood facing the man he considered his son. He held in both outstretched hands a war club of cherry burl.

"This was my father's," Little Turtle said, "given to him by his father."

The prized weapon had fine workmanship. It had been rubbed smooth and polished with beeswax. Wild Carrot stood and accepted it gravely.

"Stay here and think on these things that I have spoken," Little Turtle admonished. "Remember the plans that we have discussed. When you are ready, go to the men that are entrusted to you. Lead them!"

Again, Little Turtle was gone in an instant. Pushing off with the two canoes, the guard paddled him to the French Landing wharf. One of the guard remained standing beside the third canoe. Wild Carrot did have a lot to think about. He sat again upon the little ledge. His mind saw his arrival at the lake, Sweet Breeze waiting by the walnut tree. He thought of lying on the hillside beside her, the full moon making shadows through the branches. Two nights, her father had said, "Sleep there two nights." Perhaps the baby had already been born! It sometimes did happen this early. He hoped that Tulip Leaf would stay and be there with her daughter. He imagined the baby arriving in this world while he engaged the Americans, the battle swirling around him. The battle! He should be thinking about preparing for war, not fatherhood. So, it was Chief Charley gathering the army at the Wabash forks. Yes, Charley was bold, yet wise.

He rubbed his hands across the war club. What an honor it was to hold it! With its possession also came responsibilities. Surely Black Loon, Little Turtle's own son, should be the one holding it. Sweet Breeze's oldest brother had shown great courage at Pumpkinheads. Her second brother, Crescent Moon, forsook the ways of war while residing in the war camps as a civic leader.

There were too many thoughts crowding his head. He must concentrate first on one then another. His chief had given him full access to the stores to prepare his force. He and Withered Hand had worked together in guarding, numbering, and distributing the supplies warehoused in the French Town of Kekionga. He kept charts in his headquarters in the old French house. He recounted each storehouse and its contents. What items would be useful? How would he conduct this demonstration? Certainly his chief deemed it an important event. Would his warriors participate in the farce? Where should it be held? The torture grounds just below the St. Joseph River at the confluence would be significant. But it still held the decaying bodies of the slaughtered American regulars. He hated the torture grounds anyway.

Against his will, his mind flashed to the image that he constantly tried to suppress. How, as a captive, he had been tied to the post with leather thongs. How he had seen the captive at the next post scream and wail while being roasted by the fire in front of him. How the women taunted the wretched burly man as they poked with firebrands. He again saw the knife expose the man's bowels, how they puffed and oozed at the heat. The frenzied mob turned their attention to him, a mere boy. Burning sticks from the death fire of the first victim were used to touch off the fuel piled in front of his own post. He would not die like the helpless man beside him. He would stare at the glow bouncing in the leaves high in the trees in the distance. He would welcome release from the life of starvation and beatings he had lived throughout the fall and winter. He felt the heat on his nose and chin and genitals. Could he hold without flinching? He heard the sharp whack of the knife against the post. He heard the woman say, "Do not burn this boy! I claim him for my Swift Foot!" He shook off the image and the chill that came with it.

He spoke into the wind to Sweet Breeze as if she could hear, "How shall I do this thing for your father?"

He looked up as if following the north wind carrying his voice across the waters, resting it upon the pasture meadow. He saw another vision, not of the distant past, but of what was to come. He narrated to his absent wife the plan of the mock battle, step by step, detail by detail. He found himself with his feet in the waters of the St. Marys, a twig flapping in the current against his ankles. His outstretched right arm was pointing the war club at a shrub in the pasture on the opposite shore. The lone guard was giving him puzzled looks as Wild Carrot followed the soft ground around the base of the knoll.

Though the guard knew him well, the big man greeted him formally, "I am Buffalo Man; I am your guard."

Wild Carrot sheepishly stepped into the canoe and grabbed a paddle. They crossed to the meadow and beached on the sands inside the bend just as Little Turtle's entourage paddled past, headed upstream to the main portage. Wild Carrot jogged up the grade to his cabin. Buffalo Man was close on his heels and stood outside the cabin door. Wild Carrot was somewhat irritated by this close attention. This would take some getting used to.

He laid his war club, tomahawk, and knife upon the table. He removed his cornhusk-colored loose blouse. Setting up a mirror, he clipped and shaved his head. The long queue he combed and braided with a red ribbon. Opening a carved maple box, he removed his headdress of two fine feathers. This he fastened to the top of the queue with sinew strings. The feathers curved jauntily down and to the right. He retained his medicine bag and amulet that hung by thongs from his neck. The medicine bag was of simple doeskin. The amulet was a thin, flat greenish stone that he had picked up from the sands of the grand lake Michigan to the north. He removed his buckskin leggings and put on a red wool pair made with blue fringe. A blue breechcloth completed his costume. In addition to the three weapons of his war belt, he attached a second knife to the calf of his right leg. Sweet Breeze had stitched this sheath and decorated it with paint and quillwork.

From a second maple box he laid out his paints. He carefully traced his signature white diagonal line across his face. Above the line he smeared with red. Below, down onto his neck and onto his shoulders, he rubbed black. Red lateral smears on his ribs completed the ritual. He placed some crumpled dry leaves into a copper cup and added a pinch of tobacco. Lighting it with flint and steel, he let it smolder while he went about the next task. From three long guns he selected the fancy rifle. He inspected it and checked the load, flint, and prime. Replacing the priming powder, he looped the horn about his neck and shoulder, as he did the leather pouch. When Wild Carrot emerged from the cabin, Buffalo Man grinned profusely. The guard gave a loud whoop. His strong arm buried his tomahawk in the end of the neighboring cabin log, sending chips and splinters flying.

CHAPTER 4
Kekionga

The canoe carrying Chief Five Medals bumped against the pier at French Landing in Kekionga. It was soon followed by those of two other Pottawatomie chiefs. The group made a little stately procession up the steep, short path to the former trading post. Upon reaching the top they were immediately greeted by the Miami chiefs Little Turtle, Charley, and Richardville. The Pottawatomie chiefs were surprised to find their Miami counterparts decked out in war dress complete with body paint. They were wondering if they had missed something in the invitation and would be out of place in their decorated buckskin attire. Under a brilliant morning sun, they were led to the west side of French Town. They greeted Withered Hand who was also in war paint, as were his men guarding the storehouses. Their destination was a row of tents that had been captured from Harmar. Each tent was closed on three sides with the open side facing a meadow of tall grass that sloped gently to the waters. The St. Marys made a sweeping curve enclosing the timber to the west, the bowl of the meadow, and then French Town to the right.

The back side of the tents blocked a whipping stiff breeze while the canopy absorbed the warmth of the bright sun. Long colorful ribbons of cloth fluttered from the poles of the tents as well as from a long row of tall poles set in a curve at the crest of the meadow. The wind played with the ribbon flags, creating an unending variety of ripples, occasionally snapping the cloth with a sharp whack. The Pottawatomie were warmly greeted by a contingent from each of their allied nations as they passed down the row of tents. They were pleased to find the others were not in their war dress or formal apparel. The exchange of looks after each greeting indicated that none knew what events to expect. They took their place upon the benches in front of the last tent. A smiling maiden emerged from the tent and directed their attention to the table inside bearing large turtle-shell bowls of berries and nuts. These she offered, or if they preferred, there were four bottles of wine and a jug of cider. Five Medals directed his personal guard to station themselves behind the tent. He chose wine.

The dignified audience was waiting, lounging, expecting to soon be addressed by Little Turtle. Chiefs frequently directed peeks to the easternmost tent to see if their host was rousing. A long canoe of five warriors flowed with the current and expertly beached at the meadow. The warriors trotted up the slope where they divided and stood in front of each tent. The man in front of Five Medals was tall and lean, dressed and armed for war. The stoic figure did not speak or look at anything. His outstretched arms offered a long gun horizontally resting upon his palms. This the chief took and carefully examined. The scene was repeated down the line.

When Five Medals looked up, the bearer was gone. A second canoe appeared. Six warriors walked abreast up through the tall grass. A seventh followed, hidden by those in front. On they came with the sun full in their faces. At fifty paces from the crest they stopped and parted, three to the left, three to the right. The warrior that was following kept his pace through the midst of them. Five Medals soon recognized the war paint of Wild Carrot. His battle attire was augmented by blue-dyed feathers on both upper arms. He carried a lance decorated with beads, ribbon, and feathers. At ten paces he stopped and thrust the lance forcefully into the ground. The sun caught the sharp edge of his tomahawk with a piercing gleam.

Wild Carrot stood alone facing the greatest chiefs of the lands stretching from the mountains of the east to the great river to the west. He would rather be charging with his riflemen into the mouth of cannon in real battle than directing this mock one. With only one half and one full day to prepare, he had seen to every detail that he could. Tents, food, and targets had been assigned to teams. A squad had occupied itself setting up the cannon and learning to fire it. He decided only one firing was necessary to create the needed effect. Reloading would require too much time to teach and might still result in failure.

Much time had been consumed in finding the appropriate mixture of powder to give suitable rapport without causing harm to charging warriors. Bombs had been prepared with fist-sized doeskin pouches filled with the poorer American powder. These were placed into cloth bags of flour. With everything in place there had been time for one practice drill with his men in the evening. Knowing the warriors were wondering at the strange occurrences, he had led them back towards the training grounds at the place of great sycamores. He stopped them short at the site of the old French fort. Here he told them to begin a fast and to be ready for battle when the moon rose. Upon returning the warriors had found a large bonfire lighting a war post covered in blue. Ample war paint was laid out for them. They heard Wild Carrot tell them that the next day they must please the Creator with a show of their skills. He told them that the eyes of Little Turtle would be upon them. He told them that the eyes of the chiefs of other nations would be upon Little Turtle. The warriors had burst into their war dances with shouts and chanting. The fire had burned high well into the night. The drums had kept their rhythm until the last hatchet struck deep into the painted post.

Now, facing the great war chiefs of the nations, doubts shot like arrows into Wild Carrot's head. What if the powder was too weak to ignite? What if the boys were afraid to set the marks? What if the warriors participated sluggishly, or even refused to join the action? Would the signals get mixed up? He wanted to inspect the field one more time, but had to fix his gaze on the dignitaries. He could see the one thing that the chiefs could not see. High within an oak behind the tents perched a signalman. Yes, at least the signal flags were ready. He took a deep breath. His voice must be strong and clear, "Chief Five Medals of the Pottawatomie."

He stood straight and tall as he faced the chief. He noticed that one of the Pottawatomie chiefs had a wide grin. It was the young man who had stopped at the lake camp, Metea. This unexpected sighting nearly caused him to forget the next dignitary's name. He managed to say, "Chief Turkey Foot of the Ottawa, Chief Buckongahelas of the Delaware." He turned his body square to each as he addressed them, "Chief Blue Jacket of the Shawnee, Chief Little Turtle of the Miami."

Events were now unfolding; there was no turning back. "You hold in your hands the same long guns as these warriors," Wild Carrot said. He swept both arms back while still facing his audience. "They are new to us. They are truer than any long guns we possess. The rifled barrels send the ball to its target at the command of my riflemen."

He pulled his war club from his belt and slowly raised it with an outstretched arm towards the heavens, actually towards the signalman. Five Medals was shocked to recognize it as the sacred war club of Little Turtle. Two yellow flags unfurled in the tall oak. A bomb exploded on the left side of the field followed quickly by one on the right. The startled spectators jumped to their feet as puffs of smoke and flour rose against the trees. Boys with long sticks topped by green apples ran forth from the brush and set the sticks into the ground, three on the left and three on the right. At the sign of a blue flag in the tree the warriors behind Wild Carrot turned to the targets. Each swiftly cocked, sighted at the assigned target eighty paces distant. Firing sent bits of apple flying. Still looking past the end of his war club, Wild Carrot saw the lone white flag indicating no misses. He lowered his arm and the warriors behind him exited to each side of the old pasture.

"I am Wild Carrot,"he exclaimed in the fashion of his nation,"I bring three hundred warriors with such weapons. The guns are all of the same construction. They all use the same caliber of balls."

He paused for the interpreters. There was some commotion among the chiefs at this telling. Their tribes hardly had one gun for each three warriors. They were of all shapes and sizes. Nearly all were muskets that could hail the enemy with one to four balls. The few rifles required balls to match the bore, and there were many bores. The chiefs inspected the guns again. Yes, they were well made, but three hundred was surely a boastful exaggeration.

"Keep your eyes on the enemy position," Wild Carrot again addressed the gathering.

He steeled himself to keep his eyes forward until all was played out behind him. A large red flag raced across the field below, near the river. The boy carrying it ran along an irregular fence line of rails and limbs. Logs were placed at intervals resembling cannon. Small blue flags signified the enemy. Several boys ran out from the woods and set up bundles of rushes made to resemble soldiers. Some were wrapped in blue cloth, some had hats. When the boys disappeared into the trees the red flag traversed to its original side. The black signal flag was displayed behind the tents. Wild Carrot took a deep breath and circled his war club over his head. He then held both arms straight out to the sides. A green flag then joined the black, signaling to the cast below to begin the show.

Shots erupted from the treetops far to the left. Splinters flew and blue flags fell. A series of bombs boomed from the enemy formation. Wild Carrot saw all the men gasp, even his mentor. There was a rustling in the tall grass one hundred and fifty paces in front of the assembled audience. One hundred warriors rose and fired. Hats flew, more blue flags fell. The riflemen disappeared into the grass. The chiefs could hear the rattling of ramrods as a second wave of gun-wielding warriors rose thirty paces farther down the slope. The effect of their balls was clearly seen on the targets. As these men disappeared, a third line another thirty paces ahead, organized in pockets, trained their rifles on the close by enemy. Reed bundles shattered and fell. A second round of firing began from the top, then the middle, and then the lower line. Smoke began filling the vale.

A third round began, but the top line did not dive into the grass this time. They dropped their guns and ran forward, reaching the heels of the middle line as those guns cracked. These warriors, too, wielded tomahawks and knives and joined the charge. The farthest line groups sent their balls to the enemy as their comrades flew past. These lower groups held their positions while reloading. The assailants reached the enemy as more bombs burst nearby. They hacked at the sticks and limbs. They turned over a log-cannon on the left and drove a large spike into one on the right with a stone battle-axe. Some of the young chiefs at the tents began to whoop. From the center of the enemy came a thunderous roar of a live cannon. Some of the warriors played dead as their comrades fell back. The front line provided cover fire with help from the trees as retreating warriors took up their previous positions. A few of the observers on the hill missed this latest action since they had dropped to the ground at the belching of the big gun.

The red flag again appeared and the field grew quiet. Reed and flag targets were again positioned. The whole was repeated with the Miami successfully routing the enemy. The riflemen retrieved their guns and gathered in the middle of the hazy meadow. In unison they cheered and fired a volley into the sky. They then noisily moved off towards their camp. Upon hearing this, Wild Carrot finally lowered his arms. He simply walked after his men.

Once through a curtain of brush, he looked for a place to sit. His emotions were drained as much as were his arms drained of strength. He had done all that he could. The reactions of the viewing chiefs indicated that his warrior-riflemen had performed superbly. Had he fulfilled Little Turtle's expectations? Had he overlooked any instructions? For now, he just wanted to sit.

The warriors would not have it. They dragged him off to celebrate. They all showed good humor as they rallied at the old fort site. Jesting and laughing, they crowded to the waiting feast. Some joked at the ability to walk the earth after "dying" in front of the cannon. Each told where they were when the mammoth gun blasted forth, some pretending deafness. One said that he was immediately in front of the horrible bellow. He told how the smoke and powder entered his mouth and came out his ears. Wild Carrot surmised that the air thick with gun smoke must bring out a feeling of well-being in men.

As were his instructions from Little Turtle, Wild Carrot kept squads of men firing at targets on a rotating basis until darkness set in. A second bonfire was piled high as he produced two kegs of rum. The celebration eventually subsided as groups of two and three drifted upstream to their campfires. Strolling through the camp, he stopped here and there conversing and congratulating the men on their unique performance. Three kinsmen invited him to use their room in the trunk of a huge sycamore, but he refused. He would sleep under the twinkling stars, listening to the gurgle of the rolling waters and dreaming of a lake visit. Buffalo Man kept his vigil.

After the wondrous display by the riflemen the attendees had lingered among the tents, visiting in various groups. There too, jesting and laughing were in order. There was wonderment at how these guns were procured. They wondered about the cannon. There was not known to be a single cannon located anywhere between the British camps along the Maumee's lower rapids and the American's Fort Knox at Vincennes. The chiefs who had hoped that no one had seen them dive to the ground were disappointed to hear the repeating renditions of their acts.

Little Turtle did not reveal that had he known that Wild Carrot was intent on firing the old cracked French cannon, he would have recommended against it. It was a dangerous stunt; but all proved well. The demonstration had created the desired effects. None of the chiefs had seen such a coordinated attack by men of the forest. The way of the tribes was to fight in small bands of family members or trusted friends. Warriors would swarm in and about the enemy's position dartingly. They could maneuver quickly in the forest, swamp, brush, or meadow. Surprise, terror, and trickery were esteemed. Each warrior within his band was intent upon displaying personal bravery, even desiring death on the battlefield. For the remainder of their time on earth, returning warriors would tell and retell of their triumphs in battle. They would display their captured scalps and spoils as they pointed to their battle scars.

The chiefs also saw who had prepared these Miami riflemen. The trusted interpreter was more than they had supposed. His three hundred men were wicked with their shooting. What training this required! He united them into a power unknown in their own tribes. The man who had held Little Turtle's war club had maneuvered his riflemen without words, without drums or arm signals, even without seeing with his eyes, as if by his will alone. Beyond that, he had honored his chief by presenting this grand spectacle for their gathering.

The southern wind had settled to a light breeze, yet it quickly cleared the little valley of gun smoke. The chiefs enjoyed a meal of roasted grouse and fresh perch from the lakes region. A canoe had arrived with an ember from the fire of Little Turtle to light the evening council fire. The lighting ceremony took place in the old pasture. Blankets formed a semicircle facing down towards the river. The Miami Chief Pecan assisted Chief Little Turtle in initiating the first formal council within the confines of Kekionga since the Battle of Pumpkinheads.

All chiefs spoke favorably on the use of the new rifles. Blue Jacket spoke last with astounding news from McKee. The American General St. Clair had sent writing to Detroit. This writing declared the intentions of the American government to establish a fort at Kekionga. The Americans did not want the British to misinterpret their intentions as being an attack on the British posts. The English officers had never in the past received such a communication from the blue-coat army. Any pretension of a peaceful resolution with the enemy was swept away. The enemy was resolved to claim in deed, as they had claimed in words, the entire region as their own.

Historically the French, and later the English, had garrisoned small forts at Kekionga. These had been welcomed as business headquarters. They served to control the traders and the French population. Occasionally a larger contingent of soldiers would accompany an official touring the area with the king's proclamations. All knew that the Americans were different. They desired the land for themselves. They would cut and burn the forests to establish their plantations. They would build their ugly towns on the sacred grounds of the tribes. Virginians had preached the annihilation of tribes; now it seemed to be the policy of General Washington's council of thirteen fires.

The chiefs could see the council fire's reflection on the white canvas of the tents above them to the south. They could envision that it was Washington's fort. In their minds they could see the blue-clad soldiers drilling in this hillside meadow. They could hear the cannon's echo rolling over the waters of the three rivers, the smell of spent gunpowder filling the valley. They could hear the trees cracking, crashing to the ground. A fort here would mean the end of resistance for the Shawnee and the Canadian tribes. The Miami and their brothers the Wea, the Piankashaw, and the wandering Delaware would be completely displaced. The Pottawatomie lands would be fronted by the Americans on three sides. It must not happen! The tribes would fight as one! They would unite under one leader; the leader would not be an Englishman!

* * *

The sun was well up when a group of canoes landed at the training grounds. Wild Carrot immediately recognized Little Turtle accompanied by ten Miami warriors. As they approached across the soft ground, he saw a contingent of Pottawatomie beach their canoes and mill about the water's edge.

Little Turtle stepped directly to his son-in-law, "Be prepared to move to the advance camp in six days."

Wild Carrot quickly calculated. That would be the day after his return from the lake. His captains were fully capable of making the preparations without his direction. There were no women or children in this elite compound; the camp could move quickly when and where needed.

"I have brought Chief Metea of the Pottawatomie. He pleaded with Five Medals to join your riflemen."

Wild Carrot gave a startled look and was preparing to protest.

Little Turtle cut him off, "There is little time. They cannot expect to achieve the skills of your men. He has forty chosen men. Do you have enough guns?"

"I have thirty in reserve," Wild Carrot stated.

Little Turtle weighed the knowledge, "Test these men; keep twenty and send me twenty. Metea will serve as a captain under you. Do this for me." Then he added, "Tell your men that they have made their chief proud."

Watching the elder walk towards the canoes the young war chief pondered. Move in six days. Train these newcomers, these outsiders. Was he expected to forego his jaunt to the lake? Would he not see his Sweet Breeze until after the battle? No, he was to take Tulip Leaf to the lake. If he were to stay, he would have been told that her escort was changed.

Little Turtle stopped and returned. He instructed, "I will tell this Pottawatomie chief and his followers that if any of them do not follow your command they will be tied to a tree. An apple will be placed upon the violator's head. Ten Miami riflemen will stand at seventy paces and fire at the apple. If the culprit survives, a second apple will be targeted by a second ten. If he survives, he will be free to return to his people."

"Perhaps a walnut,"Wild Carrot suggested.

The men embraced and parted. Tests were soon underway. The Pottawatomie warriors sat in a huddle as their chief was led through a thicket. Metea joined Wild Carrot in a clearing.

Wild Carrot asked,"Why do you suppose that post was selected to hold the apple?"

At seventy paces Metea saw five straight, thick limbs planted in the ground. The bark had been removed and each was painted a solid color. Thinking that he would be asked to fire at the apple he replied,"The red pole indicates the color of the blood of the Americans."

"You have chosen well. Now ask the question of each of your men in turn."

A warrior appeared and moved the apple to a different post. One of his men was escorted from the brush to Metea's side. The question was posed.

"The green post makes it the most difficult to site the target."

And so it went, with Metea becoming more perplexed. Finally one of the contestants spoke of the white post while the apple was on the blue. This individual was escorted in a separate direction from the clearing. Metea wondered at this happening. One man spoke of a trick, as he could see no apple. And so it went until eleven of the group were eliminated. Metea was astonished to learn the meaning of the puzzle; some men simply could not see the apple at this distance.

Those who passed the first test were led in groups of four to sycamore trees with four colored ribbons tied high in the branches. The men of the squads would compete at once to reach a ribbon, untie it, and deliver it to Metea. One fell, two were very slow, and one refused to climb. Five more were eliminated in the throwing-rocks-at-the-turtle-shell event. Those who were escorted back to the canoes protested that they had not had a chance to shoot an arrow or fire a gun.

The selected Pottawatomie warriors were anxious to fire the new long rifles. They sat impatiently through instruction of caring for the valuable weapon. They were shown how to inspect it, how to clean it. They were shown the proper load. They learned to properly mold and trim lead balls. They were instructed that they could use only the balls from the molds provided to them, yet they could share or could use those retrieved from a fallen comrade.

On the second day, the trainees were taught the signals and how to move together. Finally they were given powder and balls, each under the direction of a proven marksman. The third day it was load, fire, reload, fire, reload, fire, inspect, reload, fire. Over and over they drilled. Their loading was clumsy and slow. They could not grasp how the Miami instructors could effortlessly reload while moving with their eyes focused on a distant target. The novelty of the new gun vanished. Some Pottawatomie occasionally thought about standing against a large tree steadily balancing an apple.

Metea was thrilled at partaking in each endeavor. He rallied his men, reminding them what a great opportunity this was. He hid his disappointment at not seeing Wild Carrot that day.

Wild Carrot was having a busy day preparing for the relocation of the camp. He had conferred with the fifteen captains who were under him, excluding Metea. He showed Withered Hand the maple sticks he had painted with colored bands. These sticks would be sent from the front with runners to authenticate a report or request. He separated personal items into those that he would need at the lake from those that should be ready to go to the advance camp. Three times he checked that he had the necklace purchased at silversmith Kinzie's post on the Auglaize. He instructed Buffalo Man on procuring food for the two of them for the march.

A runner arrived bringing a red stick. The message was from Little Turtle to all of the Miami camps. The runner recited, "We will move in four days. Send away any remaining children. Any stragglers who will not be in the field camps should go to the lakes region. All others should prepare to move with the warriors."

Now the whole nation would know what several Miami chiefs knew. The time was at hand. Wild Carrot selected four young warriors to participate in the excursion to the lake. He had not yet decided which two would stay there to watch over the refugees. He would observe their behavior during the trip. He sent these men with supplies ahead to Turtle Town. He arranged to have horses sent ahead to meet them farther down the Eel River.

Having attended to all the necessities, Wild Carrot headed down the Maumee to Little Turtle's camp. Arriving there, he was pleased to see Tulip Leaf had her bundles piled upon a rack beside her wigwam. The whole village was alive with activity.

"Are you well, Mother?" He had never before called her "mother." He surprised himself as he said it.

"Yes," Tulip Leaf said, "all is well. Do not worry, I am prepared to travel before dawn. We will want an early start."

He smiled. Indeed she was anxious to see her pregnant daughter. She showed that she understood how much he desired to be there.

Tulip Leaf asked, "I have food prepared. How many will be traveling?"

"I have four young warriors with huge appetites, but they have gone to the village of your home to prepare their own food. They have taken with them Blind Man. He will stay at the lake camp." A rifle had exploded in the man's face, burning him badly and blinding him. He would forever be known simply as Blind Man.

"This man here," Wild Carrot pointed directly at his guard, "eats an elk each day."

Buffalo Man could not contain his laugh.

Tulip Leaf held up a fistful of loose wool, "It is hard to know what clothes to wear this time of year. One day is sweating hot, the next is shivering cold."

The two men grabbed gourd bowls and filled them with steaming stew. Their hostess disappeared into the wigwam. Wild Carrot began to relax, glad to be done with the preparations. Once again his mind ran through the events since the mock battle. Everything seemed to be in order, that is, as long as the squad of Pottawatomie did not blunder.

Tulip Leaf reappeared, "My husband inquires about your preparations."

He began reciting the events he had just contemplated.

She stopped him with a wave, "Do not fill him with details. He, too, has been very active. This is a big day for him; he needs to meditate. I will tell him you are pleased with your preparations."

She retrieved a small bundle from the pile and headed for the opening of her abode. Raising a hand gently she instructed them, "There is enough noise around here, do not add to it."

The two men stole away to a vacant hut. The nights had been short and Wild Carrot needed some rest. Soon the young war chief's snoring added to the village noise.

Buffalo Man kept his watch while his charge took a respite. When activity in the compound picked up, he hesitatingly gave his boss a shake, then another. Finally he resorted to poking him with a stick.

Buffalo Man urged, "It is time. The sun grows old in the sky."

Wild Carrot sprang to his feet. He ran to the river and briskly bathed. Returning to the hut, he set out his mirror and paints. He renewed the pattern that he had worn constantly for five and one-half days. Could he persuade his mother-in-law to leave this night immediately after the council? No, she would want to stay with her husband. She did say they would depart before dawn. He could see it now. At the crown of the crest they would look down upon the valley bowl and glistening lake. The inhabitants would have a banquet prepared for their arrival. Sweet Breeze would be standing by the walnut tree, waiting for his approach. He would embrace her, then place the engraved silver necklace about her long neck. He could feel her warmth and the softness of her skin.

He heard laughter. Charley had told some hilarious story enjoyed by LeGris and Richardville. Behind them Chief Soldier was rummaging in a pouch. When had these men arrived? Perhaps he should be paying more attention to the business at hand. He noticed that these chiefs were dressed in finely fashioned buckskin, not war dress. Porcupine and a Wea chief that he did not know by name were now joining the group.

Wild Carrot greeted Porcupine, "You look well, Father."

"You also, my son."

"What is the news on the prisoners?"

Porcupine answered, "None, there is nothing. Our search goes unanswered." After a moment he declared with a laugh, "I hear from Charley that you have been busy."

"That I have. These are exciting times."

"Charley says that our chief was quite pleased with your pageant."

Wild Carrot allowed a grin. Tulip Leaf stepped out to meet her guests. She was beaming radiantly showing off her best outfit. There were greetings all around. A maiden poured wine. A young warrior fed the fire so eagerly that it nearly engulfed the limbs overhead. Everyone had to move back from the heat.

Shouts rang forth when Little Turtle joined them. His tall frame was clothed in newly decorated buckskin crafted by his wife. Quillwork of red and blue and white covered the chest and ran down the arms. Fringe at the forearms and the bottom of the tunic were accented with beads and colorful thread. A woven thread chord laced the neck. The leggings and breechcloth were of crimson cloth, again with fringe tied with beads. On the side of the moccasins was quillwork matching the arms. The tops of the moccasins showed embroidered black cloth.

Little Turtle's five feathers were expertly positioned above and to the side of his head. He wore his signature bear-claw necklace and silver French medal. This medal he had repeatedly worn to English councils, never giving in to demands that it be put away. A wide armband of engraved silver was about his left bicep. The great chief danced once around the bright fire in boyish fashion. He then extended personal greetings to each person present, including the seconds, the guards, the wine maiden, and the fire boy.

* * *

A fleet of canoes moved down the Maumee as if in battle formation. Chanting accompanied the rhythm of the strokes. There were howls and whoops. There were calls of elation at the accomplishments of their great chief. As they passed fire after fire, their calls were returned from the shore by revelers who joined in. The landing at the village of Five Medals was lit by two fires. Drumming and chanting were rising from a fire beyond the longhouse. Emerging from their canoes, the Miami war chiefs were escorted up the torch-lit path to the longhouse.

Nearing the longhouse, Wild Carrot saw the great chief stop, allowing the others to pass. This was not customary, but Wild Carrot did as the others did. Taking his place behind his father he saw that the other great chiefs had already assembled. The council lodge was packed with colorfully dressed leaders of many nations. He noticed that the council fire was augmented by bear-oil lamps hung from the roof. Red ribbons were also fastened to the roof. No one spoke. Drums and merriment drifted in from the feast outside. It was only a moment until Little Turtle entered.

Five Medals stood. He lifted the calumet of the Pottawatomie. He declared, "Welcome, Chief of All Nations!"

Everyone stood. The calumet was received and smoked by Little Turtle. It was smoked by Five Medals. The calumet began to make the rounds. Richardville presented the calumet of the Miami to Five Medals. This was also passed down the line, consuming a long while.

Wild Carrot now realized what apparently everyone else knew. His deprivation of sleep had apparently muddled his mind. It was a foregone conclusion. It did not require a vote. Little Turtle would lead the army of the nations. If the last council had elected to follow the English, then most likely Blue Jacket would have been the leader. But now his mentor was the one.

Little Turtle was the natural leader of the close group of leaders. His fame was known to all the villages of all the tribes. Though each tribe's great chief had proven himself in battle as a warrior and chief, this man had defeated American invaders three times. Little Turtle was supported by a well defined government of his people. Each of the others had a tenuous hold on their claim as their nation's head. Only Little Turtle and his father before him had been known to hold the symbols of both sagamore and war chief. He was not bound to the English as were Turkey Foot and Blue Jacket. He fielded the greatest amount of warriors. All were conscious that the intended destination of the invaders was at the heart of the Miami nation.

Little Turtle stood and held forth his arms. Richardville produced many wampum belts and draped them over the arms of the appointed Chief of All Nations. They were each identically patterned with fine rows of glass beads. The field was bright red with blue border. A pattern of blue arrows and hatchets ran the length of the center. A yellow sun dotted each border at the ends. Richardville sat to hear the address.

Little Turtle's speech was amazingly short. He said, "In three days we will meet at the mouth of the Auglaize, opposite the point. We will meet at the place where we honor Great Chief Pontiac. There we will light a new fire using neither flint nor steel. There we will lay out plans to meet the enemy."

That was it. It contained no oration of his triumphs, no listing of his nation's accomplishments. There was no soliciting the vanity of the assembled dignitaries, no demand for loyalty. Richardville again rose. He lifted the belts one at a time and presented them around the room. A belt was stoically given to each nation, even to the Iroquois who had come with only eight warriors.

After the last belt was given, Little Turtle sat. The orations began with each chief presenting a wampum belt to Little Turtle. So it went into the night. Wild Carrot was glad he had napped earlier. Finally, Five Medals honored the Chief of All Nations with his wampum. Then the passing of pipes began in earnest. Tribes from the east, the north, and the west each wanted their calumet shared by all.

Wild Carrot began to wonder if he would be able to get away before sunrise. He would have to make fast tracks in order to travel to the lake and return for the Auglaize council. Smoke faster, faster, he was wishing.

CHAPTER 5
Eel River

Four young warriors were in good spirits powering the laden log canoes downstream. The sun was providing just enough light to dodge the limbs protruding into the narrow stream. There had been a night of carousing in Turtle Town. Still, they had the canoes loaded and ready when their war chief and the woman arrived. Of course this was not just any woman. She was the head of the village where they had spent the night. She was the wife of the head of the Miami nation, today the wife of the Chief of All Nations. They would perform their duties well and see what little extras they could provide for her. Yet, each intended to enjoy this excursion away from the war camp.

The canoes of the warriors formed single file. They were followed by a light canoe with Buffalo Man, Tulip Leaf, and a young nephew of hers. At the tail was Wild Carrot and Blind Man in a fourth transport. Blind Man could feel the surging of the craft with each stroke of the man behind him. He could hear the ripples generated by the paddle as well as the dripping during the return stroke. He joined the rhythm with his own strokes. How refreshing it was to feel the cool waters of the river Eel trickle down the ash wood paddle. He breathed deeply to capture the smells in the moisture-laden air. The chatter of the boy in the canoe ahead gave a sense of direction; Buffalo Man called out obstacles. Wild Carrot and Blind Man worked out simple commands to improve coordination of movement: left, right, power, easy, hold.

Talk turned to the herds of buffalo they each had seen: thousands on the trace between Vincennes and the Falls of the Ohio, at the salt licks and cane fields of the Kentucky lands, and on the Illinois plains. They spoke of how the Virginians were blocking off the licks and turning them into salt factories. Can the reports be true that out of every ten buffalo on the plains, nine had not survived the terrible harsh winter? They determined that woodland buffalo numbers had been reduced by over-hunting. Blind Man had once seen a herd of four hundred of these eastern buffalo along the Auglaize, often two to three hundred. Recently the herds were more widely scattered and lower in number. He had recently killed a lone bull as he was traveling to the war camp with friends.

It was turning out to be a gray day. Treetops were doing what they could to add a bit of crimson, yellow, gold and orange. Otter and beaver hesitated briefly to view the passing parade. The waters of Blue Creek entered, swelling the stream. Tulip Leaf informed the boy that her husband was born on the lake to the north at the head of that creek, living there until"just about your age."

The canoes of the warriors doubled up. Wild Carrot moved forward beside the bark canoe.

He asked his mother-in-law,"How is the paddling?"

"I love it! I do not get to do it much these days. I am just now getting the feel of it."

They exchanged smiles,"Blind Man informs me that he is quite the buffalo hunter."

"Welcome, buffalo hunter,"Tulip Leaf said. "I hope that you find my river to your liking."

Blind Man responded,"I am sorry to say that I have not been to your village or this river. I like the feel of it. My village is on the upper Mississinewa."

Stroke after stroke, on they went. Though enjoyable, this was no leisure outing. There was business and a destination to be had. Wild Carrot steered near to Buffalo Man and gestured to pick up the pace. Several brooks added to the current's strength. They were hailed by a sentinel at the mouth of a creek on the right, later by one on the left.

The plan was to enter the lake camp from the east rather than from the south. This trail was slightly longer than ascending the creek from Squirrel's Village, but better for horses. Knowing that horses would be waiting not far distant, Wild Carrot took the lead. At a bluff straight ahead the river took a sharp left. He scanned the bluff-top to see if a sentinel was posted; he saw none. Rounding the bend a hill rose on the left as the one on the right fell away to a gentle slope. There they were!

"To the right hard,"he instructed Blind Man. "Hold."

The prow slipped into the sand and held. Wild Carrot stepped with a splash into the knee-deep eddy. He helped Blind Man out and guided him to a grassy seat. Quickly returning to grasp the canoe, he lifted and pulled it solidly ashore. He walked upstream to where the bark canoe was landing, extending a hand to Tulip Leaf. She ignored the gesture and disembarked.

The four warriors, plus two who had advanced the horses, went about the business of unloading canoes and packing horses. The others walked up the long low slope of a meadow. Reaching the little summit they stopped to look back at the progress of the packers. The hill top was something of a ridge that stretched from the river bluff due west to the horizon. The river flowed away to the southwest. The north side of the ridge sloped gradually into a wide valley. Close by was a small round lake choked with reeds on its south and west shores. Forest pushed against the lake from the other directions. A clutch of huts stood where the prairie and woods collided.

Wild Carrot headed the horse-train along the ridge-top. Two warriors ran up and joined Buffalo Man to form a semblance of a guard. They were wagering who would kill the first bear, no guns allowed. They were excited at the signs of buffalo, very fresh signs as a matter of fact. The little caravan moved cross-country through briars and brambles. Thin sod was interspersed with bare gravel and rocks. Thorns and burrs poked at their leggings. Sharp stones seemed intent on piercing their moccasins.

A series of peat and marl bogs lined the bottom along the north edge of the ridge. The ridge and valley gave way to rolling hills. Up and down four times they went. The fifth rise formed the bowl of the brilliant spring-fed lake. Wild Carrot quickened his step. For the third time during the trek he checked his pouch to feel the silver necklace. He stretched his neck to see over the crest. The view was not as he imagined. There was no sparkle on the lake this day. Wind whipped circular pockets of leaves on the hillside. Ten huts surrounded the original encampment. The big old walnut tree was there, but there was no one under it watching, waiting. Two elderly men were sitting beside the frame of a wigwam. Children were husking a pile of corn. Women were upon their knees scraping skins. Was one Sweet Breeze? He could not tell. As his traveling companions caught up from behind, he took Tulip Leaf by the hand and again forged ahead.

The stiff fall-season saplings were not cooperating with the two men building the wigwam. Lashings were not holding. They were contemplating their next move when they saw the string of horses descending. The men abandoned their work and approached the visitors. They expressed their joy at seeing someone from the outside world. What was the news of the war? No, they did not know visitors would be coming. How long could they stay? Yes, Sweet Breeze was residing in the new wigwam by the shore; she was resting. The men went to the packhorses to examine the bundles.

Wild Carrot strode to the new wigwam. He had one foot inside, then pulled back.

He thought it best to call, "Sweet Breeze!" Again, "Sweet Breeze!"

He heard rustling inside. Out she came. Her eyes looked at his then danced away. She laid her head on his chest. He embraced her and sighed. He held her at arms length and reached into his pouch, bringing forth the prized necklace. She presented a faint smile as he dropped it over her head. To him her skin felt as cold as the silver chain. He bent to look for a smile on her face. Sweet Breeze stepped back from her husband. Spotting her mother, she ran to her. The two women embraced fully. Sweet Breeze sobbed and trembled.

Wild Carrot stood there dumbfounded, not knowing whether to turn left or right. At Kekionga scores of men move at his command, but here he was helpless. Mother and daughter staggered to the wigwam and went inside. Wild Carrot wandered over to witness the elderly men celebrating the arrival of canvas and rope. He went to the spring and got a drink. He went to the beach and sat near the lapping waves. He idly hoped the waves would sooth his mind. The two men slapped his shoulders as they seated themselves beside him. They thanked him for bringing the material, saying how much it was needed. The three sat quietly facing the stiff cold wind.

The two residents departed when Tulip Leaf approached. She reached into the sand and picked up some flat pebbles, plinking them into the water one at a time.

"There will be no baby," she said as she peered over the waters.

Wild Carrot rose silently and went to the packs. Brandishing his knife he opened one and lifted out three wool blankets. These he took to the new dwelling. Inside, he placed them upon the mats and lay beside his wife.

"I am sorry," Sweet Breeze finally spoke, "I wanted to be strong, but I could not face you."

"There should be nothing that you cannot bring to me." He pulled her closer. After awhile he said, "Tomorrow is a new day. Another day the Creator will grant us a child."

She sobbed softly, "Indeed, it will be so. But today it is a hard thing."

Wild Carrot wanted to talk some more, but kept drifting asleep. He had not slept since the afternoon nap the day before. "Do you know that your father is now Chief of All Nations for the war against the invading army?"

She whispered, "No, we receive little news."

"It happened only last night," he said. He nodded off, then caught himself, "The captives from Eel Town remain a mystery. We have heard nothing." He slept.

Sweet Breeze pulled the blankets around them. She could tell that he was exhausted from the weight of his duties, yet he was strong and warm. His heart pulsed against her as if lifting the whole wigwam with each rhythm. She had failed him by thinking only of herself. She would pull herself together and be the strong wife that he deserves. Surely her father could only spare him for a few days, then he would be off to war, serving his nation, protecting her. She did not sleep. She tried to think of the things she must do to help her husband, to support her people in the war, to break out of her mourning.

The night was black and cold as she found her way to the lake. She placed a piece of bark upon the sand before setting down her basket. She disrobed in the unrelenting cool breeze. Briskly, she plunged in and rubbed her body with handfuls of sand. The frigid lake waters gave her whole body gooseflesh. Drying quickly, she wrapped herself in one of the blankets sent by her father.

She lit a candle from the coals and entered her mother's hut. She said softly, "Mother, Mother, I need your help."

"Yes my child, that is what I came for, to help," Tulip Leaf replied.

"Brush my hair and braid in this ribbon."

Sweet Breeze knelt as her mother brushed a long while. The tugs on her hair in the candle's flickering dim light took her back to her childhood. First separately, then together they reminisced happy times that only they knew. Soon there was glee and laughter. Tulip Leaf rubbed her daughter's shoulders with scented oil. After completing the task, she displayed a skein of light blue cotton cloth.

"I have nothing prepared for you," the daughter protested.

"Seeing you smile is my present, child." She unfolded the cloth and draped it around her offspring. "Something else, wait." Tulip Leaf rummaged through her things and came up with a dark blue sash adorned with gold pattern. "Here, take this. Now be gone. Later I will set some food by your wigwam."

* * *

By the time Sweet Breeze and Wild Carrot thought of food, sunbeams were piercing around the canvas opening. Wild Carrot poked out his head and one arm to find the food. Cold corn cakes would do fine when topped with the maple syrup and blueberries. Milk, three kinds of nuts, and tea were wolfed down.

"The camp is empty," he mused, "They must all have gone to the cornfields."

"Come here," was all that she replied.

When the sun reached its zenith, they were both hungry again. Rousing about the cook fire, Sweet Breeze noticed activity on a steep slope on the lake's far side. Gazing, she saw that it was indeed buffalo grazing. She counted, twenty-four, twenty-five, twenty-six. Small dark figures advanced from the woods towards the animals and stopped. Again they advanced and stopped. No, they were not wolves.

"Husband!" she called. She pointed, "There is a buffalo hunt going on!"

They took bowls of stew to the beach and sat next to each other. One animal fell to the arrows of the stalkers, then another. The herd began to roam about. A bull staggered. He bellowed and kicked to his feet with great commotion, then fell still. Cows, calves, and bulls were scattering. Puffs of smoke rose as shots popped from scattered bushes. The last of the beasts disappeared over the crest leaving three more lifeless dark brown masses on the ground. Hunters approached each of the fallen animals with weapons held high in the air. Standing over the fallen prey, they chanted prayers of thanksgiving. Women and youth rushed from the trees with shouts of joy. A boy led a man, Blind Man it must be, into the midst of the celebration. Blind Man sat and began beating a drum, chanting to the rhythm. The carcasses were skinned and quartered. Hides and meat were packed on horses and the procession began to round the lake.

"I must leave after sunrise tomorrow," Wild Carrot told Sweet Breeze in a low voice.

She looked at him with a start. So soon, too soon, she thought.

"Your father will have a war council at the Auglaize in the evening."

She knew his presence was required. The sun warmed their backs as they looked over the placid waters of their beloved lake. Buffalo Man sat far beyond the walnut tree, envious of those who took part in the hunt.

Blind Man had taken charge of the short expedition. He addressed Wild Carrot, "We will keep only one of our prizes here at the village. Elk and deer will provide meat aplenty for this little village. Take one buffalo to the village of Tulip Leaf and the four to my brother warriors in your camp. The hides, and the brains to tan them, will stay at this place."

"That is generous of you," his war chief replied. "You have brought good fortune to this place."

Tulip Leaf approached, "I will be staying. Sweet Breeze has need of me for a season. Little Turtle need not be concerned about me. Let his head be full of war only. We will work the patches of corn and send as much as we can."

She turned and left before he could respond.

* * *

The horse under Wild Carrot splashed into the Eel River, swam a distance, and found footing on the far side. The riding horses for him and his ever-present companion had been obtained at the little round lake near the river. They galloped due east over a wide flat open prairie. They dipped into Little Pony Creek's narrow winding valley. They found the crossing easy and were once more moving swiftly across the flatlands. Wild Carrot never felt comfortable in the open lands. He preferred the wooded hills with their streams and lakes. Eventually, they were in the forest once again. Soon, they struck the trail that connected the Forks of the Wabash with Kekionga. They tested the endurance of the animals. Fording the St. Marys, they entered the riflemen's training grounds at the sycamore grove.

Wild Carrot found the training camp packed for the big move. Hundreds of horses had been brought in to haul the loads. Taking care of business with two captains of the riflemen, he directed them to secure good riding horses. The horses were to be delivered promptly to his French Town cabin. At the cabin, he shed buckskin for war garb. He lashed his war club to the saddle. The two riders were soon again making tracks to the Auglaize.

Wild Carrot and Buffalo Man found the crowd was already gathered. They sought out the Miami chiefs. Wild Carrot took his place in the large semicircle. The north bank of the Maumee provided a natural amphitheater facing the river. On the opposite shore the Auglaize joined the mighty river. Dancers could be seen on the point formed by the two rivers.

The focal point of the gathering was a large stack of sticks. The war-council fire was to be lit here by the water's edge. The fire would later be moved beyond the little bluff.

Drums from the point began beating a fast rhythm. Five torch-lit canoes appeared from the mouth of the Auglaize. Front and center was Turkey Foot, the gathering's host. Paddling and chanting as one, the warriors gave their best show. Turkey Foot stepped ashore followed by the torchbearers. The torches were set upright in the mud along the waterline; the warrior-paddlers formed between them. Turkey Foot displayed a brightly decorated white pipe. This he dramatically broke in two and threw the pieces far into the waters behind him. He pulled a polished red-handled tomahawk from his belt and laid it on top of the stick-pile.

Drums beat from behind the gathering as two men ran out, one from either side, and began working their fire-lighting spools. The chief of the Ottawa began his discourse on the vile conduct of the enemy. One of the spools showed some smoke but could not maintain it. The story of the slaughter of peaceful Christian Delaware families was told. Tinder burst into a tiny flame that was carefully nursed. Turkey Foot narrated the wanton killing of game animals, the stripping of the forests, the gouging of the salt licks. The smoldering tinder was transferred to a box of shavings. The litany told how the Americans violated sacred grounds of the dead and robbed their possessions. The fire-lighter handed the burning tinder box to the chief who raised it high and handed it to the man serving as his second. He told of the Americans making treaties with minor chiefs and trying to force the words upon entire nations. Turkey Foot's second lit the council fire with the flaming tinder box. The orator lamented the Americans inviting chiefs to council, and then murdering them while yet under truce.

A shaman of the Shawnee sprang forth fidgeting in the sands around the fire. This chanting and convulsing man apparently had never bathed in his lifetime. He spat into the fire and leaped over it. A poof of green sparks shot up high into the night air. The listing of American transgressions went on unabated. A shaman of the northern Pottawatomie took four fancy feathers from a pouch. These he placed at the four points of the compass, quills pointing to the fire. He studied them seriously for a time, then placed strips of tobacco where the quills pointed to the fire. With great ceremony he tossed and sprinkled finely chopped tobacco over the entire fire. Satisfied, he picked up his feathers and left. A third holy man that no tribe seemed to claim shook rattles at the fire and danced wildly. He overstepped his bounds by kicking sand on the chief and shaking a turtle-shell rattle in Turkey Foot's face during the old chief's speech.

The fire grew as did the oration until the flame caught the hatchet. The discourse stopped abruptly. All watched the burning tomahawk handle while listening to the slow methodical beat on the hill. When the tomahawk's head fell with a burst of sparks, a cheer went up from the crowd. Little Turtle emerged from behind dressed for war. He stately walked through the midst of the seated chiefs directly to the fire. Stopping briefly, he stepped around it and drew his own tomahawk. This he buried deeply into a red-painted post. Another cheer went up, louder than the first. The war was on! Shouts and whoops and chanting were augmented by musket fire from the point across the way.

Little Turtle raised his new black-walnut war club to silence the celebration. He shouted, "This fire will light the new war-council house tonight! There the Great Spirit will reveal his war plan!"

He lowered his club and festivity resumed. He passed through the crowd followed closely by invited chiefs.

The war chiefs huddled tightly in the council house. Calumets were offered and passed, but the long speeches were eliminated. When all were satisfied that the spirits were pleased Little Turtle stood and addressed each chief by name. He gave the arranged sign to Wild Carrot that he wanted him to interpret. Wild Carrot took a prominent place and recognized the other interpreters. Two Miami warriors of the guard entered and spread a large blanket near the fire. They set some rocks and turtle-shell bowls of colored powders upon its edge. A large white stone was placed in the middle of the edge nearest Little Turtle.

Finally, Little Turtle spoke, "This is the war plan that was revealed to me!"

A large red stone was placed midway between the white stone and the left edge. A blue line of powder was traced from the white stone past the red and to the left edge.

"We are gathered here on the Maumee," the Chief of All Nations pointed to the red stone with a stick of hickory. "The intent of the American army is to build a fort at Kekionga." He touched the white stone. Leaving a gap to the right of Kekionga a blue line was drawn slanting away to the right. "This is the Wabash," he said.

At the edge nearest the fire, directly across from the red, a large black stone was placed. A blue line looped away. Little Turtle said, "The American Fort Washington is at the north bend of the Ohio." There was silence as the two assistants filled in the smaller rivers with green. He continued, "The march of the enemy will be along this route."

A wide black mark began at the black rock and stretched across the blanket. The line passed in turn the source of the Mississinewa, the Salamonie, and the main south branch of the Wabash until finally intersecting the St. Marys. The chiefs were all craning their necks to witness. They each knew the lay of the lands and rivers. Raids on the Kentucky settlements, and more recently on their sorties to harass the American camp, had hardened their knowledge.

A rock was placed at the Forks of the Wabash. Little Turtle instructed, "Chief Porcupine has his war camp at these forks. He will split his forces retaining the tribesmen from the lower Wabash as well as a few of his own. These will remain at his current camp where he can move in any direction to block the enemy or support our forward camps. Chief Soldier will descend the Wabash with warriors of the Miami, and then ascend the Mississinewa to near its source." A green stone was positioned to designate the place. "He will be joined by the Delaware of Chief Buckongahelas. Chief Charley will take his Miami now at the forks down the Wabash, and ascend the Salamonie to its head." Green stone. "My Miami from this place will cross to the south branch of the Wabash to establish a forward camp where it turns to the south." Green stone. "Chief Five Medals and the consolidated Pottawatomie will ascend the St. Marys from Kekionga to near the path of the Americans." Green stone. Little Turtle announced, "These four forward camps form the mighty talons of an eagle."

All present bumped and shuffled trying to see. Each was satisfied that the four rivers with the green rocks looked indeed like the talons of an eagle reaching for its prey.

Little Turtle touched his stick again upon the large red rock. He continued instructing, "From the camps on the Maumee the Shawnee will move up the Auglaize. Blue Jacket will set up at the little bluffs and at the old Wapakoneta villages where that river turns to the east." Two green rocks were placed on the blanket. "Black Hoof will move across to the bend of the river called Great Miami." Another green rock. "Turkey Foot will head all Canadian and eastern tribes. He will advance to the little rapids of the Auglaize which are downstream from Blue Jacket's first camp. These form the other talons."

76

Again, there was jostling for position to view. These did not look so much like eagle's talons, but were passable. The lair was obvious. The enemy would march unknowingly into the snare. Black Hoof could close the trap from one side and Buckongahelas with Soldier from the other. If the Americans pushed through ahead they could be guided into the expansive Black Swamp.

Little Turtle spoke boldly, "I will lead the attack from the west, Blue Jacket from the east. All must remain in the war camps until I give the order to advance. No one will attack until my signal, or the bird will fly and we will lose our opportunity. Do not be responsible for sending the enemy to flight due to your impulse to show your bravery. Many have sacrificed to come and stand against the Americans; honor them with your patience.

"The Americans have been filling their stores since the time of the blossom of the tulip poplars. They will bring all of their materials with them: cannon, forges, carpentry tools, nails and their food and tents. There will be many horses and cattle. They will move slowly, cutting a wide path and building bridges. Their weight will be like a man carrying a boulder in a marsh. They may fall under their own weight and retreat to their fort. In this case we will press them hard. The Miami and Pottawatomie will bind them within their fort and the Delaware will destroy their boats. Blue Jacket with all of his forces will slip away to attack the American town at Marietta and wreck havoc along the length of the Ohio." The eastern tribes were greatly excited at this option; the possibility had never occurred to them. "The Wea will destroy the isolated forts at Vincennes and at the Falls of the Ohio."

Little Turtle checked his audience. All were keen to his words. He continued with the plan. In a lower tone, he said, "If the Americans succeed in advancing with their materials, we will watch them march into the talons. We will all be patient. Black Hoof will let them pass by. Buckongahelas and The Soldier will let them pass by. We will not trip the trap until they are deep within the snare. The farther they are from their fort, the more difficulty they will face. There will be many brooks to cross. The ground will become softer under their boots. The season will turn colder. When the time is right, you will receive a signal from me, and from Blue Jacket, to leave your war camps. You will then join the tribes to your left and to your right. When the time is right, our war clubs and our tomahawks, our arrows and our muskets will strike them as one!"

Little Turtle began to quickly pace before the fire. His words also quickened. He encouraged, "If the Creator provides us with a blizzard or with heavy rains, we will welcome it. If the invading army becomes bogged down, we will not wait for the snare, but will attack quickly before they can move."

The war chiefs were all amazed at the comprehensiveness of the plan. The obvious simplicity was astounding. With the scattered camps each group could forage for themselves. Their backs were to their homelands allowing for the flow of communication and supplies. Traveling lightly they could concentrate quickly for the attack.

Little Turtle coached, "Do not look for the American General St. Clair to divide his army. He is a veteran of Washington's campaigns. He will be arrogant in his strength. He will hope his show of power will chase us away. When engaged he will concentrate his forces. This we will encourage. You have been taught to scatter the enemy and to conquer the pieces. This we will not do! That would only break our trap and allow the bear to escape. He will stand and fight! We will stand and fight! Their general will rely solely on his cannon and muskets. We will silence his cannon! His muskets will use up their balls and powder! Our tomahawks will end the days of the Americans north of the Ohio!"

Blue Jacket stood and shouted. The lodge erupted with joyous howling. Blue Jacket let the celebration continue awhile. He then called for order.

Little Turtle pointed to each green rock in succession. He continued, "Each war camp will release twenty men to independently harass the enemy camps and supplies. These warriors are not to know our strategy. In the event that they are captured, they cannot betray our cause. They should do nothing to change the direction of the enemy army's march. The Americans will have deserters. That is good. Follow them and kill them at a distance so others may also desert." Addressing his worst fear he concluded, "If mounted horsemen break off to strike at our homelands, as did the raiders Scott and Wilkinson, we must let them go. Send the alarm to Porcupine and to the Wea and Piankashaw villages. It will be left to them to confront the horsemen. The claws of the eagle must remain sharp to rip into the enemy's flesh."

Little Turtle was certain that the Virginian volunteers would want to employ the raiding tactic. He was also sure that the old general would not permit anything that would reduce the American army's strength.

Little Turtle complimented, "Buckongahelas will keep his spies in the field. They have done us great service. They understand the enemy. They penetrate deeply into American camps. Now they tell us that the General St. Clair has sent soldiers to prepare bridges to his north. They are beginning to make a fort above their Fort Washington. This new fort is on the Great Miami River. Soon their columns will be on the path to our lands. Do not delay! Move now to your advance camps!"

With this the chiefs were dismissed. They left in single file, each nodding to their leader, but neither speaking nor touching. An Ottawa paused and shook his prized eagle foot that he wore about his neck. Only Wild Carrot and Blue Jacket remained. Wild Carrot was dismissed.

Wild Carrot took the opportunity to briefly say, "Tulip Leaf stays at the lake." He soon found his horse and trotted in the dim moonlight for Kekionga.

Blue Jacket spoke, "The plan was received well by the chiefs. They will be loyal until the attack is under way."

"You must see that the Wyandot and the Chippewa warriors do not attack too soon and give up the surprise. When we advance from the war camps, crowd in upon them from the east. I will have Five Medals crowd from the west."

"I will keep them down the Auglaize as far as I dare where they will have farther to travel and will be crossing the swamps."

The two men smiled and smacked each other on the arm.

Blue Jacket added, "We must preach to the warriors to not stop for prizes during battle. They must maintain the fight. This is not their way. We need to convince them that the spoils will be distributed equitably after all of the Americans have been chased beyond the Ohio."

"Agreed!"

CHAPTER 6
Head of the Wabash

Large puffy snowflakes fluttered down to add another touch of frigidness to the black waters of the marsh. Wild Carrot was sloshing along, testing the bottom with each step. The swamp varied in depth from ankle deep up to mid-thigh. Trudging through the muck was actually a relief to him; finally he was moving towards the enemy. He turned to survey the progress of his warriors. Three hundred and twenty bumps were silhouetted by an orange sky of the setting sun. Tromp, splash, plop, on they came. A thicket of shaggy birch ahead was his immediate destination. There he would rally these riflemen one last time before the assault. He looked to the left to see if he could detect the movement of Little Turtle's main forces, nothing. He looked to the right for signs of Chief Charley, nothing. He knew that they were there, it was just as well that they were invisible.

The sun's display was overcome by heavy clouds. Black water was joined by black bushes, black muskrat dens with their domes of sticks, and black trees. The waters became shallow, but the muck deepened. Thick brush choked the edge of the thicket, each man finding his own way through. Reaching ground that was partly firm, Wild Carrot wrapped himself in his blanket. He anxiously waited for the tail of the procession. Listening intently he was surprised that he could not hear the sloshing more than an arrow flight away. He gave the call of a quail to signal the location of the assembly. He felt a fist pressing against his back signaling Buffalo Man's presence. The darkness could not hide the grin of Metea who was, as always, front and center.

Wild Carrot was pleased to hear the men joking about missing appendages. Some claimed to have left them floating in the frigid waters. These men had been dedicated to their mission throughout the campaign. They had progressed from outcasts to something of an elite unit.

Little Turtle had to constantly visit the other camps to keep them from charging ahead to engage the Americans, or from wandering away in disappointment at continual waiting. Who could have predicted that it would take the foreign army forty-two days to reach the headwaters of the Wabash? The chiefs organized a rotation of days of hunting, war training, and contests. But still, the warriors were restless. Little Turtle organized a network of news about the enemy's movements. He held open councils each evening to dispel rumors.

Wild Carrot had endeavored to keep his squads occupied during those days of waiting. The riflemen once organized a deer-drive in the flatlands between the Wabash and the Salamonie. Taking three days, it generated so much meat that they had to call in other camps to carry it away. Once, Wild Carrot was directed to take his most mobile force to sweep behind the advance camps. His force traveled from the Wabash forks to the mouth of the Auglaize in order to confirm that there were no renegades or stragglers bent on pillaging the defenseless home camps. He had taken several opportunities to exchange visits with Porcupine. He encouraged other war camps to view his riflemen's war games.

The Delaware spies knew the enemy camp inside and out. General St. Clair had massed an army of nearly three thousand. Of these, well under three hundred were experienced soldiers. Somewhat over four hundred were militia from the Kentucky lands. The vast majority were short-term enlistees. Hamtramck's presence was noted. Richard Butler, the nemesis of the Shawnee and Delaware, was with the American army. He was a general, second in command only to St. Clair. His scalp would be a prize above all others.

It took their army five days to move the short distance from the Ohio to their new Fort Hamilton. It took another ten days to finish the fort and resupply themselves before again heading north. At five days' march they built a stockade to guard their supplies, and at another four days they formed a great encampment. At this place they built a larger fort, named after Jefferson, holding two cannon. On the ninth day at this camp a pack train of one hundred horses arrived with food, but the train and the escort had consumed much of it on the way.

The spies reported that the march resumed from their new Fort Jefferson on the third day after the supplies arrived. After only two days they again stopped, awaiting more food. At this camp there was much wrangling among the officers and the men. Butler was reported to be arguing with St. Clair about the slowness of the progress. The strength was now seventeen hundred, diminished by leaving many behind to bring supplies, and some men left to garrison each of the three new forts. On the third day, a string of eighty packhorses arrived, but the advance did not renew for another five days. The following night was the night of the great storms. In the morning the general was furious at learning that there were a great many deserters from the militia. He sent many soldiers under Hamtramck to bring them back. He did not move forward that day, but received a caravan with two hundred packhorses loaded with food for men and animals.

Butler had wanted to advance to Kekionga with five hundred mounted riflemen. St. Clair demanded to keep his strength intact. He boasted that when he had the opportunity to show the tribes his powerful army, they would melt away. That strength was now gauged by the Delaware spies at twelve hundred uniformed, plus two hundred fifty militia. In their midst they carried six large cannon bound for the grand fort of General Washington's intent. Additionally, eight smaller cannon moved with the formation. Nearly seventy women served the men with daily chores. Over one hundred spare horses and sixty cows followed. The last report from the spies told that the American scouts were venturing out only a short distance beyond the army. They did not know the land. They were being directed by their compass.

The warriors surrounding the red-haired chief had heard the daily reports. Now gathered on the little rise, they were eager to engage the enemy. The dank musty smell of the swamp water hung heavily on them.

Wild Carrot addressed his men, "It sounds like you have enjoyed our trek this night. We have only to the next timberline until we form our position. Your patience will be rewarded. The attack will not be at sunrise; that is when their sentries will be vigilant. We will wait until they have filled their bellies and are milling about. The soldiers have been marching in the swamps for three days. Snows have beaten them in the face. They will be looking to their comfort, not to their duty. Watch for the signal, fire well, make the charge, destroy the cannon! Remember what you have practiced. Once we control the cannon you may allow your anger to flow to the soldiers!"

A warrior shouted from the left, "I will fill their mouths with the sod they came to seek!"

From the right, "I will fill a cannon with their private parts and touch it off!"

This brought a cheer from all around.

Wild Carrot called for quiet, "No more shouts until the cannon are silenced. Remember, officers and cannon first."

They pushed off through the brush and gained a narrow neck of the marsh. The waters became shallow and pocketed with brambles. The snow turned to ice pellets, then back to puffy snow. Wild Carrot hoped for scattered snow cover that would be ideal for his men to conceal themselves. Too much ice would make it difficult to climb the trees and to rush the cannon.

When they reached the forest they were met by a waiting messenger from Little Turtle. The simple message was that the attack should proceed as planned. They moved to higher ground and found protection under a grove of giant oaks.

A second messenger arrived, "This message is from Little Turtle, Chief of All Nations. The plan has changed; you are not to be the first to begin firing. The militia of the enemy has camped on the north side of the Wabash. The regulars are crowded upon a knoll on the south side. Chief Little Turtle and Chief Five Medals will strike the militia quickly and drive them into the main camp. This will impede the cannon-fire and cause confusion in the lines of the regulars. You can easily locate your position near the Wabash River. The enemy's bonfires will guide you. Hold your attack until the militiamen are in front of the cannon." The messenger gave Wild Carrot the coded stick and asked if he should repeat the message.

Wild Carrot quizzed, "Bonfires?"

"Yes, the enemy is trying to warm the entire swamp with their fires," the young man's lips crept into a broad smile. Obviously the generals had no idea about the circle of tribes closing upon them.

He handed the boy a stick from his pouch and told the courier, "My message is: I understand. I will hold. The riflemen will be in position by the time this message is received."

He sent two scouts to reconnoiter the crest of the hill, two to locate the warriors of Little Turtle to the left, and two to the position of Charley to the right. The two from the front were not long in returning with muffled laughter.

The scouts reported, "From there we can see many fires of the enemy camp. The hill falls sharply from the top. There is a small marsh and winding brook. A smooth short hill rises to their cannon. We could find no sentries on this side of the brook."

The scouts looked at each other and giggled. The other scouts reported that friends were close by and were moving closer.

"We will rest here for a time," their chief instructed. "You have fasted two days; today you will eat the cattle of the Americans."

Nothing more could be accomplished until the passing of the deepest of the night. Waiting became the hardest part. Occasional noises from the American camp caused a stir. But each alarm proved hollow.

Finally, Wild Carrot signaled the captains of the tree-climbing sharpshooters to move their men ahead. He called the captains of the first line to assemble to his right, the second line to his front, and the third to the left. Here the men stripped to their loincloths and checked their weapons. He waited agonizingly long periods before releasing each of the groups.

A Miami warrior was not to think of loved ones once he was in the camp of war. However, Sweet Breeze was ever present in Wild Carrot's mind. He vowed aloud to her, "I will follow the path that the Creator has laid before me." He smacked Buffalo Man on the shoulder and scurried to find a place to command.

Metea led his band of riflemen to position on the front line's right. He had badgered his friend and war chief into providing a special assignment. His Pottawatomie riflemen would creep ahead of the front of the three lines. They would hold their fire until the conclusion of the third volley. At close range they would rise and eliminate any officers or artillerymen that survived the barrage. They would charge and loop behind the cannon to destroy powder and materials. They would break the swabbing poles and overturn the swabbing buckets while the Miami were eliminating the defenders.

The chief from the prairie beyond the Tippecanoe smeared his blanket with mud, as did all of the stealthy force. He dabbed the mire with reeds, leathery brown oak leaves, and weed straws. Covering with this canopy he motioned forward with his rifle. Off they went, hovering low to the bottom-ground. Twenty steps and halt, twenty steps and halt. Check the lay of the terrain; check for sentries; move on. Ice pellets pinged against his cover. The precipitation aided the sly approach. Metea reached the flooded brook's edge. Here he paused, then biting his lip, moved on into the icy waters. Finding a little rise where the reeds ended at the current, he signaled to hold. He made a nest in the muck, lining it with a deerskin.

Metea did not need to hear or see his companions; he could sense their presence. He did not need to watch for the signal flare; only count the rifle volleys, three, three, three, shoot. He hoped there would be enough light to see the targets on the knoll above. He would know the officers and the artillerymen by their hats.

Metea waited through the night. He thought back to when he met the red-haired man at the lake. How their trust and friendship grew at the war camp. Now he had the opportunity to prove his bravery. Nearby, two men began speaking in English. He determined that they were below the bluff ahead, close enough to hit with a stone. If they splashed into the brook, he would have to silently eliminate them with his knife. He wished he understood more of their language. Soon, he concluded that the men had come to the brook to relieve themselves. With much commotion, they slipped and slid up the hill.

Wild Carrot surveyed the bottomlands. He could detect the dimples forming broken lines. The lines were not perfect, but certainly acceptable. The ice and snow were obliterating their presence. He found a place where the signalman could light his fire between two fallen trees. The left signalman assured him that the elements posed no problem; the fire would be ready. The chief again checked his weapons. He sat against rotting twin stumps overlooking the little valley. Waiting would be the game.

The bonfires in the distance were burning low. They reminded Wild Carrot of Ouiatenon's fires. He recalled how the Miami had set the trap hoping to snare Hamtramck. He reminisced about his visit to Small Cloud and his son. He had intended for them to be safe at the lake camp. Captured at Eel Town, their whereabouts were still unknown. Were they alive? He recalled defeating the Americans under Hardin, the waiting on the bluff at the Eel crossing. At Kekionga he had also waited along the St. Marys for the enemy to attack. This time he would be the one to attack. He thought about the branch saving him from the sword. He thought about the knife cutting him loose from the stake at the torture grounds. He thought about the fires burning, roasting his knees. He thought about the girl poking a stick into his ribs.

Buffalo Man poked again, "Chief, Chief! There is movement at the enemy's fires. There is the banging of metal pots. They are rousting."

Wild Carrot jerked with a start. His mind was muddled; how long had he been asleep? He could see women dressed in their white bonnets and collars, some with white aprons. A silvery glow permeated the mist behind them. It was not long until the entire hilltop was lighted. A tapping of drums came from the center. The Delaware spies had informed him of the routine of the enemy camp. He had in turn instructed his warriors to not misinterpret the drumming to be an alarm. The soldiers wandered about with much racket. At the sound of a second tapping of the drums, they formed their ranks. Officers shouted; drums beat; a volley was fired. The sentries were changed, unintentionally giving the watching warriors a clear understanding of their posting. The soldiers broke their ranks and went to chores and eating. He watched to the north and listened, waiting for the results of the initial arrow attack by Little Turtle's forces.

A lone horseman came galloping from the north. He crashed through the narrow stream of the Wabash. He rushed to the nearest finger of the hill. A lad with a high pitched voice, he continually yelled, "Indians!"

Apparently the rider never thought to yell that the attack was in progress. A stampede of horses, some mounted, many not, soon traced his trail. The popping of uncoordinated shooting could be heard, then the thunder of a volley. The air carried sounds of shouts, whoops, and gunfire as the engagement quickly escalated.

"Wait, wait for the militia to be driven in," Wild Carrot coached himself.

Across the vale there was shouting and the rattling of metal. Drums beat and soldiers formed in rank and file. Cannoneers were busy about their weapons. Three cannon were turned northward, four remained directed across the valley, and one somewhat southward.

He could now see a mob dashing to the river as the militia abandoned its position. The Virginians were offering no resistance. Many were empty-handed, desiring only the cover of the army on the hill. On and on they came, obstructing the field of the trained cannon, pushing into the lines of the regulars. Loose horses were creating disorder. Some militiamen were held up by the throng at the base of the hill. They began pushing along the brook.

"Ready your flare!" Wild Carrot ordered.

He could now see the line of smoke from the firing of his comrades to the left. The regulars and cannon were positioning to counter.

"Signal the flare!"

A flaming arrow arced high over the little valley. Before it landed, an arrow from the left side of the riflemen's front line made a strange glowing arc. Next came one from the right. The rear line rose and fired.

Soldiers tending the cannon fell. Firing exploded from the Miami riflemen's middle line. Soldiers in their dark blue coats, crossed with white, made perfect targets. One cannon belched, raking several of the militia. Confusion reigned on the hillside. The Virginians who had not made it to the top stopped and looked about. The soldiers did not know whether to fire or hold. The front line of the Miami marksmen exposed themselves and fired, taking many at the cannon. The militia stragglers on the bank now made pell-mell for the top.

The three lines of Miami riflemen made a second wave of firing. The cannon began a somewhat organized barrage. Their grapeshot, shattering trees around Wild Carrot, told him that their aim was to his ridge top, not the bottomlands. Lines of soldiers were organizing a return fire. His sharpshooters in the trees began eliminating the officers. Smoke began to fill the valley. The rear line fired and began the charge. They moved quickly forward, gathering up the middle line. The front line fired a devastating blast and disappeared into a patch of rushes. The horde of tomahawk-wielding warriors rushed past using their best war cry. Boom! Boom! Boom! Not a single Miami fell to the cannon fire.

Metea threw off his blanket and raised his war cry. In an instant he charged through the creek and onto the hillside. His war club bashed a cowering buckskin-clad youth in the temple. Metea made for the hill top. Intent on penetrating to the caissons, he dove through a line of astonished uniformed men as they reloaded. He stepped on two dead soldiers and dove over some baggage. A fellow Pottawatomie followed his lead. A band of soldiers turned to fire. These soldiers received Miami tomahawks in their backs, muskets discharging as they fell. The battle became general mayhem. A cannon blasted the shoulders, head, and arms of a Miami high into the air; the rest of him went elsewhere.

Soldiers were focusing on protecting the big guns from the charging warriors. With a handful of his warriors, Metea began wrecking the materials behind the cannon. With his war club, he deflected a bayonet driving for his chest. He chopped into the top of the assailant's shoulder with his tomahawk. The war club smashed the side of the man's face to mush. He picked up the man's musket and looked for a target. A squad of soldiers was running up from the south. Metea took quick aim on the leader and fired, dropping the man, though not fatally. He led his band along the line of stores behind each cannon. He was surprised that the guns were smaller than he had expected.

Miami warriors broke a cannon loose and sent it tumbling down the hill. The next in line was receiving a metal spike driven into its fire-hole by a Miami wielding a stone mace. Three lines of blue uniformed soldiers moved up quickly from behind. Metea leaned against the kegs and pulled a canvas over him.

Wild Carrot saw masses of soldiers approaching. He signaled retreat. His warriors withdrew in good order and slipped into their hiding places. The soldiers attended to the dead and wounded while their replacements came up. This second force was larger than the first. Few of the first had withstood the charge. Survivors struggled to the rear. The new lines fired ineffectively into the field and trees. Four of the cannon had been silenced.

Wild Carrot's marksmen in the trees continued to pepper the officers across the way. He detected a line of warriors to his left advancing through tall grass near the river. Farther away Little Turtle's main force was massing behind a neck of woods. He waited for his men to find their weapons and reload, and for Little Turtle's forces to concentrate.

Not wanting to give the Americans too much time to organize, Wild Carrot signaled to attack. The Miami riflemen fired in orderly waves. He tried counting the puffs of smoke; the loss of his warriors was amazingly small. Should he rush down and join this charge? No, there may be a message from the great chief. He had a role to play and he would stick to it. His men made their second rush to the summit. He could see Little Turtle's multitude of warriors on his left taking up the charge. He could not see to the right, but could hear the moaning roar of battle building in that direction.

From his hiding place, Metea again counted the volleys. He heard the wailing of dying soldiers. He could hear the clanking as the soldiers turned from balls to bayonets. He crept from the canvas and located six Pottawatomie. With hand signals he directed three to assault the gunners from behind, and the remainder to continue trashing the stores. He could hear battle sounds coming from all directions. Two gunners were astonished to find the enemy behind them. One met with Metea's tomahawk in his chest. The other had his gut slashed open by the knife of the warrior to Metea's right. Several blocks of soldiers from somewhere began concentrating on the area.

Metea dove under a bush and pulled oak leaves around him. Again he heard the Miami fall back. He listened to the commotion all around. The moaning drone of dying men palled over the ground. Officers were striving to organize new groups to serve the cannon and the musket lines. He could faintly hear the engagement to the east. Was it getting closer? The fight to the north continued.

Wild Carrot saw the battle being hotly contested to his left. To his right, the warriors had fallen back as his did. He ran down the bluff and began passing instructions. There would be one volley and reload. All would charge at once with rifles in hand. They were to discharge at contact with the enemy and continue the charge through the lines. Enemy balls whizzed around him as he darted back and forth over the mushy ground. He made it to the signal station on the right and fired the flare himself. The Miami volley was returned by two from the hilltop. A third time the warriors made for the hillside.

The war cry of a Pottawatomie rang above the din as a warrior sprang from a bush near Metea and lunged at a soldier. The chief saw a musket barrel club his comrade's head. He could hear or sense a bayonet stick the warrior to the ground. Soldiers began poking about the thicket. Metea decided if he were to die here, he would do as much damage to the enemy as possible. He grabbed a stone in one hand and a fist of soggy sod in the other. He burst like a quail from his nest directly for the cannon. He thrust the sod on the firing hole of one cannon and the rock into the mouth of another. He felt a rod smack him across the back. He fell draped over the second cannon. The cannon fired before he had time to move. His innards shook and his teeth rattled. He found himself sprawled on the hillside minus his belt of weapons.

A strong hand grasped Metea's elbow and pulled him to his feet. A rifle was smacked into his hands as he was pulled up the slope. "It is primed," the man said. It was Wild Carrot.

All around, Miami warriors fired into the soldiers at close range. The warriors reached the crest. They threw their rifles into the uniformed ranks. They dashed ahead shattering the line with their tomahawks. The soldiers could no longer hold the ridge; they gave way. The Miami howled as they pushed cannon and ammunition over the brink.

The Americans refused to panic. They conducted an organized retreat. They fired, fell behind the second line, and reloaded. Time and again they fell back.

Warriors swarmed from tree to log to bush. Tribesmen carrying bows joined the rifleless riflemen. Fallen limbs and low oak branches provided ample cover for the advancing warriors. Warriors with muskets joined the methodical chase.

The soldiers were trying to fend off the attack from their front. Arrows and balls were flying in from the flanks also. It became apparent that the entire army was surrounded. Men and officers continued to fall at a constant rate. Officers were rallying the tired men and reforming squads. One group of soldiers made a charge and successfully pressed through the ring of warriors. Their ammunition spent and isolated from the remaining army, they were hacked to bits by war hatchets. The main force of soldiers retreated until their backs formed a ring around the baggage in the center of the camp. Their concentrated fire held off the advance of the tribes.

One officer formed a company and forced open the road that had led them to this fateful knoll. Soldiers and packers and women fled through the opening. The rout was on! Wild Carrot tried to direct bands of warriors to focus on the few soldiers determined to cover the retreat. He soon left the chase of the fleeing mob to the Delaware and Shawnee. Some took up the chase while others roamed the battlefield looking for prize weapons. Metea circled the north end of the melee to meet up with the Pottawatomie of Five Medals.

Wild Carrot went in search of the officers' tents. He stepped carefully around bodies knowing that some would be alive and wounded, or alive and playing dead. Either could be as dangerous as a panther in its lair. There were so many bodies of the enemy that it was necessary to proceed slowly. Just as well, there might be stragglers lurking behind any tree.

Seeing a red and blue flag and a large white tent, Wild Carrot moved to the south. He heard whimpering from the backside of a large beech tree. Stepping around silently, he saw a young man with blond hair and pale complexion sitting against the tree. The youth looked up at him with wide eyes and half-raised a pistol. Wild Carrot's arm swung down and the fair skull popped open under the weight of his war club. He continued towards the officer's tent. Rounding a massive oak, he looked straight into the face of a woman. She was tall and strong with fiery red hair braided atop her head. Her blank stare revealed shock at what she had witnessed. Startled at the sight, hardly more than a stride away, Wild Carrot paused. Before he could react, an arrow pierced her neck. She fell at his feet. Her arm stretched out across his moccasin; her hand released a butcher knife. He looked around for the source of the arrow, but saw no one.

Arriving at the tent, Wild Carrot studied it intently. He satisfied himself that it was vacant. Entering, he found the pouches, leather-bound papers, and rolls he had hoped for. He cleared a table to stack selected items. He called to three warriors who were scavenging bodies for coins. They ignored him and went about stringing one fallen man's intestines in some branches.

He went to the back of the tent and found a keg and some cups. He set these upon the table. He called, "Whiskey!" The three joined him shortly. Imploring the name Little Turtle, he persuaded them to help him carry the merchandise.

Wild Carrot witnessed the ridding of the battlefield while leading the way back to the cannon position. Warriors would approach each fallen soldier and, after scalping, either bash in the skull or sever the head, marking the enemy as permanently dead. Others were plastering innards or private parts on branches. Warriors were pushing sod into mouths, nostrils, eye sockets, and ears rewarding the invaders with the ground that they had so desired. Some Ottawa were gathered around an officer who had been propped against an oak. They had the fallen man's heart tagged to the tree trunk above his scalped head.

"Butler! Butler!" they cheered.

They cut the heart into strips and ate.

"Butler," they repeated the name of the acclaimed officer who had been their nemesis.

Wild Carrot waited while his three assistants partook. They desired to increase their bravery by ingesting this man's heart.

"I have no need of it," Wild Carrot declined.

He walked on, keeping an eye for a fine long rifle. He approached the overlook where the field-cannon had been. There he found women of the tribes already on the battlefield. They went about collecting weapons, stripping the clothes from the dead, and searching pouches for anything of value. Discarded paper money fluttered in the breeze. Guns, knives, powder, and cartridges were gathered into piles. Brass buttons, combs, necklaces, compasses, and trinkets were placed in baskets. Food and clothing were laid out upon logs. The aftermath of the battle was one huge treasure hunt. Items that may be common in the east could hold wealth on the frontier.

Wild Carrot leveled a spot and parked his wares. He instructed the men to guard the papers. Promising a reward, he informed them that Little Turtle would value the knowledge that the items contained.

Wild Carrot looked back at the little ridge where he had started his day. Why had the cannon been so ineffective? How resolute his men were in storming this place! He congratulated the captains and men when they straggled back. Some of them brought horses to carry dead warriors to their relatives' camps.

The sun began to peek high overhead through the clouds. Wild Carrot was exhausted. He watched the hat of an artilleryman float down the meandering stream near the base of the hill. He watched it enter the Wabash and drift around a bend. He pulled a similar hat from between two bodies and stuffed some of the papers into it. The enemy's papers would be his souvenir.

CHAPTER 7
Vincennes

Sweet Breeze walked the trail leading from the river Eel to the Wabash. Borrowing a vacant canoe, she crossed the swiftly flowing waters to the medicine rocks on the south bank. She had come to think. There were too many distractions in the village. The clean up and rebuilding at Eel Town was sporadic. It had become apparent that the town would not be its former self. French residents had moved on to the western lands before the raid. Since the war had reached its tentacles to this land, no traders had returned. Many of the townsfolk had not returned, remaining, at least for the time being, up the Wabash at the forks, on the Salamonie, and the Mississinewa. Some had joined the new Miami villages on the Maumee or farther up the St. Joseph.

The ones who had returned were those weary of war. They only wanted to mend their homes and plant their crops. They desired to fish the waters and hunt the hills and valleys that they knew. Charred remains of the destroyed buildings were constant reminders of their lost loved ones. For three generations the population of the Miami nation had been reduced by poxes and by the beaver wars with the Iroquois. More were lost to the battles with the Pottawatomie and in raids to the Kentucky lands. Over the years, many families had replaced missing members with captives from other tribes and from the Virginians. Still the population dwindled.

No one could look at the blackened logs and not wonder about the fate of the women and children swept from their midst by Wilkinson. Residents would pause and look across the river to the trail from the south; how many days could they live in peace before raiders returned? How long until their soil was again soaked with the blood of war?

Many families had deep roots drawing them home to the old town. After all, the revered council fire had been maintained by youth maintaining a home guard. A wealth of merchandise had flowed into the vil-

95

lage from the captured camp of the Americans. Every wigwam was covered with canvas; every fire had a copper pot; salt was plentiful. Blue jackets trimmed in white and red had become fashionable. In addition to guns provided by the English, many had been captured in the Battle of the Pumpkinheads, plus hundreds more were secured from the defeat of St. Clair's army. Each man and boy had his choice of firearms with ample powder, lead, and flint. Canoes arrived from upstream regularly with cargo of corn and beans.

Returning families and new residents began looking to Sweet Breeze for guidance. Earlier she had only been a visitor; now, somehow, she was becoming the matriarch. What part of the town should be inhabited? Where should a newly arriving family erect their wigwam? Who gets first choice on a batch of incoming provisions? Who gets the rhubarb from the French gardens? She had never realized the responsibilities that Primrose had overseen. Now she, the niece of Primrose and Porcupine, the daughter of Little Turtle, the wife of a war chief, was asked to decide for the village.

Here at this isolated weird little outcropping of limestone she had to make a decision about her own future. She could stay and guide the villagers, she could go up to her childhood home of Turtle Town, or accompany her husband to the region of the lower Wabash. She knew that she was not the leader that Wild Carrot was. With him gone she might not bear up like she had done thus far. It was tempting to return to Turtle Town, but that was impractical. That village of her childhood was now a village of refugees. Her mother and father were at the new villages on the Maumee. Those new villages remained very much a war camp, and she was tired of war.

She was drained by war pushing her about. She was weary of war calling her man into battle and war business calling him away from her. Her enemies were the councils that demanded his presence at Kekionga, the Wabash forks, the Auglaize, the Maumee rapids, and Detroit. She knew that the call had gone out to all the known nations for a grand council to be held late in the summer. If she wanted to be with him at that season it would mean at least two moons living in the war camps on the Maumee. Now, in the spring when the trees had not yet found their leaves, he was called the opposite direction, down to the lower Wabash to counsel for peace.

She wanted to reach a decision before she would surely be discovered by the sentinels on the nearby island. They would tell her that she should not perch atop the sacred table rock of the diminutive summit. She cocked her head to listen for their approach. Whippoorwills filled the morning air in the little meadow behind her. She heard ducks on the river not a stone's throw ahead. With her bare feet she caressed a clutch of buttercups that poked up their yellow petals. She noticed how they thrived on only a handful of soil between the rocks. The medicine rocks did not speak to her, but seemingly the little flowers did. If they could display their beauty with so little nourishment, could not she blossom in the midst of turmoil? The gurgle of the current of the Wabash beckoned to her, "Follow me, follow your heart, I will renew your soul."

That was it. She had decided. She would let the current carry her to a new life. She would leave the resettlement of Eel Town to others. She would follow her husband on his journeys. She would conceive and begin their new family. And, ha, she had not been discovered! She considered going to the island on behalf of the village to chastise the incompetent watchmen.

* * *

As was their way, the men of Eel Town had spent several days in their new council house deciding the issue. The question being if the village should join those on the lower Wabash in offering a wampum belt of peace to the Americans. An earlier council of the entire Miami confederation had been called at the Forks of the Wabash. Their brethren of the Wea and Piankashaw tribes requested pardon from the war councils to seek the recovery of their families taken captivate by the Americans. They had been invited by Hamtramck to visit Vincennes to plant the seeds of peace. Having suffered from two surprise attacks that leveled their towns and crops, their lust for war had abated. Chief Pecan took up their cause and persuaded the council in their favor. Any town that had been raided was free to join the peace quest.

Eel Town, having been raided with captives taken, needed to decide whether or not to participate. The village held as many of those who had loyalties to the Wea located downriver as there were those whose loyalties were to the greater Miami tribe upstream. However, most of the long-time resident warriors and their families had not returned. They remained at the camps upriver.

Eventually, the Eel Town chiefs opted for peace. The process shifted to selecting the chiefs who would represent the community, and who would stay to govern. It would surely be an extended process of counseling with other tribes followed by supplicating to the Americans. The contingent would need to be gone well past the planting season. Nearly all of the families that had relatives taken by the Americans wanted to participate.

Finally, the delegates were named. Porcupine and The Soldier would lead the talks with chiefs Grasshopper, Squirrel, and Wave attending. Wild Carrot would participate in the tribe's councils. In parley with the Americans, he would serve as no more than their interpreter.

* * *

Sweet Breeze rearranged her packs in the canoe. She was ready to depart, but the others were slow in loading.

"Do not be anxious," Wild Carrot soothed her. "It will be an easy trip to Ouiatenon. The spring run-off always provides ample flow at this season. Our load is light since the tribes of the lower Wabash have offered us accommodations."

"I am eager to go," she said. "I anticipate the adventure. I have never been south and west beyond the stone-faced point of the Eel and Wabash confluence." She added, "I am concerned not about our travel, but what we travel towards."

Twenty-two canoes glided over the limestone bottom of the Eel as it churned its capacity into the current of the Wabash.

She pointed side to side with her paddle as she said to her husband, "Show me the landmarks like my father always did when I was a child. Tell me about your voyages."

Wild Carrot thought, but did not say, "I have told you, you just were not there to hear the words."

He showed her the island where a family of bears refused to evict so that he could make his camp. He showed her the sandbar where he had to make a quick escape from a company of French voyagers. They traveled past the camp where men dug into the north bank for coal. There were rocks that had names given by the tribes, many by the French, some by the English. The sun was still well above the tree line when the entourage pulled into the mouth of a stream on the left bank known simply as Stony Creek. They would spend the night here at an old trading grounds along the south shore.

Buffalo Man secured his canoe and offered to carry some of Sweet

Breeze's things to the top. She had brought more on the trip than essential because this man allowed space in his vessel. Brush was cleared and piled for a bonfire. Cooking fires would not be needed since they had brought a cold meal for this one night. She chose a place under the wide arms of a sugar maple to spread out a large buffalo hide. On this she placed the pouches and blankets. A smaller buffalo hide would be reserved in case the night proved cold.

Her husband hung his long rifle and pouch in the limbs before he strolled the circuit of the camp. She headed for a gravel bar at the creek to wash off the mud from the landing. By the time she returned, he had made it only half-way around. A change of clothes from doeskin tunic to loose blouse and skirt of cloth refreshed her. She tied on the blue-with-gold sash given by her mother. Crushing herbs into a salve of bear fat and honey, she brushed it into her hair. Off she went to join the gathering women. Some of the women had prepared blankets for the men's banquet when she arrived.

"Get more branches for the fire!" she shouted cheerfully. "Bring out your bells and rattles! Put ribbons in your hair! Tonight there will be dancing! Make a second fire for the children; let them have their own fun. We will eat with the men! We will have a feast of peace this night."

She directed some women to gather wood and other contingents to rearrange the seating, locate the second fire, instruct the children. The men had filled their clay pipes and were exchanging stories about their past escapades in Vincennes when they saw the approaching females. Neither married man nor bachelor dared protest as he was dragged off to the festivities. Sweet Breeze saw to it that men whose wives had been taken away by Wilkinson were attended to by relatives. Soon all joined the affair of food and frolic.

* * *

With legs weary from dancing, Wild Carrot sat studying the embers. He knew from the looks the women were giving his wife that she was the instigator. How perceptive it was of her to know that this was the first opportunity for this community to celebrate since the Virginians had raided their town. Certainly many of them had been in war camps that celebrated the victory over the American army. However, the Eel Town community had been strewn among several camps. Many had scattered to the winter camps to distance themselves from the war. As they had slowly congregated at their old town they were burdened with reorganizing. Yes, it was good to celebrate being together. Over the winter he and his wife had never really celebrated being together. He would appear at the lake for a few days, then be off to Detroit or the Auglaize. Again, on this venture he would be in a series of councils. But, this time she would be with him. He would endeavor to find opportunities to enjoy being together.

With her head against his arm, she, too, was studying the red and white coals. "Are you for peace?" she asked.

What a strange question this was to him, "How can I be for peace when Little Turtle is for war?"

"You will be interpreting for Porcupine in all of the councils. Listen to the arguments for peace."

"I am just an interpreter, not a participant."

"You have never been 'just an interpreter.' My father and my uncle have always taken your comments to heart. My mother has told me this; I have seen it. They know that you understand a man's intentions, not just his words. That is why they want you in their councils. Other interpreters can deliver words, though, of course, not to your degree. You give the words meaning. You are also a war chief of the Miami; you have been honored with three feathers. The warriors sing your praises. The one who is called Chief of All Miami and Chief of All Nations has given the hand of his daughter to you in marriage. You are not 'just an interpreter.'"

He was completely taken aback by her firmness and sincerity.

He did not have long to reflect before she went on, "Listen to the arguments for peace and take them back to my father. Five Medals and Blue Jacket and the other chiefs of war have his ear. Let him hear that there are Miami who look for peace. You are wrong when you say that 'Little Turtle is for war.' He is for what is best for the Miami nation. If it is war, he will do it. If peace is best for his people, he will seek it. If no one speaks to him about peace, how is he to decide for it?"

He was no longer studying the embers. He was not aware of the drums or the fire or the dancing. Ideas were swimming in his head like fish in a trap. It was as if Primrose was speaking through his wife. That thought was partially scary and at the same time gratifying.

He was searching for a response when she said softly, "Do it for us and our family. Now come to my blanket and we will have peace tonight."

He followed.

* * *

It was near midday when the flotilla was met by two canoes emerging from the high bank opposite the Tippecanoe's mouth. A painted deer skin stretched on a pole identified the canoes as an escort provided by the Wea hosts. It was a fine day for paddling, chanting, and light-hearted water games. The Miami had intended on stopping at the old Ouiatenon fort, but the escort cruised past the vacant site. Sweet Breeze would have to wait until later for Wild Carrot's Ouiatenon tales. They quickly passed the ruined landing of the Wea towns on the south bank. Shortly they came upon a wide new landing lined with canoes. Both sides of the opening were outlined by white-flowering dogwood. Here they were greeted by a multitude of jabbering children and barking dogs. Boys offered beverages of local tea. Girls placed delicate flowers in the hair of arriving women and girls. After their hands emptied, the children began tugging baggage to a level place up the slope. The Eel Town chiefs grabbed their wares and were directed to a greeting ceremony farther ahead.

A new town had sprung up to replace the Wea villages demolished by the Virginians Scott and Wilkinson in the late spring, and again by Wilkinson in the summer. The huge fields of the Wea plains had been trampled, but a portion of the crop survived to maturity. Some hidden fields remained untouched by the invaders. Relief food had flowed down the streams and creeks and river tributaries of the Wabash from villages large and small. The town had received an ample share of the spoils of the victory over the American army, though only a few Wea warriors had participated.

The population, after dispersing over the winter to find shelter, had returned en masse to build anew. They were augmented by a segment of the dwindling Piankashaw tribe, the remainder residing in the vicinity of Vincennes. A handful of Pottawatomie and Kickapoo residents were joined by Mascouten and stragglers from the lower Illinois country.

Sweet Breeze heard rumors bouncing around the town. The essence was that the captives were alive. The answer to their whereabouts could be found at Vincennes where the Americans were seeking peace. Chief Young Beaver and Chief Little Fox were anxious to lead their Wea and those who would join them to a grand parley as soon as possible.

Young Beaver ascended to the position of spokesman for all chiefs after Porcupine declined. Their position would be for a pact of non-aggression on both sides after the safe return of the captives. The Ohio River would be the division between the Americans and the tribes. The Americans would be allowed to maintain the fort at Vincennes. Traders would be allowed there and at Ouiatenon. The Americans would be asked to send a blacksmith to Ouiatenon. Wild Carrot would be the interpreter for all tribes. He would dress in the French style and converse with the French population to confirm their understanding of the American position as gathered by Crazy Legs.

Within days the Wabash was full of convoys carrying five hundred villagers to join the over one hundred Piankashaw residing at Vincennes. Where the river bent southward, Wild Carrot showed his wife the location of the trap that her father had laid for Hamtramck before the Battle of Pumpkinheads. As they swept past the Vermillion River he told her of the legendary silver mines and of the plains beyond where he had participated in the great buffalo hunts. For four days they rode the current; for three nights she hoped to conceive.

Fort Knox, perched upon a sandy hill, was smaller than she had imagined. The town to its south was larger. Certainly not comparable to the English town of Detroit with its fine homes and shops, this ancient town did have a certain charm. The expansive orchards were starting their time of blossom, adding fragrance and color to the scene. There were cows and sheep, fields and fenced gardens, warehouses and flatboats. There were whitewashed log homes and barns, plus a few painted clapboard homes. Taverns, traders, carpenters, and blacksmiths dotted the riverfront. She felt at ease here more than she had ever experienced at Detroit.

The Piankashaw had prepared a camp on a plain north of the fort. She selected a wigwam and began laying out their things.

Wild Carrot called her out, "Hamtramck has offered us a cabin in the town. Would you be willing to live among the Frenchmen during our stay? You can travel to this camp as much as you like, I will find an escort. Buffalo Man will discretely stay with me doing his duty in a fashion not to display my authority. The French will provide meals and all we need. Hamtramck will be paying me in coin to be the official interpreter for the council."

"Stay in the town?"

"Yes, there is a cabin. If you do not want to eat their pig meat, I will arrange for meals to be brought from here. It will be a great help to me if you will agree to Hamtramck's arrangements."

She had come here for new life, new experiences, this would be one for sure. "I will sleep where you sleep; I will eat what you eat. When do we go?"

"Now."

"Just give me time to tell Porcupine and our friends."

"Our chief knows, he is now arranging for your protection. He wishes us to be among the French."

By the time she stacked the last of the bundles outside the wigwam, six young Eel Town Miami men had arrived to be a bearer-escort.

Gathering herself she said, "Wait, one more thing."

She grabbed one of the bundles and disappeared into the hut. Soon she reappeared wearing a finely decorated cloth dress with shawl. Her hair was rolled up in back and fastened with decorated bone pins in the Miami fashion. She donned her engraved silver pendant necklace and looped silver earrings.

"Now, to the town!"

Their cabin was in the second row from the north side of the town. They were met by a small polite man.

He greeted them in French, "Welcome to your home, I am Pierre Renault."

He bowed. They bowed slightly. Sweet Breeze took a palm-full of corn pollen from a pouch and sprinkled it around the flat rock stoop.

The little man grinned, "If you please, call me Shorty. It is a name given by my friends. I will take care of your needs. You will find your firewood here. You may take what you want from the garden. Let me know what needs you may have." Again he bowed.

Sweet Breeze replied in perfect French, "I am pleased. I am certain that we will have a comfortable stay."

She stepped inside and Wild Carrot motioned in the bearers. The cabin was warm and dry with a fire burning in its stone-lined fireplace. The front and rear walls each had a single glass-paned window. The open rafters revealed a sleeping loft reached by ladder. There were randomly spaced shelves and pegs on the walls. Furniture consisted of a table with three chairs, a sidetable, a cupboard with eating utensils, and a second small cupboard.

She went to the door, "Shorty, I ask a favor. Would you remove the bed?"

The bed completely filled the space of the loft and she had no need of it. Besides, her mother had frequently warned her as a child about the uncleanliness of beds.

Shorty nodded and smiled. He was eager to please this Miami princess. It was common in Vincennes to see tribesmen about town. Only occasionally did they bring their women past the perimeter. One of radiant beauty and graceful bearing such as this must surely be of royal lineage. Her husband, too, had a confident poise. For Major John Francis Hamtramck to have made these arrangements, the man must be important to the parley. Anyway, Shorty knew of families willing to buy the mattress.

Pierre, Shorty, secured two companions to remove the bed. That done, he said upon exiting, "My wife will prepare morning and evening meals. If you are to have guests let me know, if you please. If you are to be gone, place this block in the window."

"That is fine," Wild Carrot stated, "We will be eating in the camp tonight."

All bowed. Upon exiting, Shorty noted a huge Miami and two smaller of the tribe sitting idly, resting with their backs against the wall, watching the traffic in the street. Surely, he thought, the occupants of the cabin are an important couple.

"Husband, I will be happy here. I sense that significant events will happen here," she embraced him.

"Yes, we must bring Primrose and the others home from captivity. A treaty is to be consummated."

"Indeed, of course. I meant significant to you and me."

Four days it took to establish the bulk of the camp. A few French visited the new village, amazed at the number of people pouring in. Tribesmen in turn visited the town. The French were cordial enough; the Yankees were not so amiable. The Virginians were nothing short of inhospitable, frequently shouting insults at the natives. The soldiers flew their flags and beat their drums. They paraded on the fort grounds between the town and the encampment of the tribes.

At noon of the fifth day the fort cannon were fired signaling the assembly for the conference. A double column of troops marched to the clearing beyond the parade grounds and formed a line. Four officers and two flag bearers rode out and dismounted. The officers took their seats at a plank table as the flags formed behind. Twelve chiefs stood motionless facing them. Wild Carrot stepped inconspicuously into the gap to translate.

Hamtramck stood, as did his fellow officers, "Welcome to Fort Knox. I am Major John Francis Hamtramck, commandant. It pleases me to see the tribes are so well represented."

"I am Young Beaver, chief of the Ouiatenon villages. We have come to find if the heart of the commander of this fort is for war or for peace."

Hamtramck was taken aback by the forthrightness of the chief. He was a veteran officer experienced in the ways of the tribes. He was accustomed to the chiefs trying the patience of officers with days of pre-council rhetoric and positioning. Here was a chief asking for war or peace in his opening statement. Undoubtedly, the overwhelming victory over St. Clair emboldened the tribes even more than he had feared.

Shaking off his jitters he commenced, "Let us counsel and speak of peace. Let us discover if the men of the forest and the men of the fort can walk the same path in friendship. On these grounds there will be no aggression from one to another. This day I will deliver to you one wagon filled with fine blankets. Four milk cows and twenty steers will be delivered. Each day I will provide ground corn for your camp. These are presents of our peace. I apologize that I cannot provide more meat for your meals. There are many more in your camp than I was prepared to count."

Little Fox stepped forward and prepared the formal presentation of the wampum belt of white with a pattern of blue and brown diagonals.

Hamtramck held up his hand, "I am not authorized by my government to accept your wampum. I have no wampum to return. Putnam is the name of the man who has it. He is at our great council of thirteen fires in Philadelphia. He wishes each of the tribes to send two chiefs to him so that he can present his wampum. He has the authority of our government to hold council at that place."

Wild Carrot was stunned. The chiefs could see in his eyes that something was wrong before they heard him interpret the words. There was much consternation among the chiefs as they heard the translation. How can this be? Had they not been invited here for peace talks? Had they not supplicated to the Miami council for the privilege to attend? Was there any chance to recover the captives? Two Wea chiefs walked off the field in disgust. Little Fox did not know what to do with the belt. He wanted to drop it into the dirt, but that would mean immediate war. If he laid it upon the table then the tribes were bound to peace without obtaining any concession. He conferred with Young Beaver then folded the belt in a doeskin.

Young Beaver addressed the officer, "We will hold our belt. We will be at peace while we are on these grounds. We will talk here again in two days. If you are for talks of peace, do not bring your soldiers with guns to face us."

The chief did not wait for a reply, but turned about and headed off accompanied by his compatriots.

Wild Carrot was unsure if he should leave or stay. If he had his tomahawk he may have left it buried in the planks of the table and never returned. Again his mind heard the words of Sweet Breeze, "Listen to the arguments for peace." Yet, the audacity of the Americans gave little room for peace.

"That did not go very well, did it?" Hamtramck glanced at the interpreter as he spoke.

"No sir," the man in fancy buckskin replied.

"Will they attack us while we sleep?" the commandant asked of him.

"Young Beaver is the spokesman for all chiefs. He said that he accepted your offer of truce while in your camp. You have no fear of the tribes as long as you encourage negotiations. It would be well to plant a white flag where we stand."

"Will they accept the gifts I send?"

"They have already accepted. If you do not deliver the gifts, or if you deliver less than stated, you will have broken the covenant and then the truce is cancelled, and yes, then they may attack you."

"Go to them, Wild Carrot, and tell them that we will meet here in two days. I will leave my soldiers at the fort, but they should be represented by only four chiefs and two attendants so the two sides of the table will balance. Tell them that we will talk as man to man and not as representative of one to representative of another. We will eat together and share cups of rum."

Wild Carrot asked, "Am I to have a paper to read to them?"

"No," the commandant waved his hand over the pouch of papers, "just tell them."

Wild Carrot nodded that he understood, he was to be a go-between, an off-the-record messenger. "I will make them understand, 'man to man.'"

* * *

The parties met in two days as designated. Hamtramck followed Wild Carrot's suggestion that the meeting be in an open circle sans table.

The chiefs passed a calumet decorated specifically for the occasion. The fort commandant passed out miniature American flags with red and white stripes and a field of blue with thirteen stars in alternating rows of twos and threes.

The chiefs made their position clear that they, being many, had traveled the first part of the path. Putnam, being one, would need to travel the remainder of the path. They had come this far for peace, but would go no farther. They would remain in camp until the American negotiator arrived or until he sent word that he would not come. A second stance was that the captives would be reunited with their families before they would parley with Putnam.

For his part, Major Hamtramck understood that failing to treat meant a resumption of hostilities. He told the chiefs that he would do all in his power to get the ambassador to come to Vincennes. He assured that one hundred and forty captives were being held at Fort Hamilton. This fort was on the Great Miami River north of Fort Washington. He personally had seen them and knew that they were being well cared for. He was perplexed at the excited reaction to this, not realizing that the tribes were completely devoid of knowledge concerning the captives' location. Conferences continued to be held every second day with the major sending out couriers periodically. Mutual trust was built to the point where they swapped tales of their experiences, omitting reference to the battles at Kekionga and the Head of the Wabash. They cooperated in keeping the peace between the townspeople and the camp. Feeding and supplying the camp became regular topics of discussion.

Wild Carrot found the French citizens to hold Hamtramck in high regard, pointing out that he was a Canadian by birth and upbringing. He had helped to protect their farmland rights from the intruding Yankees. He had corralled the waywardness of the Virginians and established a representative civil government. The French all thought that the fort commander would personally seek justice for the tribes. However, they also understood that he would do whatever was asked of him by his superiors in the east.

The town was essentially divided with the French, both longstanding and new, living in poor homes and eking out subsistence. The Americans that he met seemed cold and secretive. Hardly an American spoke the French language and the French population was essentially ignorant of English.

Sweet Breeze enjoyed having time to stroll about the town and the village camp making friends. She concentrated on her crafts. Her husband purchased what manufactured goods she needed. For natural products she had to simply ask in the tribes' camp and it was provided. She was trying to get accustomed to eating most meals inside the cabin, but preferred to eat and work outside when possible.

One cool day she was sitting at the table staining a stack of quills that had been boiled and flattened.

Her husband sat down opposite her and lit his clay pipe, "A message has come."

"So soon? It has been only a little more than a moon since we came to this place. Philadelphia is so far. Everyone was saying it would take longer to hear from the ambassador." She continued her work.

"Not from Philadelphia. From the Falls of the Ohio. Hamtramck spoke to me today in confidence," he was speaking solemnly.

"That man shares so much with you. He holds you in high esteem."

"This meeting was personal. A trader named Cartey Wells supplies him with horses and salt and such. This Wells had often inquired about his youngest brother who had been taken captive as a boy. He said the man looks a lot like me."

She bumped a cup and spilled yellow stain on her hand and on the table. She had no response other than to look at him with wonder.

"Hamtramck sent him a dispatch after we arrived. Yesterday, he received a message from the man's brother. A man by the name of Samuel Wells is coming to meet with me," his voice was unsteady during the last sentence.

Only the light crackling of the fire and the occasional dropping of ashes broke the silence in the cabin.

"Will you meet with him?"

"Yes, I should. Hamtramck says the man has great influence in the Kentucky lands. I will meet with him," he was almost whispering as a single tear moistened one cheek.

Sweet Breeze instinctively leaned across the table, spilling more stain in the process. She moved around behind him and held him tightly.

CHAPTER 8
Buffalo Trace

Sweet Breeze lifted the creek's waters in her cupped hands and tasted. The slightly bitter taste was not so bad, but the smell was that of a pig wallow. Ancient legends told how the licks region waters held healing powers. She took two gulps and waited, but felt no miracle occurring in her body. Normally she would heat the water and make her special tea, but here it was said to drink without heating. She filled her gourds and returned up the path to the hilltop camp.

It was her third night out from Vincennes on the Buffalo Trace, destined for the falls of the river Ohio. The undulating trace had entered hills much larger than she had ever seen. She was told that it would be rough country the remainder of the journey. This night's camp was on a maple-covered knob. Stories of people being trampled in their sleep by buffalo roaming the flats encouraged them to seek higher ground. Herds of buffalo were known to frequent the valley fingers that penetrated the forested hills, waylaying on their migrations to lick the salty creek bottoms. They had not spied any of the beasts, but their signs were present. The camp hill was bounded on the east and north by a stream known as Lick Creek and on the west by one called Stink.

Their destination was the home of Captain Samuel Wells beyond the Falls of the Ohio. Sweet Breeze surmised that the Americans admired the French as much as did the Miami. They had named the town at the falls Louisville in honor of the French king. Samuel told her that Putnam had led a band of men to found Marietta. The settlement on the north side of the Ohio below Fort Pitt was named for the French queen. She supposed that Louisville would more resemble Vincennes than Detroit. After all, Vincennes was established on ancient council grounds by a French diplomat to the tribes. She encouraged her eagerness to supersede her fear in anticipating what waited for them on the south side of the Ohio.

As one of the first Virginian settlers in that area, Captain Samuel Wells had accumulated land. His plantation was now flourishing. He had always felt responsible that his little brother was kidnapped by the Indians. When he married he had sent the orphaned boy to be raised and schooled by friends of the Wells family. He should have kept the boy under his wing to raise him properly. As it turned out, the boy was raised by the very Indians who had killed their father. Samuel understood the reluctance of William to come to Kentucky. However, he was certain that once there his little brother would choose to stay.

Hamtramck had encouraged Wild Carrot to go to Louisville. At that advanced position he would be in a better position to assist in the return of the captives if Putnam so directed.

Sweet Breeze had told her husband that from behind, the two men walked with the same gait and swing of the arms; they possessed the same confident stance in front of men. It was the scar on the back of Samuel's head that finally convinced Wild Carrot that this was indeed his older brother. One of the few memories of the younger brother's childhood was hitting his oldest brother with a thrown sharp stone.

To Wild Carrot, the dignified man's character was a mixture of Yankee, Virginian, and English officer. At least that was his public side. In private he spoke and smiled with a warm friendliness. The stranger-brother obviously meant them no harm. He agreed to go to the plantation while waiting for word from Putnam.

Raising horses was a large part of Samuel's business. The well-dressed Kentucky man had brought fine-looking horses for the trip. Wild Carrot thought himself to be a good horseman, but this man was his superior in riding skills. Trying out these horses was one of several inducements to undertake the journey. There was, also, the pull of the child within him to see once again the cliffs and fishing holes that flittered in his mind. There was the curiosity to verify the reports of the Ohio country that he had heard in Detroit. He would learn what he could about the intentions of the American army and diplomats. Most of all, he wished to confirm that the captives were unharmed at Fort Hamilton.

Wild Carrot had originally wished Sweet Breeze to stay in Vincennes. But now, as she sat down upon the root protruding from the cut-bank beside him, he was glad she was near. She removed his hat and pulled a blanket over their heads and around their sides. She raised a water-filled gourd to his nose, then handed it to him. They nudged tightly together to share their warmth.

The spring rains had been light. This shower was not much more than a drizzle. Occasional droplets found their way through a massive oak under which the travelers sought shelter. Grease sizzled and popped in iron skillets.

"That old boy would make a heap of barrels," Samuel set forth for conversation, gesturing with his pipe stem to the tree trunk.

"What do you see in this tree Captain Wells?" Wild Carrot queried.

"Samuel. Call me Samuel, Brother William. Oh, this monster is fine timber. He could frame an entire mill. The slabs and limbs undoubtedly have extra fine grain for cabinets and tables. There are plenty of smaller limbs and branches for barrel staves to store new whiskey. The scrap would be reduced to charcoal for filtering, not to mention the fire wood. In Louisville this timber would bring a tidy sum. Out here, well, I guess it is good for keeping some rain off a person."

He puffed on his pipe, then added, "I wager that there is good boat lumber in there, too."

Wild Carrot, with a wink, asked of Sweet Breeze, "And what do you see, my wife?"

"I thank the Creator for placing this mother of the forest here to protect us and to give us this seat for our meal. Tomorrow her arms will protect the bear from wind and rain. In her branches are homes for squirrels, for bees, for birds of song and birds of prey. Under her roots are homes for badgers and foxes. Her fallen limbs provide cover for chipmunks and rabbits. Her leaves nourish the caterpillars which in turn nourish the birds." She bent to scoop up a handful of leaves and acorns, "The leaves keep the rains from washing the soil from this hill and filling the streams with mud. The old leaves crumble and turn black to renew the soil." Brushing off the leaves she fingered the acorns, "Her fruit provides food for the deer and elk and bear and also the little animals. Squaws may happen by and gather the nuts and dry them and grind them into meal. Some of the fruit will put down root and shoot up a stem and become her sapling children. Some will not survive, but one day one of these," she waved around towards the seedlings and saplings, "perhaps this one, will become a new mother of the forest."

Samuel puffed on his pipe and stoked the coals under the skillets.

"And you, Buffalo Man, what do you see?" Wild Carrot wondered.

"Here beside us, high overhead, and deep within the earth below is a sentinel of the forest," Buffalo Man's eyes gazed far into the distance to the unseen. "His roots feel the trembling earth as buffalo herds pass to and fro for season upon season. His trunk was a sapling in the time of my grandfather's grandfather. He will become hollow and perish in the time of my grandson's grandson. In his life he has seen days when only the tribes followed the buffalo trace, then he saw Frenchmen follow the path. Now Englishmen and Americans hurry past on their quests. He drops his branches for the cook fires for all men alike, and he will continue to do so if we only let him be what he is."

"Still make a heap of whiskey barrels," Samuel huffed to himself. Aloud he asked, "And you, William, do you have a vision of this tree."

"My vision seeks the future. Will Buffalo Man's grandson camp under this tree? Or, will some American settle in the valley along the creek and come to this tree and say, 'Old Tree, I will cut you down and put you to work for me alone!' The signs are not clear. Which will it be?"

* * *

Up and down and around they rode following the old trace, heading towards every point of the compass, but always drawing closer to the falls. They crossed brooks with hard rock bottoms. They rounded looming limestone cliffs. Nary a single meadow broke the forest. They saw not a solitary man since the crossing of the White River on the first day. Sweet Breeze counted twenty-two bears plus eight cubs, six elk, and one lone bull buffalo. Early on, she gave up counting the many deer and turkeys. Beaver and otter were not as plentiful as along the Eel, at least not near the trail. Since the packhorses were laden and they had plenty of food, the game ran free, save four deer and two turkeys brought in by the braves in the evenings.

Near noon of the sixth day, Captain Samuel Wells halted the procession on a ridge and pointed to his right.

"The beautiful Ohio," Wild Carrot said to his wife.

She saw a bow of the magnificent river sweeping a wide bend to the south. In the distance it looked like a silken ribbon winding through the heavy forest.

"I have heard of its beauty, now I see with my eyes," her voice bubbled with excitement. "I am glad you brought me here, husband. We will have many tales to tell our children."

Samuel pulled back beside his younger brother, "Once we descend this ridge we will be near the falls. Your braves should go no farther.

Make sure that they cause no mischief that would jeopardize the return of the captives. There is already enough trouble upriver."

"Agreed, Captain Wells. Wait here and I will take them back to the last brook."

He signed Buffalo Man to retrace the route. He whispered some instructions to his wife, then disappeared to the west. Gathering the nine warriors and Buffalo Man in a little valley, he led them up a brook and found a miniature falls. To the right he pointed to a protruding rock.

"See the roots growing around that rock. When I need you I will put my mark on that tree. Hunt and explore as you wish. Do not go near the cabins and do not cross LaBelle Riviere. Do not molest the boats. Your good behavior ensures the return of the loved ones of our people. Buffalo Man will speak for me. Listen to his words until we are rejoined."

* * *

Water ran too high at the lower falls crossing, so Samuel elected for the ferry above the upper falls. They skirted some cabins, then trotted through Clarksville. Samuel arranged their boarding, and the ferry shoved off under the palisades of Fort Steuben. Sweet Breeze became uneasy at the strength of water rushing past the boat. The relentless power was far more than any she had experienced. She felt that she was at the mercy of strange boatmen. The looming hills on the south bank seemed to hold secrets. The narrow valleys looked dark and mysterious.

A huge flatboat crossed their course near the shore. The monstrous vessel looked like one of the shops of Detroit floating down the river. It had a full cabin with a smokestack, a pen with cows and pigs, and what appeared to be two families perched here and there on bales and kegs. The Ohio was fine to look at, but riding the waters was fearsome.

"I will keep my canoe on the Wabash," she told her husband.

He smiled, "Do you wish to carry pigs in it?"

She socked him in the chest, "No, I will carry wildcats, and I will have these wild men paddle it for me."

The ferry docked at the head of a landing that stretched far along the bank. Boats were unloading; wagons were loading; women and children huddled in groups. On shore, men with heavy hammers and iron bars broke boats into piles of lumber. Samuel purchased six roasted clams and laid them out upon a plank tray.

"Many boats today?" he asked the vendor.

"Sixteen today, seven yesterday."

Samuel motioned for them to take a seat upon some sacks of grain as he opened the mussels with his knife.

He pointed his knife to the edge of the dock, "Do you remember when we first landed here? There certainly was no wharf then. We nearly busted-up at landing on the rocks. Of course, you were just a pup then."

Wild Carrot had no recollection of the event. Samuel alternated between talking with townspeople and sharing reminisces with William.

"The horses are ready. To Wellsmont it is, unless you and Sweet Breeze want a meal at a tavern first. It is about a two-hour ride upstream, that is unless some new squatter has put a hut in the middle of my trail."

He did not wait for an answer and was already heading for the horses.

The guests from the north followed the hometown leader up the shed-lined street to the plateau and east through rows of board shops and homes. Samuel was busy returning salutes from the men and tipping his hat to the ladies. Only rarely did he look behind to see that his guests were keeping pace. Wild Carrot blended into the crowd, but Sweet Breeze received many stares ranging from pleasure to surprise to leers. Samuel struck a road that climbed a hill strewn with log huts and then headed onto a trail that led back down near the river. Later, they again steered from the river. Cottonwoods and brush gave way to locust and poplar and then to dense forest of oak, hickory, and chestnut.

Sweet Breeze was thinking about the "two-hour" ride, how the English and Americans spoke of hours, miles, pounds, and tons. How they thought everything could be measured and understood by numbers. How they divided the sun and the land, how they put the rivers on maps and carried them in pouches. How they named each day and filled it with work to make improvements.

The trail broke upon a wagon road that connected a river wharf with a clearing far up a long slope. They followed the road up to the clearing where Samuel dismounted and pushed a rail aside for passage through a fence.

"Welcome to Wellsmont, Brother William! Welcome Sweet Breeze, Princess of the Miami!" He bowed.

Wild Carrot was perplexed at the saying. Sweet Breeze kicked her horse. With a shout she darted ahead. She rode off into the field to the left scattering some grazing horses. Nearing a fence she turned about and galloped back to the road. Across she went to the fence forming the right of the long narrow rectangular field.

Returning to the road she pulled up, "A fine pasture you have, Brother Samuel."

CHAPTER 9
Kentucky

Sweet Breeze looked down upon the Ohio River from the precipice. A flatboat appeared from around a bend far in the distance. It looked like no more than a twig in a brook. It lazily swept around the lengthy curve and disappeared behind dense trees. After a very long while it reappeared in a short stretch visible closer below. Days were noticeably warmer than when they had first arrived at Wellsmont. Sweet Breeze and Wild Carrot had taken to riding up to this spot in the afternoon. They sat in a meadow near the summit letting the sun warm their backs.

"I am afraid," she softly spoke, leaning her head on his shoulder.

She looked down into the little valley to their right. Smoke was rising from the kiln, although there was no work on this day called Sunday. She could see the house with the unfinished addition behind. Nearby were the springhouse, smokehouse, slave quarters, granary, and tobacco shed. The fenced field stretching out in front of the buildings disappeared behind the chestnuts.

"That is a word I have never heard from you, 'afraid,'" her husband admonished. "You know I will protect you. If you do not like it here, I can take you back to Vincennes. We could go cross-country to Eel Town, or Turtle Town if you wish."

"It scares me that I like it too well here," she explained. "Their customs are strange; building a home of bricks, so many buildings for one family's farm, staying inside so much of the day, their music. I did not know what to do in their worship this day. There was no dancing, no drums, sitting so silently. But I do like the people; they are not what I expected. They work constantly, building constantly, always planning for something ahead. I think that in planning for the next day they miss today. It is good that they set a day aside like this to rest and enjoy their family. Your brother and Mary have been good to us. Margaret and young Mary Elizabeth adore you as do little Sam and Rebecca. I came to learn about your family, but now I am afraid I like them too much. Do you understand what I mean by this fear?"

"Yesterday I would not have understood," Wild Carrot replied, "but today I do. At the worship meeting they sang that song: Thy nature, gracious Lord, impart; come quickly from above; write thy new name upon my heart, thy new, best name of Love.* When they sang it, my chest was filled with powerful warmth."

He held her closer. "I must tell you something I have kept from you about the battle at the headwaters of the Wabash. When the fighting began to subside, I went searching for the officers' papers. I came upon a woman who stood within two paces directly in front of me. I should have killed her immediately, as a warrior must do on a battlefield, but I did not. I looked her in the face and hesitated, I do not know how long. In my head I heard this same song as if sung by the woman, but she did not move, did not sing. The next I knew, she lay dead at my feet, stricken by the arrow of an unknown warrior. To hesitate in battle is a dangerous thing."

"The Creator protects you. You have not a single blemish from the battles."

"That is not all. I gathered the papers from the officers' tent and carried them to Kekionga. There I studied them. One of the packets contained a book of songs; this song was among them."

"The Creator guided you to these papers and to these songs," she concluded.

"Some are like our chants; some are poems; in some I can read the words but not discern their meaning." He picked a single flower and handed it to her. "I wonder if their Lord and our Creator can be one and the same."

She, too, had contemplated these things, "There is but one earth, there can be but one Creator. We see the earth as the Creator providing for all his children; they see it as something to be marked off and purchased, to be changed and sold. There is one earth that is seen differently by the two peoples; there is one Creator that is understood in two ways. It is strange that they offer a prayer of thanksgiving after their food is prepared and cooked while we give thanks before harvesting and when an animal is killed. I do think that the Creator is pleased either way, perhaps we should do both."

"There is something else that I must tell you. I want to share everything with you, but this thing is not easy. Samuel has a second farm south of here. He wants me to go with him a half-day's ride to the east of the farm. That is where his father died. I declined to go there."

"It would be a proper thing to honor your father."

"Samuel said that he and his father, also named 'Samuel,' fought a battle there when I was a child. A Miami war party destined for Boonsboro came upon travelers fleeing their settlements for protection of the fort at the falls. In a short battle many Virginians were killed. The following morning local militia hastened to the site and again encountered the Miami. It is said that the elder Samuel was killed by Little Turtle."

"War is mean to all, both the Miami and the Virginian," she pronounced. Reflecting she added, "But your brother is so kind to me. He should hate the daughter of Little Turtle like I would hate the daughter of Wilkinson."

"He knows you only as a Miami princess. He does not know that you are the daughter of Little Turtle. He once asked if I was the adopted son of Little Turtle, as rumors have said. I said that I am not, that I am his interpreter. I did not elaborate. He does not know that I am the nephew and son-in-law of the Chief of All Miami."

"Then he must be told! I thought he knew."

"Yes, when you have returned to Vincennes I will tell him. I came to recover captives, not to deliver them."

"He is too honorable to think of holding me. I will tell him!" She wondered, "And your mother, what of her?"

"I only know that she died on the other side of the mountains before the family came to the western lands. I have no recollection of either of them."

They sat quietly watching three more flatboats make the bend.

She inquired, "Was Captain Samuel with St. Clair's army?"

"He led a company of militia from here. They were cut to bits in the first attack. Only two in ten returned. He told me that General Butler died standing his ground; this I knew. He said that General St. Clair fought bravely, had three horses shot from under him, and held the army together until the retreat turned into a stampede; not enough officers remained to hold the lines. He confirmed that Hamtramck's company, out rounding up deserters, never engaged in the combat. Everything he told me has been printed in newspapers, so there are no secrets to be had. The accounts say that the uniformed army lost nearly six hundred men, the militia another one hundred forty. There were sixty women killed in the camp with just seven returning to the fort.

119

"He said that the scouts were worthless once they left Fort Jefferson. The course was by compass only. The Americans thought that they were at the head of the St. Marys rather than the Wabash! I did not correct the error. He said that the Indian casualties appeared to be light and asked what I knew of it. I said that it has been told in the camps that the American army did fight well, but had not put up fortifications for the camp. I told that it was said that the artillery was ineffective. I said that it was known that the dead of the tribes numbered under forty; I did not say that five were my riflemen and six were Metea's strikers."

Staring at the wooded hills across the Ohio he continued, "He told me that in the east, President Washington went into an uncharacteristic rage when he learned of the defeat. Many of the states had not favored a national army. It was Washington's persuasion that created it. It is said that in none of the battles with the English had the great general ever lost so many men. A fortune in materials had been lost to the enemy, that would be us. There is great concern of what became of the abandoned cannon. Your father's name is known throughout the land."

"He does not know that you were at the battle?" she asked.

"No."

"What of the captives? Does he know where they are? Are they well? Will they be released?"

"I should have told you, but I have been weighing all that I have learned. Samuel saw the captives at Fort Hamilton, which is shortly above Fort Washington. Their food and shelter were good, the same as we were told by Hamtramck. Some were sick, but that is common in forts. The captives refuse to talk or even give their names. Wilkinson oversees them and does not want them released. Samuel assures me that General Washington wants them returned, and will authorize Putnam to see to it. I should wait here until the Americans at Fort Steuben hear from Putnam. It is expected that I will be needed to interpret for him; Hamtramck has recommended that I do it. It may be some long time yet."

Sweet Breeze stood, "Then I will stay until that day unless your brother sends me away; I do not think that he will. Do you think that the Americans will give up the fight for our land? I see these boats coming from the east. There are so many new arrivals. In only five days," she held out a hand with fingers spread, "as many settlers come as there are in one of our villages. In a moon there will be as many as the whole of Eel Town at festival time. The settlers will want the Wabash lands for their cows and pigs and chickens. I think that the Miami and the Americans will fight again."

Wild Carrot confirmed, "Samuel says that there are rumors the council of thirteen fires has agreed to field a new army, an army with more men and more supplies and a new general. They fight among themselves who this general will be, a Virginian, a Pennsylvanian, or of another state. All I can say is that it will not be St. Clair or Butler, and I hope that it is not Hamtramck. Many from this land want Wilkinson or Scott, and if not, then Clark. Samuel does not trust Wilkinson and says that the American council has lost faith with Clark." He stood and began pacing to and fro. "Samuel goes to many local councils, as you know. He says that this land of Kentucky will join the council of thirteen fires as a state soon, and no longer be Virginia. Samuel is likely to sit on its council. If there is to be war, he will again lead militiamen from Louisville. More than that, we cannot honorably discuss. I am here to learn the best posture for the release of Primrose and the others. I do not offer my knowledge and do not inquire the special knowledge of our host. But, if he offers information, I listen to it."

She took him by the hand and faced him squarely. She said, "Samuel knows that you will return to Little Turtle with your knowledge. However, he gains your trust hoping that you will stay at this place."

"Yes, he has spoken of needing an overseer for one of his farms. Do I look like an overseer of farms to you?" A grin crept over his face.

"It is too nice of a day to be thinking on so many things." She had a smile of her own as she pushed him flat onto the ground and jumped on him. "One more thing, I am sure that I am pregnant."

* * *

In the shade of a hickory near the house, Samuel learned the full identity of his sister-in-law. He scoffed at the guests' suggestion that they sleep in the barn that night and be gone in the morning. Though Samuel remained somber for a few days, Mary remained her charming self while concentrating on her knitting and tatting. The visiting couple took long rides through the forest. Sweet Breeze frequently donned clothes provided by Mary. Samuel was again called to Danville to a conference on organizing the state.

"The Sunday after I return we will have a garden party," the host addressed the family, "in honor of my brother, the famous government interpreter for Major Hamtramck and soon for Major General Putnam, and in honor of his bride. I will give Gabriel instructions for the preparations in my absence. Mary, take Sweet Breeze to town and find the two fanciest dresses to be had. Brother William here already has the fanciest outfit in the territory."

His reference was to the form-fitting buckskin embellished with expert quillwork that Sweet Breeze fashioned over the winter at the lake. He turned to the maker, "I wager that it would be worth a fortune in the Louisville shops."

Mary immediately started the guest list. First on the list were neighbors William and Lucy Croghan.

"You will love Lucy," Mary chatted, "she has so many interests and stories. She is the sister of George Rogers Clark, you know. I could ask her to invite the old general if you like."

"That would not be a good idea," Wild Carrot responded.

"Oh," she was surprised, "I thought you would like to meet him."

"If I meet him I will have to kill him. Every Miami warrior has sworn it."

"Are you Miami?" Samuel asked. "Are you a warrior of the Miami, or are you your father's son?"

Samuel stood, swinging his saddle bag onto his right shoulder. He left the house, and left the questions hanging in the air.

Mary, who always avoided joining deliberations on politics, business, and military matters, adhering mostly to topics of religion, education, and household issues, broke her policy. She remarked, "You need to understand that after all these years, my husband still mourns the loss of his father at the hands of the Miami. Now the bodies of neighbors and friends who were under his command lay unburied in the northern wilderness at the hands of your people. He understands that war is war and that killing is the essential business of it. His father was in the French War in the east and the War of Revolution in the west and the battles of conquest here.

"Long Run was my Samuel's first battle; he became a hero the same day his father was killed. He took it upon himself to oversee the family and to carry on his father's tradition as a soldier. When you were lost to the Indians, he blamed himself for farming you out to the Pope's rather than raising you in our home. We were so young and newly wed that it really was the proper thing to do, but it haunts him to this day. Everywhere he went, he inquired about a red-haired lad living with the

Indians. There have been dozens of youngsters taken from the settlements. Some have been ransomed in Detroit, or purchased back directly when found. A few escaped. But, the majority of them remain lost.

"Brother Cartey learned of the red-haired interpreter of Little Turtle on the upper Wabash. He tried to mount an expedition, but the area was too dangerous for travel. Your resemblance to Cartey is remarkable. Now that you are found, my husband cannot bear the thought of you returning to the wilderness, though he knows that you likely will. We are both so fond of Sweet Breeze and do wish you both to stay on. Heaven knows, there is a place for you on one of the farms. But, you have your life and we have ours. Do what you must. I only pray that a peace can be settled before you Wells brothers meet on opposite sides in war."

Wild Carrot, William, was ready to comment that they already had been on the same field of battle, but thought better of it.

Sweet Breeze rounded the table and stood behind Mary, placing both hands on Mary's shoulders, "We love you and your husband and your family. You have been kind and generous to us. We do not mean to bring trouble to your house. We do not know what fate war has for us, but my husband is here on a mission of peace for the Piankashaw, the Kickapoo, the Wea, and the Eel Town Miami. If peace can be had on the lower Wabash, then perhaps it can be so further up the Wabash as well. If there is to be peace, let it begin with my husband's mission."

"I will pray for it," Mary whispered as she returned her eyes to list-making. "Anyway, the Croghans must come if there is to be a picnic. I will subtly suggest that the old general will be too busy with the upcoming Independence Day celebration. He has been embarrassing Lucy with his bouts of drunkenness. There are rumors that he has been secretly conferring with the Spanish, or some say the French, to raise an army of conquest. There are many who would follow him if he gave the call. Mostly he spends his time mining for fossils near the falls, though he is building a mill up behind the fort. Let me work on this list, then Margaret and Mary Liz and I will teach you to dance some of our reels."

* * *

The Wells's Sunday garden party turned out to be the first in a week of celebrations. Samuel had returned with the news that Kentucky had been declared a state by the American congress. Sunday to Sunday, with Independence Day at midweek, would be a time of festival.

Sweet Breeze was struck by the differences from parties in Detroit. At English parties there were many uniformed officers. Here, only a few wore the swords and uniforms of the militia or army; many guests were farmers and merchants. The same musical instruments were used, but the music was quite different, as was the dancing. Fine tables and delicate foods were the order in Detroit. Here everything was bold and raucous. She enjoyed the food and merriment and robustly danced the reels. The knowledge quickly faded that, unlike Detroit, she was the only person of the tribes present. She was pleased that her husband, introduced to the guests as William Wells, was treated as an ambassador.

Samuel had also brought word that Putnam had left Fort Pitt and was to be at Fort Washington for the Independence Day celebration. Wild Carrot was to proceed with an army squadron to that place soon after the week of festivities.

On Wednesday a good portion of Louisville's citizens crossed to join Fort Steuben's formal ceremonies. A dignitary presented the fort commandant with a homemade flag which displayed fifteen stars. He announced, "I present to the garrison of the United States Army on this day, July 4, 1792, this flag representing the new state of Kentucky as a full partner in the United States of America."

The flag was raised. A cheer rose from the crowd. Fifteen times cannon blasts shook the surroundings. The garrison of nearly one hundred soldiers and officers marched about to the cadence of their drums. The people of Clarksville provided a dozen roasted hogs, cornbread, plus kettles of beans that had simmered in underground pits.

William Wells used the opportunity to present himself to the fort commandant and make arrangements for the trip. Inside the compound it seemed strange to him to be looking up at the new American flag on their national holiday. Was Porcupine now greeting Hamtramck under the American banner in Vincennes? Was Little Turtle meeting with McKee under the Union Jack?

In the evening he stayed on the north bank. Sweet Breeze traveled back to Wellsmont with the family. Under a full moon that night, he ran west to the Buffalo Trace and hurried across the ridge. Finding the little stream, he ascended to the small falls and found the tree he had pointed out to Buffalo Man. Here he hacked his mark, and by morning was again at the fort. After learning that the expedition to Fort Washington would leave in six days, he gained transport to Louisville and to his brother's plantation.

William and Sweet Breeze accepted from Samuel a gift of two hors- es they favored. They declined the offer of an escort to Vincennes for her. They promised Mary and the children that they would return when con- ditions were favorable. Ferrying the Ohio, they soon rendezvoused with Buffalo Man and his band of cheerful warriors. Before parting, the cou- ple spent their last night together embracing in the forest with only three deerskins laid out for a bed. The sweet smell of the grass rode a warm southern breeze.

"It is not good to spend so much time indoors like the Americans," she whispered. "I hope you find Primrose to be well. Tell her that I miss her and that there are many awaiting her return." She paused, but final- ly said, "Have you thought about what you will say to Small Cloud?"

"I will not seek her out. When she comes to me, I will inquire about her health and about my son. Then in the presence of three elders I will put her away. I will be done with her and treat her as I treat all others. Do not be concerned that I will want a second wife, it is not for me."

"In my youth I missed my father when he was gone, but I under- stood that he was important to the Miami people, and that I must share him. But, I miss you more when you are gone. I try to not be selfish knowing that you, too, are chosen."

"The Creator has joined our paths into one for his purpose. We must walk this path not only on the sunny hillsides, but also in the briar laden ravines. Though we will go in opposite directions on the trail at tomor- row's light, my heart will go with you and your heart will come with me."

"I understand."

"Buffalo Man will tell Porcupine all that I have learned. I need you to tell all the people camped at Vincennes that I will do my best to bring their families home."

"I will tell them. Now lie quietly and let our hearts speak to one another."

William Wells spent the following two nights in the fort and the next fifteen in the boat-camps on the Ohio. Two boats of twelve boatmen had been contracted to deliver sixteen soldiers, Captain Stewart of the US infantry, and the interpreter Wells to the Cincinnati landing. The captain had fought the English in the east as a boy. He had been involved in the erection of Fort Harmar where he remained for many years. He related that he was supervising the loading of wagons in Cincinnati when he learned of the disaster that befell St. Clair. The captain expected that soon there would be an all-out war with the Spanish or English.

Boatmen spoke of being secure in their trade due to army supplies once again being warehoused at Pittsburgh. Men of the river would be needed to transport war materials to Cincinnati. Yarns of the soldiers indicated all had been in St. Clair's army. Their stories conflicted with each other and with what he knew, but he pieced together a saga of their experiences. Some of the men had remained at Ft. Washington to guard supplies and occasionally escort a supply train. Others were garrisoned at Fort Jefferson, and a few were with Hamtramck chasing the deserters. None had participated in St. Clair's Defeat, as they called it. Second-hand stories of the battle were highly imaginative and provided no real substance. Two things were clear: the supplies and provisions were of poor quality, and the Americans intended to fight again.

* ["O For a Heart to Praise My God" – Charles Wesley, 1742]

CHAPTER 10
Cincinnati

Boatmen worked hard against the steady flow to gain the Cincinnati wharf. The mouth of the Licking River on the opposite side of the Ohio made the wide river seem even more expansive. After aborting the first attempt at landing, the crew wrestled their boat upstream and circled back to land with the current. Banging against the pilings, the vessel was quickly tied off. Captain Stewart wasted no time at the landing. He marched his men to the encampment on the west side of the town, keeping Interpreter Wells close at hand. By evening, the two men had been summoned to the gate of the fort. Upon arrival, they were escorted to the commandant's headquarters.

William was surprised at the size of the encampment and the strength of the fort. Fort Washington was the most magnificent structure Wells had ever seen. The main edifice was a square courtyard surrounded by buildings constructed of whitewashed heavy planking two stories tall. The red-painted shingle roofs were pierced by four tall brick chimneys in each row of buildings. Set out at each corner were five-sided blockhouses pointing away from the fort like tips of an arrows. A watchtower protruded from each blockhouse roof high above the second-story cannon. Palisades formed additional triangular enclosures attached to the north and west sides.

There was an air of business about the place that he had only slightly sensed at Vincennes' Fort Knox and the Clarksville's Fort Steuben. Each person he met seemed to be about an urgent errand. Unlike the English at Detroit, the military here was kept separate from the town. In comparison, flatboats substituted for sailing ships; squalor and disorder contrasted to the cleanliness and regimen of the English town.

Their escort led them to a room with four officers in fancy uniforms. He announced, "Captain Stewart arriving from Fort Steuben and Mr. Wells the interpreter."

Stewart exchanged salutes with each of the officers. The man behind a large desk in the center of the room had the fanciest uniform William had ever seen.

The man spoke while seated, "I am General Wilkinson, commandant here and overseer of Fort Hamilton and Fort Jefferson."

Seemingly dismissing the fact that the man standing to his left held the higher rank of brigadier general, he motioned with his hand, "My guest here is General Rufus Putnam, sent from Philadelphia to treat with the Indians. Major Stewart, you are dismissed. Mr. Wells, I understand that you have business with General Putnam."

Wells sensed coolness between the two generals. He could not know that coolness had a long history dating back to the earliest days of the War of Revolution. Putnam rose and shook the hand of the departing Major Stewart, then the hand of Wells. Putnam looked deep into William's eyes and studied his face. William wondered what would happen if he suddenly announced that he had led the charge against St. Clair's artillery and had captured the army's documents. He kept this idea buried, but could not resist a little smile.

Putnam began, "Major Hamtramck tells me that you are the man who is the most fluent in the languages of our Indian prisoners. He says that they know you and will trust what you say."

Wilkinson chimed in, "I heard that you interpreted for Little Turtle himself when he parlayed with the British."

Putnam sent a scowl towards Wilkinson letting the man know that he wanted no more interruptions.

He turned to the interpreter, "All I want from you is to get these people to understand that we will be taking them to Vincennes to be released to their people. If I can get their cooperation there should be no problems and all can arrive safely. For this the government is willing to pay you one dollar per day to represent us and interpret to the captives. If you can gain their trust, we will bring them here from Fort Hamilton and then arrange transport to Vincennes."

William looked back into the eyes of the general. There he found the calm confidence of a man in control. He recalled Samuel telling him how this man had been personally selected by President Washington and confirmed by the government to represent the United States in the west. He knew that this man had designed fortifications for Washington during the war with England. He was glad to be speaking face to face with this general. He was also glad that he was not required to converse directly with

Wilkinson. He found himself suddenly unprepared to deal with the man.

"I will do what I can to gain their release," Wells spoke confidently.

"All in good time. Right now, just get them to talk to me," the general replied. "Be here at sunrise day after next. The two of us will head to Fort Hamilton."

* * *

William returned as instructed to find the senior officers absent. Lieutenant Harrison swore him in as interpreter for the government and had him sign a paper of allegiance and a paper outlining the payment arrangements. Harrison led him to the rear of the fort where a company was forming.

He strode up to General Putnam, "Lieutenant William Henry Harrison and Interpreter Wells reporting, sir."

"Lead on," was the reply.

As it turned out, "the two of us" was a company of forty mounted soldiers and officers plus seven packhorses. Putnam invited Wells to ride beside him. Harrison with four soldiers headed the column. Along an improved road leading north into the hills, the general engaged the interpreter in conversation to assess his knowledge of the native languages and customs, and his understanding of the geography. The general shared a bit of his background and the politics of the east. Having been an officer during the entire time of the revolution, he prided himself on quickly evaluating men. Today, he found a man of ability and integrity. Actually, most men quickly accepted William Wells, Wild Carrot, as a confidant after only a conversation or two.

"I understand that you are married to a Miami woman."

"The most beautiful of them all," William responded.

"Ha! The exact words of Hamtramck." On they rode.

Late in the day, the column broke out into an expansive prairie. Fort Hamilton could be seen hugging the east bank of the Great Miami River, or River of Rocks as it was called by the French. Though as large as the fort on the Ohio, this rectangular fort was of rougher construction. The walls were of pointed log palisades backed by an earthen firing platform. Artillery platforms were mounted at each corner. Buildings were set inside apart from the wall. A triangular protrusion was added to the south wall and a large rectangular enclosure attached to the north.

The road made a wide arc, then paralleled the river as it approached the gate. An unusual sense of anxiety overcame William as he rode across the grassy plain towards the outpost. He had imagined this fort while listening to the reports of the Delaware spies. Now, it was looming large before him. Well beyond, to the north, were two more stockades, Fort St. Clair and Fort Jefferson, marking the road that the Americans intend to extend to Kekionga.

Harrison swung his horse around and came beside him, smiling broadly as if revealing a joke, "The big house is General Wilkinson's." The massive two-story log house with its veranda overhanging the fort wall, overlooking the river, seemed oddly out of place. He pointed to the northern enclosure, "Your captives are in there."

Just then, two of the fort's cannon fired a salute to the arriving Major General. A guard with drums and flags marched out through the gate and lined the entry. General Putnam took the lead and rode the column into the fort.

Putnam addressed Harrison, "Wells can bunk with you. We will meet with the captives in the morning."

"I would like to sleep with the prisoners tonight, if I may," William asserted.

The two officers looked at each other with an air close to amazement. Harrison shrugged his shoulders a bit while Putnam studied the idea.

Putnam stammered, "It's your skin." Turning to the junior officer he continued, "See to it." Again to Wells, "You will need to leave your knife and any other weapons outside the compound."

"One more thing, General," William propositioned, "extra rations this evening would put the captives in a good mood to hear your message."

The general smiled at the man's spunk, "If the fort has the provisions, Lieutenant Harrison, let it be done." Putnam headed for headquarters before any more requests could be made.

William Henry Harrison embellished the general's directive by rounding up all the spare food he could scrounge. Gladly willing to war against Indians, he did not find holding captive women and children to be good military policy; only Wilkinson seemed to endorse it. As a good officer, Harrison efficiently carried out his duties. He had left medical school to join the army in Philadelphia a year ago, shortly after his father died. His father, Benjamin, a signer of the Declaration of Independence, had been a Virginia delegate to the Continental Congress. Esteemed by many, Benjamin became the governor of Virginia.

The son, in financial need and having a zest for adventure, found St.

Clair's wilderness campaign an attractive option. His trip down the Ohio from Fort Pitt came too late to join St. Clair's advance, so he was left behind keeping inventory at Fort Washington. Wilkinson later offered Ensign Harrison an opportunity to serve in the field rather than the clerk's post. He took the offer and, although he did not like him personally, held onto the ambitious man's coattails.

Harrison quickly understood that James Wilkinson was interested in the army only as a means to high political stature. The general entertained hopes of being governor of the new state of Kentucky, or another new state to be carved out of the Northwest Territory. Harrison suspected that Wilkinson catered more to Thomas Jefferson than to Secretary of War Knox and President Washington. He somewhat doubted the general's claims to a great victory at Eel Town. For now, Harrison worked at being indispensable to his superiors. He would keep an eye toward possible land speculation and civilian posts in the territorial government still headed by St. Clair. Harrison was determined that one day he could return to Virginia as his own person of stature.

Harrison was disappointed that he would not immediately share quarters with Wells. His travels had taken him no farther west than this post. He hoped to learn more about the lands and people on the extended frontier. Typical in an army post, he had heard all sorts of rumors about this interpreter, most hardly believable. Was the interpreter really raised in the forest by the savages? Did he have children playing in the camps of the enemy? Had he in Detroit interpreted for Little Turtle, the Miami chief who confounded the entire American government and army? Was he the brother of Captain Wells of the Kentucky Militia who received the initial charge in the massacre on the St. Marys? Why had Major Hamtramck given him high praise if he was only an interpreter?

Harrison weighed the possibilities of joining the escort to the west if the prisoners were moved. Being attached to Putnam may give quicker promotion. On the other hand, the possibility of being stuck in Vincennes may stagnate a career. He knew that a new, larger army would be established at Fort Washington. He decided that was the place to stay.

Wells waited with the sentries at the gate to the north compound. He watched soldiers pile sacks of vegetables and grain and two chunks of beef. When the gate opened, he heaved a bag of meal onto his shoulder and entered with the troops. The soldiers dropped their burdens haphazardly and rushed out. A crowd began to circle the mound of provisions and the lone buckskin-clad man standing in their midst. The women wanted to get to the food while staying out of the reach of the stranger. Soldiers on the parapet were wagering whether the interpreter would first get stabbed, clobbered with a grinding rock, or simply get torn to shreds by the mob. Wells set his sack upright atop two others, tugged at the string and opened the canvas bag. He dipped in both hands and held them in front of him.

Speaking calmly in the Miami tongue he said, "I have brought you some meal."

A voice from the right near the front called his Miami name. Four times she called it, each time louder. Women rushed forward to touch him and to look into his face. Primrose pushed to the front as shouts abounded.

"It is Wild Carrot of Eel Town! He will save us! We are spared!"

As Primrose came closer, he raised a hand and signed for quiet and patience. In a low voice he said, "Surely Wilkinson has spies on the wall who understand our words. Woman, do not touch me." He did not say "mother" for fear of spies. "I will visit you after darkness grows. I will visit everyone during the night. Arrange them in groups of four and I will talk with each in turn. Now, share the food. I will get some milk for you."

He pushed through to the gate and called to the sentry. He stepped outside and demanded that all the available milk be brought to the gate. The shocked soldiers scurried away to fulfill the request as if it was an order from Washington. The interpreter needed the time for the word to be passed among the captives to not give up his full identity.

The soldiers set down their pails of milk and exited. Wells turned to find the women had organized themselves into two rows to welcome him. A youth took his hat and escorted him down the middle as each woman touched him on the head and gave him a blessing. The lines disbanded as he passed. Primrose and Small Cloud, the last in line, remained with him. Two maidens calmly distributed the milk as all prepared a bonus meal in the twilight. Nine elderly women formed a circle and danced to a slow chant.

The general and others were soon told of the miraculous reception of the interpreter. Many immediately grew suspicious of the man. Perhaps Major Hamtramck was duped. Perhaps Hamtramck sent this man to undermine Wilkinson's authority. Putnam was relieved. Finally there was someone these people would talk to. Now, if the man could only get them to cooperate, he could fulfill Washington's wishes. He could appease the Yankee congressmen that abhorred the holding of these prisoners. With the foundation that Hamtramck had laid with the tribes of the lower Wabash, the delivery of their kin could only bolster peace negotiations. Looking at a map, he imagined ascending the Wabash signing treaties of peace in village after village until the entire Miami tribe had renounced war. With the Miami denouncing war, the Shawnee would seek peace and soon the British influence would disappear. Detroit would be vacated and the entire Northwest would be open to American enterprise.

Yet, the first step would be to get these people to Vincennes without incident. He reminded himself that only two weeks earlier a band of Shawnee dressed in British coats and shirts had killed a haying detail on these very fields. One man was tortured within sight of the fort and mutilated bodies of others were strewn about; two have not yet been found. Putnam convinced himself that the strange incident was brought about by a British plan to assassinate him and wreck the peace effort. He needed to be cautious in returning the captives. If they darted for the forest or jumped overboard on the river, the whole affair would turn very messy. The fiasco would become fodder for eastern politicians.

In the morning, Putnam summoned the interpreter to join him for breakfast. He wanted to talk to him informally. Wells replied that he had already had his breakfast and was busy interviewing the prisoners. The interpreter relayed that three women had been elected as leaders. They would meet General Putnam only, with a small guard if he desired, at the river's edge in front of the fort at noon. Taken aback at the abruptness and insolence of the proposal, the general soon relented that it amounted to exactly what he had wished.

He wrote a quick message to Secretary Knox and one to General Wilkinson. Next, he ordered that a contingent be posted on the opposite side of the river, and one each upstream and downstream on the near side. A mounted unit was to crisscross the prairie to confuse any observing war parties lurking about. He asked Harrison to assign him four good soldiers and a flag bearer who "could keep their mouths shut." A party of twelve soldiers would escort the women leaders to the river. The soldiers were to retire to a distance of fifty yards.

General Putnam skipped lunch and checked his uniform in the mirror. He gave a laugh at himself dressing for a talk with savage women on the bank of a river whose name was unknown to all of his eastern friends. He thought about having a desk and paper sent ahead, but decided that would represent a formality that may hinder cordial discussions. He

smacked himself on the thighs and headed for the gate. There he followed his country's flag to the water's edge. He motioned to where he
wished the guard and flag positioned. He signaled the soldiers at the
gate to bring the captives.

Six soldiers emerged followed by the three women and another six
soldiers, then William Wells. Wells spread soiled and tattered blankets
upon the sandy gravel for the women. The women proceeded to the river
and washed their faces and arms followed by legs and feet. They then
returned and sat nonchalantly upon the blankets and looked up at the
officer without expression. Putnam was wishing that he could soak his
feet in the cool waters since the sun was heating up his polished black
boots. Actually, he felt uniformly hot all over. He was unsure whether his
discomfort was due to the sun or to the unusual negotiation session. He
realized that the interpreter was looking at him with raised eyebrows,
anticipating his opening words.

"Yes, well, I am Major General Rufus Putnam. I am here to represent
President Washington, chief of all Americans and of all the Northwest
Territory. I am glad to find you to be in good health."

The general waited for the interpretation. He was surprised at his
first hearing of the Miami language. Many of the words had several syl-
lables and sounded indistinguishable from one another, but they were
spoken delicately and in a cadence that was poetic, somewhat melodic.
The women listened without expression.

He wanted them to speak, so he asked, "Have you been treated well
here? Have you been well fed?"

After the translation, the woman nearest the river replied, "We have
survived; that is all."

The woman in the middle added, "We are concerned for our little
children. They do not get enough to eat and the foods are not the correct
ones for them. I see berries hanging at your back, but we cannot get
them."

The general responded, "Our soldiers are also short of proper food.
Tonight, have Mr. Wells make a list of foods your children need. I will
provide what I can. Now, tell me your names."

Each replied with their name and village. Wells repeated the name
only, then gave the corresponding English words: Panther Paw, Blue
Feather, Primrose.

Primrose put forth a statement that she had long imagined saying to
her captors, "We cannot gather our medicines from the forest and prairie

because we are confined at the fort. We are weak from poor food. However, more food cannot feed the hunger of our hearts to see our homes, our lands and rivers, and our families. Our legs are weak from lack of work, yet we will walk towards the setting sun for the time of a moon to reach our villages. Our minds are weak from being denied our crafts; still, we can read the signs of the land to find our way home. Release us now and we will walk naked into the forest taking nothing. We have no life here. If you cannot release us, then kill us this day. Feed our flesh to the wolves and crows. Send our bones back to our families to be buried at our villages." At the close she lowered her head into her lap as if awaiting execution.

Wells had determined that, overall, the captives were in good health. They had not been tortured or violated. He assessed that they were actually as well off physically as if they had spent the seasons in their villages. A few days of exercise out in the open would regain their strength and spirit. As usual, he interpreted fully and faithfully.

Putnam was obviously moved by Primrose's speech. He was also impressed by the detailed interpretation given by Wells. The ambassador realized that the interpreters he had experienced at Fort Pitt and at Fort Harmar were only rudimentarily conveying the conversation without any expression whatsoever. In those places, each side in turn had lowered the level of conversation to brief statements as if speaking to children.

The general again addressed the women, "I have word from Vincennes that your families are gathered there to welcome you home. They want peace with my government. We want peace with them. I will travel to Vincennes in one month, in the time of one moon, to speak for President Washington to your chiefs. If it is your desire to go with me and be freed of your bondage upon arrival at Vincennes, then each must make a vow to not attempt an escape and to follow the instructions of the soldiers. The soldiers will protect you from molestation; I will protect you from the soldiers. Think on these things. Send your list of foods that you desire with Mr. Wells. Have him convey, also, other needs that you have. I will fulfill requests that are within my ability and military policy."

He removed his hat and bowed as if at a reception in the east. He strode up the incline to the gate without waiting for the interpretation or reply.

In his office General Putnam ordered Lieutenant Harrison to form a hunting party to be sent out every third day to bring in fresh venison for the captives in addition to their normal rations. He instructed him to replace all the blankets in the captives' compound and review all sanitation measures. Harrison was to make the garrison understand that while the Indian women and children were to be kept under full guard, they were to be treated as refugees and not as enemies or criminals.

Upon entering the compound, Wells led the three women leaders to a place where they could not be heard by the guards. He congratulated them on their conduct. He advised them to put their trust in Putnam. The ambassador did indeed represent General Washington. Putnam wanted to give them safe passage to Vincennes where they would be freed to their waiting families. He recommended a prompt response, especially now while Wilkinson was away. He then asked them to remain.

Returning shortly with Small Cloud at his heels, he took her by the hand, "In Eel Town I married Small Cloud of the Wea. She has my child who is with you here. She deceived me and did not do the things of a wife. I put her away at Ouiatenon before the child entered this world. Again I say in your presence that she is not my wife and I put her away." He released her hand and turned his back.

Primrose replied stiffly, "It is so. The child will remain with Small Cloud."

Small Cloud scoffed, "You are a dog. I will have no more to do with you, nor will my child!" She stomped off to her blanket. She bundled her few possessions within the blanket and relocated against a more distant wall of the fort.

"I will do what I can for your son," Primrose promised.

"Mother," it was the first he had addressed her as such since his arrival, "I will spend the remainder of the day and this night with you. Tomorrow I must return to live with the soldiers. I must be one of them until we are home. I have heard you tell of your events since the capture at Eel Town. Now I will tell you what I saw there; I will tell you of your husband, about Sweet Breeze and Tulip Leaf. I will tell you how Little Turtle became Chief of All Nations and how I became a war chief. I will tell of the great victory at the headwaters of the Wabash. You will hear about the tribes camped at Vincennes. You will learn about my journey to the American town at the Falls of the Ohio where Sweet Breeze and I visited the brother of my childhood."

"Yes, let us go to my little camp." Primrose was filled with wonder as she spoke. "I want to hear it all."

"I can only tell you a portion now. Remember," he reminded, "that you cannot share any of it with these. If the soldiers overhear them speaking of it, and I think there are spies that know some words of our language, they will know that it came from me. I have kept many secrets from the Americans so that I may be here to guide you home."

Two weeks it would be until the supply train arrived at the outpost with enough wagons to transport the captives, refugees, as Putnam called them, south to Fort Washington. Putnam sent ahead orders on preparations to detain the refugees at that place. It would take him another two or three weeks to arrange the trip to their destination in the west. He conducted a formal ceremony where the refugees pledged cooperation. He established procedures for grievances via the interpreter. He was busting with joy at how smoothly the affair was proceeding. He was continually amazed at the abilities of the interpreter. He was anxious to greet the man's mentor, Hamtramck, who he only knew briefly during the War of Revolution. Putnam did know Hamtramck by reputation as a dedicated officer heading an isolated frontier post.

Putnam kept the garrison and attached companies busy going to and fro to dissuade enemy war parties from wrecking his plans. The general, being a military engineer, took an expedition north to inspect Fort Jefferson as well as Fort St. Clair, a way-station midway along the trail. He found the Fort St. Clair stockade design and location adequate for its purpose, though not quite the gem that General Wilkinson had described. He found the Fort Jefferson defenses, though solidly constructed of hewn timbers, woefully small and poorly situated to the surroundings. He recommended relocating the entire operation.

Before departing Fort Jefferson, the general from the east scaled a newly built free-standing blockhouse. His gaze turned northward over the top of an unbroken forest of maples. Here, he imagined the massive army of General St. Clair disappearing into the trees only to return as a broken shambles. He bit his lip at the shame of hundreds of soldiers, officers, militia, and civilians yet lying unburied in the wilderness. Farther north, the fallen men of Harmar's expedition had also been abandoned. If his peace effort could reach all the way to Kekionga, even by a wide circular loop, he would place the recovery of the fallen as the top item on the treaty. Out there, somewhere, was another concern to Putnam and all the military officers. The cannon for the fort that General St. Clair had intended to build at Kekionga had been lost at the defeat. In capable hands they could blow any of the American forts to splinters.

Peace was a fleeting hope and conflict was real. It had been six weeks since Colonel John Hardin had left this very clearing on Secretary Knox's peace overture to the chiefs in the north. Rumors were that this hardened Kentucky frontiersman was killed and scalped by the Shawnee only a two-days' ride from the fort. Still, despite rumors, hope remained that the veteran of Clark's and Harmar's expeditions and numerous raids on the Shawnee villages was still out there, working his way through the Auglaize country. The fate of Major Truman, who had left for Kekionga at the same time with the same letter, was revealed in a dispatch from Hamtramck. An Eel River chief reported that a man carrying papers and a flag had been killed on the Salamonie.

Finding his daily duties to be brief, Wells spent much of his time fishing. During the evenings he studied the books that Harrison had carried to this post. Occasionally, he accompanied the mounted sorties. From time to time he pitched in with the soldiers forming timbers and digging postholes. Other than recommending more fresh water for the captives, he was pleased with the advancements in the compound. Diet, clothing, and shelter had all been improved. The captives' requests for bathing in the river and for working in the hay fields were understandably denied.

Hot humid days that only came in brief spells on the Eel seemed to be the norm in the Great Miami River valley. At night, Wells would awaken gasping for air in the dank log room of the officers' quarters. He forsook the open air of the compound to gain the trust of the Americans. Besides, he wanted to know more about Lieutenant William Henry Harrison. In addition to his military life, this man had experienced the people, places, and politics of the east. Being only a few years younger than Wells, Harrison inquired unceasingly about the lands of the west and the ways of the tribes. The young officer wanted to know the similarities and relationships of the tribes as well as their differences. He tried a few simple words of Miami and Pottawatomie, but certainly was not a linguist. The lieutenant quizzed this walking-encyclopedia companion about the timber and plants, about the soil and rocks, about the animals and birds.

From Harrison, Wells learned that about half of the enlisted men were immigrants or sons of immigrants from across the great sea who were seeking to establish themselves in their new country. Others came west to avoid prison due to debts or crimes. A few were likely escaping oppressive homes, unhappy marriages, or overly persistent lovers. The best soldiers were the ones that came west for adventure. Several of these were keeping diaries of their travels. They studied the surroundings, hoping one day to be among the first settlers when the lands opened for sale. The ones who gained experience and learned to read and write could become officers. The new army that would soon accumulate at Cincinnati, perhaps as early as the next spring, would need officers.

Officers and enlisted men alike thought that it was inevitable that the Miami strength would be broken and the British would be pushed out of Detroit. If by peace, fine, but they just as soon it happen by military might. War meant employment for the enlisted. It offered advancement and prestige for the officers, assuming, of course, that they survived.

* * *

The women were enjoying a long day in the wagons even through bone-jarring jolts and dust that could choke a horse. The dark green of the forest canopy offered relief both from the sun and the monotonous brown and gray existence within the compound walls. On occasions, Williams Wells would ride up to each wagon and make jokes about the soldiers. He assured the women that Putnam was indeed at the head of the column and that the man had prepared for their care at Fort Washington. Staying a while there, they would be whisked away by the waters of the Ohio to their own Wabash. Some of the women made their own jokes about their dowdy appearance or about the respite from tanning hides at home.

On the twelfth morning at Fort Washington, the refugees were rousted early and told to pack. An escort walked them through a jeering crowd of the town's citizens. They could not understand the words, but the insults came through clearly enough. Soldiers pushed and butted their rifles against townspeople who pelted the procession with stones and sticks. At the wharf, Putnam's guard repelled the crowd with fixed bayonets and the threat of gunfire. Wells swiftly divided the captives and directed them into waiting flatboats. Any apprehension of boarding was outweighed by the desire to escape the mob. The horde scattered when an armed caravan of wagons arrived with the military escort that was to travel to Vincennes. Sixty soldiers and officers and one civilian joined the one hundred forty refugees in the five large boats. Within an hour, lines were tossed and oars steered the boat barges into the current of the mighty Ohio River.

CHAPTER 11
Ohio River

The waters of the Ohio seemed to sing to the captives that freedom was at hand. Low water had added a day to their journey, but today they would reach the falls which were midway to the mouth of the Wabash. Each evening the flotilla had moored on the Kentucky bank. While the soldiers set up each camp, the women waited aboard. Once ashore they could then move about gathering firewood and plants. By the second camp they were, of their own volition, assisting in the cooking. Within days, they had taken over the entire cooking duties, adding to the happiness of both parties. Each evening Primrose directed the erection of a frame to hold a canvas curtain where water could be brought for bathing.

She had gained trust in Putnam as a man of his word. He did personally accompany the convoy as he first indicated. He often sought the advice of Wild Carrot on various matters about the voyage. In addition, a Moravian missionary by the name of John Heckewelder accompanied the expedition to observe the entire operation. Having come with Putnam from Marietta, he represented the pacifists in congress. He was to verify the proper treatment of the captives. Also, he was to assure that all efforts at peace would be attempted before the next armed excursion. The man had extensively traveled the frontier of Pennsylvania and into the Ohio country since before the revolution. Having a good knowledge of the Muncee Delaware and their language, he could understand some of the Miami sayings. Constantly writing in his journal, he was personally interested in learning all he could about the lands and tribes to the west. He was thoroughly frustrated by the reluctance of the captive women to be interviewed. He turned to the interpreter with his thousand questions.

At the previous night's camp, after supper, the general ordered forth a heavy trunk. From it he produced new skirts, blouses, belts, ribbons, and combs for the women. Primrose organized the order of pick of the wares. When all were attired, the general laid out a blanket beside the bonfire and set a yellow-painted cask upon it. Opening the cask he poured out a wealth of copper and silver earrings, necklaces, and bands. Pandemonium erupted as the women scooped them up. Shrieks of glee pierced the night sky as young girls danced with their new adornments reflecting the firelight.

* * *

Under a brilliant sun, Primrose finished her corncakes with honey and dried apples. Her boat veered left into a narrow channel which was separated by a large island from the main part of the river. The general's boat boasting a large flag approached alongside and bumped heavily, causing her to drop her last morsel. Wild Carrot took two strides, leaped the rails, and landed with a thud on a crate in front of her. He held his balance a moment, then stepped to the plank floor. The tillermen effortlessly separated the vessels to a respectable distance.

"Let me get a look at you!" her adopted son proclaimed.

She stood and twirled, then spread her skirt with both hands. She turned her head from side to side to display her earrings and combs. Her silver broach with seven tiny dangling chains glistened in the sunlight.

"Porcupine will think that you have been to a festival all the while," he kidded.

"We will have festival enough when my husband and I are rejoined. I am thankful that we will not be returning in rags. The women are building strength; they are regaining their spirits. Putnam is wise to recognize our dignity."

"I am here with words from him. He wants you to remind the women that the soldiers are here to protect you from the Americans just as much as they are here to guard you from escape before our destination is reached. You have seen how he keeps a wide berth from the settlers' boats and how he camps in isolation. He wants you to remember how you were protected from the mob at Cincinnati. We will soon approach the falls. There will be settlements on both sides of the river. The American fort will be on the right with villages nearby. The main town of Louisville will be on the left. There will be some rough water and many islands as you recall from when Wilkinson brought you upstream. We will camp for two or three days on the large island near the south bank where Clark had his old fort. We will remain there until the boats can be lowered past the falls. Villagers will be kept away from this camp. However, some dignitaries from the fort and the town may visit. Our people should not be afraid. That is what he wants you to tell our people."

She acknowledged with a nod.

"We will tie up at the end of this island in a moment," he continued, "so that you may address our people. Tell them for me that I am proud of their conduct. Let them know that I will tell the story of their bravery to all the chiefs at Vincennes. I am glad that Putnam is not an officer who would parade you through the streets of the town as an exhibition. One more thing for you only, after we clear this island I will soon point to the south with an oar. There on a hillside you will see the plantation of the brother of my childhood, Samuel Wells."

He lounged at her side until the boats joined.

He laid his right arm on her shoulder and said, "You look as beautiful as you did on the day you adopted me at Kekionga."

"Yes, I remember that day. You ate the whole pot of carrot soup that was to be our supper. That is why I named you your name," she grinned. "Now go, Wild Carrot!" With a quick jump he rejoined the boat of the general-turned-admiral.

* * *

A rumbling of the thundering waters hushed all other sounds in the camp as the women prepared their temporary huts.

Wild Carrot approached his mother, "It will be good for our people to walk upon the earth again while the boats are lowered. This place will make a fine camp." He continued, "At dawn I will leave to visit the family of my brother. I will return after nightfall. Heckewelder assures me that he will remain in camp for the day to look after your needs."

"Heckewelder is a good man," she mused. "He tells me that he is neither English nor American, but disciple of Christ only. It is known by all that he was held prisoner in Detroit by the English during General Washington's war. His Christian Delaware were murdered in his absence by the Pennsylvanians. He has reason to hate both the English and the Americans and to seek revenge. But he does not. He hopes to live among us and tell our people how he worships the Creator."

She tugged at Wild Carrot's elbow to have him sit beside her on a log, "You have been a good son to this old woman. Porcupine and I lost our beloved Swift Foot in an attack not far from this place of falls. We hoped that his spirit would reside with your soul and restore our family. Whether that has come to pass or not, you have mended our hearts and filled them with joy. You have grown in strength to a man of wisdom and courage and honor. You have become the husband of my niece who adores you. You have been favored by the Creator to become a leader of the Miami like my husband and my brother. My people honor you as a war chief, and now here you are tending lost women and children."

She listened to the waters for a moment, "Here we sit, you and I, between two worlds. I will return to my village beside the Eel River, to the lands that I know. There I will one day die in peace or at the hands of the Americans, I do not know which. But I do sense that my generation will be the last to live as our people have since the Creator placed us upon this earth. You, Wild Carrot, have a choice. I know that you are thinking, 'Mother, I will go where you go,' but do not say it. You and Sweet Breeze, and your family to be, will live in a world different from what I have known, what I will have in the few winters that remain. Think on it, whether to look to the north where you will live the life of a Miami chief constantly embattled by those who seek your lands, inevitably to be trampled by the horde of settlers. Or, whether you should look to the south to live the life of your brother's family where Sweet Breeze can enjoy the rich rewards of life. I will always be your mother and you will be my child, but I tell you now that you may choose which path you will take."

Wild Carrot did not want to hear these words. How could she think he would forsake his Miami people? He could not steal Little Turtle's daughter and live among his enemy. He felt like a little boy being schooled by his mother. But, he must ponder her wisdom.

How long they sat he did not know, but finally he had a response. "You have spoken well, Mother," he said. "But, perhaps peace will flow across the lands and the Americans will learn to live beside the tribes without warfare. One side can benefit from the other and both can carry on in peace. Putnam and Heckewelder continually discuss ways for peace. They say that Washington and the council of fifteen fires prefer it."

* * *

Since his sleep was repeatedly interrupted with strange dreams, William Wells decided he might as well begin his trip prematurely. His early departure caused some commotion among the sentries. However, the paper written by the general approving his travel calmed them once they found someone to read it. The horse was good enough, though short of the quality of Samuel's steeds. Thrice William took wrong turns and had to backtrack to the proper road. He gained the fenced pasture while morning shadows still stretched to the lane.

"Miss Mary!" A black cook dashed from the out-kitchen to the porch. "Miss Mary, a lone rider is coming from the river gate!"

Mary stashed her needlework and scurried to the porch. She recognized the rider instantly.

"Margaret, children! It is your Uncle William! Wash up and come to the porch."

At the call, the children dashed about gathering the items each had made for him. Each day with Uncle William was like a holiday.

Before he could dismount Mary offered, "Come down, I have some of the coffee that you like."

"For me? How did you know that I was coming? I am traveling downriver with an army escort."

"Oh, there are no secrets on the river. It may take two months for a message to travel from Philadelphia, but it comes with every story between that place and here when it eventually arrives. You just need to backtrack the time to the source to piece it all together. Everyone knows all about the peace envoy and the Indian prisoners destined for Vincennes. Word is that the brother of Captain Samuel Wells is heading the endeavor. Is that right?"

"All except the fact that Washington's own Major General leads us and I am outranked by about ten people," he smiled. "Speaking of the Captain, where is he, is he home?"

"He is never home! He has been wearing out horses all over the territory attending meetings. If meetings make a government run, then ours will be a good one. I have to keep a chart to know where he is and how long he has been out. Lexington, five days so far, this time."

The children burst upon them and playtime ensued.

"Please, William, can you stay a few days," Mary inquired. "I am sure you can make up the lost time by going up the trace."

"No, my presence is required with the boats. Your government is paying good silver for an interpreter, you know. I have only now, and must be at the falls by nightfall."

Indeed, by nightfall he was once again William Wells the government interpreter and Wild Carrot the liberator of the prisoners.

* * *

As the boat bobbed its meandering course under an afternoon sun, missionary Heckewelder again initiated his quizzing. He inquired, "Mr. Wells, I have seen nary a soul nor dwelling in the five days since we passed the mouth of the Salt River. How far do you reckon to the Wabash? Are there any towns?"

"Only one settlement of a few cabins is to be seen. See how the hills are giving way on the right? When the low ground is on the left also, we will be within one day of the river Wabash. I would say a bit over two days at this progress."

"And how long to Vincennes?"

"That will depend on the skill of the boatmen. First they will need to gain a clear channel to the actual river; there are many reed-choked inlets to negotiate. The entire river is lined with swamps right up to Vincennes. Above there the character of the Wabash changes quickly. If the water is low like it is here on the Ohio, it will favor our progress against the current. By the time you see a dwelling we will be quite near Vincennes. You may see a party of trappers in their log canoes, or a trader, perhaps even a flatboat headed down to New Orleans."

"You have been quite helpful to me, Mr. Wells." The missionary continued his inquiry, "I want to thank you again for being there when I encountered that bear. I have been in the forest most of my days and have seen many bears, but have never felt one's breath on my neck before."

"You likely stepped into his favorite berry patch, and the berry season is nearly over. I do not think he liked that." He was going to make a joke about his brother roughly chasing off squatters, too, but let the idea pass. "Keep in mind that where you are going there is a bear behind every third tree."

"I have to ask, is the ramrod your weapon of choice with bears?" Heckewelder wondered.

"Had I fired my rifle, you would have been burnt by the powder, perhaps even struck by the ball. He would have mauled you by the time I could have lunged with my knife; that is dangerous business anyway. I did not want him to be able to reach my gun barrel, so the ramrod was the next best choice."

"At first I was startled at the teeth of the beast inches from my face,"

146

the missionary recalled, "then by its snout being poked by your ramrod as if by a lance. I think old man bear was as startled as I was. Your yank rolled me behind you and I could not see what was happening."

"I apologize for getting your face scratched by the briars, but they do not cut as deeply as do bear teeth or claws. I think the marks will fade by the time we reach Vincennes."

The missionary could not leave any untold details, "You spoke to the bear in Miami. What were you saying?"

Wild Carrot laughed, "Well, I scolded mister bear on his cowardliness at backing down without a fight. I told him that his whimpering was a poor representative of the animals of the forest. I told him that I would have to kill him and take his meat and fat and skin. I told him that if he had been brave, I would have first cut out his heart and eaten of it to gain his courage. I would have worn his claws about my neck to honor him. But he was not brave and his heart would be left for the scavengers and his claws would return to the soil."

The missionary wondered, "Yet, after you killed him you gave a prayer of thanksgiving."

"Yes, I always give thanks to the Creator when I kill an animal. It is our custom."

"And I gave a prayer of thanksgiving to the Lord for your presence and skill. Why did you choose to speak the language of the Miami and not English?"

"I could have spoken in French or any one of the tongues of the tribes as far as the bear was concerned. Miami is my natural language," Wild Carrot thought the answer should have been obvious.

"And how many languages do you have?"

"I am not sure. Let me think on it," the interpreter leaned back to ponder.

He watched a pair of eagles soar back and forth high above the river. His mind searched geographically the regions of the tribes. Reminisces of his travels caused him to lose count several times.

"I count eighteen tongues of the tribes plus French and English. I do not know the language of the Iroquois to the east nor the Creek and Choctaw to the south. The Sioux and others beyond the Mississippi I do not know, nor Spanish. You have lived among the Muncee and know their words well. Let me ask you this. The Muncee and Lanape are known as Delaware among the English, do you find their language to be the same, or are they two?"

Heckewelder replied, "They converse well with each other, but there are many words of one that are not of another. Many place-names are different. A phrase in one may not mean the same as in another. I would say that they are two."

"Agreed, they are two. Place-names are the hardest part of interpreting. The French call these waters carrying us towards the Illinois country 'LaBelle Riviere.' Yet, each tribe has its own 'Beautiful River' flowing north or south, east or west. There is but one river that carries canoes from Kekionga to the grand lake Erie, but it is known by nine different names. To interpret well between two languages one must know more than the meaning of words in one and words in the other. It is necessary to know how the people live, to hear stories of their ancestors. Omitted words are often as important as the spoken words."

The tranquility of their drifting boat was suddenly disturbed by thunderous crashing and splashing. The boat ahead of them had gone to the right of an island and they had gone to the left. Buffalo on the island were surprised by the lead boat and took to the water in the direction of the second boat. Soon the boat carrying the interpreter and the missionary was caught in the midst of a herd of swimming beasts. Oars and tiller banged into the animals. Boatmen were in a frenzy to avoid capsizing. The vessel swung sideways to the current, then spun a complete circle. Once clear of the animals, they drifted stern-first long enough for everyone to recover their wits.

"We did everything but ride those big ponies!" the tillerman offered.

"I did not get a single shot off," Wells lamented.

At that evening's camp he atoned for it by downing two large wooly cows.

* * *

The late-summer lull was apparent at the Vincennes wharf. Low rivers above and swarming insects in the swamps below brought activity to nearly a standstill. The coming autumn would find them unloading cargoes of grain and pelts from the canoes. Wares for exchange would overflow the traders' shacks, vying for the attention of the native peoples. Merchants would consolidate loads onto flatboats, hawking for crews to descend to the cash market at New Orleans. Today the hot sun trapped a steamy humidity over the town, limiting action to only essential tasks. Makeshift tables under spreading limbs hosted tradesmen and traders with cards in hand. An occasional shout or roar of laughter was the only evidence of activity.

"Here comes our princess," the dealer of the northernmost set informed his companions, "and that big bull of an Indian. Guess what she will want."

A giant stevedore spoke in a high-pitched voice, "Has any word come up today about the military convoy?" The effect aroused the laughter he sought.

A merchant in a white shirt chimed in, "Make your fun, but I for one will be disappointed when those boats do come in. Her daily visit does more for me than these cards have done lately."

"Amen to that, brother," came from the dealer's left. "Crazy cards anyway! A few more soldiers added to the post cannot be bad for business. I need to up my stash so I can keep on losing to you pirates. I am banking on this general coming from the east with some silver for the garrison's back wages. I intend to settle some accounts; it is going on near a year now."

He twisted around to observe the sway of the embroidered cotton tunic as graceful steps of bare feet descended the dusty street. The card game came to a halt. "Good afternoon, madam. Come share our shade."

Sweet Breeze smiled at each in turn then inquired, "Has anyone come up from below today?"

"Only a load of raccoon and fox," came the reply. "Those boys have been deep within the marshes and have no knowledge of river travel, sorry to say."

She bowed and moved to the next cluster, and the next, overlooking no opportunity to find any bit of news. From the landing she walked north to the fort where she stopped to get a drink from the well. By being seen there, she ensured that she would be informed if any military dispatches concerning the captives had arrived.

General Putnam had sent word from Fort Washington to set the peace conference date for the twentieth of September. Hamtramck had shown her his calendar with the days marked to that event. Sweet Breeze placed that number of twigs beside her tent and ceremoniously removed one each day. Putnam confirmed the date in a dispatch sent overland from Fort Steuben. Both messages verified that Wild Carrot was in the party. Satisfied that there was no new information to be had, she completed her circuit back at the encampment of the tribes.

She had informed Pierre Renault to keep the cabin prepared for them when her husband arrived. Meanwhile, she had taken up residence in a canvas tent next to Porcupine's wigwam. The temporary village, nearly abandoned on her return from Louisville, was once again alive with daily arrivals for the peace council. She tied back the tent flaps to catch what breeze was stirring. She went about her needlework. She had completed one pair of fancy moccasins for her and had started a second pair for her husband. With the quantities of trade-goods in the town, she had turned to beadwork instead of her traditional quillwork. The beads allowed for more fanciful designs and progressed more rapidly. The council would surely last many days and her husband would, as always, be in the middle of it. He should be dressed to match the important event.

* * *

A majority of the soldiers lay in the bottom of the boat delirious from fever. Their comrades labored with the boatmen on the poles urging the barges north. They had elected to push on through the night in hopes of gaining their destination before another nightfall. Another night of camp within the dismal swamps would neither guarantee rest for the healthy nor relief for the sick. Each shove on the poles or tug on the oars under the stars shortened the time spent among the snakes and bugs. A sliver of moon provided enough light to negotiate the waters. Wildcats screeched their eerie cries at the passing parade of lanterns hung from corner-stakes. Infantrymen answered the chorus with curses as they lost footing and crashed shins or forearms on plank edges.

"Bang my head if we did not pass that island before, I swear we must be going backward!" one called out.

"To think I left my father's ox and plow for this!" bellowed another.

A third, "Keep at it boys! I smell that ox roasting up ahead!"

"Not so," came another voice from the darkness. "That smell is my oar-lock burning up from friction. I say the harder you work, the more you sweat, and the more you sweat the better you keep the fever away."

All available hands pressed on throughout the night. They paused for a brief meal at sunrise, then resumed the rhythm at the oars, trading off and on by teams. Before midday they passed a vacant cabin resting on the eastern bank. By noon they neared a second cabin where two farmers and two boys in unison fired a salute. The salute was returned by three rifles at the front of the lead boat. The sight of golden fields of grain stubble alternating with fields of maturing corn renewed the strength of the weary men. The boats surged with each stroke.

"Canoe!" rang out from the lead boat.

The three riflemen shouldered their arms. Wild Carrot released his oar and stood in the second boat, but could not see. He motioned to have the boat edge to the right to get a view. In the distance, he recognized the diminutive form in the light bark canoe plying towards them.

"No harm! No harm! Waylay your arms!" he broke military protocol by ordering directly.

Actually, no one was certain who was in charge since all of the officers were under the fever. The light canoe closed the gap quickly.

A lone female yelled to the lead boat, "Wild Carrot?"

The men looked at each other in puzzlement.

The woman called again, "Interpreter Wells!"

Arms pointed to the second boat. She swiftly maneuvered the canoe alongside the vessel. She rolled over the gunwale, allowing the canoe to float free. A boatman secured the canoe with an oar and tied it off. She found herself sprawled on her back in the bottom of the boat. Sweet Breeze called her husband's Miami name. Some of the captive women recognized her and pulled her to her feet. Showering her with hugs and kisses, their tears ran freely.

The helmsman took evasive action to avoid striking the rear boat as they drifted backwards. He yelled to the oarsmen to quit gawking and direct their attention to their duty before they became a mass of driftwood. Wild Carrot regained his oar. He resigned himself to the idea that the reunion of the women would need to subside before he could hold his wife.

* * *

Major Hamtramck stood in front of the national flag flanked by two junior officers. The welcoming ceremony for Brigadier General Rufus Putnam would be held at the town wharf since the size and number of boats would overwhelm the little pier at the fort. His men were thoroughly drilled for the review. Half his garrison, in spruced-up uniforms, was formed in two lines of twenty. Civilians had been hired to unload the boats. Wagons had been contracted to supplement those of the fort to transport the new supplies and the captives. When a line was thrown to the lead boat, the major drew his sword signaling the commencement.

Drums rolled as a detail of six men stepped off to the left and six to the right. They fired a volley with their rifles and returned to the lines. This was repeated a second and a third time. These were answered by three rumbling echoes rolling down the valley from the fort's cannon. Spotting the general seated on the far side of the lead boat, Hamtramck stood waiting for the man's salute. An infantryman leaped onto the wharf from the boat and trotted up to the garrison commander.

"The general is ill with the fever," the soldier said while looking at his feet, "as are the other officers and half the force." The nameless soldier shifted his weight nervously.

"Understood, soldier," Hamtramck loudly replied. "My officers will assist you with the general."

The officers responded and briskly stepped to the boat. The major efficiently organized the front line into a rescue squad. Half the second line was to guard the materials and half to hold the prisoners in place until the emergency was settled. These frontier soldiers were accustomed to plans going awry and proficiently went about the business at hand. Two officers of the expedition were aroused enough to supervise the unloading. A number of freight wagons were designated to become ambulances.

A pair of the new arrivals produced a crate and the general was plopped down upon it. Hamtramck formed a curtain of ten men to shield the dignitary from onlookers. Interviewing the ailing man, he assessed that the ambassador would need to ride a wagon to the fort. He assigned a fort officer, the flag barer, and twelve men to accompany the wagon. The general had two requests: release the captives today in an orderly manner, and give him five days to recuperate before holding negotiations.

Primrose's legs buckled under her as she stood upon the wharf. She, and most of the women, had escaped the fever. However, she had not been on her feet for two days, and had not walked any distance for many days. The women and children were directed to join the procession behind the slow creaking wagons. They huddled along with a column of soldiers on either side. The townspeople neither jeered nor cheered, but looked upon them solemnly.

As they cleared the last of the houses, Primrose raised her eyes to the fort. She forgot about her pains. From the right a mournful wail surmounted the clanking of the wagons. She saw the camp of the tribes lined five deep with chiefs and women, men and children. She saw men shouting with arms upraised to the sky. Some of the waiting women dropped to their knees, holding their stomachs as they moaned. A few were rolling in the dust, flailing haphazardly. She fought tears for a moment, then let them stream down her cheeks. Sweet Breeze put her left arm around Primrose's waist; Wild Carrot placed his right arm on her shoulder.

"Soon," is all he said.

Hamtramck had the captives held outside the gate in sight of their relatives. He ordered water and rations for them. When the rear guard had entered the gates, he called to Captain Doyle.

"Quickly," he ordered, "ride to the encampment and tell them to listen for a cannon to fire. At that time they are to send chiefs to the fort to receive the captives. They are to bring only two each of the Eel River Miami, the Wea, the Piankashaw, and the Kickapoo. No others are to come to the fort."

"Four tribes, two each," the captain responded. He headed to the gate to gather Rene Coder, the fort interpreter.

"There is Wells," Hamtramck interrupted, "take him. Go now!"

With the sun hanging low in the sky, the wagons returned towards the town. The major moved the captives across the parade grounds away from the fort and formed a square. With Putnam too sick to attend, Hamtramck decided to dispense with ceremony. There was no point in having soldiers separate the women and children from their people any longer. He signaled the firing of the cannon. As the chiefs approached he simply ordered the guard back to the gates. The former captives hesitated for a moment, looked about, than ran to the startled chiefs.

* * *

Hamtramck lit his pipe and leaned on the parapet of Fort Knox. Across the way he saw blazing fires lighting patches of the encampment. He told the sentry next to him to relax. He offered the soldier some tobacco fresh from downriver.

Hamtramck mused, "Well, the day did not go as expected, but the result is as intended."

The sentry rested his musket against the wall and stuffed his pipe.

His commander continued, "The sounds of those bells and rattles dancing to the drums mean a period of peace for you and me. I think I will stay here and listen to the chanting if it is all the same to you."

The soldier nodded slowly, hoping his commandant would remain long enough to fill his bowl a second time.

CHAPTER 12
Fort Knox

Wild Carrot let his canoe drift down the west edge of the Wabash in the darkness. Below the fort he circled and landed in seclusion. Silently he found a place to spend the remainder of the night. Drums and dancing still filled his head. His time in the tent of Sweet Breeze was too short, but would suffice until they settled at the cabin. For now, he needed to get some sleep before dawn. He would walk to the fort from the direction of the town. He expected his duties would be light until Putnam got back onto his feet. The interim would be beneficial in giving the now-freed captives time to reunite with family and friends.

It was a fitful night for Wild Carrot. Cool dew saturated the grass where he lay. Through the night his mind had traced the trail of Primrose. First was the capture at the hands of Wilkinson at Eel Town. Wea and Kickapoo captives were added as they ventured down the Wabash. Overland they went to Fort Steuben, then up by boats to Cincinnati. The women united in defiance of Wilkinson's interrogation. They gave one another mutual support in the face of the angry soldiers after St. Clair's defeat. He had visions of his own reunion with Primrose, as if seen by a soldier on the fort wall. The long trip home mixed emotions of fear, puzzlement, hope, and joy. Over and over his mind repeated the scenes. Then faces appeared: Wilkinson, Samuel and Mary, Putnam, Little Turtle. He saw an arrow flying through the forest. On and on it went between tall trees. A tall woman emerged from the shadows. Her freckled round face was topped by braided red hair. She whispered to him, "Are you a Miami warrior, or are you your father's son?" The tip of the arrow broke out from the left of her neck, spurting blood on the tree trunk at her side. Wild Carrot sat up with a start and looked about. He settled back to sleep only to have the scene repeated. The third time he decided to forgo another attempt at sleep. In the first rays of the sun, he cleaned himself and headed for the fort.

Major John Francis Hamtramck had his best night of sleep in years. The successful return of the women and children of the tribes culminated months of apprehension. Having a superior officer at the post was surprisingly calming. The arrival of the paymaster was having a good effect on everyone garrisoned at the fort. He decided to go outside to have the morning meal with his men. The cool air caught him off-guard, but did not dampen his spirits. He chuckled at the disheveled appearance of Interpreter Wells sitting quietly at the opposite end of the table. He had never seen the man other than fully composed and poised. Best to give him some rest after the trip, and allow the man some time with his wife.

The commandant left his plate and went to the opposite end of the table, "I have nothing for you today. Check in twice each day and take some time for yourself. Organize procedures with the other interpreters and bring them all to me Monday morning."

* * *

Beads of sweat covered Brigadier General Rufus Putnam's face as the interpreters filed in. Major Hamtramck gave introductions and began the session.

"Welcome, gentlemen," the major said. "We are going to delay deliberations with the chiefs for a few days. We will commence on the twenty-fourth day of September. William Wells, you will be head interpreter and interpret for the Eel River Miami. Rene Coder will interpret for the Wea and Piankashaw chiefs, Captain Mayet for the Pottawatomie. John Baptist Constant will handle the Kickapoo and the various chiefs from the Illinois country. If at any time you are unsure of your chiefs' meaning, or if they do not understand the proceedings, take time to clarify it with them; we want to get it right. If there is a problem, Wells will mediate. Understand that General Putnam personally represents President Washington. At the conclusion, any treaty agreed to here will be carried to Philadelphia to be ratified by Congress before it becomes binding.

"Some of you have close ties to the tribes and to the chiefs involved. Remember that you represent the government of the United States in this affair. Interpret faithfully. If you must share opinions, relate them to me only, privately. You will remain at the fort until the conclusion; you will not speak with the chiefs beyond the council grounds until its conclusion. Now stand and Lieutenant Prior will swear you in."

Captain Mayet joined the three frontiersmen in pledging to faithfully execute their duties as United States government interpreters for the duration of the peace negotiations. Putnam congratulated the interpreters. He instructed that three milk cows had already been delivered to the encampment. He vowed to send a head of beef for butcher each day to keep the village in good spirits. He asked if the interpreters had any suggestions that would help in the negotiations.

"Two things," Wells offered. "Keep the townsfolk out of the village, and the tribes out of the town. Order that no whiskey or spirits be traded. Set up a field of exchange so that trade may be carried on in view of the troops. This will keep alcohol away from the chiefs. It will prevent charges of cheating or thievery, and it will keep English or Spanish spies from agitating those seeking peace."

"Good idea," the general indicated, lifting his cigar high overhead as if indicating a vote. "Do you suspect spies?"

"There are always informants, sometimes agitators. Rumors say that even Clark has been recruited by foreign governments. The Frenchmen of this place give loyalty to no one; most will hold hands with anyone. That brings my second point. Many of the chiefs remember when the French soldiers oversaw Vincennes. They long to return to those days. They did not welcome the English any more than they do you. My point is that the English officers always call them 'children' while the French called them 'brothers.' I recommend 'brother' as the preferred term."

"You have spoken freely; I appreciate that. Your insights are helpful, as usual." The general was growing weak. He motioned with his cigar towards Hamtramck encouraging a conclusion.

Hamtramck read a list of thirty-two chiefs who would be welcomed to the council. Mayet would handle the invitations.

"That is all," the major instructed. "Lieutenant Prior will see you to the quartermaster to sign the arrangements. Each of you should check in morning and afternoon daily. You are dismissed."

Wells hesitated, then spoke, "Rene and myself would like a word in private, if we may."

The others were chased out by Hamtramck.

"What is it?," he queried.

William explained, "Coder, or as he is sometimes called Rene Loderts, and I have both lived amongst the tribes many years. We were adopted into their families and have wives who are their kin. We do not wish General Putnam to be deceived about these things."

"This I know," the general calmly replied as he leaned back the legs of his chair.

"One thing you may not know," William continued, "We have each been honored as a chief among them."

The general and the major exchanged glances at the revelation.

Putnam looked out the window and blew a long puff of smoke, "Will this affect either of you in representing me during the negotiations?"

"No, sir."

"No, sir."

"Is there anyone else available that can do the job as well as you?"

"No, sir, nary a soul."

"Not one."

"Well, then, just remember that it is the other chiefs with which we negotiate, not you. Carry on."

The general wished to know more, but understood that on the frontier, as in the army, inquiring into a man's background too far did not always produce the best results.

* * *

Chiefs of the Eel River Miami, the Wea, the Piankashaw, the Kickapoo, and some of the Plains Pottawatomie and the Kaskaskia sat in a semicircle three rows deep under an azure sky. Three of the interpreters interspersed themselves in their midst. William Wells stood in front of the officers' table with Brigadier General Rufus Putnam and Major John Francis Hamtramck seated behind. The missionary observer John Heckewelder sat at one end of the table. Clerk William MacIntosh sat at the opposite end prepared to record the proceedings. A second table, behind and at an angle to the left, held five additional officers of the army. The American flag hung limply to their right. Putnam checked his watch: two minutes until ten o'clock. He looked around to find all was in order. He gazed into the eyes of each chief in turn. Finally he nodded to Wells who took an ember from a pail and lit a tinder box. The general stood and presented the lead interpreter with a new peace pipe prepared for the occasion. Wells lit it and returned it to the general for the first puff. He then sent it around the council for all to share. Putnam followed it around and shook the hand of each chief.

At the completion of the circuit, Putnam stood behind the table and spoke his first words to the chiefs.

Putnam proclaimed, "Brothers, finally we meet face to face. Together we smoke the pipe of friendship. Look to the sky, the Great Spirit has blessed us with a clear day to meet and talk of peace. Four moons ago I left General Washington to bring you his words. I will return to him with the words you speak at this place. It is an honor to stand on this ground that has been made sacred by your ancestors. Your fathers welcomed the French and made treaties at this place of council.

"Once there was a dark cloud in the sky. Your people and my people struck each other's heads with the tomahawk. Today the sky is clear. Let us dig a hole under the roots of a tree and bury the tomahawk. Your women and children are with you now. Let us join hands one to another and hold tightly."

Porcupine was the first of the chiefs to stand and speak. He replied that this council ground was indeed holy. He welcomed the ambassador from the east, then yielded to the next chief. Nearly all elected to speak, some with brief statements, some longer orations. There were many references to the good relations the tribes had with the French who lived among them, who married their daughters, and who never asked them to give up their land. By two o'clock, the speeches concluded, Putnam brought the session to a close with an invitation to all to celebrate with a pint of rum.

The session of the second day certified the articles established previously by Hamtramck on nonaggression and trade. Putnam expressed that he was not there to take their lands, but if any tribes should choose to sell lands, the sale must be to the United States government only. The chiefs held that the Ohio River should divide the lands of the tribes and the lands of the Americans; only recognized traders should cross over. The third day again commenced under a cloudless sky. Clarification was made on the lands the tribes had long-ago granted to the French farmers. The chiefs approved the maintenance of the American garrison at the fort as inherited from the English who had inherited the right from the French. With all issues settled, the next day, September 27, 1792, was declared to be the day for the signing ceremony.

* * *

"Look, husband, at what I prepared for you to wear to the ceremony of this day," Sweet Breeze held out the pair of moccasins. "I wanted to add some more detail; I did not think that the council would conclude so soon. But here they are, I want you to wear them today."

"I will wear them in the midst of the ceremony with my father at one hand and the ambassador of General Washington on the other. The tribes will be presented in order from the east to the west as is our custom. The Eel River Miami are the eastern-most and will be the first to sign; Porcupine will be the first to sign for peace with the Americans."

"It is good that I have been invited to observe the ceremony," she cheered.

Her face was full of wonder and hope. Formal ceremonies involving war or peace had always been the domain of men only.

"Will Primrose be present?" she asked. "I have stayed here at our cabin these four days and am anxious to see her. Should we return to the village tonight or remain at this place?"

"The chiefs are allowed to bring one or two persons each. I do not know if Primrose will come to be in the presence of soldiers again." He turned to domestic issues, "Let us remain here within the town until the encampment is deserted. I will have some business at the fort after which we can decide our destination. I presume that we will be going to Eel Town and on to Turtle Town. I will travel to find Little Turtle at the grand conference of all tribes at the Auglaize. We have much to discuss, he and I. Do you mind staying in Vincennes a few more days?"

"I do not mind being here," her eyes widened and lifted to the log rafters. "I could spend a year in this town, I like it here. Now with the peace, it has many advantages. When the rains come it will not be so hot and dusty. If the many nations that have heeded father's call continue to shout for war, I wish to remain here. Our baby will arrive in this world when the winds blow cold with snow. Vincennes could be the child's first home. However, if the grand council at the Auglaize wishes to seek peace with the Americans, I would wish the baby to be born at Turtle Town, no matter the snows. I do want to see Primrose settled back in her home. I want to see my mother and father and brothers."

Her thoughts were jumping from one possibility to another. She caught herself, "Most of all, I want to stay near to you. Do not leave me behind when you go to Little Turtle. I am the daughter of a war chief. I am the wife of a war chief. My brother and uncles are war chiefs. I do not require to be shielded from harm."

With a laugh Wild Carrot added, "You forgot to claim that you are the sister-in-law of Captain Samuel Wells, a war chief of the Kentucky militia. This night we will have our own celebration! My business at the fort will be short each day. We will have many days to talk about our future without the concerns of our people clouding our minds."

They walked the path to the fort as though it were their path to a new life, swinging their joined hands between them as do children joyous in the present. At the head of the path the Americans were marching out from the fort on the left with their brightly striped banner fluttering high in the breeze. From the right came a colorful array of chiefs with staffs decorated with feathers and ribbons. Husband and wife stood hand in hand for a moment watching gathering dignitaries. Eventually General Putnam waved Interpreter Wells over to begin the ceremony.

Sweet Breeze had tears shining on both cheeks. All she could say was, "Go to your duty!"

She gave him a shove and followed him with her eyes. He took his assigned position between the two parties. Standing alone on the fringe of the council of peace she was overcome by wave after wave of emotions she did not comprehend. Freed captives, harmony among nations, tranquility for Eel Town warmed her heart, and then her entire body. She sat upon a tuft of grass that had turned brown by the summer sun and let the tears flow openly. As her husband lighted the pipe presented by the general, she sensed the Creator looking upon him and her. They were favored by the Great Spirit and in turn they had pleased him. The world was good.

The Miami princess and the army interpreter went directly to their cabin after the final chief placed his mark on the treaty. The last wampum belt had been exchanged and the last calumet had been passed. They shared their love and emotions with few words throughout the following night and day. Only Shorty, bringing meals, interrupted their self-imposed isolation. Their souls joined together in complete devotion.

* * *

In the morning of the second day, Buffalo Man called from outside the closed door. Wild Carrot opened to find Primrose holding a bunch of wildflowers.

"You must come with me tonight," his mother invited. "Porcupine will hold a special ritual on the mound east of the town."

Wild Carrot thought it best to keep a distance from the camps even after the conclusion of the negotiations. He sensed the importance to the rite for the Eel Town community.

"We will be there," he answered. "Now come, join us here in our Vincennes home. We can talk freely without ears all around. From our reunion on the Great Miami River to our arrival at this place, we could only converse briefly. Our speech was in circles. Now we can follow the straight line of an arrow and fill in the unsaid words."

He gave her a long hug. He led her by the hand into his home.

Late in the day, Wells reported to Hamtramck that he was invited to a celebration by the people from the town of his youth and was compelled to attend. The major was pleased that the interpreter informed him of it.

Hamtramck encouraged him to attend, "Your relations with these people have greased the wheel of our endeavors. Go and enjoy yourself, take Sunday off, also. The general is down with the fever again. Come Monday and I will have prepared a message to the encampment. The clothing and powder has all been delivered as General Putnam promised. I will inform them that we can provide no more beef. Wednesday will be the final day of rations. That should encourage them to disperse, I would think."

* * *

In the light of a blazing bonfire, Porcupine motioned to Wild Carrot to be seated on his right for the ceremony. A bright full moon lit the faces of Chief Soldier and Chief Grasshopper to his left. Drumming and chanting filled the night as each chief, elder, and warrior slowly drew on the calumet. Wild Carrot anticipated that Porcupine would be presented with a sixth feather for directing the peace negotiations. After all, having the Americans agree to remain south of the Ohio River was a significant accomplishment. He thought on what he would say to honor his adoptive father.

It was The Soldier, who had led the right wing of the Miami attack at the head of the Wabash, who spoke first. He rose and looked around the circle. Taking his tomahawk from his belt, he laid it under his blanket.

He exclaimed loudly, "The name of Wild Carrot will be honored in Eel Town until the sun sets in the west on the final day. Wild Carrot broke the back of the American soldiers at the great victory at the headwaters of the Wabash. Our chief Little Turtle honored him with a third feather for his deeds. Now it is Wild Carrot who has returned our women and

162

children to us."

The oration paused. The circle of men opened to allow all the freed captives to walk in a procession in front of the chiefs. They disappeared as quietly as they came. The circle closed.

Soldier continued, "It is Wild Carrot who spoke our words in truth to the Americans at this council. He spoke for us fully as men, not the words of children used by the other interpreters. He helped us understand the desires of the Americans, not just their words. We signed the papers of the American treaty. We signed in confidence that the paper recorded our desires accurately due to the assurance of Wild Carrot."

Grasshopper, too, spoke in praise of Wild Carrot. When Porcupine stood for his oration, Wild Carrot began to suspect that the ceremony was not what he had anticipated. The head chief of Eel Town gave a long speech relating the achievements of his adopted son. At the conclusion, he took Wild Carrot by the arm and raised him to his side. A maiden came forward with a white cloth and held it out. Porcupine unfolded the cloth and lifted high a fan of feathers, the symbol reserved for a sachem, a wise man greater in stature than a war chief.

Grasshopper and The Soldier lit torches and led the way slowly up the ancient mound. Porcupine took Wild Carrot by the hand and stately followed. At the summit the four alone looked over the plain to the west. Moonlight outlined the structures of Vincennes. The small fort sitting upon the sand-hill had little significance from this vantage. The two chiefs lifted their torches to the four directions and put them to a prepared stack of wood.

"Surely the townsfolk could see this fire atop the mound." Wild Carrot wondered to himself, "Will they send out an alarm to arouse the militia?"

Porcupine addressed the entire community gathered below. He declared, "We have a sagamore among us! Whenever he speaks, the people of the Wabash will turn their ears and listen to his wisdom! It is your duty to do whatever he asks of you!"

He pompously placed the fan in Wild Carrot's hands. The new sachem was embarrassed to receive this highest of honors. He knew of only a few who bore the title, and they were all well aged or dead. Not knowing the appropriate response, he managed to hold forward the fan and direct its presence to the crowd. Sweet Breeze and Primrose beamed. The others hurried to assemble for a dance at the base of the mound.

Sagamore Wild Carrot joined Sweet Breeze in the second dance. Afterwards he sat upon a blanket between his wife and his adoptive mother.

Sweet Breeze spoke in admiration, "I know of only one other who holds both titles of War Chief and Sagamore. That is my father."

Primrose added, "And my father was so known before my brother."

Wild Carrot said in a near-panic, "Do not compare me to Little Turtle. The Great Spirit favors him as no other. I know of no man like him. My mother, I did not know the father of you and Little Turtle, the grandfather of my wife. I only know of his deeds through the legends of the Miami. No, do not speak my name beside the names of these men."

Primrose expressed her own wisdom, "It is good that you say that the Great Spirit favored my father and continues to favor my brother. Fools think that exceptional men excel by their own strength. Those who are wise understand that the path is chosen for great leaders. Just as the moon of this night can enter the eyes and penetrate the heart to make it mellow in knowledge of the spirit of the Creator, like the full sun at midday penetrates the flesh, so too, the Great Spirit lays a path on the mind of one who is chosen to lead. The wise leader will stay on the designated path no matter the footing, no matter the ruggedness, no matter the burden on his back. To leave the path for his own comfort or desires would be to displease the Creator. When he who is chosen discovers the correct path and stays on it, not only he becomes blessed, but he passes the blessings along to all whom he leads."

The wise woman sensed that her red-haired son felt less worthy with each sentence. She concluded, "The best leaders are those who are the most humble. Do not esteem boldness over humbleness."

"Dear Aunt," Sweet Breeze implored, "you understand many things that we do not know. Help us to find the path of which you have spoken. My husband knows that he has his duty first to Little Turtle, after that we do not know. So many things are unsettled; we do not know which path to take."

"My child," she replied, "see this night that your husband holds the fan of a sagamore. All vows and obligations are dismissed. He has duties to no one but himself. If the Great Spirit leads him to Little Turtle, he must go there, but in his own authority, not in obligation. Yes, many things are unsettled for you and for our people. When there is tranquility all about, the Creator has no need for a sagamore. It is in times of turmoil that great leaders are called forth to deny themselves and carry the burdens of their people."

Sweet Breeze was stunned at the tone of her aunt's voice. Her Aunt Talking Bird, the elder sister of Primrose and Little Turtle, often spoke in this manner. The old woman was the sage of Turtle Town. As a child, Sweet Breeze would crouch out of sight behind the wares when her father took her with him to Talking Bird's trading post. The elder aunt's eyes and voice gave her the jitters.

It was not until Sweet Breeze became a woman that her mother informed her about her aunt. Talking Bird had been abandoned by her husband, the noted trader Antoine Joseph Drouet de Richerville. Talking Bird maintained the trading post on the Eel. It was the same post that was the intended target of LaBalme's little French-American army. Continuing in the Catholic faith, she raised their son, Jean Baptiste, accordingly. The boy took Wildcat as his Miami name, but was referred to by all as Richardville. Chief Pecan assisted in raising the boy, and Little Turtle taught him to become a warrior. It was Richardville who had taught Sweet Breeze how to fire a gun.

The younger aunt continued, "If a broad passageway cannot be seen, it is best to meditate. The course may appear as when lightning strikes a tree, splitting it into two trunks with chunks and splinters flying at your head. So too, it may appear as when a calmness passes over a lake, the waves diminishing to ripples, the ripples giving way to the flatness of a mirror."

Sweet Breeze said softly, "I shall stay with you here at Vincennes, husband, until the way is made clear." She laid her head on his shoulder.

* * *

Interpreter Wells had light duties at the fort during the following week. Putnam, though ill, was leaving by the Buffalo Trace on Friday. William Wells had been informed to report for a meeting with the general and the fort commandant early in the morning of that day. When the door closed behind him, he found it uncustomary that the three were the only ones in the room. The usually relaxed major had a look of seriousness. The general looked ashen and weak.

Hamtramck began succinctly, "The general has some words for you."

"Mr. Wells," General Putnam addressed him, "you have exceeded my expectations by your deeds and conduct. I will convey these sentiments to President Washington and to Secretary Knox. I will also convey them to General Anthony Wayne. Remember that name. He is the one who has taken over the task of defeating the Miami Confederacy.

"Wayne is a revered general of the War of Revolution. He is esteemed by the President Washington, Secretary Knox, myself, Major Hamtramck, and anyone who has seen him in combat. He is known to be the toughest of all generals. He will carry out his mission to an honorable conclusion! I am going to him at Fort Pitt to tell him what I am going to tell you.

"It is good to have peace established at Vincennes; we will send no army to the lower Wabash. I, and the president, wish to have peace extended to the upper Wabash and to the Maumee. War benefits neither us nor the tribes. It is well known that the consolidated Miami and the Shawnee are welcoming chiefs from the Iroquois in the east to the Osage in the west, from Canada to the Winnebago. Even the Sioux are attending the great council on the Maumee as we speak. It would be best for them and for us to have their council decide for peace. The chiefs at this council need to know that the American government desires peace more than war. Mr. Wells, you know me as a man who speaks the truth. You know my words are endorsed by the president. It is no secret that Wayne is assembling a powerful army at Fort Pitt. There is still time to counsel for peace before the army centers on Fort Washington.

"Our government has sent out four ambassadors to the chiefs on the Maumee with messages of peace. We have reason to believe that each has been murdered en route. I have sought out a trustworthy messenger that I can send from this post. Only the Gamelin brothers showed interest, and they have refused. All who refused recommended you as the one who would get through. You were the first choice of Major Hamtramck. I should have listened to him.

"I have observed you for the past three months. I see how men of every persuasion call you 'friend.' I, too, shall call you 'friend.' I understand that you have loyalties to the Miami, and even that they call you 'chief.' Yet, you have faithfully fulfilled the duties that you swore to as government interpreter for the return of the captives and interpreter for the treaty council. That job, along with the oath of treaty interpreter, ends now. You will be paid in full as of this day."

General Putnam lit a cigar. He leaned across the table towards Wells. He sternly stated his business, "I now ask you to be a courier for the government of the United States. I wish to have you deliver a message from Secretary Knox to the head chiefs of the council gathered on the

Maumee. The message will express our desire for peace and offer options to meet with us in council."

The general leaned back and took a deep draw on his cigar. He blew a pair of smoke rings and watched them drift until they became void.

Again Washington's ambassador addressed the frontiersman,"Know that it is a dangerous undertaking. Those who are for war will stop at nothing to keep our peace overtures away. It is also well known that the British continue to create mischief among the tribes. They continually use those who are loyal to them to undermine the others. The British are bound by treaty to relinquish Detroit and Niagara to the United States, yet they continue to dishonor themselves by maintaining their garrisons. They deceive no one in arming and supplying the tribes for their own purposes. If they know of your mission, there will likely be a bounty for your scalp. There was even a plan to assassinate me on my way down the Ohio from Marietta!"

The general sharply stood and leaned his face close to William's, "What say you? You are the last hope for peace in the Northwest Territory. Are you the man for it?"

Wells firmly replied,"I will take your message. I am the only one who can succeed."

Putnam took his chair and responded,"God go with you. Deliver the message to the head chiefs and return to this post with an answer from them. For this you will be paid three hundred dollars upon your return. If their answer is for peace, and they agree to sit in council with us, the amount will be five hundred dollars. Your life depends upon complete secrecy. There will be no written contract. Only the three of us, the commandant of this post if Major Hamtramck is relocated, and General Wayne will have knowledge of the arrangement. Of course, Secretary Knox and President Washington will be informed.

"If you need to seek refuge you can invoke our names at this post, Fort Steuben, Fort Washington, Fort Harmar at Marietta where I will establish my office, or Fort Pitt. The preferred place for treaty council is Philadelphia. Any of the forts mentioned will suffice if need be. We are not inclined to go to the Maumee or the Erie country where the British continue to stir the pot.

"Three days after my departure you are to come here to settle your pay. At that time Major Hamtramck will deliver the pouch for your mission. To waylay any suspicion, you may claim that this meeting was over a difference in pay. Now go and remain clear of the fort for a time. I will pray to God for your safety and for the prospect of peace."

William Wells made for his cabin where he found Sweet Breeze sitting in the sun with her needlework.

"This morning lightning struck a tree," he said with a grin, "chunks and splinters went flying about my head."

CHAPTER 13
Salamonie

Sweet Breeze searched the stony river bottom with her bare feet for matted leaves to cushion each step. The cold waters were refreshing after a day of harvesting corn. She crossed to the Eel Town village where she dumped the bounty of her latest basketful onto a husking pile. She plopped down upon the nearest bench. There she massaged her bulging abdomen and her aching feet. Content to sit for a spell, she eyed her husband sitting on a flat rock at the water's edge near the council house.

Plink. Plink. Wild Carrot tossed pebbles into a ripple and watched them twirl and sink. The Eel River was running low and clear as was usual in late October. Round rocks lifted their heads high enough to stay dry. They caused little swells to dance around each side, bubbling and laughing a little song. Each pebble settled into one of the ripples only to be swept along below the rock. An eddy hooked it back towards the rock and deposited it in a pool of still water.

Sweet Breeze lifted herself from her bench and traipsed the short walk downstream to the flat rock. She placed her right hand on the rock's edge and sat next to her husband.

With her feet dangling in the cool water she asked, "What troubles you, my husband?"

"What troubles me?" he repeated. "What troubles me I do not know. That is what troubles me."

"Perhaps I can help you. What are you thinking right now?"

"As a boy I used to sit upon this rock and think. After I met you I would sit on this rock and think about you."

"Did I give you a lot to think about?" she laughed.

"That you did," he shared her laugh. Then after a pause, "Look at what once was my village. Once I could not see the entire length of the town upstream or the length downstream. Now it is only a shadow of that town. The traders have moved on. War parties from the north no longer assemble here for their raids to Kentucky. Many of the people have not returned from the Forks of the Wabash. Some who are for peace have moved down to reside amongst the Wea. Some who are for war have moved to the Maumee. Those who remain will scatter to the lakes if the war comes this way."

"Indeed, and now there are not enough women to bring in the pumpkins and corn."

Wild Carrot looked to the massive clump of cottonwood trees up the bank to the left. He asked, "Do you remember talking with Old Wolf's wife, his widow, on the night of the raid?"

"Yes, of course I remember," she replied softly.

"His charred body was over there," he pointed towards the council house, "stacked with four others like logs on a bonfire. I vowed to avenge the deaths and desecration of each of those men. This I did at the great battle at the Head of the Wabash."

"This I know." She pulled her feet from the water and leaned tightly against him, "It was the honorable thing to do."

"I return here and remember those men. I think of the revenge I have taken to honor them," his voice tailed off, "but there is no fulfillment. When the battle was over and others were reeking vengeance on the dead and dying, I took no part in it. Simon Girty was rousting all the warriors to gain satisfaction in defiling the corpses. I did nothing to stop them. I told myself, 'It is done,' and went about gathering the officers' papers and maps. Of necessity I slew another, a young officer with a cocked pistol. The red-haired woman I have told you about."

He looked again in the direction of the council house, "In the battle I had no emotion; I had no awareness of my actions. It was as if I were a hawk watching myself move from clash to clash. In the aftermath I waited for achievement to fill me at having fulfilled my vow to these men." He released a long slow sigh, "None came."

"You are held in high regard by all the warriors and chiefs who were in the field of battle. My father reserved his highest praise for you," she assured him.

"I had thoughts of killing Wilkinson at Fort Jefferson," he confessed.

"But you could not. The captives would have been slaughtered, if not by the soldiers, then by the townspeople," she argued.

"No, I did not. Yes, to secure my mother and the others. But, mainly, because it would do no good. The deaths on the battlefield gave me no satisfaction; neither would the murder of an army officer I despised."

"You did well in overseeing the return of the captives. Again you have received the highest praise for accomplishing what no other could do."

"The raiders burned our town and destroyed our corn. In the spring a new crop was planted, nourished by the ashes, grew to maturity, and is now for harvest. It took me from then until now to know that my fulfillment is not in the tomahawk of vengeance. I found the satisfaction I sought in the faces of women and children when they were released from confinement, when they were free to join their families."

She placed his hand on her belly, "I will have my fulfillment before the third moon." They shared a kiss.

Wild Carrot held her close. He said, "I have never traveled alone. I have always felt you with me at my side."

She jumped up and pulled his arm, "You are free to sit by my side and husk some corn."

He picked her up and dashed up the river, nearly sending both for a soaking when he lost his footing on a loose rock. He set her on a stool by the corn pile and draped a blanket over her shoulders. He pulled up a second stool and whistled a tune as he joined in the women's work.

"I know you are impatient waiting here," Sweet Breeze consoled her husband, "but you know that you cannot proceed until my father returns from the south. The Wyandot will surely carry out their death threat if you go near the Maumee. They saw you at Fort Hamilton with Putnam and Wilkinson. They do not care what your business was. They would enjoy binding you. They would parade you bound in front of the great council of all tribes. They would relish torturing you!"

"While you were in the fields today, Buffalo Man came with a message from Little Turtle." He pulled the decorated message stick from his pouch and showed her. "He is in the area of Fort Jefferson watching the Americans. He intends to capture their supplies. He will later send a message as to when we can meet privately. We will confer for three days before he returns to the great council."

"How privately?" she asked.

"You cannot go. It is too dangerous with bands from so many nations traveling about. If you like you can go to Turtle Town, or the lake. We can inquire if Tulip Leaf will be with you for the birth."

"Then Turtle Town is where our child will be born. It is a good place and will be closer to the travels of you and my father. The cabins will be warm for the winter."

"Turtle Town it is," he affirmed.

Buffalo Man came from meeting with Porcupine and greeted the two huskers. He kept enough distance so as to not make the work crew a threesome.

Buffalo Man said, "I have again been appointed to be your guard, if you will have me. Chief Porcupine will appoint two others when we prepare to leave this place. Sweet Breeze is to have her own guard of three."

Sweet Breeze responded, "I need hands to shuck these ears more than I need hands to wield tomahawks. Join us, if you will."

The big man replied, "I am off to get some turkeys that are calling from beyond the field."

Her reply, "Then return with one arm full of turkeys and the other full of ears of corn."

The hunter inspected an arrow and trotted off without comment.

* * *

At first light, a runner set out from Eel Town for the vicinity of Fort Jefferson. He quickly traversed the neck to the Wabash. He crossed the wide river by canoe. He followed a good trail on the high ground up the Wabash to the mouth of the Mississinewa. He engaged the trail along that river to the southeast. Tied to his belt was a pouch of nuggets prepared with meal, honey, maple syrup, dried berries, herbs, and pollen. He carried no water, using his knowledge of brooks and springs to supply his needs, drinking frequently before thirst set in. His only weapon was a sheathed knife.

A third item at his waist was a small pouch carrying two talking-sticks. One, painted white at both ends with a blue stripe in the middle, a blue jay feather attached, would verify a message from Porcupine to Little Turtle. The second had the prearranged sign of Wild Carrot to Little Turtle: blue at both ends and a red stripe with a string of eight blue beads attached. He skirted the small Miami villages and camps. Eventually, he reached a Delaware camp where the river makes a sweeping south bend. Here, he ate and bedded for the night after burying the talking-stick pouch underneath a mat and blanket provided by his host.

In the morning, he was off again, heading east through the flatlands to the headwaters of the Mississinewa. In the springtime the footing would be spongy, if not wet, and it would be necessary to stay on the beaten course to avoid the marshes. Today, the ground was hard and the marshes were nearly dried up. He reckoned across the countryside to cut some distance. The runner located Little Turtle's camp while the sun was still well up. He held his decorated pouch high as he was led to the great chief.

"A message from Chief Porcupine," the runner retrieved the stick and presented it. "Your message was received by him in good order. The guards will be assigned. Chief Porcupine will remain at Eel Town."

Little Turtle replied, "Well said."

"A message from Chief Wild Carrot the Sagamore," he presented the second stick. "Chief Wild Carrot will remain at Eel Town until he receives your return message. He suggests the place of many springs on the Salamonie where you killed the panther."

"Well said, take your rest."

"Another message," he removed a silver bracelet from his wrist and gave it to the chief. "The destination of Sweet Breeze is Turtle Town."

The runner headed for the stewpot to eat his fill. He was free to roam at his leisure. Customarily, he would rest until the next evening. He was given the respect equal to a seasoned warrior. He freely moved about their assemblies. Light and swift, he was proud of his ability to outdistance a horseman in a day's journey or longer. No one dared inquire about the messages he transported under the penalty of death. Of course, the same penalty awaited him if he ever divulged a communiqué, even if years outdated. He used a little trick of repeating nonsensical phrases to remove the message from his thoughts as soon as it was delivered.

Little Turtle understood that his sister's husband, Porcupine, would honor the Vincennes treaty and avoid the approaching conflict. His sister's adopted son, his daughter's husband, Wild Carrot, would meet him for the three-day retreat. The suggested location, where a little stream makes a trickle falls as it joins the Salamonie, seemed ideal. Situated on the west side of that river near the confluence with the Wabash, it offered isolated hollows for seclusion while yet being near enough to communication lines in case of emergency: Kekionga only a day away; an extended day's travel within anywhere on the Mississinewa, Salamonie, or upper Wabash; Fort Jefferson two days. Little Turtle, his two sons, and Wild Carrot had often hunted the area and knew each undulation. Yes, that is where they should meet after the business at hand was concluded.

Little Turtle could not contemplate these thoughts for very long because two additional runners had come in. The first carried details from events at Fort Washington. General Putnam had arrived at the fort having ascended from Vincennes. He had with him Captain Prior and the missionary Heckewelder. Chief Soldier and Chief Crazy Legs, plus thirteen chiefs of the Illinois tribes, were in the expedition headed for Philadelphia to meet General Washington and General Knox. Wilkinson had extended a big welcome to the voyagers.

The second messenger came from Chief Richardville, the son of Little Turtle's sister Talking Bird. A contingent of warriors had captured two soldiers who had information about a supply train. The captives would be brought to his camp by morning. At this news, he immediately assembled all available runners, including the arrival from Eel Town, to direct them to each of the advance camps. He needed to consolidate his marauding force of three hundred warriors to prepare an attack.

* * *

The first attempt at snaring the American convoy was foiled when the militia escort discovered a contingent of the ambush party. A small skirmish ended with both sides backing off without loss. Little Turtle had fully instructed the chiefs and warriors to not take excessive risks. The time would come when a full assault could be made. The intent was to harass the enemy, to keep them penned up in their forts.

All attempts by the Americans to scout the countryside had been turned back. Even American hunting parties were at risk. Their forces were fully occupied with simply advancing supplies to Fort Jefferson. A stockade called Fort St. Clair had been erected midway between Forts Hamilton and Jefferson to guard the packers overnight. This garrison, too, required supplies. Little Turtle observed that the men and animals of the convoys ate the majority of the provisions they carried. Very little net product arrived at the destination.

The unloading of the packhorses at Fort Jefferson was easily viewed by the Chief of the Miami and his scouts. The rounded hill that held the small fort was not the highest in the area. It was undoubtedly chosen because of a good spring. The spring provided fresh water near to the southwestern blockhouse. A clear stream two arrow-shots farther west watered cattle and horses. Patches of prairie provided ample grass.

The fort's livestock provided a tempting prize to those men watching from the forest. To return home with such a herd would be a grand event. More importantly, it would be a twofold loss to the Americans: a raid within sight of the fort would be humiliating to their efforts; the expense and time to replace the animals would heighten their failures. Still, the fort was solid and capably manned. Cannon in the blockhouses were the determining factor. Well-fired cannon would be devastating to the tribes' effort. An unsuccessful attack would have the opposite of the desired effect, boosting American moral and lessening the resolve of the warriors.

The chiefs waiting on the far side of the knoll anxiously watched their acclaimed chief descend through the thick hickory and cherry forest.

Little Turtle instructed, "Only a few scouts will stay. We will all move north then west to the head of the Mississinewa. We will move loudly with many tracks and litter. Once there, we will leave a few men to make fires while secretly we turn south. The Americans of the returning convoy will remain vigilant until they have passed the site where they fought Black Loon's warriors." He gave his listeners a large smile, "We will let them gain Fort St. Clair. There they will feel safe."

Miami warriors usually travel in small bands, but this day they moved as one force. After making a ruse camp, eight warriors remained to tend fires and the horse-herd. The warrior-force headed south quickly on foot, then arced around to approach Fort St. Clair from the opposite direction. This stockade was not as solid as its brother to the north. It rested upon small bluffs of a stream on the north and west. Flats of broken woods and prairie reached out from the other two walls. The small garrison was aided by two light cannon. One mounted in the bastion overlooking a spring at the northeast corner, and one at the opposite corner.

During the night, the chiefs began laying their plans in earnest. The opportunity had passed to seize the supplies carried to Fort Jefferson. However, there were still horses to be had. With good fortune, even the Fort St. Clair stockade could be taken. Successful or not, an attack would force the enemy to divert even more resources to defend their supply lines. An army looking backward could not move forward.

Reports from the scouts placed the camp of the packers and militia on the plain east and south of the fort. Their fires were burning brightly. Only a handful of pickets had been posted. Their horses were positioned between the camp and the fort. The gates of the fort were closed.

It was determined to have one-third of the warriors conceal themselves in the wooded area directly in front of the gate. They would send fifteen warriors to drive the horses northward down the bank and across the creek. The main force would directly attack the camp to push the militia to the fort. When the gates opened to receive the fleeing militia-men, the concealed band would charge directly into the compound.

A sentry of the militia sensed a commotion among the horses. He woke Major Adair. The major got to his feet just as the first muskets popped from atop the walls of the fort. Chaos ensued as shouts and gunfire stampeded the horses, some breaking through the camp. Pickets shouted the alarm as they pulled back, rousting their comrades.

The major ducked as a wave of arrows fell from the sky, "To your posts, men! We are under attack!"

A volley of muskets blasted from attackers concealed in the forest, then a second. The major ordered the fires to be extinguished. He formed a line of battle. His men fired two volleys before three of them were dropped by the enemy. Sensing the Indians were ready to charge, he fell back to the walls to gain the support of the garrison. The warriors were upon them quickly with vicious hand-to-hand fighting. Darkness merged friend with foe; the fort's soldiers could not fire into the melee.

As attackers were driven back, militiamen called to the soldiers above, "Open the gates! Open! In we come!"

The gates remained closed. The warriors in the neck of woods held their urge to attack. Major Adair reformed his line to receive a second wave of attackers. The anticipated attack came quickly. This time, they repulsed the assailants at thirty yards. Muskets on the walls sent the Miami into retreat. The militia followed. They reached their former posi-tion and held. Fingers of sunlight began peeking through the dense trees. Adair had his men move their baggage against the poles of the fort wall under cover fire. The firing from the forest melted away.

Still, the gates remained closed. The disappointed hidden reserve of the Miami crept away without engagement.

* * *

Yellow leaves and a white sheen of frost-covered grasses glistened under beams of piercing sun. Soldiers laid a row of six bodies outside the fort walls. Adair's men grumbled and cursed at the lack of support from the garrison. Adair knew that Wilkinson's orders prevented the men inside from opening the gates or sallying forth. Darkness had prevented the cannoneers from determining the position of the enemy until they were too close to the defenders to fire. He was grateful that his loses were not greater, but was disappointed that only two of the enemy had fallen. Without a single horse to be found, he would have to send a squad on foot to Fort Hamilton for relief. In the meanwhile, he would arrange a burial detail.

The Miami took the horses north to the creeks that fed the Auglaize. Here they waited until Wyandot scouts arrived to replace those of the Miami. The Wyandot were to take a turn at the harassment tactics and would, in turn, be followed by Shawnee. Little Turtle turned the war party over to Chief Richardville and Chief Owl. They would move slowly north to the Maumee, grazing the herd as they went. Little Turtle advised that he would be at the great council in eight days. Meanwhile, he could be contacted at the Forks of the Wabash.

* * *

Somewhat below the Forks of the Wabash, and a bit above the mouth of the Salamonie, Sugar Loaf Rock loomed as a prominent landmark on the south bank of the Wabash. As did most landmarks, it had many names assigned by the various tribes and the Frenchmen. This label was by former Canadian Governor Hamilton, given when he had made his way down the Wabash to retake Vincennes during the American Revolution. Travelers frequently paused here to climb to the cap jutting over the river. Atop, they would make a tobacco offering. Below they might eat a meal or camp for the night.

Below Sugar Loaf Rock, Little Turtle and Wild Carrot embraced after a long absence. Having discarded his warrior garb, the great chief was dressed in a hunting shirt and plain buckskin jacket. His younger companion was similarly dressed but with fringed jacket and fur cap.

"You are well, Wild Carrot. I can see it in your face and eyes," the elder spoke first.

"And you," the younger replied, "You appear well, you have that gleam in your eyes."

"I am eager to hear about your journeys. Porcupine has kept me informed; now I want to hear it from you. And what of my daughter, a child soon? But first, we will depart from our guards. We will hunt and tell our stories. Now, let us climb this rock."

After their little ceremony atop Sugar Loaf Rock, the two men set off into the forest. They carried only bows, arrows, knives, tomahawks, flint, and blankets. Leaving their attendants behind, they headed due south. They soon scampered down a cliff face to the Salamonie. They crossed on a rill of the limestone bottom and headed into a ravine. Two turkeys were flushed from under an overhanging ledge. These were felled as they beat their wings furiously trying to gain the crest. Assured of a meal, they cached the birds and went in search of larger game. The day yielded two honorable bears, but no elk. They passed on opportunities for deer, squirrels, rabbits and burrowing animals. The gray sky did nothing to diminish the spirits of the pair of hunters. This was the way the Creator intended for things to be.

Late in the day, Wild Carrot prepared the birds and gutted the bears while Little Turtle readied the camp. The mighty chief bent on his knees to clear dry leaves and sticks from against a recently fallen tree trunk. He tore some inner bark into shreds and kindled a fire. He added leaves and twigs until the flame could sustain itself on larger sticks. He allowed these sticks to burn down to embers before adding more fuel. Meanwhile, he cut a sapling and lashed it between two beech trees with strips of braided bark to begin a lean-to. Alternating between tending the fire and fashioning the shelter, he had the little hunting camp arranged when his red-haired companion brought the skewered turkey meat. He stoked the coals with a green stick and fanned them to a bright red glow.

Placing the skewers into notches of prepared stakes, Wild Carrot sat beside his father-in-law near the fire. He looked deep into its glow and thought of all the things he had to share. He should tell not only the events of his journey, but the observations he alone could relate. His feelings were unsettled. He held a jumble of ideas he had not yet sorted out. Little Turtle had been wise to arrange this wonderful day when the two of them could roam carefree as in days not too far past.

Wild Carrot waited for the elder to lead the conversation towards his report. It was not to be this day. Little Turtle would talk only of hunts near and far. The fiercest bear, the greatest buffalo herd, the largest elk rack, and the wiliest panther were the stories that carried them into the night. They recounted days past at this, their favorite hunting camp. Wild Carrot ended with the tale of Heckewelder and the timid bear.

* * *

Wild Carrot lifted himself on his right elbow and looked about. Gray light filtered through the trees in the moist morning haze. He heard steel creaking in the gully below. Feeling for his tomahawk he jumped to his feet. In a moment, he recognized the sound for what it was. Little Turtle had located their old hunting cache and was returning with an iron pot, the heavy weight swinging on its bale with a squeak-bang rhythm as he mounted the steep slope. The leader of the Miami nation appeared at the crest with the full grin of a boy who has found a silver coin.

"Gather some wood and we will get this pot boiling before morning prayers," he instructed with a hint of glee.

Off he went to gather acorns and onions and the many fruits of the forest for the bear stew. Ample firewood was soon stacked.

The forest air remained cool and damp until well past the high sun. Wild Carrot edged near the little fire. Little Turtle seemed impervious to the chill.

"I have not seen my sister Primrose for two years," the great chief spoke in an unusual melancholy tone. "That is when we went to the Wea towns to cut off the path of Hamtramck's army. Porcupine and I met four times while you journeyed from Vincennes to recover the captives. He sent frequent messages about the captives and the treaty. In each he tells of his admiration of your skills. My daughter, I have not seen her since the snows of the past winter. First tell me about my family, then you may tell of meeting the Americans."

Wild Carrot was not sure if "meeting the Americans" meant his Kentucky family, the soldiers at Fort Washington, or the treaty at Vincennes.

"Sweet Breeze was the blossom of Vincennes for our people, for the French, and for the Americans as well. We think as one, your daughter and I, though sometimes she is a step ahead of me. She traveled with me to meet my Kentucky family." He wondered if he should have rephrased "Kentucky family", but pressed on. "She speaks the English tongue well now and has insights into their ways. When I returned to Vincennes with the captives, I saw that she had taken on the role of Primrose in the camp of the Eel Town people," he laughed, "and gained some of Primrose's independence, too. She carries the child well and has had no sickness. Today Porcupine personally escorts her up the river Eel to Turtle Town where she will stay for the winter. She will be glad to be there and to see Tulip Leaf. Her heart waits to see you.

"Primrose led the captives in defiance of the soldiers. She complete-ly frustrated General Wilkinson," another laugh. "The confinement was hard, but they were fed well enough and not harmed. Upon our arrival, General Putnam greatly improved the conditions of their captivity. He was kind and generous. During the return to Vincennes he was attentive to their needs. By the time we reached the falls, Primrose was restored to her usual self. I must say, the reunion at Vincennes was grand!"

While skinning and butchering the bear pair, the red-haired adopted Miami narrated his saga in detail. He began with the last time the two men were together at the interpretation of St. Clair's papers. He recited the events one by one, envisioning them as though they were floating by on a progression of rafts in a summer stream. Perhaps he dwelled too long on Samuel Wells's plantation with its magnificent horses and tobacco. He described every aspect of the forts Knox, Steuben, Washington, and Hamilton. He told how Putnam kept referring to a new fort named Fayette that was to replace Fort Pitt. Observations of military facets were interspersed throughout the telling. He gave account of his oaths and duties and pay arrangements with Putnam.

Butchering completed, Wild Carrot cleaned his knife and began sharpening it on a flat stone. He was surprised to find that he had talked the day away. Darkness engulfed them as he related the speeches of the treaty negotiations. He ended with the location near Squirrel Village where he stashed Putnam's peace letter.

Little Turtle took a quick puff on a reed stem to test the bowl of a pipe he had carved from a walnut branch. He said, "You left out one part."

The saga teller tensed as he wondered what it could be. Did the great chief feel betrayed by an omission?

"You forgot to tell that you are now a sagamore," he noted as he stuffed more of his mixture of tobacco into the bowl.

Looking away, Wild Carrot said sheepishly, "I feel that it is Primrose that has made me a sagamore. Surely she prodded the others into it."

"Perhaps that is so. Cannot the Creator smile upon Primrose to straighten his path?"

This he had not considered. He felt unworthy of the title and kept the fan hidden away. A sagamore should be certain of more things than he was. His path seemed to him like walking in wet clay, alternately sticking and sliding.

The elder chief spoke as would a sage, "Now you have no chief over you. You must find your own way, a new way for you, a new way for our people."

"You will always be my chief!" was the quick reply. "Porcupine will always be my chief."

"That is not the way of our people. Do not say of me 'my chief.' You may address me with the title 'Chief' when we are with others, but I am no longer your chief. It would dishonor the title of sagamore for you to have a chief over you. You may use 'Fellow Sagamore' if you wish."

"That would be hard for me to say," he paused, then uttered, "Chief."

"Then 'Chief' it is. With us and with only our family you may say 'my father'. Here, take this pipe and I will make another."

"Thank you, my father, a fine pipe it is."

Wild Carrot hoped that his fellow sagamore would now tell him about the events on the Maumee since his departure. He especially wanted to hear about the great gathering of tribes on the Maumee. Roaming Pottawatomie brought reports to Eel Town about exotic tribes arriving at their village on the Chicago River. Bound for the Maumee assembly place, travelers requested guides to see them to their destination. Every known tribe, and some unknown, was sending ambassadors to discuss the "American Question."

Little Turtle shared only generalizations, "Our many eyes in the woods and the English spies at the American council of fifteen fires have already informed us on the military matters. We have drawings of American forts made by their own officers. We possess their guns to see how well and how far they shoot. We know the names of their officers, their posts, and the numbers of soldiers. We know how much the American council will spend for supplies. Their newspapers tell us of the desires of the populace. These things we know." Little Turtle leaned towards his companion and held out two cupped hands. "What I wish to learn is the nature of the officers you have met. Tell me of their people in their towns and farms. Help me know their thinking."

"The spies of the Miami and Delaware are good," Wild Carrot retorted, "but they misinterpret much. The spies of the Shawnee and others cannot always be trusted. The English officers do not tell you all. They shape the truth like you shape this pipe, cutting out and throwing away the parts they do not want. Did the English tell you of the treaty that ended their war with the Americans? Did they tell you they promised to leave Detroit and Niagara and all posts south of the grand lake Erie? Did they tell you that their king dishonors himself by reneging on these pledges? No, they continue to tell you that they will fight with you against the Americans. I tell you that every American officer, every American soldier, every settler and merchant feels violated by the English presence on soil that was relinquished by treaty. They distain the English and will not step back from them. They will fight them!"

Wild Carrot felt warm blood rushing to his head. Perhaps he had spoken too forcefully. Perhaps not.

Little Turtle, while taken aback momentarily, was pleased that now he was getting what he hoped for, though not what he expected. Suddenly many dealings with the English made sense. The English had ignored his request to build a fort at the Auglaize to station soldiers and materials. The cannon abandoned by St. Clair's army should have been directed back at the Americans. Instead they lay buried, hidden and useless, at the site of victory. He now realized the building of a fort, or the firing of cannon on the Americans, would violate the treaty between the two governments. The English prodding tribes to war, their continual promises of military support, was a woeful sham beyond what he had suspected.

What everyone on both sides called a great victory for Little Turtle he, himself, recognized as a failure. With St. Clair's American army routed, Fort Jefferson should have been overrun and the American army hemmed in on the banks of the Ohio at Fort Washington. The eastern tribes should have overwhelmed Fort Harmar and the town of Marietta to cut off the Ohio River traffic. Forts Washington, Steuben, and Knox would have been isolated and eventually abandoned. A few English soldiers did come to the battle, not the regiment that was promised, no cannon to blast the vulnerable Fort Jefferson. Had the English fulfilled their promises, the tribes would now control all lands north of the Ohio and west of the Muskingum.

Little Turtle instructed, "Tomorrow we will talk about the American people. Afterward we will see if the Creator will provide some elk for us."

On their third day, the hunters greeted the rising sun on the cliffs overlooking the river Salamonie. The unnamed run below their hunting camp dropped over a ledge into a deep limestone horseshoe bowl that opened to the river's edge. Little Turtle stationed himself on the left promontory where the horseshoe met the river cliff. Wild Carrot descended the ravine, crossed above the falls, and scampered up the opposite side, pulling himself up by tree roots. When he gained the southern promontory, they faced the silvery orb glowing through a curtain of clouds. They sent their chants drifting above the ripples of the Salamonie and into treetops to the east.

The day's mist turned to drizzle. They allowed themselves a larger fire. The smoke contained by the droplets kept their hideaway secure.

Little Turtle reworked a portion of the shelter covering, stirred the leaves under his blanket-seat, and stuffed his pipe.

Now settled, he inquired, "The man Putnam, what is his character?"

"General Putnam was given the highest rank of their army to represent General Washington, whom he referred to as 'the President,' in these lands they call the Northwest Territory. It is obvious that Washington wanted the prisoners released without incident. Putnam took great pains to shield the captives from the Kentuckians, as the settlers from Virginia now call themselves. He was determined to quickly finish what Hamtramck had prepared, and return to Philadelphia with a treaty in hand. He encouraged a large number of the assembled chiefs to return to the American council with him. Fifteen boarded boats for the trip to the east. Putnam had caught a fever in the swamps and was sick during the peace talks. He remained quite ill when he left."

Little Turtle held his cupped hands in front of the younger man's chest and motioned them up and down. Wild Carrot understood that he wanted something more about the man, something deeper.

"The soldiers liked Putnam as a man, and as an officer. Throughout the revolution he had designed defenses for Washington. After the war, he supervised the establishment and settlement of Marietta in partnership with Washington and others. During my presence he was an ambassador and did not always follow military protocol. I liked him and thought he played his part well. He put his trust in me and never asked more of me than I could deliver. He knows that I am a Miami chief, yet he put his confidence in me. He acted upon my suggestions at Fort Hamilton in spite of Wilkinson's protests. At Vincennes, he and I met following the council closing ceremony each day. He would ask questions such as, 'What did Young Beaver mean by his speech?' He definitely wanted to understand the full meaning of their words and the intent of them. He did not talk to the chiefs in circles as the English officers do. His words were plain and straight. He spoke with power and confidence; he never threatened. Peace was his business and peace he attended to. Now he sends his words with me. He asks the great gathering of tribes for a council to be had among the many nations and the Americans. He will do what he can to prevent war if a council can be had."

Wild Carrot shared his favorable impression of Hamtramck, "Who only desires to be a good officer and is respected by his soldiers." He expressed his distain for Wilkinson, "Who is a vain braggart and is liked by not one person." "Many of the junior officers are dullards." He singled out William Henry Harrison as an exception. "A likable fellow eager to learn the ways of the tribes. He possesses sound judgment and sizes up people quickly. He will surely become a senior officer one day."

"The soldiers will fight; they will not shy from the field of battle. Some wish to avenge their defeat on the Wabash." Wild Carrot interrupted himself, "To this day they all think they were at the river St. Marys which would take them to Kekionga. I wonder what would have happened if they had descended the stream in search of the Miami towns." He fed the fire then resumed, "Some of the soldiers have personal vendettas against the tribes. Many are simply adventurers or those seeking the opportunities of the frontier. They have their scoundrels who will bail when the lark plays out, but all in all, they will fight. The officers and soldiers are convinced that they will prevail in the end."

He told about Samuel and Mary and the gentlemen and ladies of their social circle. He expounded on the new government for Kentucky, their local militia, their worship, their trade. He told of how the people are exasperated at the ineffectiveness of the army. They hold little hope for peace without conquest. "Every gathering of men leads to talk of finding the right general to push the tribes into Canada or beyond the river Mississippi to the Spanish lands. Hamtramck places his confidence in Wayne, who has won the position."

With a leap to his feet Little Turtle cut off the narration, "Now, let us see about that elk!"

Little Turtle led west and south across one creek and into a second. This they followed in twists and turns north to where it joined the Wabash. All along they were presented with opportunities at game large and small, but no elk. Not even a sign of elk was to be seen. The winds whipped up and swept the drizzle away on their return to camp. They scouted its perimeter before settling down to another repast of bear stew.

Little Turtle brushed back some leaves with his hand to expose a patch of ground. With a stick he drew a line in the bare dirt. On one side he placed two piles of twigs and did the same on the other side.

He offered, "You have said that the Americans have good and bad officers; they have good and bad soldiers. You know that the tribes too have good and bad chiefs, good and bad warriors."

With the stick he pushed two piles together on the left side and mingled the twigs. Deliberately, he repeated the process opposite the line.

"Often it is difficult to tell the good from the bad," Little Turtle kept pointing his stick. "Who do the people from the north to the south, from the east to the west, call the greatest military leader in all of the lands?"

"It is Little Turtle, Chief of the Miami,"Wild Carrot gave his answer. "This day tribes from every direction gather at his call. The English king gives him guns and powder. The Spanish king sends him silver. The Americans quake at his name."

"You honor me. But I ask again, who is the greatest of all military leaders?"

"Then, General Washington,"Wild Carrot replied.

"None would dispute your answer. Where were his first battles?"

"At the river Monongahela above where it merges with the Allegheny. There the Miami and others joined the French to drive the enemy from Fort Duquesne, now called Fort Pitt. The army of the enemy opposing the French was routed."

"And who was his general?"

"Braddock was the general." The red-haired hunter wondered at the asking of such trivial questions.

"Who sent General Braddock to claim the Forks of the Ohio?"

"The king of the English sent him."

"General Washington served in this army of the English king?"

"Yes, he fought there and in the Virginia mountains."

"And whose army did General Washington lead later in the towns beyond the mountains?"

"He achieved great fame leading the Americans in council and in war."

"What army did he fight in this war?"

"He opposed the English king and threw him off."

Little Turtle brushed the dirt with his hand, erasing the line. He took all of the twigs in his hands and scattered them across the patch of dirt.

He looked carefully at the twigs for a time,"Which is good, which is bad?" He picked up one twig and eyed it closely then returned it.

He drew a circle around all of the twigs,"Is Washington reviled as a traitor?"

"He is recognized by all the tribes and all the countries as the greatest general and wisest leader. The few who despise him are fools."

Little Turtle took out his favorite knife and began whetting it on a flat stone. "A good chief must please his people or he will no longer be their chief. There may be a time when he must lead them on a path his people do not like. If he knows the path will benefit his people, he must choose it."

He spat on the stone and rubbed away, leaving his fellow sagamore to ponder these words. The younger man sat in silence puzzling over the story of the sticks and the line. Perhaps sleep would bring an answer in a dream.

Sleep was fleeting. Cold damp air penetrated Wild Carrot's bones. In his head ran a series of visions. He saw Primrose seated in the front of a flatboat, her form bouncing with the waves. She reached her left arm out wide, then her right, "Which will it be for you, Wild Carrot, the bank on the north or the one on the south. You are free to choose." Next Harrison sitting on his bunk, "How do the Wea differ from the Piankashaw?" Metea appeared with his wide smile. Sweaty and soiled, the Pottawatomie chief stepped forward and raised his fist with a yelp of celebration. Samuel, in his militia captain's uniform, strapped on his sword, donned his hat, mounted a muscular chestnut steed, and rode away. Porcupine sat alone in the Eel Town council house and stared solemnly at the smoke rising from the council fire. Sticks rose off a pile and danced in a circle then fell to the ground. He saw Sweet Breeze facing a beaver pond, standing with her back to him. She turned to him with a soft smile and held out a bundle, "Here is your son. Where is his home?" A strong red-haired woman emerged from behind the trunk of a straight tree. With a long knife she cut off a length of his warlock. She spat on it and washed the greased ash from it. "Look, it is red. Are you a Miami warrior or are you your father's son?" An arrow tip protruded from her gullet and blood spurted onto his face.

Sitting up quickly, Wild Carrot struck his head on a pole supporting the makeshift roof. The jolt sent two raccoons off the roof onto the ground, disappearing into the darkness. He wiped his face with both hands and looked at his palms. There was no blood, only sweat. It was a relief, but, in a strange sense, a disappointment. Looking around there was nothing but the usual sounds of the night forest and the sleeping chief. He walked about to ensure that the camp was secure. Finding nothing of concern, he fed the fire and curled inside his blanket.

Still drowsy, he hoped sleep would come if he thought about going to Sweet Breeze. In the morning he would part from Little Turtle to find his wife at Turtle Town. He thought about the tricks he used in his youth to show off for her. How he had yearned to see if she was watching, but dared not turn his head. His mind wandered to Primrose on the flatboat, and all the scenes in succession as if written in Heckewelder's journal.

"The tea is ready. Have some, the air is cold," Little Turtle called.

Wild Carrot felt paralyzed and moved only his eyes. Not wanting to have the elder chief think of him as lazy, he managed to stir his muscles and drink the warm tea.

"It appears the rains have ended," the elder chief affirmed, "After the mist has cleared, we will have sun for our separate journeys today. We will take only the bear skins; the rest we will scatter for the crows and wolves." Both knew that the warriors waiting at Sugarloaf Rock would have prepared all the meat they could transport. "We will break camp before our prayers." He had already doused the fire and began dismantling the lean-to.

The sun did show promise of an appearance if only the fog would loosen its grip on the valley of the Salamonie. On his rock-ledge, Wild Carrot could hear the ripples below, but could not see the stream. His prayers centered around favor for completing his current mission so that he could then focus on becoming wise in the ways to help the Miami people. He sought favor for Sweet Breeze to deliver a strong child. He picked up his bow and looked across the narrow chasm where Little Turtle was motioning down to the bowl below the falls.

Laying their weapons and clothing aside they bathed on the sloping ledge under the falling water.

"Do not go to Turtle Town from here. It is too dangerous," Little Turtle warned. "Four times the Americans have sent ambassadors to the grand council. Four times empty pouches arrived at McKee's post without their bearers. The scalp of one lost bearer was said to have been that of the soldier Hardin who you and I defeated on the Eel. Surely Simon Girty is paying a bounty for these pouches. He excites all to war. He will do all in his power to prevent peace. It is no secret that his power comes from the English, though they often deny knowledge of his actions. Be wary of renegades who will do his bidding. Retrieve your letter sent by Putnam. Be at your cabin at the storehouses in Kekionga in six days. Do not travel on the streams or on the beaten path. It will be best to stay in the lands between the Eel and the Wabash until that day."

The cold falling water kept Wild Carrot's senses keen. Cold air blew into the opening from the Salamonie and swirled the mist across dark mossy cliffs.

Little Turtle's voice resonated against the limestone walls of the narrow bowl, "The grand council will receive no person that is not of the tribes. I will prepare the council to receive you and Putnam's message, and will pledge my protection for you. They will know you are a Miami who is delivering a message from the American treaty-signer of Vincennes. After you address the council you must leave, you may not visit my lodge nor confer with anyone other than your escort. I will tell the council that you are my guest and will reside in my town on the Eel to await the response. I will tell them that you have my protection until you receive the response. You must stay in Turtle Town until I call. Do not go out to hunt, or for any purpose. I will have fifty warriors reside at Turtle Town until that time. I will send for you when it is time to hear the answer from the council. Once you have the answer, I can escort you to the Forks of the Wabash. You will need to find your own way to the Americans. Vincennes is the only route that may be achieved, and that with great care. All other routes will be blocked."

Wild Carrot poked his head through the neck of his hunting shirt and tugged at the laces, "When I appear, I will dress not as a Miami warrior or chief, but as do the French voyagers."

His father-in-law nodded approvingly.

Lifting his bow and testing its strength, the younger asked, "My father, which is best for our Miami people, war or peace?"

"Peace is always the better if the two choices are offered on a scale that is in balance. But, that is never the case. I hope for peace. By offering my protection to the bearer of the letter from Putnam, I am casting for peace in the council. Most of the older chiefs would welcome a council with the Americans, but are afraid to speak because their younger chiefs and warriors want only to fight. Some are bribed by the Spanish or the English to speak for war. With such a great number of tribes, it will be difficult to settle on one answer."

The great chief continued, "I look upon our cousins the Delaware who fought in the eastern lands near the great ocean, only to be driven into the mountains. And from the mountains they were driven to the Allegheny, and into the Ohio lands. We asked them to come and live on our lands along the White River. They stand among us continuing to wage war on the invaders. Each time they fight, and each time they move, they are fewer in number. They live only to fight, and do not tend their crops as they should; they do not have fine clothes or good possessions. Our Miami warriors say, 'We will not be driven away. We will stand and fight to death, until there is not a Miami warrior standing.' I ask them, 'What good is that? The Miami nation will be no more and the Americans will plow the soil where we died.' No! The Miami nation will not be driven from this land. We will live on! We will fight when there is something to be won that cannot be achieved in a council of peace. If the council of peace does not lay a happy path, then we will need wise men to find a new path through brambles and thorns."

With their business settled, their retreat came to a close. Together they stepped out of the little chasm into the open waters of the Salamonie. When they cleared the cliffs, they were startled by a loud snort on their right. A huge stag elk was trotting downstream directly towards them. With a start, it turned its full rack upstream and bellowed. Three trailing females bolted and were herded by the stag back upstream. The two hunters laughed and howled at their inability to notch an arrow.

"The Creator has played a trick on us!"

CHAPTER 14
Turtle Town

It took an extra tug to break their canoe free from the thin clear ice along the bank. Wild Carrot and Buffalo Man backed their canoe into the current and expertly swung it upriver. They headed at an angle to cross to the low ground on the opposite bank of the St. Marys. They had entered Kekionga from the west and traversed to the place where warrior Wild Carrot had narrowly escaped the sword of death. Turning right at the creek they had trotted to the ever-present canoes opposite the old French landing.

Moon shadows added eeriness to the assemblage of nearly vacant villages. Those who had not moved down the Maumee for the safety and excitement of the new consolidated villages of many tribes, or who had not withdrawn north to the lakes to avoid diseases from the remains of battle, had been forced out of Kekionga during the past spring by a terrible flood.

Stepping out of the canoe, Wild Carrot saw three fires burning at the crest of the slope. Undoubtedly, the fires were made by those guarding supplies still kept in the old French cabins. The pasture that was once trodden by his drilling riflemen was now thick with tall brown grass. Halfway up he stopped and raised his hand.

"We are on a mission for Little Turtle," he called ahead.

Five warriors arose from the grass on either side. They directed the intruders to proceed to the fire. An interrogation commenced until one of the warriors removed Wild Carrot's floppy hat and looked close in his face.

"It is Chief Wild Carrot who smashed the cannon on the Wabash! Bring some warm food and water. Warm the fire. Give these men your blankets."

"That is my cabin over there," Wild Carrot pointed. "My companions and I must go there now. Bring some food and water. We have no need

191

of blankets."

The cabin still proved to be solid, though the contents were dirty and disorganized. Buffalo Man was invited inside. The chief of the sentries posted a guard at the door and one at each corner of the little log house. Wild Carrot lit an oil lamp and began tidying up. Realizing that they would be there only a short while, he put his hat on one peg and his decorated pouch and his leather currier pouch on another. He lay down upon a canvas cot, likely one that once held an American officer whose corpse now mingled with the soil at the Head of the Wabash.

"Are you keeping that document safe from harm?"

Buffalo Man replied by tapping his quiver with two fingers, "I carry it like a baby."

Soon a pail of water arrived. Wild Carrot moved close to the mirror. He washed his face and neck and hands and combed his hair. He paced the cabin until the morning meal arrived. He and Buffalo Man quickly downed roasted turkey and venison and squash, corn cakes and bean soup, cow's milk and tea. At the last drop of milk a commotion was heard outside.

A man called, "I am Metea, chief of the Pottawatomie beyond the Tippecanoe!" The voice was loud, firm and solid, "Who is it that makes his camp in this cabin of the Pottawatomie?"

Buffalo Man heard a bang on the door. He watched it break loose from its leather hinges and thump to the dirt floor. He jumped, knife in hand, to shield his ward from the finely dressed intruder.

Wild Carrot grabbed his defender's arm and lowered the knife, "I am Wild Carrot, a warrior of Little Turtle. You are mistaken to call this a cabin of the Pottawatomie. It is known that the waters of the three rivers flow through Miami villages."

Buffalo Man knew Metea, but was puzzled at this exchange. He watched the two chiefs hug and slap each other's back. He stared as they danced a little jig.

"How do you happen to be in Kekionga this day?" the red-hair asked.

"I am with your escort to the grand council lodge. We have Little Turtle's sons and Pecan's son and thirty warriors. Five war canoes await you. We will make a grand sight on the Maumee!"

A grand sight they were. The war chief-sagamore-courier sat in the bow of the long canoe. He wore a plain long elk-hide coat and felt hat. The canoe was powered by six flamboyant warriors adorned with paint, feathers, and ribbons. White banners fluttered from long poles at each end of the canoe. On the left and right were similar canoes with red banners. Front and rear canoes completed the ensemble with blue banners. They maintained a tight formation as they plied swiftly with the current. Stroke upon stroke the pace remained steady. They were soon passing villages where people ran to the water's edge and pointed. Oncoming canoeists pulled in their paddles, silently gliding while watching the unexpected procession. How Wild Carrot wished that Sweet Breeze could be beside him, or sitting in the bow and he among those propelling the sleek vessel!

Wild Carrot soon realized that there were many more people than when he was last present in these waters. The villages they passed grew closer and closer together until one could not be distinguished from another. He counted twelve tall decorated teepees of the tribes from beyond the great western river. Stories of the grand encampment proved to be true. The number of inhabitants was beyond counting. Wild Carrot glanced over his shoulder and raised his eyebrows to Metea. His friend only flashed his usual broad smile and continued stroking in rhythm.

The parade of war canoes rounded a point and entered the mouth of the Auglaize. They moved from the full sun of the Maumee into the late afternoon shadows. Cold air sent a shiver through Wild Carrot despite his long elk-hide coat, buckskin jacket, and hunting shirt. He was glad for the cloth lining of his leggings and moccasins. There was no welcoming party on the merchant's wharf other than curiosity seekers. Metea led him directly to a cabin built into the hillside. Wild Carrot recognized it as the cabin of the young silversmith Kinzie from whom he had obtained the necklace for Sweet Breeze two years ago. Three women had stew and roasted duck waiting for the hungry men. Metea, Wild Carrot, and Buffalo Man took their full bowls inside. The others were served and sat on the slope along the path. A large open hearth in the center of the back wall radiated warmth throughout. Kinzie had removed everything to Detroit other than heavy furniture and his metal-covered smithy's bench.

"Why are we on this side?" Wild Carrot inquired.

Metea finished his bite, "Little Turtle will now be informed by his sons of your arrival. He will send for you when it is time. Perhaps tonight, perhaps tomorrow night. It may be longer. He will send for you. You must remain inside the cabin."

Metea had heard the rumor that his friend was carrying a message from General Washington. He wanted to ask if it was fact. Even chiefs that were close friends did not inquire into the other's business unless it was first brought forth by the one whose business it was. He had eyed his friend's leather pouch and wondered at its contents.

The courier for the Americans shared, "I am anxious to have this business concluded. Of course, councils never move as smoothly or swiftly as our war canoes did today. I wish that now I was across the Maumee."

"Where?" the Pottawatomie chief asked.

"In the council lodge, to hear and feel the direction of the talk."

"Ha! You would be lost without me! The council lodge has been moved across from us, on the east side of the Auglaize. A new fire was struck for this council of all councils. The new council house is wider and longer. The sun and the moon have never seen such a gathering of great chiefs. It is a wondrous thing to be here this day."

Metea and Buffalo Man went outside to refill their bowls.

Wild Carrot moved his chair closer to the hearth. The chill in his bones continued. He had little shiver spasms. Was he getting sick? Perhaps he should have insisted on paddling in order to warm his body. No, he now recognized the feeling was in his stomach and heart, not in his muscles and bones. It was the same feeling he had on his wedding day when he sat alone in the cabin anticipating the little ceremony. Was he worthy of her trust? How would he provide for a family? Would her love one day leave him and turn to another? He had never felt as alone as he had that day. Now that aloneness had returned. Here in the midst of a multitude he was alone in the cabin; he was alone in his being. He could not turn to Little Turtle or the other chiefs of the Miami as he had always done. He appreciated the companionship of Metea and Buffalo Man, but they could be no help in preparing for stepping before the council. Even the constant sensation of the presence of his wife abandoned him.

He said aloud, "Sweet Breeze, how I wish you were here to look at, to talk to, to touch!"

The two men returned laughing loudly.

"We have fish," Metea held out a bowl. "Here, take this, it is for you!"

Wild Carrot stood limply with his hands at his side, "No, I cannot eat. I must meditate."

He added wood to the fire and sat on the board floor just beyond the hearth. There he crossed his arms on his knees and lowered his head.

Buffalo Man was not disappointed in the rejection of the food.

A messenger arrived at dusk with instructions to wait until the full moon clears the horizon. When its light shows through the tree limbs, they should proceed to the council house. Wild Carrot rose from his stupor. He arose from the floor. He resolved that the Creator had sent him to this place and he would leave the burden in the Creator's hands. He was only a messenger; that he could be.

"Metea, my friend, see if you can find some milk and some corn cakes with maple syrup or honey."

He lit the two lamps hanging by chain from the ceiling. "Buffalo Man, what do you think? Are we ready?"

The big man nodded affirmatively and banged his chest with a clenched fist and then banged the table.

The dome of the moon rose slowly, large and red. For a moment it seemed to resist releasing from the earth. Breaking free, it gradually grew smaller and paler. As the Miami guard ferried Wild Carrot to the east bank of the Auglaize, the last leaves clinging stubbornly to the branches were silhouetted by a full pink moon. The Miami did not delve in magic and superstitions to the extent of some of their neighbors, but they did recognize omens. A blood moon could be sinister; a rose moon could be promising. Either way, their senses were keen as flaming torches were ushering the way up the path to the grand council lodge. A rhythm of drums drifting from across the Maumee on the still air blended with a more powerful rhythm and chanting coming from up the Auglaize. The crowd parted before them like the wake of a canoe until they reached a stick fence marking the clearing around the council lodge. The Miami warriors entered the compound and moved left off the path.

Wild Carrot, Buffalo Man, and Chief Metea were escorted to the entrance where they stood silently waiting for admission. Wild Carrot drew his knife from its leather sheath and surrendered it handle-first to one of the escorts. The escort denied it with a wave. He handed it to Buffalo Man. They could faintly hear portions of the talking inside. Every saying was interpreted loudly into three languages. These in turn were repeatedly interpreted in lower tones to groups or individuals.

The men became restless awaiting their first view of the pageantry gathered inside. The air was cold and completely still. Every person looked as though they were smoking a pipe as they created a cloud with each exhale. Wild Carrot focused on the breath of the tallest of the guards. His moisture froze and sparkled in a moonbeam. It drifted slowly upwards, then swirled about his face and head. A few crystals clung to large silver earrings while the remainder disappeared into nothingness just as the next cloud blew from his lips.

Through the blanket cover of the entrance Wild Carrot heard his name spoken by Little Turtle. He could hear that the Chief of the Miami was recounting his deeds in battle against the Americans. He heard "Vincennes" and "General Washington" and "Putnam." Upon the conclusion of the interpreting, Chief Richardville appeared through the blanketed opening and resolutely said, "Come."

The three stepped forward, but Richardville held out a hand to halt Metea, motioning the other two inside. Expressionless faces that were dimly lit inside the lodge gave no hint of the mood of their reception of him. He was surprised that the faces that he had never seen before outnumbered those that he had seen at countless council fires. Even friends kept solemn faces, neither winking nor smiling. In the cramped space he had to stand directly in front of Little Turtle, with his toes near the fire. He stood erect but relaxed; he did not assume the haughty stance of a chief about to make a great oration. He took in all of the faces while giving those who had traveled far a chance to inspect him. He thought about removing his hat, but decided no, that is what an American would do.

He turned about and faced Little Turtle. He had no calumet to hold forth, no wampum nor feather. He looked him in the eyes and extended both arms forward, palms down. He turned slightly to the right and similarly addressed the chiefs, first the tribes from the east and on around the arranged assemblage to the tribes from the west. He held his hands in the direction of the fire and turned his palms up. He remained silent until an attendant came forward and fanned smoke over his hands and face.

He spoke in the Miami tongue, "I am Wild Carrot, War Chief of the Miami, Sagamore of the Wabash Tribes. I would address each of you, but I do not know your names, or even all of your nations. I come with a message from the Americans. I do not come as an ambassador. You can see that I bring no wampum, no gifts. I bring only a letter."

He did not wait for the interpreters, but repeated for himself in Shawnee, then Pottawatomie and French.

He waited for the chain of interpreting to taper off, "Do not focus your attention on me. I am like a mist appearing here briefly, only to vanish into nothingness."

The listeners began to look around at each other. Not one had ever heard a chief address himself thus. Wild Carrot was pleased with the reaction. He did not wish to speak to unemotional faces.

"What deserves the attention of the chiefs of this council is the letter I carry. I bring you a letter from General Putnam, ambassador for General Washington."

He lifted a document from his leather pouch, reached forward, and laid it on the fire. Hushed gasps went up as it was consumed quickly by a green flame. He stepped briskly to Buffalo Man who handed him his quiver. Wild Carrot removed the arrows and handed them one by one to Richardville. He reached into the quiver and withdrew a leather tube. Assuming his previous position he pulled the actual letter out of the tube. The ruse-letter had served its purpose. It had been a substitute for the genuine paper, useful if the bearer was accosted. Paper covered with pine pitch and copper shavings had heightened the flame and the attention of his audience. He showed around the circle the authentic document with its seal and ribbon. Reading its entirety in English, he followed with his translations.

Feeling that he had successfully conveyed the message, he fanned himself in the smoke and again recognized Little Turtle and each sector of the circle. Richardville stepped forward and ceremoniously received the document. Little Turtle glanced around the lodge and saw that no chief rose to comment.

"Chief Wild Carrot, you will reside as my guest in my town on the river Eel," he spoke forcefully, "until the day you are recalled to this council to receive a reply to be delivered to the Americans."

* * *

Paddlers worked hard against the current through the night and well into the daylight to gain Kekionga. Fifty-three men stepped ashore, leaving twelve to take the large canoes back downstream. The foot-squad trekked the portage towards Turtle Town. They met a party of Wea transporting corn on eight packhorses.

"A runner reached us this morning with the news of your coming," the small man in the lead of the pack train declared. "We heard of your speech to the council and the stir it caused. We heard of these many warriors coming to reside at Eel Town. We are happy they are here. The women are cooking for them now, but there is only enough for one meal.

There are not enough huts for so many men. The strong men are occupied unloading canoes and transporting corn to the Maumee; there is no time for hunting. Only the old men fish and trap."

"You carry enough corn to feed the town for many days. How can you say there is little food?" inquired the red-haired chief.

"We portage this amount each day. It comes from the villages below. It is for the towns on the Maumee, so many camps of all nations."

"Surely there is enough to feed Turtle Town. Is not Tulip Leaf there to direct things?"

"We have often expected her, but she is always delayed. No person is in charge of the town, save young Sweet Breeze who recently arrived, and she is great with child. We, I live there now, I am Red Bow of Ouiatenon, we sacrifice so others may eat."

"What of Sweet Breeze, is she well?"

Red Bow now made the connection that he was talking to the husband of Sweet Breeze, "Yes, I assure you she is well. She works hard to prepare her cabin for your arrival. As the rest of us, she struggles to find food."

"Then there will be a toll on this portage, just as there has always been on the Wabash portage."

The little man looked down, "Unless Little Turtle returns and declares it, there can be no toll."

"Are you aware that you are speaking to a sagamore?"

"Yes! Yes, that is correct. Say it, and it will be so."

"Well then, Red Bow, leave one horse with his load. You and your men deliver the remainder of this cargo today. Come to me in the morning with three leaders of the men of the town and we will set a fair toll."

Red Bow barked some orders, then led the procession, whistling his way down the trail.

Wild Carrot organized the warriors into six groups of eight with each group electing a leader. Three groups would enter the town to protect it and the portage. The three others would set up hunting camps at a distance from the town. They were instructed to alternate with the town guard every fifth day. Dispatching the bands to favored hunting sites, he pushed ahead towards the town.

Metea was awed by his friend's decisiveness. He recalled that he was on his first journey to Turtle Town when he first saw the red-hair. The audacity of the interloper had immediately impressed him. That same characteristic was cloaked in the beauty of his wife. He was contemplating that beauty when he saw it walking towards him from the crest of the trail ahead. He looked a second time to be sure it was not a mirage. It had to be her. Though wrapped in a robe of animal skins, the gait of the step was unmistakable.

He poked the shoulder of his companion and pointed ahead, "Look yonder." He looked for the quick smile, but, instead, found tears filling the man's eyes. He took Wild Carrot's bundle and tucked it under his free arm allowing the interpreter, warrior, chief, diplomat, wise counselor, friend, to stride ahead and embrace the vision.

Sweet Breeze put both arms around her husband's neck and let him hold her a long time. Releasing, she turned to the nearing troop. She opened her coat and showed off the form of her belly under a blue dress. A smile and a wave brought a cheer from the encircling warriors.

She saw the face of her husband turn the color of his hair. "Look what he did to me. Can you believe it?"

She said to her embarrassed husband, "Let us wait behind. I am tired and need some rest."

Overhearing, Metea interjected, "Then all will rest."

Upon calling a halt, Metea took some men into the trees. They soon returned with sapling poles and created a litter. Sweet Breeze was placed upon it and hoisted to their shoulders. She felt the jostling may throw her to the ground, but she would not diminish the joy of the doting tribesmen. She soon learned to shift her weight with each stride and began to enjoy the ride.

* * *

As brisk late-fall days turned to bleak winter, Wild Carrot felt like he was a prisoner of Turtle Town. He busied himself with organizing and improving the town. The population had overturned during the past two years. Families with deep roots in the land had given way to refugees and transients. Social structure had broken down to near chaos. Having stabilized the food supply, he focused on wood to fuel the fires of winter. One of the three bands of warriors in town was daily detailed to bring in wood from the forest. Balking at women's work, they had to be convinced that it was an honor to restore Little Turtle's hometown. An efficiently working town could support the camps at the grand council and the warriors on their raids. The refugees were families of their fellow warriors who could not be present to care for them. Finally, their own comfort, and perhaps survival, depended on a coordinated effort much like in a hunting camp. A second band was given the task of repairing cabins and wigwams and building new shelters.

The third squad worked directly under the direction of Wild Carrot on civic improvements. Breastworks were placed overlooking the flood-plain at the south and east edges of the community. Across the river defenses were constructed along the portage trail. The portage landing was improved and a toll house erected. A granary and storehouse were built on the high ground to the north, new latrines farther on. Inhabitants were evicted from the council house. It was returned to its intended purpose. A new council was formed including the captain of the portage, three captains from the warrior guard, three long-time residents, and three men elected by the refugees. Wild Carrot and a cousin of Sweet Breeze held the places of honor.

Sweet Breeze declared that all food was to be communal. She set up cooking stations at four strategic locations. All women were to cook, grind, or chop wood until the high sun, with the afternoons available for personal tasks. Two women were selected each day to accompany Sweet Breeze on a tour of the town to police policies on sanitation and rubbish removal. Repeat offenders would be threatened with loss of food. She encouraged those with unsound dwellings to make improvements; if they could not, her husband would send assistance.

On the day the first snow fell, she was pleased that the day's tour had produced no violations. She could now call each woman by name, just as she could when here as a child. She knew the names of the villages displaced families called home.

She did not know the number of days until her husband would hear from the grand council and leave for Vincennes. She did know that the number of days were few until her birthing time. Sweet Breeze lingered under the blankets of their snug cabin. She had come here to the home of her family for this birth. She had not found the town that she knew; only two cousins remained. Her mother and father sent messages, but were unable to come. Yet, she felt satisfied. She was with her husband. The town had become cohesive and was beginning to function like a family. Midwives vied for her attention. She looked around the stark cabin. She had patched, chinked, fixed, and cleaned, but it was bleak. There were no adornments, no bundles of herbs drying under the rafters, no color.

The door opened with a draft of cold air. She watched Wild Carrot track snow the length of the floor to the fireplace. A full armload of wood he laid on the coals. Flames began to warm the room with heat and light. He came to her and sat upon a bench near the bed.

Leaving his coat on he said, "The snow is deep. Stay here and I will bring your breakfast. I will tell the women there will be no tour of the town today."

He started to rise, but she held his hand and kept him, "The river will be frozen solid soon. No more corn will be coming. Is there enough food for the winter?"

"There is enough for those here now, and a little more for travelers. Not enough for a new wave of refugees."

"Is there enough for a festival? The people have worked hard. Those who were quarrelsome have left; those now here are good. They have not had a celebration for so long. We should have a festival."

He sat quietly watching the flames flicker yellow streaks of light on the walls.

After a time he said, "I have been thinking the same about our warriors. I will send a runner to ask for replacements so these men may go west on a buffalo hunt. For now, I will give all six bands extra powder and send them into the woods for two days. On the third day there will be a contest as to which camp can bring in the most meat. The festival may begin that day. We will allow twice the corn and vegetables."

"For three days?"

"For three days there shall be no work."

She kissed his hand.

He started to get up, but sat back again, "What is the name of this festival?"

They thought.

He offered, "Festival of the Toll Station. Without the extra corn from below there would be no festival."

"One does not celebrate a toll building!" She threw off her blankets and sat up sharply. Her eyes danced and gleamed, "Mary told me that they decorate with pine boughs in the winter. She puts ribbons on them and hangs them in her home. They fill the room with a sweet scent. Let us have a Festival of the Pine Boughs. All of the people of our village should bring newly cut boughs into their dwellings and place some over their openings. On the last evening each person can bring a branch from their home and throw it on a bonfire in exchange for a handful of corn."

"I had better go quickly and tell them this before your head fills with thoughts too grand," he started for the door.

"One more thing, tell the women to elect three of their own to do the tour today," she paused, "and each succeeding day."

* * *

The captain of the winning band was presented with a bow finely crafted by one of the elder men. The warriors of the band whooped and danced when Wild Carrot gave them a cask of gunpowder. The surplus of bear meat and venison was such that it would take many days to consume. There were so many rabbits that it should have been called Festival of Rabbits. On the first day, large fluffy puffs of snow piled quickly, covering everything of nature and man in its whiteness. During the night the winds howled through the town, whipping the snow into drifts and mounds. The morning of the second day brought sleet. It created a hard crust on top of the snow-cover and coated branches with ice.

By midday only patches of white clouds dotted the blue sky. Tiny sparkly ice-crystals danced in the air. Straws poking above the white blanket appeared to be made of glass. Wild Carrot wore a pair of borrowed snowshoes and carried a pair on his shoulder.

He entered the cabin noisily and sat upon the bench by the bed, "Get dressed. Five days inside this room is too long. The sun is now bright and our neighbors are out frolicking. Come now, you need to be up and moving."

She knew he was right and managed to get moving. Her walk had become a waddle and she was unsure what it might become on snowshoes. She pictured herself face-down rocking back and forth on her belly like she had done over a rolled-up snowball when she was a child.

"I will join you if you will get me a stick to keep my balance."

He disappeared. He returned with two stout poles. Helping her with her coat and snowshoes, he stood her up and ushered her outside. He measured the poles against her; he chopped them off breast high.

He guided towards the center of town, but she pointed to the south, "This way."

She surprised herself as she moved towards a promontory overlooking the narrow valley. Scoot, step, pole, scoot, step, pole. The walk was exhilarating, but tiring. She reached a breastwork and plopped down upon the logs. Snow crunched and flew. She bent over and caught some breaths.

She lifted her head and gazed towards the river. She became breathless, not from exertion, but from surprise and joy.

"It is so beautiful!"

Wild Carrot maneuvered his snowshoes to get close behind her. He leaned against her back and placed his arms around her. They watched rivulets of snow dance and swirl across the icy crust. To the right an eagle swooped in low under the branches, caught a rabbit, and vanished into the sun. Behind them they could hear the muffled shrill sounds of children playing. Before them they heard only the rippling water where it bubbled in stretches between sheets of ice. A red fox trotted downriver at the edge of the ice unaware of the watching humans.

Wild Carrot teased, "If you sit here too long you will become frozen to the logs. I will have to leave you as part of the defenses."

"Do you think these defenses will be needed?" she asked.

She was immediately sorry that she had mentioned war.

"If nothing else, they kept our warriors busy and away from making trouble in the town. Those men now feel attached to the townspeople."

"Do you think the chiefs' council message will say that they will meet with the Americans to talk of peace?"

"I think there are too many in the council lodge to decide anything. Runners bring news and Metea shares during his visits, but I am tired of waiting. Soon the second full moon will be here since they heard the letter from Putnam."

"Tired of waiting? You should be a woman carrying a child in her womb, then you would understand 'tired of waiting.'"

"I just wish the days would pass more quickly."

"Do not wish your days away, my husband. Do you not know that the Creator fashioned this moment just for us to share. Never again will that whisk of snow curl just so. Only now will the lip of this snowdrift hold its shape. The shadow of that cloud moves silently over the whiteness once, and it is gone. A ripple may one day resemble that one below the rock, but it cannot recover an exact likeness. Even now, it is not the same water that was there when the fox passed by. The sparkles in the snow change with the movement of the sun, gleaming first here, then there. The Creator put the sun in place; he brought the snow and the blowing of the wind to make a little mound behind that stalk. All this he did so that you and I can see one gleam for a brief moment. We cannot go and find others and say, 'Come, see this!' for it will be gone, never to return. But he also makes sparkles, and shadows, and wind in their hair that only they can experience. This moment he has made for us. All that is required is to stop and look and thank the Creator for thinking of us."

Her husband began to realize that as much as they thought alike, he would never be able to see the world as she did. He leaned around and looked into her face. It was her eyes, her face, her form, her moving that mesmerized him.

"The beautiful creation that I see is here," he kissed her forehead. "Come, let us get you back to the fire."

* * *

That night a new sound filled the cabin. One of the three midwives led him in and held the lamp high, "A girl," she beamed, "healthy in all ways! She came to join the Festival of the Pine Boughs." Wild Carrot beheld a sight more wondrous than glistening snow.

Day upon day the snows fell and the winds blew. Few travelers came or went. The buffalo hunt was successful in bringing in meat and robes. It was also successful in cheering the warriors assigned to Wild Carrot at Turtle Town. The guard that had relieved them during the hunt was waiting out the blizzard.

The storm did not keep Metea from his faithful visits to his friend. This friend was now silhouetted by flickers of the cabin fire. "I left two within this cabin and now I find three!" Metea picked up the infant.

Lying on his back in front of the hearth, the guest hummed to the naked baby prone on his chest. Sweet Breeze sat at his feet on a folded buffalo robe. The cloth she was working was taking the form of a skirt. She laid her work aside and wrapped the child in rabbit fur.

She presented the bundle again to Metea, "Pine Bough, this is Metea. Do not listen to anything he tells you. He charms all the girls."

"And you, Pine Bough, are the loveliest of them all."

He tried to hand her to Sweet Breeze, but the mother turned away to her sewing. He placed the furry bundle with the sleeping baby upon the father's chest.

Metea said, "My friend, I have a plan."

"A plan to seduce my daughter?"

"Five Medals has told me what he hears from Chief Black Hoof of the Shawnee. Simon Girty has bands of renegades ready to assassinate you when you make your return trip to Vincennes with the message from the grand council."

"If there is a message," Wild Carrot tersely stated. "If a multitude of chiefs can agree on one answer. The third full moon is here and still I wait."

He glanced at his wife. He did enjoy the time with family, but walls made him restless.

She continued her stitching, "I expect that one day soon my husband will take his war club to the Auglaize and shake it in the faces of the chiefs."

"Girty tells his hired killers that you will be escorted as far as Kekionga. That you will traverse to the Wabash or Eel to start for Vincennes. That you will seek assistance at Eel Town and the Wea villages. That you may trick them and go north to the Tippecanoe or make a straight path through the forests south of the Wabash."

Wild Carrot sat up and gently placed the child upon a blanket covering fresh pine boughs. Pine Bough let out a wail and fussed. Her mother caressed her and began nursing. Her father gave his full attention to the visitor.

The visitor continued, "I have a plan. They will not attack while you are near Kekionga or Turtle Town where they would be subject to revenge. You will have a personal guard of three. You will instruct two of them to remain with your baggage at Kekionga and wait for your return while you visit your wife. I will have a strong and fast horse waiting for you here. You will leave during the night on the Yellow River trail. I will meet you at the crossing of the Tippecanoe. Together we will move swiftly to the Yellow. This we will follow into the grand Kankakee marsh."

The hearer leaned closer. He had not hunted in the marshes for years. In the autumn they were teeming with ducks and geese and every waterfowl known. The bewildering maze of swamps, ponds, and streams were choked with thick brush. In places trees grew so close together that a man could not negotiate a path.

"I know the marsh," the Pottawatomie related, "and have trusted friends who know it better than I. My people will take our horses north as though we are bound for the Sauk Trail to the river Chicago. You and I will head into the marsh to the west and south. We will have camps stationed ahead of us. We will have horses waiting beyond. South we will ride across the flatlands, keeping to the west of the Wabash."

Metea's eyes grew wider with excitement as he laid out each detail. It was a good plan, a superb plan.

"These friends," Wild Carrot inquired, "you trust them well?"

"The Pottawatomie of the marsh live their own way. They care nothing of events beyond their realm. They are loyal to their own kind and count me among them."

"You would risk your name and your life for a message to Vincennes?" Sweet Breeze asked of their friend.

"For your husband, not for a message," he replied as a matter of fact.

Wild Carrot smacked him on the shoulder, "Most likely for the adventure!" He paused, "Agreed! I hope for a night of storms when I ride."

KANKAKEE

CHAPTER 15
Kankakee

A crashing sound alerted Metea to the peak of his senses. He rose from his nest he had hacked under the low branches of a spruce. He parted the boughs enough to peer over a snowdrift. A horse and rider were struggling to gain the north side of the Tippecanoe. Surely it was the companion he had waited for. Darkness would not reveal the form of the rider. He would need to act quickly before the rider passed by. Letting the horse find its footing up the low bank, the rider proceeded slowly and stopped, then trotted into the trees. Seeing that the dark form had no pack or blanket, Metea tumbled clear of the spruce. He threw his spear in front of the horse. The man dismounted. Metea drew his tomahawk at the unfamiliar figure covered in furs. He heard a familiar voice calling in his own tongue, "My friend!"

In an instant they continued the flight together. Metea took the lead through broken woods and meadows. Morning light found them chopping a hole in the ice of a round lake to water their horses. Walking their horses to the top of the hill to the west, they mounted and rode through grasses of an open prairie.

They neared the Yellow River at midday. Their horses began breaking through an icy crust into deep mud. Dismounting, they led the tiring steeds at an agonizingly slow pace. Here, the river was a mere creek with hardly a bank to direct its course. The water was low with a thin layer of ice. The bottom was too soft to cross as planned, forcing them to turn west along the south side. Eventually, the course of the stream turned to the south leading to firmer ground. Soon, they gained their crossing. Threading westward between the river on the left and a series of ponds on the right, they soon reached oak covered sand hills.

"Not far," were the first words Wild Carrot heard from his companion.

Once again they crossed the Yellow River, this time much easier on a smooth sandy bottom. The pair of men and the pair of horses trudged

207

into a waiting camp provided by the marsh people.

Night closed quickly upon them. Wild Carrot heard the screech of a panther to the west, then another to the north. Soon the marsh was full of the eerie cries coming from near and far. He watched the four locals move about the camp in the firelight. Their ghostly forms appeared as though they were moving bushes. Their porridge and tea were seasoned with a strange mixture of bitter herbs. He lay back and wondered about these men and their customs. He contemplated this plan of foiling his pursuers. He wondered about the future of his tiny daughter.

Something began tapping the souls of his feet. He sat up with knife in hand. It was Metea standing over him, kicking with the toes of his moccasins.

"Up, man, up! We are ready to move."

Wild Carrot wondered why they would move after supper, then realized that he had already slept the night. A short drink of tea, a stretch of the muscles and leisure time was over. He was handed a pouch of mixed grain, a gourd filled with herb water, and a sword that had twice the reach of his tomahawk. One of the men silently stepped into the brush with Metea close behind. Wild Carrot dove after them. He was followed by a second man of the marsh tribe.

By the time he downed his second handful of meal, Wild Carrot realized that he had lost his reckoning. He looked left and right, ahead and behind. He was now totally dependant upon his guides. If abandoned, he could not return whence they came. He imagined himself wandering aimlessly under the dark canopy day upon day, year upon year, finally abandoning all hope of recovering the world of his past. He could remember only once in his life that he had lost his sense of position and direction. The feeling was so unsettling that he began carrying a brass French compass.

He reached his right hand into his leather pouch. He felt the little cotton bag of Sweet Breeze's tea mixture that she had handed him at his departure. There was the miniature sheath of the sewing kit, cold steel and flint, a short string of wampum, a chunk of beeswax, and in the bottom the cold, smooth circular compass. He tested it and found north. He continued down the trail carrying it in his hand, checking his bearing from time to time. Certainly no pursuer could track them here, even if they dared. Eventually the compass returned to its quarters; it served no useful purpose.

Sleep was much slower coming the second night. He sat back and listened to the exchange of stories among the three Pottawatomie. Usually he would participate, but he simply sat. He was becoming moody, restless, like being cooped in a cabin during a blizzard.

After a third camp, they were led to two small gray horses. Metea resupplied them from caches of food and weapons. They were soon speeding over frozen ground of an endless flat prairie, gladly leaving the marsh behind. Wild Carrot could not discern the landmarks that his Pottawatomie friend used for reckoning. He simply trusted the leader's skill. The second day on the plains took them to a camp of eight Pottawatomie hunters.

"Here we will rest," Metea instructed. "We can afford a day at least."

"Yes, we can afford it, and I can use it. I compliment you on your plan. If those devils are looking for me, they are chasing their tails from the sands of great lake Michigan to the salt streams of the Buffalo trace."

"I say differently," Metea offered. "I say they sit in Kekionga drinking whiskey, waiting for you to return from pleasing your wife."

* * *

Metea guided to fording places for crossing the Vermilion north and Vermilion south. They continued southward paralleling at a distance the western bank of the Wabash. A warm southern breeze brought showers, turning frozen ground to slush, and eventually, to a quagmire. With nothing but swamps and muck ahead, and the pace becoming laboriously slow, a new strategy was needed. At a Kickapoo hunting camp, they traded a horse and a silver armband for a log canoe and bundles of furs. Wild Carrot would continue alone. He assumed the guise of a trapper. Metea made his way back north to his homeland.

Gaining the Wabash, the lone trapper kept to the right bank as much as the ice-flow would allow. Melting into the landscape, he pulled ashore the first afternoon when the sun poked through the overcast. Even if he limited his paddling to morning and evening, progress would be greater than an overland attempt, that is, if there were no ice-jams. The second and third days on the river produced continual drizzle, allowing enough concealment for full days of river travel. He moved quickly enough that he did not risk being overtaken by travelers from behind. He moved cautiously enough to spot the few laboring upstream travelers in time to duck under overhanging branches.

Unexpectedly passing close to a camp of Illinois hunters, Wild Carrot tapped his packs with the paddle and called in French, "Good day, my friends! Look, the winter has been good to me!"

They shouted in the language of the Kaskaskia for him to come in to their camp. He pretended not to hear clearly.

"Yes, the ice is broken up and flowing well!"he called over his shoulder.

He did not quicken his paddling stokes, but steered into swifter current to make some speed. He whistled and sang a bawdy French tune in rhythm with his paddle. Downstream he looked back to verify that they were not following.

* * *

Secluded in the brush of a lagoon, Wild Carrot could smell the fires of Vincennes. After being exposed to two days of cold showers, he longed for the warmth of those fires burning within the cabins and homes and the fort. The log canoe and the elk hide would suffice for a bit longer. He waited for darkness to envelop the river from tree line to tree line before slipping from his quiet cove. Lying as flat to the log canoe as he was able, he let it float close to the eastern bank. The bleating of goats mixed with the tinkling of their bells told that his destination was near. The banging of cabin shutters being closed was close by. Soon he was passing the fort, barely missing the little pier. A bit farther down he made his landing. He pulled his furs and meager goods into the brush, and released the canoe to find its own destination. A canopy of hide draped over two packs would be his shelter for the remainder of the night. The thought of Sweet Breeze nursing their daughter was the only warmth to comfort him.

The din on the hill became a rumble as the fort came alive. Wild Carrot held his place until soldiers accompanying two rattling wagons passed, apparently a firewood detail. He shouldered his packs and tramped through a foggy mist directly to one of the sentries at the gate.

"State your name and business,"the soldier demanded.

"William Wells, come to see Major Hamtramck."

The soldier was startled.

He peered into the trapper's face, "Remove your hat." Recognizing the trapper as the interpreter, he exclaimed, "What a story this will be! We have been on the lookout for your scalp, but had given up on even that." Inspecting the man in front of him again, he corrected, "Lieutenant Colonel Hamtramck it is now. Follow me."

Hamtramck half looked up at the sentry, "What is it?"

"Wells has arrived, sir."

He looked up, "Cartey or Samuel?"

"Wells the interpreter, sir."

"The interpreter? Are you sure?"

"Yes, sir, either him or his ghost."

Wells had already been relieved of the musket that had proudly been presented to him by Pottawatomie hunters, one they had scavenged after the battle at the Head of the Wabash. He handed the men posted at the door his tomahawk, the sword, and two knives.

Colonel Hamtramck stood behind his table checking his urge to rush forward and embrace the man, "Welcome to Fort Knox, Mr. Wells. It has been a long winter."

Wells said simply, "I have the message from the grand council."

"Good!" He gestured to a row of pegs, "Hang your coat and hat. We will first have some peach brandy."

He set out two cut glass mugs and poured. He chopped a nub from a plug of tobacco and offered it to his guest.

Wells declined the offer, "It is an oral message. I should present it now."

"Then tell it now. Later I will have you repeat its entirety in front of the officers and a clerk."

William rummaged for the single short strand of wampum. He held it out saying, "This message was presented in the lodge of the grand council on the Maumee at the mouth of the Auglaize. It was delivered by Chief Tarhe of the Wyandot, Chief Turkey Foot of the Ottawa served as his second."

He held the wampum high and looked at the ceiling beams, "The Grand Council of All Nations has received the message from General Putnam to come in peace to sit in council with the Americans. The nations desire peace so that our children and our elders may have a happy life. Our nations desire peace so that our men may go the path to hunt game rather than go the path of war. The tribes will meet with the Americans to find a lasting peace."

Hamtramck felt a rush of excitement. What fortune it would be to halt the war before the great clash that, until now, was a certainty.

The speech continued, "Our chiefs will not come to your forts. The council will be held at the Forks of the Wabash. You will know it is time for the council when you see three staffs decorated with white feathers and white ribbons standing at the Falls of the Ohio. When you see this sign, your ambassadors will be escorted under truce to the place of council."

Hamtramck grew apprehensive. The government would never send a contingent to such a remote place. The Forks of the Wabash was obviously picked because of its isolation from the established posts.

Wells continued to recite in a low-toned cadence, "A staff will be erected when it is seen that the Americans have torn down all of their forts north of the river Ohio and between the river Allegheny in the east and the great river Mississippi in the west. A second staff will be erected when it is known that the Americans have ceased from measuring the lands north of the river Ohio and have ceased placing their marks upon the lands. The third staff will be erected when all settlers north of the river Ohio have moved to the south of the river. When you see the three staffs, then we will hold council." Wells lowered his arms and held out the wampum, "That is the message from the Grand Council of All Nations."

Hamtramck pounded his fist on the table making the decanter rattle.

He kicked his chair, "Blasted coot scoundrels! They want it both ways! Saying they want peace while drawing a line for war!"

He spat into the ashes of the hearth.

He spoke to the stones of the fireplace, "War it will be! There is no hope for a council now! Do they think I will tear down this fort! Do they think I will say to the people of Vincennes, 'Come, follow me, I will lead you back to the lands of Kentucky.' I will be surprised if Washington does not strap on his own sword when he hears this message!" Turning in rage to Wells he proclaimed, "Get out! You are not welcome here!"

Wells stepped forward and laid the pittance of wampum on the table. He dutifully secured his coat and hat while calculating how far "out" he should get. Unlatching the door, he opened just as a flash of lightning cracked and rumbled.

The thunder almost drowned out Hamtramck's calm voice, "Wait. Hold on. I have feared for your safety and cannot now send you off. I will make accommodations within the walls. Join me for breakfast tomorrow and tell me about your journey. Then we will get this on paper, and you will have your pay as promised."

* * *

Contented with the completion of the project he had accepted from

General Putnam, William Wells reported to the commandant's office in the morning. He did not take Hamtramck's tirade personally. It had shown that the professional military man preferred a stab at a peaceful resolution rather than rush to battle. It was clear to Wells that the Lieutenant Colonel would prefer to accommodate, rather than subjugate, the tribes. Through the years at this most remote of all posts, Hamtramck, along with his wife and children, called the banks of the Wabash his home. He had skillfully overseen relations between the tribes, the French farmers, traders, voyagers, trappers, Virginians, and more recently, Yankees.

A banquet for two was laid out on the board. Hamtramck was embarrassed by his conduct the previous morn. Short of a verbal apology, he did all he could to show respect for his guest. He inquired about Sweet Breeze, who was pregnant upon her departure in the fall, and Porcupine.

"Chief Porcupine has relinquished control of Eel Town to Chief Charley. Primrose, the wife of Porcupine, my adoption mother, died of a pestilence. Sweet Breeze resides at Turtle Town where we have a cabin. It was there we waited on the decision of the council. In that cabin she bore us a fine daughter." He tried to say it matter-of-factly, but a smile and laugh accompanied the word "daughter." "Pine Bough is her name."

"A fine name for a fine girl. I ask you to stay at my fort for a couple of weeks so we can talk and share. You cannot travel upstream against the ice flow; surely you do not intend to travel cross-country in the spring." The officer refilled his plate, "Besides, I expect a supply convoy soon. Your brothers Cartey and Samuel may be with it. We had reports of your death, and I passed them on to Fort Steuben."

"Let it be known in Vincennes that the message from the Grand Council of All Tribes has arrived at this place. I will let myself be seen in the streets of the town. The news will get back to the Maumee soon enough. I will depart in two weeks."

Hamtramck was pleased with the answer. "I tell you now so you can think on your answers. I will need to interrogate you in front of the officers and a clerk to validate the authenticity of your message."

"The string of wampum validates it, meager though it be."

"Your word is good enough for me. But for me to shell out three hundred dollars in silver of the United States treasury, I will need to enclose documentation with the voucher that General Knox can show the politicians. You and I know the power of wampum among the tribes, but in Philadelphia they want signed documents. Wampum and calumets lose their power as they travel east. Once they held power there, but now it is a different land."

* * *

The clerk took down every word of the frontiersman's story, beginning with the October departure of Putnam from Vincennes and continuing through to facing Hamtramck the day previous. As was the way on the frontier, Wells expertly blended fact with fiction until they could not be sifted apart. No mention was given of the private rendezvous with Little Turtle at the Salamonie. He omitted the role Sweet Breeze and he had played in the rebuilding of Turtle Town. His private guard and the name "Metea" were left out. Names and locations were slightly altered to suit his fancy. He fabricated stories of close escapes from assassins bent upon severing communication with the Americans. At the close, he recited the message word for word as he had the day before.

"You did not interpret at the council nor attend the discussions?" a uniform asked.

"I attended the delivery of the letter from General Putnam and the response of the council. That is all."

"How many chiefs participated in the council?"

"I can name over thirty, and there were that many more that I do not know. Some I do not even know the name or abode of their tribes."

The four officers all gave Colonel Hamtramck looks of surprise. Rumors had set the number much lower.

"A council of that size should send a large and expertly decorated belt of wampum with such an important message to such a great nation as the United States. What do you make of that little string that you bring?"

"What do you make of it?" Wells returned the question.

"It is an insult to our country!" a captain huffed.

"Then that is what you should make of it," the red-haired courier, still in trapper's garb, calmly replied.

A second captain kicked back his chair and stood, "An insult to the army!"

The colonel brought the meeting to a close, "I am satisfied that Mr. Wells has completed his duties as set forth by Major General Rufus Putnam in my presence in this very room, and shall be paid under the conditions set forth at that time. Mr. Wells, I commend you on the completion of your mission in the service of the United States government. A mission, I dare say, that could have been accomplished by no other person. Mr. Wells, step here and sign where indicated. Stay close at hand. We will have breakfast again tomorrow. In the meanwhile, you may draw against your pay at the stores of the quartermaster."

The second breakfast was ample, though less extravagant than the previous. The fort commandant obviously had issues to present.

Hamtramck said, "The cabin in town is available if you wish to locate your family here. I know that Sweet Breeze enjoyed her stay; it would make a fine home for a family. My wife and children have become attached to this frontier; it is our home." He absentmindedly shifted his food with his broad dinner knife, "I am certain that I will be called to Fort Washington when the legion descends the Ohio from Legionville."

Seeing that the terms were lost on the listener, he explained, "The new army is called the Legion of the United States." He assessed what the British spies already knew, "General Wayne established Legionville below Pittsburgh as his winter camp. There he drills twenty-five hundred men in his war techniques. In the spring he will consolidate four thousand uniformed soldiers and two thousand militiamen at Fort Washington. He will march to Kekionga and establish a fort to govern the region."

He paused to sip his milk, "Yes, yes, you think that the warriors on the Maumee are more numerous than those that stopped St. Clair. Hear what I say. I know Wayne, I served with him in the east. Have no illusions about it, Wayne is no St. Clair. He will not repeat the folly of St. Clair. His preparations will be thorough; his strategy will be refined; his discipline will be stiff; his determination will be unfaltering. The British fear his name. I saw him hold his Pennsylvania line at Monmouth Court House when those on both flanks withdrew and fled. Did he falter? No. Did he conduct an orderly retreat? No. Did he stand his line in the face of overwhelming strength of the redcoats? No. What did he do? He charged. His men obeyed his orders and charged into the mass of the enemy, sending the British into confusion and disarray until they were forced to withdraw. 'Mad' they called him, and the name 'Mad' took. In Washington's war councils when others were timid, his advice was always to attack. And attack he did in other battles brandishing his distain for the enemy. These were not feverish reckless attacks, but cold and calculated, and ever effective."

Wells knew the look in the colonel's eyes. It was a look of a seasoned man who had seen wondrous events. Samuel had spoken highly of Wayne, but his knowledge was not the same of Hamtramck's. William wanted to match his admiration of Little Turtle and tell of his qualities, but dared not.

Hamtramck warned, "You would do well not to underestimate General Wayne. Congress has given him a clean slate in forming the legion. He answers only to General Knox and President Washington, and they are giving him free-rein."

Wells quietly countered, "Until he proves himself against the tribes, they will remain defiant. They will fight his every step."

"Will the tribes of the lower Wabash honor the treaty of this place?"

"The chiefs who signed will honor it. They will stay in their villages and encourage their warriors to stay. But, each warrior will decide his own path. Many stay. Some have gone to join the war parties, and the chiefs will not stop them." He could have said "cannot stop them." He reassured the colonel, "The Piankashaw, the Wea, and the Miami of Eel Town who remain will not fight. Others have come to make their homes among them in pursuit of a peaceful life."

Hamtramck seized his opportunity, "And you, where is your home? Is it Eel Town or Turtle Town? Which end of the Eel River is home?"

Wells, Wild Carrot, started to answer. Warm blood rushing to his head made him lightheaded. Home? Where is home? He had always felt that Eel Town was his home. However, the Eel Town of today did not feel like home. The buildings, the people, the sense of belonging had changed. Porcupine was no longer the head and Primrose had joined its earth. Turtle Town had always been home for Sweet Breeze. They had intended to make their home there. But, he knew that his wife felt like a stranger, an intruder, in her own town. Kekionga, even in its current desolate condition, had always felt like home. Neither of them would be satisfied in the new villages on the Maumee. He thought of the other places they had lodged as husband and wife: the lake near Squirrel's Town, Vincennes, Wellsmont with Samuel and Mary.

Wells answered, "Wherever Sweet Breeze and I lay our heads together we call home."

Hamtramck urged, "Cast your lot with us, William. Wayne will not go off blind into the wilderness following only a compass. He will seek scouts who know the region, and I dare say, he will find none better than you. I can hire you on as fort interpreter until such time as I am called to headquarters. Think beyond the war, man. Fort Kekionga will need an interpreter. Would it not be best to have someone who would interpret fairly, even one who could be a spokesman for the Miami nation? One who could guard their interests in peace negotiations when arms of war have been laid down? Who else could fill that role? Your brothers are raising a company of militia in Kentucky. Join us in this time of war. When it is finished, you will be in a position to help build a lasting peace."

Wells was taken aback by the forthrightness of his trusted associate. He was shocked at the certainty with which he referred to "Fort Kekionga." For an instant his mind transcended the little fort office. A vision erased his thoughts. He saw Little Turtle take a pile of tiny twigs in his left hand and a second pile in his right. The great chief joined them together, dropped them to the ground, and drew a circle around them. He wondered to himself, "Was this the answer to the riddle of the twigs?" He had stood on these very boards when the Creator presented him, through Putnam, with the peace mission. Was the Creator using Hamtramck to direct him to a new path? Was this a continuation of the same path?

Revelation was replaced with bewilderment. He regained his senses.

William Wells said, "I will think on the words you have spoken. Know that I will not be as Chief Joseph Brant of the Iroquois who, on a given day, has his loyalty pledged to the tribes and to the Americans and to the English. I will declare my intentions and you will know my heart."

On the tenth day, a hard freeze allowed passage over the trails. Wild Carrot did not wait for the arrival of the convoy. He left instructions that if his brothers arrived in Vincennes they should not attempt a hazardous journey to follow him, not to contact him. He would return to Vincennes before the heat of summer. He threw in with eleven warriors of the Wea intent on ascending to Kekionga. He departed with them at dawn.

He needed Sweet Breeze to assure him that his thinking was right. Did he interpret correctly the meaning of Little Turtle's riddle and the instructions given by Primrose while on the Ohio. All the signs indicated it was so, but the idea was too foreign to fully accept.

* * *

Sweet Breeze saw the door open and her husband enter. She tried to smile, but it was faint and full of longing. She laid the suckling baby aside and went to him. She helped him remove his coat. She pressed herself tightly against him, locking both hands behind his neck. She did not look up at him; rather, she buried her face in his chest.

"Take me from this place," she muttered, almost sobbing.

They stood there embracing each other's body, each other's heart. After a time, he held her back with his left hand and raised her chin with his right. He looked into her teary eyes, but she did not look back.

"The people demand so much of me," she sniffed, "They repeat the lies that are told about you by those wicked Shawnee warriors staying at Kekionga."

He tried to reassure her, "I faced them and they fled. They are no longer there. They are not warriors of the Shawnee, only a pack of wolves in search of prey."

"Yesterday a man came across the portage. He said he had seen your scalp on a pole in Detroit. I knew it was not true, but it hurt. Some of the town believed. That hurt more."

A bawl from Pine Bough announced that she was not finished nursing. Father lifted her and returned her to her mother's breast. He undressed and they all lay on the husk mattress. Through the evening and into the night they nudged next to each other and caressed. They rested and talked. Would she follow him to Vincennes? Yes. Beyond the Ohio? Yes. She, too, had seen the signs. He could no longer fight the Americans. Their minds were tugged by the tranquility of Vincennes; what a lovely place to nurture their daughter. To remain passive in the villages on the lower Wabash was not in their nature. The path that the Creator has prepared for them leads even beyond.

If the tribes were able to defeat the invaders in the coming season, it would only be another victory in an eternal war. Even a series of victories would weigh down the Miami nation like a packhorse on the portage that worked long and hard, but eventually gave out. Attrition would diminish the people as surely as a defeat. A single defeat could crush the tribes. The Miami nation could vanish as some of the eastern nations had. Would their people survive as have the Delaware, pushed from land to land? Would they become fragmented like the Shawnee, half moving far to the west, the remnant struggling for survival, suffering the effects of war year upon year? If Little Turtle was killed in battle, would the people remain united or splinter into factions?

Sweet Breeze fixed her eyes upon a beam of light that entered through a crack in the shutters. It brightly shined on the log wall near her head. They had talked the night away. They were now of one mind and one heart.

She forced a cheery voice, "We are agreed upon the path that is before us. It will be a lonely, arduous course. If we are to take it, let us do so cheerfully! Let us proceed with vigor and not look back! To lie here idly or to act timidly would be the way of cowards. A new bed awaits us. Arise, call the town council! I will pack."

By midday the council was gathered. Those attending anticipated hearing words from the war council, perhaps a message directly from Little Turtle. Wild Carrot addressed the council of elders and warrior captains.

He stated, "I must journey far from this place where we sit. No matter what you hear about me, know that the Great Spirit leads me. The Great Spirit will one day lead me back to you. I hope for peace. I hope that one day all may live in the villages of their families. Follow the ways that have been established for this town until the time that Little Turtle may return."

He immediately left the council house and rejoined his wife. They ferried their possessions to the south bank and procured a packhorse at the portage landing. Sweet Breeze resolutely walked up the trail. She did not glance back at the town of her birth. The town of her childhood and youth, the town where she had wed the man beside her was left behind.

* * *

Glorious pink blossoms adorned the crabapple trees in Kekionga. The purplish hue of redbud blossoms was beginning to fade; the bold white of the dogwood was bursting forth. Wild Carrot saw other signs of new life. The villages that had been burned in the Battle of the Pumpkinheads, nearly two and one-half years past, were being repopulated one family at a time. Daily he walked about, encouraging the people, lending a hand here and there. Up the east side of the St. Joseph and down the west he strolled. Twenty-one days, three weeks American, he had waited at the three rivers town while Sweet Breeze and their child went down the Maumee to visit her mother and father. She wanted to have a parting ceremony at Kekionga, a formal, yet simple, departure for when one leaves to join another tribe. Would her parents come? Would they accept their plan for their daughter and him to be among the Americans, to grow in stature with the enemy of the Miami nation, to be in a position to influence a just peace? It was a lonely wait with little to occupy his time.

Crossing to the French Landing, he saw a familiar figure on the wharf. Porcupine had arrived in response to his invitation. He found his adoptive father frail from his bout with the illness that claimed Primrose. The elder chief would not let a feeble body diminish his spirits. He recited past events of French Town as they walked slowly up to the cabin. They stowed his things and laid out his accommodations while reminiscing happy days. They joined the guard camp meal and stayed into the night for storytelling. Wild Carrot was surprised to hear Porcupine relate stories he had never heard: a buffalo stampede leveling Eel Town, a summer without rain when Eel River went dry. He masterfully told of a wondrous journey to Montreal, leaving the warriors spellbound as he rose to part from the light of the fire.

The following morning, Wild Carrot skipped his trek about town. He hosted as Porcupine received visitors. In the afternoon they toured the warehouses and walked to the site of the old French fort. Upon returning, a messenger relayed that Little Turtle would arrive in five days. The ceremony was to be at high sun.

"Four days of fishing for us," Porcupine beamed.

* * *

Two canoes brought Sweet Breeze to the wharf early on the fifth day. She had traveled with her guard of three, plus two of her husband's guard. Only Buffalo Man had remained in Kekionga. The flurry of activity of her arrival, preparations for the ceremony, and preparations for their departure left little occasion for conversation.

"Buffalo Man, here is the last pack," Wild Carrot handed it over. "Is everything arranged?"

"Everything will be waiting at the Wabash end of the portage."

"Good. My wife and I need to be together. Leave a canoe for us and go ahead to the point. We will follow shortly, no guard."

Wild Carrot was dressed in his warrior garb, except with a full head of hair tied back with a dark blue ribbon. Before applying his paints, he looked at the woman who was about to leave the people she loved to be with him on his perilous quest. She wore a pale white dress of doeskin decorated with silver brooches and red with black braided thread chord. She wore the finely worked silver necklace and long earrings. She wore shell combs that she had made while in Vincennes to hold up her hair in the back.

Embracing her, he could not hold back his tears, "I cannot ask you to do this."

"You did not ask. I demanded it. I am ready. Get your fan and we will go."

"Little Turtle understands, and Tulip Leaf?"

"My father sacrifices much for our people, but he says that your sacrifice is greater. If he dies in battle and you live, he will be honored by our people and you can reconcile yourself to the people. If you die in battle and he lives, he will reconcile you to the people. If you both die, he will be honored by the people, but your name will be defiled forever. Therefore, your sacrifice is greater."

"Then, let us all live so that I may return your hand to the hand of your father."

She cooed to the child, "And so that this little one may grow to know his father and grandfather."

* * *

The sun was shining brightly on the gathering on the hill crest. Short green grasses of spring gave a scent of freshness to the air. Eight chiefs of the Miami stood overlooking the confluence. The gathering required neither fire nor tobacco.

Wild Carrot began the proceedings, "Buffalo Man, stand by me!"

The burly warrior trotted up the hillside and joined the chiefs and family.

Wild Carrot spoke as if in council, "All see that Buffalo Man wears a feather presented for his deeds in the battle at the Head of the Wabash."

He removed a feather from his own head and fanned it with his sagamore feather-fan.

He handed it to Sweet Breeze, saying, "I award Buffalo Man with a second feather in honor of the deeds I have seen him perform for the Miami nation."

She carefully tucked it into the embarrassed man's hair.

Wild Carrot removed the polished cherry war club from his belt, "This club I have carried into battle. It was given to me by Chief Little Turtle and was given to him by his father. It has seen only victory! This club I give to Chief Richardville at whose side I defended Kekionga."

The two men exchanged it stoically.

He removed his remaining two feathers and extended them to Little Turtle, "Let it be known that I am no longer a war chief of the Miami."

Little Turtle did not take the feathers, but took Wild Carrot's arm and lowered it. Wild Carrot stepped to his right and handed them to Tulip Leaf.

Sweet Breeze gazed at her mother, her father, then all of the persons gathered. She handed her mother and her father each a basket containing an embroidered sash.

She proclaimed, "My husband and I now leave this tribe to reside in other lands."

They turned and walked down the slope to the waiting canoe. Wild Carrot paused at the water's edge. He washed red and black paint from his face and body. The colors blended into the mixed waters of the St. Joseph and the St. Marys. He pushed off and the two began paddling against the current towards the portage to the Wabash.

CHAPTER 16
Louisville

Experience did not diminish the fear that grew within Sweet Breeze while ferrying across the Ohio. She clutched Pine Bough in the center of the boat. Smelly gruff men nudged the boat through the mighty current. A boatman with tobacco stained whiskers tried to comfort the child, much to the mother's dislike. The ferry caught an eddy near the shore and bucked wildly. Wild Carrot reached to hold fast a crate that teetered near them. The boat swung around hard and hit the pier with a thud. As soon as the men tied off and laid the plank, mother and child dashed ashore.

The American flag flying over Fort Steuben was barely distinguishable in the evening light. William Wells had not stopped at the fort before boarding the ferry. The letter with instructions, signed by Hamtramck, was tucked securely within his pouch. Hamtramck had long since left Vincennes for duties at Fort Washington. He had left the letter in the care of Captain Pasteur who relieved his command of Fort Knox. The letter would ensure employment for Wells at the fort at the head of the falls until Hamtramck issued further orders from Fort Washington. Before reporting, though, he would see to family matters and settle in at Wellsmont. The immediate concern was finding room and board for the night in the town of Louisville.

Taverns ranged from rough and tumble to somewhat refined. They soon found an inn with private accommodations suitable for a gentleman and lady. They welcomed a meal of smoked ham with green beans and plum cake served with coffee and brandy. They spent the evening in their room resting from the extensive journey. Retiring early and sleeping late, they decided to spend the new day shopping for new clothes. They would spend a second night in the town.

William hired a messenger to inform Samuel and Mary of their impending arrival. In the afternoon they purchased trunks to contain the clothes, accessories, and boots, plus gifts for the children. A freight wagon was hired to meet them in the morning. That evening they gorged on beef steaks, sauerkraut, wheat biscuits, and cobbler. They whiled away the evening thinking of an English name for little Pine Bough, settling eventually on "Anne."

Sweet Breeze asked thoughtfully, "William, Anne, what about me?"

Her husband pulled her close and held her, "Sweet Breeze is your essence and Sweet Breeze you will always be. The Americans cannot pronounce it in Miami, but the English saying of it is like a song. Everyone loves your name as much as they love the woman it belongs to."

During breakfast they were approached by the innkeeper, "A slave awaits you out front."

William went out to find a finely dressed servant standing beside a polished black carriage with brass fittings. A matched team of roans was harnessed in black leather and more shiny brass.

The man removed his hat and bowed deeply, "I am to deliver you to Wellsmont. I will be here when you are ready."

A plainly clothed slave boy peeked a toothy smile from around the back of the carriage.

William stammered, "Well, yes, I did not expect it. Yes, I will send down the luggage." He winked at the boy and gave the man a coin, "I will be awhile. Have a meal while you wait."

* * *

Sweet Breeze laughed with gaiety at the rocking and swaying of the carriage. She teased the driver up front and the boy perched on the back.

"Come in here and save me from bouncing into the treetops. Was that a rock or a buffalo we went over?"

She laughed with her husband that only a month ago they were forlorn travelers up to their armpits in the muck of the Wabash portage. Now they were the king and queen of England being whisked away to their palace.

At midday they sat upon a blanket in a clearing beside the river. The servant Joshua produced a basket with a prepared meal. Joshua and the boy tended the resting horses as the young family lounged on the south side of the Ohio.

"I can see why the Virginians want to cross this river. There is a magic pull arousing the spirit," William said, more to himself than to his wife.

"We will have no talk of conflict today. This day is to enjoy."

"Ha! You are sounding like Mary already."

"Let us speak in English the rest of the way, I need more practice."

"I heard many in Louisville whose English is less than yours, people from many countries beyond the sea."

"Indeed, but I need more practice," she repeated with determination.

* * *

They hardly had a foot on the ground when Mary and the children descended from the white porch to greet them at the foot of the steps. Each child vied for the attention of their Indian uncle and their princess aunt. All the while Mary was chattering instructions to everyone and telling the visitors about their room and when to expect supper. Samuel was expected back from Tennessee soon. He had gone in search of horses since they had sold all but their breeding stock to the army. Not a spare horse was to be had in the state of Kentucky. She had really expected him home before now. She apologized for his absence. Colonel Hamtramck had told Samuel to expect their arrival, but had no idea when it would be. She was just glad that they had arrived safely. She would see that they had a chance to recover from their travels. She paused only when she backed into one of their trunks and sat down upon it with a thump. She looked at it and the other two trunks. She looked at their tailored clothing, and wondered.

"We are pleased to be here," the visiting princess responded. "I am sure the room will be fine. After supper we will open that trunk you are sitting on and see what we may find for the children."

Squeals and shouts of glee erupted. William made it up the steps with Margaret, Mary Liz, and little Rebecca dangling from his person. Sweet Breeze carried her Anne in one arm while Sammy hung from the other. Infant Levi scurried up the steps as best he could.

Mary called after the entourage, "There are cakes and tea on the table!"

* * *

Samuel arrived on the third day with a mixed lot of thirty-two horses. "Not the quality nor the number that I had hoped," he told William, "but, with a month in our pasture, plus some grain, they will be in nice shape. General Wayne should be in the Ohio country by then. Horseflesh will be at a premium."

William did not have the eye for horses that his brother had developed from years of breeding and trading. To him, they all looked fine as is.

"That stallion," Samuel pointed with a leather crop, "will never leave this farm. He makes the trip south worth the while."

Samuel verbally evaluated each animal, setting a mental picture of the herd in his mind while educating his brother.

"I would like to stand here all day, but I best be checking that the fields are ready for planting. I expect by the time planting is done I will be attaching my mounted riflemen to Wayne's legion. The expedition will likely last the entire summer. Are you looking to throw in with us?"

"I am to have duties at the fort," the younger brother replied. "I do not expect it to amount to much until I hear further from Hamtramck."

"If one thing under heaven is certain, it is that you have a friend in Hamtramck. He tells that you are the best frontiersman of the Northwest Territory, the best diplomat, the best interpreter. He marvels at how smoothly the peace talks went at Vincennes. He tells how you were the only one able to get in and out of the great gathering of tribes in the north-country. You can wager that he will be telling that to Wayne, too. Your skills will be in demand soon enough. Levy a good wage for them."

They mounted and rode towards the house.

Samuel continued, "Do you know the murky streams of the marsh-country north of Fort Jefferson? They defy the plan of nature and the logic of man by seeming to cross one another. St. Clair's scouts were worthless in that quagmire. They say it gets worse farther to the north. You can wager that old General Wayne will not tromp an army into that ground at the point of a compass. Mad Anthony is a stickler for detail. He will want to know every tree between Cincinnati and Kekionga."

The saying of "Kekionga" made William wince. However, he liked the idea of a general laying meticulous plans. He thought that the American military leaders were too reckless with the lives of their men.

William spoke as if to the wind, "St. Clair's maps deceived him. He was more lost than he knew."

Samuel looked across at his brother and wondered at what was left unsaid.

* * *

All of the strong healthy men of Fort Steuben had been attached to Colonel Hamtramck on his upstream trip. They were replaced by maimed and sickly troops who had been a burden to the growing encampment at Fort Washington. The main activity of the garrison was the passing of rumors about Wayne's actions, and speculation about future actions. It was said that Wayne's flotilla was a sight never seen before in all the time the mighty waters of the Ohio flowed. Shoving off from their winter camp Legionville below Pittsburgh on the thirtieth of April, thirty huge flatboats carried over two thousand soldiers. Eight boats carried horses and oxen, fourteen for artillery and stores, ten loaded with hay. Each boat was assigned a position in the single line that stretched for five miles.

Signaling with flags by day and lanterns by night, they rode the spring waters swiftly. On the sixth of May they reached Cincinnati in the same order they began, traveling the five hundred miles without incident. If it was to be believed, it was an achievement of the highest order. A Pennsylvanian who had fought under Wayne during the revolution predicted that the legion would have a fort built in Kekionga before the sweet corn ripened.

Wells was the only interpreter available to Fort Steuben since every frontiersman who had ever been employed by the army headed for Fort Washington to get in on the action. Lieutenant Hunter, in command of the little fort, expecting no dealings with the Indians, negotiated Wells's duties at three days a week, enough to satisfy orders and agreeable to both parties. William interviewed travelers at the landing for news of any activity by the tribes. He kept informed of the legion news from the soldiers. Weeks passed with him dividing his days between the fort and Wellsmont. Sweet Breeze relished the freedom to nurture her child. She pursued needlework, studied the proceedings in the cookhouse, and rode the countryside with her husband.

The only military action at Fort Steuben was the late June arrival of keelboats carrying five hundred muskets and munitions to the Chickasaw nation. The expedition under Lieutenant William Clark was to descend the Mississippi, slip past the Spanish posts, deliver their goods, then return cross-country to Louisville. In three days the boats of Clark's expedition were below the falls and the stir subsided.

William Clark, being the youngest brother of George Rogers Clark, was well known in Louisville. He had conducted extensive business on behalf of his aging sibling. Wells took an immediate liking to the lieutenant. He recalled seeing him the previous summer during Putnam's portage. He had witnessed the young officer, he did not know him by name then, fending for the needs of the captives.

Two weeks later, a column of mounted riflemen kicked up clouds of dust in the streets of Louisville. Captain Samuel Wells paraded them through a cheering crowd. These were fine men, well mounted, well armed, well uniformed, and disciplined. This was not the rag-tag corps that went off to join St. Clair. Finally, his militia company was off to the Ohio country where Samuel had already visited the splendid Legion of the United States. Wayne was advancing from the valley up to Fort Hamilton. William knew that Hamtramck was leading one of the four sub-legions, Wilkinson another. He was frustrated at not hearing from Hamtramck. The colonel's duties surely were highly demanding, taking his thoughts far from a lowly interpreter at a minor outpost. He feared that the war would pass him by. Still, he waited.

Samuel was even more dejected than William when he and his men returned after only eleven days. They had no sooner crossed the Ohio than they were turned back. The word was that General Knox had ordered the legion back to the river's edge. They could not advance while a peace mission was in Detroit awaiting an impending meeting with the chiefs. Nothing could be ventured that may upset the peace effort. Wayne had gone into a rage at the order to desist. He let it be known to all that he had no doubt that the peace mission would be fruitless. It played into the enemy's hands by assuring delay.

Late in the evening of the fifth day after Samuel's return, Sweet Breeze saw her husband riding briskly up the lane. She had been watching for him from the porch. Not that she was worried about him, but he had routinely returned in the afternoon of his third day at the fort. In his absence she had picked a mess of raspberries and had prepared a special treat for him. He handed the reins to the servant and sprang up the steps in two strides.

He took her hand and said, "Come."

He led her around the house to the orchard.

He held both of her hands, "It is time."

She held her breath expectantly. He knew his mission. What would it be?

"I left the fort this afternoon. When I got out into the river I saw three keelboats heading down, one with the American flag. I returned and met them as they landed. Hamtramck hailed me and said it was good fortune to find me. He took me aside even before going to the fort. That told me that I was his primary business. He confirmed all that we have heard of the grand legion. The delay caused by the peace mission causes grave concern among the officers."

Excitement and apprehension mixed within her chest. Hamtramck was among the highest officers, reporting only to Wayne. He could have sent a messenger. But, no, he had come himself to speak directly to her husband.

"I am to go to Sandusky to spy on the council of chiefs. Wayne wants to know if they entertain overtures of peace, or are they only using the prospect to entice the government in order to affect delay."

They leaned against a low limb of an apple tree, remaining silent for a long while. She had grown accustomed to their carefree sojourn. But, it was for this purpose they had come.

All she could think to say was, "Perhaps the war can be averted."

"I will cross the river tomorrow night. There I will hunt and prepare some fresh skins. I will arrive at the Delaware villages on the White River saying I want to take my skins to Detroit. I will fall in with warriors returning to the Maumee. I will stay at the edges of small villages until I can become close to one who has access to the council."

He envisioned his route and the villages he would encounter. He said, "Hamtramck said to return to Marietta, but I find that way to be too dangerous. I will dash into the Black Swamp and head south directly to the American forts."

"What shall we tell Mary and Samuel?"

"It will be no secret that Hamtramck was at Fort Steuben. They know I have waited for him. Simply say that he calls, and I go."

"Leave in the morning as if for the fort. Circle back to the squatter's shack in the east timber. I will meet you there to cut your hair and help you prepare." She showed him her stained hands. "Look, I will dye your lock." She leaned against him, "I will fear only for your crossing the river at night in a canoe." She tugged his arm, "Come with me. I have your favorite treat."

* * *

At midnight on a warm July night, a lone figure stepped out of a canoe on the north shore of the Ohio and merged silently with the foliage, allowing the canoe to drift free.

Upriver, Wayne drilled his troops with an iron discipline. He built up his materials, forwarding what he could, without contradicting Knox, to the advance posts of Hamilton, St. Clair, and Jefferson.

Far to the north, three peace commissioners waited in Detroit under the protection of the British. When would the chiefs be ready to meet at Sandusky?

Dry heat of August filled the lands. In Louisville, Lieutenant Clark visited with family after a successful mission to the Chickasaw. Samuel Wells drove his herd of horses upriver under protection of an army escort.

Every day Mary Wells commented on the likeness of Anne to Rebecca when she was that age, "I fear that Rebecca is bound to be nothing but a tomboy, and little Anne appears to be her in every way. How the children do love having you here. Your animal stories fill their heads with wonder."

Each day Sweet Breeze rode to the woods with Anne, her little Pine Bough. The dank air of the house could not be healthy for her child. She could not understand how Mary and her family could stay within the house, not wandering further than the porch for days at a time. This day she sat at a favorite venue overlooking a calm beaver pond close by the powerful river. The little stream below the beaver dam created a slot between the trees where she viewed a portion of the big river. Looking at the opposite forest made her wonder about her loved ones far beyond. She held onto her hope that her father would find a way to halt the oncoming clash. Perhaps her husband would connect with the American peace commissioners, interpreting for them, advising them.

She sat upon a fallen log to nurse her child. Her eyes rested upon a beaver going about his work on the dam.

"Old Beaver," she spoke aloud, "I see a trapper plying that big river in a canoe. He will journey far to the west to trap your cousins. Yet, here you keep your home within shouting distance of him. How have you managed to stay and raise your family in this place?"

She looked to her baby for a moment, then back to the animal which sat up and eyed her.

She spoke boldly to the animal, "If I were at the council of chiefs, I would say, 'Behold the beaver. He dams up a little stream. When flood-waters breech what he has made, he repairs the damage and continues his ways. He does not dam the mighty river, for it is too strong to be restrained. It would wash away his every attempt, leaving him without a home. Be wise like the beaver. Know that you cannot resist every flood, or you will be left without a home.' Now back to your work, Old Beaver, I will not harm you nor betray you. I come only to admire your work."

* * *

An express boat arrived at the Cincinnati dock on September eleventh. It came from the new Fort Finney at Pittsburgh. An army courier was ushered immediately to General Wayne. The letter was from the peace commissioners saying that they were returning without ever meeting with the Indians. Wayne unhesitatingly sent a message to Scott to bring up the Kentucky mounted volunteers. He called his officers to assemble. Every passing day he had refined his strategy; now his plan would be put into motion.

While Wayne was reading that letter, Colonel Hamtramck was idly overlooking the northern wall of Fort Jefferson, the northernmost post. He saw an unusual motion at the edge of a clearing.

"What is that?" Hamtramck called to a sentry.

The soldier looked where his commandant pointed, but saw nothing. Suddenly a man, nearly naked, lifted up and stepped a few lumbering strides towards them.

The sentry spotted him with a spyglass just as the man went to his knees, "A man, looks hurt, he is unarmed, sir!"

The colonel called below to send out a rescue party, "Proceed with caution. Do not overdo it. If it is a ruse, do not go chasing off after the scoundrel."

He watched as the man was drug inside the gates of Fort Jefferson without any sign of treachery. The man was muddy and bloody and battered from traipsing through the brush. Apparently he had been pursued for many days.

Hamtramck commanded, "Fix him up and get his story. Let me know if the man knows anything." He puffed his pipe while continuing to eye the woods for signs of hostiles. "See anything?" he asked the sentry.

"Nothing"

"Well, stay alert, something is up."

Shortly, an ensign climbed to the ramparts and addressed the colonel, "The rescued man asks for you. He calls himself Wells."

A tobacco pouch Hamtramck had been twirling caught on the top of the wall. He reached for it, but it fell. Rushing down the steps he turned a heel, nearly falling himself. He dashed into the infirmary.

The man did not wince at the whiskey the surgeon swabbed on his wounds. Welts covered his face and shaved head. The long dark warlock gave no trace of his identity. If the man would open his eyes to reveal the soft blue hue, it would help to identify him.

Hamtramck tentatively asked, "Wells?"

A smile replaced the grimace on the man's face, "I bring greetings from the peace council, Major. Sorry, no wampum this time."

The ensign was about to strike the man's face with the butt of his musket at the insolence to the colonel.

"Hold on, Ensign! Bring him to my quarters," Hamtramck looked around the gathering, "say nothing of this to anyone!"

William Wells related his story between sips of beef broth. Hamtramck wasted no time sending an express rider to Wilkinson at Fort Hamilton. He told of the rejection of peace by the tribes. He requested an escort to be sent up to take the spy down to General Wayne for interrogation.

The escort arrived the following evening. By morning it was headed south with the newly clad spy and a letter from Hamtramck to Wayne. In the lengthy letter, Hamtramck attested to his faith in Wells and his belief of the spy's story.

Colonel Hamtramck called his quartermaster, "Go over the entire inventory again. You do not want to have to explain to General Wayne if you are an ounce short on musket balls."

The quartermaster grasped the meaning. The rumor spread that the full army would soon catch up to them here at Fort Jefferson.

* * *

Military rigor was everywhere in evidence as William Wells was led through Hobson's Choice, the main camp north of Fort Washington and the town of Cincinnati. Such an orderly camp, village, or town, he had never seen, even in Detroit. Like the English, the officers paid as much attention to their uniforms as they did their duties.

"I should be nervous," he thought, "soon to be interrogated by General Washington's counterpart." But, his mind was too full of his recent experience and what he was now seeing. "I will simply tell what I have seen in a straightforward manner, no embellishments. Surely, Wayne has other spies; lay out only what cannot be contradicted."

At headquarters his party was stopped by pickets three times before reaching the general's tent. At the final station a sentry held out his palm to William. Wells unsheathed his knife and laid it into the man's hand, who in turn laid it on a bench.

"Not as intimidating as waiting outside the Grand Council of All Nations at the Auglaize," he thought. "Major General Anthony Wayne could be no sterner than those solemn chiefs."

The flap opened. It was Lieutenant William Clark who motioned him inside. Clark was all business, making no acknowledgement of acquaintance. The large stout general sat behind a table littered with papers. Other officers were standing, except a clerk at a little table to the general's left. Clark joined two junior officers to Wells's left. One he recognized as young Lieutenant William Henry Harrison. Three senior officers stood to his right.

"The spy Wells!" Clark announced while producing a folding camp chair. He sat it in front of the table and indicated for the spy to station himself there. After a little commotion, all were seated. Wells was somewhat surrounded.

"Have you recovered from your time in the wilderness, Mr. Wells?" General Wayne opened.

"A few scrapes do not deter me," he would let the general deduce the double meaning for himself.

"So you made it to Sandusky and back in one piece?"

"Actually, there was no need to travel to Sandusky. The tribes held council at McKee's post." He noticed Wayne glancing around at his officers. He clarified, "McKee's post is at the rapids of the Maumee, on this side of the river, a short way above the new stockade at the head of navigable waters for the big ships, Fort Miamis."

Wayne set his jaw at the mention of the fort. The idea of British soldiers stationed on American soil was a thorn in Wayne's side. His contempt for the British had continually grown throughout his lifetime. He secretly planned to dislodge the British trespassers from Detroit before turning his attention to Kekionga. Tensions between the American government and the British were high. Knox had warned him not to open a general conflict. He also knew that the Canadians were under orders from the crown not to start warfare. However, if the British could pretend to not be aiding the Indians in fighting the Americans, he could pretend his pursuit of the Indians led him to the walls of their fort. He knew that pompous, blustering bluff was the main weapon employed by the British. These things he would keep to himself, declaring Kekionga as his destination.

The general queried, "Did those chiefs meet with the American peace commissioners sent from Detroit?"

"They kept the three Americans waiting in Detroit under a flag of truce. After four weeks they sent a message that as long as there was an American army and American settlements north of the Ohio, there would be no peace council. The commissioners sailed away twenty-four days ago without talking with a single chief. Five days after the departure of the ambassadors, McKee's council broke up. All chiefs headed to the Auglaize, not far distant."

Wells noticed Clark studying his words and nodding to the general as if endorsing the facts. Clark unrolled a large map that covered the table, securing it with metal weights. The lieutenant fixed his eyes on the map, leaning with both hands upon the end of the table. Wells had an innate fascination with maps, studying each he encountered in detail. He recognized this one had the same errors and omissions as St. Clair's. It held only a few minor improvements. As requested, he pointed out the site of Fort Miamis. He identified the location of McKee's post. With cupped hand he indicated the length of the new villages along the Maumee. He verified that "under no conditions" could the British lake ships ascend the Maumee farther than Fort Miamis.

"Was the council unanimous for war?" an officer asked from behind.

"The majority of the tribes wanted to negotiate with the American delegation. The Wyandot, Shawnee, and Delaware spoke against it. Simon Girty sat at the council. McKee, Elliot, and two English officers were at the post. Each day McKee would invite chiefs to visit with him. He would give to them gifts of silver, fine knives, and pistols. Several times the council would resolve to meet the Americans to talk of peace. Each time the English would make promises of food and clothing and weapons. They promised to send soldiers and offered the protection of the fort. They continued building Fort Miamis, making a big show of it; a blockhouse with cannon was completed in my time there. They promised to send more cannon and build another fort on the Auglaize. They said the Spanish would incite the Creek nation and other southern tribes to war, causing the Americans to split their army. The voices of peace waned and grew silent."

Wayne saw that his officers were entranced by the knowledge of the spy. They had been able to only feebly imagine what transpired beyond their own domain.

"How many warriors can they field?" the general asked forcefully.

"When I left, there were nearly two thousand warriors prepared for battle. The number grew by two hundred a week while I was present."

"Which of the tribes will fight?" a tall officer at Wells's right elbow demanded.

"The council has decided for war. They will all fight under Little Turtle. Only those tribes who met with Putnam in Vincennes will refrain. The chiefs who signed will honor the treaty."

"What do they know of our camp?" the officer continued the questioning.

"Everything. They know the number of your men, arms, and cannon. They know all your movements. They know your officers by name," Wells spoke as a matter of fact.

The questioning officer gave a snort to demonstrate his doubt.

"They know how many pigs you slaughter each day," he continued. Looking at Lieutenant Harrison, "They know how many fish you take from the Great Miami when your men drive them into the weir at Fort Hamilton."

Harrison's mouth went agape.

Wayne inquired, "How frequently are the chiefs informed?"

"Runners arrive daily with the latest information."

Wayne leaned forward and pointed at Wells "And how old is the news, how long does it take for a message to relay to the Maumee?"

Wells was surprised at the question. Did the general not know the basic facts?

"A single runner will be given a message at first light at the camp of scouts near Fort Hamilton. Before nightfall he will arrive at the council of chiefs on the Maumee."

The officers looked at each other in amazement. Their messages took days to travel between forts. Could the enemy be as well informed as this man indicated?

Clark asked permission to question.

Granted, he inquired, "After you left the Maumee rapids, by what route did you arrive here? Would not it have been simpler to travel easterly to Marietta?"

"When the council broke up, the camps headed west up the Maumee. I fell in with a band of Delaware planning to return through their villages on the White River to the Falls of the Ohio. I was recognized by a Shawnee who was with them returning to the village of his Delaware wife. He sounded the alarm. I made my escape to the south, gaining the Black Swamp with a hot pursuit. Once within the swamp I shunned the trails, concealing myself for days at a time between jaunts. Once I had traveled the entire length of the swamp, I circled west evading the favorite camps of the warriors watching the forts."

Wells was partially standing, hunched over the map gesturing.

His response turned to answering the second question, "The Scioto and the Muskingum country is covered with bands of roving Wyandot and Shawnee that cut off any travelers."

"So you know the country north of Fort Jefferson?" Wayne asked with piqued interest. "You know the streams and paths of the marshlands? Our scouts cannot make head nor tail of the region. There is not a soul who can guide us with any certainty. St. Clair merely followed a compass to end up on the St. Marys."

In an instant William Wells drew a dagger with his left hand, flashed it under the nose of the general, and slammed it into the desk, pinning the map to the planks.

"The Wabash!" Wells shouted.

Everyone leaned back in their chairs, nearly tumbling, save Clark who seized Well's left arm and pressed close to him.

Again he shouted, "Little Turtle's victory was on the Wabash!"

The officers recovered from their surprise and bolted forward to grasp the assailant.

Wayne, standing, raised his hand. "Hold on!" he told his men. Looking Wells in the eye, "Explain yourself!"

"St. Clair's report that the site of the battle was on the St. Marys is in error. Your map is marked wrong. It is here," he pointed to the tip of his dagger piercing the headwaters of the Wabash, "that General Butler died. This is where the rout began."

Wayne looked around the gathering and settled his eyes on Harrison. Harrison had been stationed at Fort Jefferson when General Wilkinson set out to inspect the battlefield the winter before last. He had no answer to divert the General's gaze. Wayne tugged on the map, rent it in two and threw half on the floor.

"I will not take my legion into an unknown wilderness!" he raged.

Pointing to Clark and Harrison, he bellowed, "You two lock yourselves inside a cabin with this man until you can produce a map that is worthy of our government's trust!" Regaining his composure, he calmly pulled the dagger loose and handed it to Wells, "That is all. General Posey, you will remain."

Outside, Wells stood alone while Clark and Harrison conferred. They did not know how literal to take their instructions, but dared not inquire.

After assigning a squad to guard Wells "confined within the bounds of the first and second pickets", they promptly set out to locate a cabin suitable for their work.

* * *

Lieutenant William Clark placed a smooth broad board upon the dirt floor. From a box of carved cherry wood he produced drawing instruments. Next, he laid out two pieces of the army's map, aligning north on the map with his compass. Three men surrounded the maps on their knees.

"Are there any faults with the main rivers?" Clark asked. "We will begin with the larger and work to the smaller."

William Wells answered quickly, "The Illinois lays too far north. The river called Chicago is absent. It is not large, but it is important. The St. Josephs of the Lake is too short and the St. Joseph of the Maumee is too long. The Tippecanoe and the Eel are indistinguishably confused. The Forks of the Wabash should be farther east, the north branch not so long and nearer to the St. Marys. The Salamonie is absent between the south fork of the Wabash and the Mississinewa. This northern tributary between the forks and the Eel does not exist."

Clark sat back on his haunches in bewilderment. He wanted to believe the frontiersman, but he found it difficult not to trust what he saw on paper.

Lieutenant William Henry Harrison offered a new approach, "Show us the trail of General St. Clair. Show us how he became confused about the location of the defeat of his army. Show us Harmar's trail. He arrived successfully at Kekionga, though his effect was wanting. Start at Fort Jefferson and work us through the creeks. We will expand out from Fort Jefferson one stream at a time."

Wells did not look at the map. He held his left hand in front of his face, palm out, fingers apart. His thumb was pointed mostly downward.

"A traveler who follows a compass north from the mouth of the Great Miami River, where it gives its waters to the river Ohio, will cross the beginnings of five rivers near Fort Jefferson. The first is the White River," he wiggled his thumb, "that begins northerly then loops west and south through the villages that are recently settled by the Delaware. This river continues a long journey until it comes near Vincennes, joining the Wabash below that town. Next is the Mississinewa," he wiggled his index finger, "then the Salamonie, both flowing north and west to join the Wabash. Next the river Wabash itself twists and turns every direction, eventually settling north and west. Finally, the St. Marys begins northerly then parallels the previous three on its journey to Kekionga. If St. Clair's scouts did not account for the absent Salamonie, then they would call the Salamonie the Wabash and the Wabash would be called the St. Marys."

Clark hastily sketched all that was described. Wells nodded approvingly, but indicated the reach of the St. Marys to be farther east and south.

"Where is Fort Jefferson?" Clark asked.

Penciling its position he inquired further, "What else in this area?"

"Two small branches of the Great Miami rise near the Mississinewa. They flow eastward across the path between Fort Jefferson and the battlefield on the Wabash. Another branch of the Great Miami begins south of the start of the St. Marys. To the north, three fingers of the Auglaize reach out to near the St. Marys."

"Like so?"

"Move that one closer to the St. Marys, that one a bit to the north."

Clark, realizing the importance of his work, was meticulous with the refinements. Harrison paced the room glancing at the paper from time to time. He beheld seven rivers originating from within one pocket of land, all draining the same marshy countryside. Some of the fingers drained southward towards their cabin. Some drained westward to the Wabash, others northward to the Maumee. Finally satisfied, Clark made a copy in ink for himself and one for Wayne.

"It is late," remarked Harrison. "Tomorrow I will go over this map with Wayne while you two draw up the territory from here to Kekionga, and to the British Fort Miamis."

The three Williams ate, bunked, and shared stories together within the cabin. Harrison was a descendant of notable Virginia planters who had served the king in various positions. His father had sided with the revolution, became president of the Continental Congress, and signed the Declaration of Independence. Their property was decimated by Tories during the war of revolution. Upon the death of his father, William Harrison left his medical studies in Philadelphia and joined the army. Having an insatiable thirst for knowledge, Harrison constantly questioned Clark and Wells on the ways of the west.

Clark's family, too, was from Virginia. His famous older brother was the ultimate frontiersman to the admiring younger brother. William practiced surveying and some law in Virginia, then came west to assist his brother with his muddled business affairs.

Through his sister Lucy in Louisville, he had heard the story of the Wells family who also originated from Virginia. That family headed west to claim land awarded for military service, the mother dying in Pennsylvania, the father being killed by Miami raiders east of Louisville.

Clark was well acquainted with Samuel and Cartey Wells.

William Wells limited his stories to events of his youth among the tribes. Upon Harrison's questioning, he presented the differences and likeness of the various tribes. He described the land, the trees, the animals and birds, all the wonders of nature he had experienced.

When they finished with the rivers and streams on the larger map, they went about placing a name on each. All were known by various tribal names; the Maumee alone was referred to by six well-established phrasings. Available maps employed mostly French wording. Wayne wanted to establish simple English names to avoid confusion in issuing orders. The many replications of "Miami" and "St. Joseph" had to be pared down.

Clark spread out his copy of the larger map, "Indicate the route of Harmar and I will draw it in."

Wells traced the path along the Great Miami River to Loramie's post then west to the St. Marys.

"He followed the south bank for half its length, then crossed, taking a direct path to Kekionga. This is it as I have been told by witnesses."

"That is fairly well the way I remember it," Clark offered while finishing his sketch.

Wells soaked in the thought.

"You were with Harmar?" Harrison wondered aloud.

"It was my first engagement in uniform. Still wet behind the ears, was I. We were to be the reserves, expecting to follow up Wylles. We ended up standing our ground to cover the retreat. We lost many a good man that day."

Clark abruptly cut off his remarks. Harrison wanted to know more about this experience, but would leave it be for now. Wells thought it best not to offer his knowledge of the action at Pumpkinheads.

"Harmar's trail," Harrison inquired, "is the preferred route for the legion?"

"I would not recommend it," came Wells's reply. "There is too much low ground. The feet of an army this size would chop the path into pudding. The horses and wagons could not get through. If they could, the column would stretch out single file for twenty miles. They could not group if attacked. There is no easy way. If you want to keep your cannon and you want steady supplies, then turn east from St. Clair's battle and build a log road through the swamps to the Auglaize. Follow it to the Maumee and up to Kekionga."

Clark recalled his trip into the wilderness three years earlier. He concurred, "Even in the dry season the trail was but a narrow causeway through a series of marshes. It would never hold up to the traffic."

Wells waved his hand across the region on the map, "There is no hospitable place for a heavy army between Fort Jefferson and any locale on the Maumee."

For five days William Wells had not been more than ten strides from the cabin. The afternoon heat forced him outside. No shade, no breeze, the dusty air of the valley was still preferred to the stifling heat inside. The summer had lingered through most of September, refusing to give way to autumn. Harrison had taken what they hoped to be the final revision of the maps to General Wayne. Clark had found an excuse to go down to the boats where it was likely to be cooler.

Wells was thinking of the pawpaws and grapes of the forest that should be ripe for picking. He thought of the fine meals that Sweet Breeze must be enjoying; he wondered if she had added any new foods to Mary's table. If the general gave his nod to the conclusion of their project, he would request to first be allowed time to visit his wife, then be assigned to Hamtramck.

Clark appeared. He carried a melon which he shared with Wells.

"No cooler by the docks," Clark reported. "From what I can see, we will be moving north within a week."

Harrison quickly strode to their station. He saw the last chunk of melon disappear. The two melon-eaters read his smile to mean the general was satisfied with their work.

"You, sir," Harrison spoke to Wells, "are to have a captain's commission, Chief of Spies!"

CHAPTER 17
Fort Jefferson

Cool sweet water from the trickling spring washed the dust from his throat. He moistened his scarf and wiped his face. The trees were hinting of an autumn hue, yet the heat held on. William Wells, Captain of Spies of the Legion of the Unites States, looked up at the cannon of Fort Jefferson on the hill above. To any onlooker, whether fort soldier or hidden scout of the tribes, he appeared no different than any drover of the newly arrived supply caravan. Yet this drover carried within his pouch orders written by none other than Major General Anthony Wayne.

Wayne's orders were read and reread by Lieutenant Colonel John Francis Hamtramck somewhat in disbelief. Hamtramck had requested Wells to be assigned to him as a scout. The orders stated clearly that Wells was to be under the command of none of the four sub-legions, but to report only to Wayne's headquarters. Wells was to head a contingent of scouts that he would be shortly assembling at Fort Jefferson. He was to distribute scouts to each of the sub-legions, direct a party of scouts to determine route alternatives, and to form a small group of elite spies to penetrate enemy camps. Hamtramck was left to wonder how Wells had gained the confidence of the general in such short order.

An express dispatch had been received two days earlier by Hamtramck. Wayne informed him that the full army would be under way within a week, and, barring severe weather, should arrive at Fort Jefferson by the fourteenth of October. General Scott's mounted Kentucky volunteers had been called and should catch up to the army soon after the fourteenth. Hamtramck was unsure as to whether he was to remain in command of the fort, or return south to bring up his sub-legion. He determined that maintaining the fort was essential to the over-all operation, and decided to stay until the march reached his position.

An exterior blockhouse had recently been erected overlooking the

241

corral. Hamtramck provided the lower room of this structure for Captain William Wells to direct his operations. Tents were situated close behind the blockhouse in a manner to conceal the scouts' activities. Wells inquired of Hamtramck his opinion of the current corps of scouts.

"Worthless", "dregs of the frontier", "lying braggarts", "riff-raff" dotted his pronouncement. "You will have your hands full with that lot."

The scouts began arriving by ones and twos with their secret orders. Each was quizzed by Wells in detail. He spoke only in Shawnee or Delaware as long as the woodsmen could follow. He interrogated them on their knowledge of villages, chiefs, streams, and landmarks. Those who were weak in the languages and those who were bent on revenge, plunder, or taking scalps were assigned to the four sub-legions where they could be held in check. From those who were more successful in the interview, he formed a band of six advance scouts to reconnoiter to the east, and a second band of six to the north and west. Nicholas Miller, who had lived among the Shawnee, and William May, an audacious frontiersman of the Ohio country, were to accompany Wells on daring forays as spies. To this last group he added Robert McClellan, a drover with the pack trains renown for exceptional athletic ability.

Initially, Wells, Miller, and May each led the advance scouts, two at a time, on initiation missions into the country to the north. Cool evenings signaled the end of the extended heat. Days were passing quickly when it was learned that the army would reach Fort Jefferson two days ahead of schedule. Wells dispersed his scouts to their assigned positions, then rode south to find Wayne encamped on a rise of dry ground north of Fort St. Clair. He advised the general that there was no concentration of the enemy within the vicinity as far north as the St. Marys River. Miller and May kept in contact with the advance scouts while Wells and McClellan returned to the Fort Jefferson blockhouse.

The following day, the army proceeded directly past Fort Jefferson without so much as a pause. The sub-legions moved in parallel columns nearly three miles in length. Each sub-legion was a fully equipped army with infantry, mounted riflemen, artillery, and mounted dragoons. Each sub-legion was designated by the color of its banners. Matching color trim highlighted splendid uniforms.

The orderly march terminated mid-afternoon in an orderly camp six miles beyond the fort. Ax-men felled trees all around. A temporary palisade, four logs high, secured the camp as it had each previous night. Bastions at each corner for cannon and outer breastworks for sentries

were engineered to repel any possible attack. Safe within their little for-
tification, the men turned their attention to pitching tents and preparing
meals.

Wells marveled at the efficiency of the movement of men and materials. He could only compare it to British seamen setting sail to leave
Detroit, but with the number of men many times over. Harrison and
Clark had belittled the general's constant drilling of the men. All now
witnessed the fruits of the training.

Wayne halted here to wait on the Kentucky volunteers. The night-
camp evolved into Grand Camp. The camp was on the edge of a large
prairie that could sustain the animals. The improved road reaching to the
Ohio River could supply the army.

* * *

Wells sent spies ahead to penetrate the enemy camps to ascertain
their intent. Slipping in and out of the camps and villages, they concluded that the tribes would not mount an attack until spring unless Wayne
advanced as far as the St. Marys. The tribes would continue to pester the
supply convoys, foraging parties, scouts, and settlers. Indeed, Little Otter
of the Ottawa returned to the Maumee with over fifty horses and eleven
prisoners and as many scalps from a raid near Fort St. Clair.

William Wells entered headquarters to make his report to General
Wayne. He met Lieutenant William Henry Harrison who was coming
out clutching a courier pouch.

"The Kentuckians will be here today," Wayne's aide hurriedly
informed. "They will form at an island of woods on the prairie west of
here, nine hundred in all."

"Is Captain Samuel Wells among them?" William Wells asked.

"I will have a full report tomorrow. General Scott is bringing up his
whole force, so I expect your brother will be in the mix."

"When I have finished here, I will ride out on the prairie and welcome the lot."

After concluding his report to the general, William Wells rode out to
inspect the location designated "Island Camp." A swift deep creek, flowing easterly through flat open prairie, reached to the main channel of the
Great Miami River many miles to the east. An oblong patch of hard-
woods did indeed appear as an island within a sea of grass. He thought
back to his youth when, at this time of year, men and boys would set the

grasses aflame. Great arcs of red would march across the prairie under billows of gray smoke. Tree seedlings and brush indicated that this grassland had not been burned for several years. Tribes occupied by war had not tended the grazing areas which nourished deer, elk, and buffalo. The tribes could burn it this season to deprive the army of fodder. But the benefits would be short since the following spring, and the next, the ashes would nourish waves of sweet grasses.

Shouts and rattling announced the arrival of the Kentucky horsemen. They broke free of the timber and galloped out onto the plain, straight into a blustery north wind. Noisily they crossed the hard dry ground, each man bracing against the wind. They approached William's position, easing up when they caught the lee of the island of woods. The Kentucky general rode directly to William. Wells for the first time saw the face of the man who had destroyed the Ouiatenon towns and the villages of the lower Wabash.

"A beautiful site for a camp," General Scott roared. "Almost as good as Kentucky!"

He wheeled and immediately began issuing orders. After the men saw to the needs of their horses, the camp began taking shape. William observed that they formed irregular groups of circles rather than the rows and columns of Wayne's rigid camp. The men tended to tents and saddles. Soon they began heading for the trees to collect wood. A lone officer strode directly towards William.

The stride was that of Samuel, "Ho! Brother William!"

William slid to the ground and led his horse forward, "Welcome to the war, Samuel!"

The two did not embrace, but held out tokens to each other. William presented a newly carved walnut pipe and Samuel a plug of his best tobacco. The older brother stretched his body and indicated that a walk was in order. Samuel lead easterly, somewhat parallel to the woods.

Samuel said, "Mary received your letter. She shared what news there was with Sweet Breeze."

William took a few steps while thinking about his wife residing in a land foreign to her. Samuel was accustomed to writing long letters to Mary while out on campaigns. Miami women did not expect to hear directly from their men who were off to war. Thinking of home and family was thought to be a weakness in a warrior. Of course, Sweet Breeze could not read a letter written in any language.

William apologized, "I could not tell more than that I had returned from the Maumee and had additional business with the army."

Samuel asked, "Why the big secret? Could you not get away for even a few days?"

"I wished to visit Wellsmont after my reception at Fort Washington, but it was not to be. It is secret. It must not get out. I am Chief of Spies for Wayne. I report to him."

Samuel stopped and looked his younger brother up and down. For the first time in his life he was at a loss for words. He thought the mission to Sandusky was foolhardy, but this was beyond comprehension. Armies based their designs upon mutual support. Spies were, by definition, beyond support. The slightest misstep was an invitation for death.

Samuel asked, "Are you certain you want to do this?"

William looked his older brother in the eyes, "All my life the Lord has prepared me for this, at this place, at this time."

As Wild Carrot speaking to Little Turtle, he may have said, "The Creator has laid a straight path for me that I must follow." He had learned in the cabin with Harrison and Clark that if he used "Lord" in place of "Creator" and avoided reference to "his path," that his meaning was better received. He felt comfortable saying this for even Heckewelder, the most reverent man he knew, made no distinction between the "Lord" of the Christians and the "Creator" of the tribes. The missionary did maintain a separation, not understood fully by William, between "Jesus" and "Great Spirit." He also insisted, as did the French priests, in baptism.

Sweet Breeze had discovered the same in her stay at Wellsmont. Since she had duly separated from the Miami nation, she viewed baptism as a ritual of joining her new community. Substituting a few words did not change her view of the world, or her understanding of the Lord God, Creator of All Things. The singing at the worship services continued to seem strange, often sad, but the experience of women praying more earnestly than men emboldened her. Besides, Mary was overjoyed at seeing her sister-in-law baptized, and all the community doted on her.

Samuel placed his right hand on William's shoulder. "It is a good man who knows his duty on this earth and is willing to see it through."

They resumed their walk silently. They diverted to plucking straws and lighting their pipes from a new campfire.

Samuel again stretched, then strode on, "What if you meet with one of your Miami friends? With Little Turtle even?"

"Until there is a truce, the whole countryside is a battlefield. On a battlefield there is only the side you have taken and the enemy. Miami warriors understand this as clearly as do you. They would expect to kill or be killed. There remains opportunity for peace, but if there is to be battle, I hope it to be swift and decisive."

Samuel pondered that his brother did not say for whom victory should reign.

The second morning after the arrival of the Kentucky volunteers, Wayne sent out a troop on a swift recognizance of the frontier. Eighty mounted riflemen of the regulars were under the command of Major William McMahon, a trusted officer with experience on the Pennsylvania frontier. They were joined by a select group of sixty Kentuckians under Captain Simon Kenton. Both officers had notable experience in the Indian campaigns. Both officers were hoping to be in the opening engagement of this campaign. The spies led them through the tangle of marshes and gained the Auglaize without seeing any of the enemy. As they descended the Auglaize, signs were clear that there were villages ahead. Kenton and McMahon were discussing an assault directly into the villages. Wells the Spy, as he had become known to differentiate him from Captain Wells of the militia, halted the column. He advised the officers that these were not isolated villages, but rather encampments holding more than two thousand warriors.

Detecting doubt, he simply said, "Leave your men here. Follow me."

Wells the Spy and William May left Nicholas Miller behind. They led the two Indian-fighters, now officers, on a circuitous route to the left. Eventually they settled on the left bank of a run that in time led them to an overlook of the Maumee. Major McMahon and Captain Kenton were dumbfounded at what they saw. The "village" covered the far bank of the river as far as they could see, both upstream and down.

"It goes on like that for miles," Wells said as a matter-of-fact. "Not far to our right it covers this side, too, and up the Auglaize to within three miles of where your men wait."

A withdrawal was decided to be in order. A large sweep to the west through the Black Swamp came up empty. Under the first snow of the season, they returned to their respective camps. Wells the Spy was certain that Wayne would get his verification of the conditions north of his position.

On the last day of October, Wayne sought the advice of his lead officers in a council of war. The question was posed: Was the legion in a position to advance on the enemy yet this season? The one favorable point was that lower water levels during the late autumn season would provide solid footing for man and beast. Concerns were: forage for horses was inadequate; the possibility of entrapment in a winter snowstorm; the wanting for necessary supplies to sustain the army at a longer distance from their base on the Ohio. Arguments for the negative carried the day. Wayne kicked at a chair and sent it flying into a wall of the tent. Its rebound struck Hamtramck in the back of the leg.

"Pardon me, gentlemen," he growled. "I have no qualms with you. You each have shown good prudence. It is those blasted peace commissioners, and those who sent them, that delayed our movements. Had I been given full authority, we could have been in possession of our objective by now." He viewed all in the tent nodding in agreement, "Here is our position." He laid a copper weight upon the map, "It will do no good to linger on what could have been. You and your men have performed admirably to get us here. We shall look forward, hunker for winter, prepare for spring."

Wells kept his thoughts to himself. His mind was telling him that the chiefs to the north were hoping the general would disregard caution and plunge ahead in eagerness. Overlooking any one of the officers' cautionary statements could snarl the army and provide the tribes with sudden advantage.

Wayne immediately ordered the erection of a huge fortress facing the creek to their front. The dragoons and mounted volunteers would be returned to Kentucky for the winter. Wells the Spy was assigned to direct Scott's men south and west to sweep away any encampments of warriors between Fort Jefferson and Fort Steuben at the Falls of the Ohio. William Wells could have one week in Louisville. He was to return thereafter to the new fort location at Grand Camp.

* * *

Metea tugged on another grapevine and freed it from the branches overhead. He chopped it loose with his tomahawk and dragged it, and others he had cut, to the little camp. He covered the twin shelters with the vines, not so much for protection from the elements, but to conceal the low lean-to coverings. Nearby were three trails that crossed at the forks of the upper Muscatatuck. He and his companions stayed close where they could observe any traffic by trail or by stream.

His trusted band of five Pottawatomie warriors had left the mouth of the Great Miami River three days previous. There they had spent a moon watching traffic on the Ohio. They reported events to Chief Sturgeon who, with a force of forty warriors, was harassing Fort Hamilton and the settlers about Cincinnati. When Chief Sturgeon headed north to the Maumee, Metea and his friends were released from their spying duties. They determined to return home west of the Tippecanoe. They first rode west. They planned to swing by the salt licks to procure salt and buffalo robes for the winter.

They were waylaid when Red Sky was pounced upon by two panthers. His face and shoulder were mangled. Raw muscle was exposed from his neck to his elbow. His right ear was gone. Tiosa rescued him by charging his horse into that of Red Sky. He struck one of the panthers with his musket barrel. He managed to fire at the fleeing panthers, but they were gone in a flash. Moans arose from the shelter as Tiosa and Metea draped the last of their vines onto the roof.

Metea called inside to Corn Tassel, "Has there been any improvement?"

"There is now only a trickle of bleeding," came the reply. If I had more thread I could get it stopped. It may be several days until Red Sky can continue the journey. Can you bring some more mosses?"

Tiosa nodded and scurried off. Metea looked about. Perhaps they were too close to the trails. They could have used the cave just up the south fork, but surely it was known to the Virginians. Aubbeenaubbee had secreted the horses east to the hills between the stream's forks. Red Sky's favorite horse was lame with a patch of flesh gone from its rump. They had several extra horses absconded from the Americans. Though of poor quality, they would do for carrying them and their wares home. Since they could not advance, Metea wished to use the days to continue spying duties.

Swiftly, but stealthily, Swan approached the camp, "My Chief, something is not right."

Metea gave Swan his full attention. The warrior had been assigned the duty of watching the trails. He would not have left if he had not deemed it important.

"How so?" Metea asked.

"The animals have been rushing past from the north and the east as though fleeing before a prairie fire. Now the birds have taken wing. I think riders are approaching."

The two men quickly returned to where the trail crossed the south fork and dissolved into the rushes. They barely had concealed themselves when they heard horses splashing across the north fork. Four horsemen came crashing two abreast through the branches into the waters of the south fork. The riders pulled up nearly on top of the crouching Pottawatomie. The horsemen relaxed their reins to allow their horses to drink. The two in front, each with fiery red hair, searched the woods with penetrating eyes. The two in the rear raised their canteens. Metea could see only parts of the action. Each pair had a uniformed man on the right and a man in buckskin nearer on the left.

The buckskinned man in the rear dismounted and filled his canteen with cold flowing water.

"Anyone else for water?" he called to his companions.

Having no takers, he returned to his saddle. He removed his hat freeing long wavy white hair. Metea tensed. He recognized this man. It was Simon Kenton! He should have rushed ahead wielding knife in hand when Kenton was in the water. His life for that of the notorious raider! The opportunity had passed. Perhaps another would be offered.

"These creeks form the Muscatatuck. Here would make a good camp for tonight," the lead scout told the red-haired officer.

Metea knew the voice, and then knew the man. It was Wild Carrot who he had followed into battle. His comrade-in-arms was with these invaders!

"Well, Brother William," the officer replied, "We will wait here until the column comes up."

Metea understood the language enough to know that meant there were more horsemen behind. He wanted to signal Swan to contain his impulses, but could not see him. For a moment he wondered if Swan had been trampled under the horses. His thoughts were cut short by the thundering of hooves and crashing of water. A large man in the fancy uniform of a leading officer pulled up behind the scouts. Metea instantly recognized General Scott, a man he had spied on many times.

"Lead on men!" the general shouted with a ring of joy. "I promised the boys we would make Clark's Grant tomorrow. Several of them have land there they want to look over before we make the falls."

"I do not like this pace," Kenton protested. "I have a patch of ground there myself from my service with Clark. But what is to keep us from running headlong into a force of Delaware?"

Scott urged, "Do you really expect to see any sizeable force this far south? The Delaware are all with the gathered tribes up north on the Maumee. Am I right, Wells?"

"With Little Turtle, expect the unexpected," the scout replied calmly.

The general quietly pondered the rebuff. He took a swig from his canteen, "Lead on. We will take advantage of the daylight we have left."

Nearly three hundred armed men forded the stream past the concealed Pottawatomie. They were followed by a drove of as many spare horses that passed on both sides of the spies. Five horsemen brought up the rear. The herd faded into the forest. The two men dragged themselves to the rocks. They looked at each other, then both burst into uncontrolled laughter.

Tiosa came at a run, "We shall raid a hundred horses tonight!"

"No," Metea instructed. "You and Aubbeenaubbee and I will immediately head for Kekionga and on to the council house at the Auglaize. The others will see Red Sky safely home. Now go, we must begin immediately. I have much to tell Little Turtle."

* * *

The cannon of Fort Steuben fired salutes as the column crested the hill overlooking the fort. A rider had been sent ahead to ensure that a proper ceremony greeted the returning heroes. The column, four abreast, descended slowly behind General Scott and the flags of the United States and of the Kentucky Militia. William Wells had fallen out of line and sat upon his mount atop a knob to the right. His little promontory provided a clear view of the fort, the village of Clarksville, the Ohio River, and the town of Louisville beyond.

The menacing, powerful, unrelenting waters of the Ohio did not seem so haunting from this vantage. Instead, the river appeared placid and serene. The sun, shining through a fog slowly rising from the liquid surface, provided a mystical enchantment. That silvery ribbon separated him from Sweet Breeze and their daughter. On scores of maps, lines trace its route between Virginia and the Indian lands, now between the State of Kentucky and the Northwest Territory. The French, the Spanish, the English, the Americans, and all the tribes recognized this demarcation as though the Creator had placed it as a division between two entities. Soon he would witness what all the people of the tribes hoped to see: enemy soldiers crossing to the south. What if their crossing was permanent? What if the war was canceled? What if the Americans all withdrew from the lands of the tribes, and the English returned to Canada? Sweet Breeze and he could return to their beloved Eel River lands. A new generation could live undisturbed. He envisioned the soldiers abandoning their fort, torching it as they left. He imagined streams of settlers joining the townspeople of Clarksville to be ferried to the American side. Chiefs would erect three white poles on this knoll proclaiming peace to all. Prosperity would reign on both banks as hatred was supplanted by harmony.

Fifes and drums from the fort signaled the end of his fantasy. The illusions were replaced with the knowledge that General Wayne was firmly planted midway between Cincinnati and Kekionga.

He looked to see Samuel galloping his way. Days spent with Samuel had kindled a kinship within William that he had never before experienced. There was something to this "blood thicker than water," as his brother often quoted. He did not understand it fully, but it was real. It held fast to his being. Porcupine and Little Turtle were his mentors. Buffalo Man, Metea, and others were comrades. Sweet Breeze was his lover and soul mate, intimate beyond comprehension. With his newfound brother there was a deep bond of trust, unique in understanding, that transcended place and time.

Samuel rode up with a boyish grin, "Ride beside me through the streets of Louisville. There is sure to be a grand parade!"

He beckoned William to follow.

"Thank you, but, no. It is your town and your people. I will not cross with the army, but will cross over this evening when the ruckus has subsided. My position requires that I remain in the shadows for now."

"Very well, Brother William. One day I will see that you get your due reward!"

"Very well, Brother Samuel."

CHAPTER 18
Greene Ville

The infant did not wince at the coldness of the water. She only stared at the lean pale face of the man with the booming voice. The man was pouring the water over her head. He held her head back and down to allow the icy liquid to be caught in a porcelain basin.

The voice proclaimed, "Anne Wells, I baptize you in the name of the Father, in the name of the Son, in the name of the Holy Ghost. May Christ pour out his blessings upon you as you grow in his care." A course hand wiped across her face and wrung her hair. Strong hands lifted her high as if reaching to the heavens. "I charge the family of this child to nurture her in the ways of our faith, amen."

The pastor turned and faced his congregation. He held the child for his flock to admire. He looked at Sweet Breeze and then at William Wells. He held Anne firmly as if contemplating not giving her back to her parents. The mother he had baptized; the father he suspected of being a heathen.

The child's aunt Mary wished the pastor would hurry up a bit. The blanket she had knitted for her niece lay on the board floor against the boot of the clumsy clergyman. She did want the gathering to see the delicate white baptismal gown that she had made for her Rachael. However, the gown loaned to her niece would not keep the child warm in this unheated church. She had warmed the child in front of the fire while her parents were dressing this morning. She had worried all night that Anne would catch her death of cold in the night air and not be able to be at church today. Perhaps Easter would have been a better time for the event.

Sweet Breeze had been insistent that the night of William's return would be spent by the three of them at her lean-to. She built the little shelter at the overlook high on the hill where they spent much of their time on their first visit to Wellsmont. Here she took Anne, her little Pine

253

Bough, to tell stories of the girl's father, of her grandfather and others who were living among the Miami. Sweet Breeze had fashioned a bed of buffalo robes and blankets. She had built a stone-lined fire pit to warm meals and to drive away the damp air. Mary's protests did not deter her despite the prospects of a stormy night.

Sweet Breeze stood and stepped the four steps to the rail. She picked up the gift blanket and shook it. She slid an arm under her daughter.

"Thank you, Reverend," Sweet Breeze said. "We will see that she receives the proper instruction."

Anne was kicking and squealing with glee as her mother wrapped her and held her tightly. Sweet Breeze proudly placed the child in the arms of her husband. The pastor invited the congregation to stand. He instructed them on a song to sing to consecrate the event. The child's mother did not hear the song; she was transfixed upon her child and her husband. She knew that William was self-conscious at wearing his military uniform, but he did look quite dignified. She was glad that she had joined Samuel and Mary in encouraging it.

The Sunday's service came to a close with Samuel reminding everyone that a feast awaited in his barn. He was assured of good attendance since the entire community was eager to hear tales of the militia's expedition into the wilderness. With the crowd nearly dispersed, the pastor directed William to the pulpit to sign the baptismal registry for his daughter and wife.

Sweet Breeze leaned in, "I will sign for myself. Show me where."

A smile crept over William's face as he, for the first time, witnessed his wife stroke her name. She gave a smile. A wink was returned.

* * *

"Five days!" Samuel retorted using exaggerated gestures. "Wayne can do without Scott and me for the winter. He sent away his own mounted corps. He let General Posey off to pursue business in Philadelphia, and Hamtramck off to Vincennes. I will wager that Mad Anthony wishes to see Wilkinson go away, maybe to France. But, my little brother only gets five days. Now I ask you, who is important to this campaign? Certainly it is not me. William has not been home long enough to see his baby girl wiggle her toes. But, Wayne calls, and you best not keep that man waiting!"

Sweet Breeze forced a laugh at the little show. Samuel had a way of summing up with a joke or story things he would not say directly. Wild Carrot, William, always seemed to be pulled to the center of important endeavors. Like her father, events cannot unfold without him. It is futile for her to resist; the course left is to encourage.

She had not inquired about the war, about his responsibilities. He deserved a respite, and she had seen to it. He would take with him the joy of playing with Pine Bough and with Mary's children. She provided her husband with his favorite foods, her stories of the animals, time with her. He would carry with him these things and a pouch of her tea blend.

Sweet Breeze stood beside the horse that would carry her husband away, "I wish Pine Bough to learn the English tongue, to read books and write words on paper. I wish her to be free of the hunger and sickness our people have known. I do not want her to be driven from one village to another by war. I do not want her to grow old in her youth."

He was surprised at the earnestness of this saying. "I understand," he softly replied, "She is no longer Pine Bough. Wherever she goes, 'Anne Wells' she will always be. Only, do not hide her pretty face under a bonnet and her arms under long sleeves like Mary's children. Her skin needs to greet the sun so one day she will be as beautiful as her mother."

He slipped a pouch brimming with river pearls into her hand. He rode down the lane at a trot.

* * *

Thudding axes and crashing trees announced to William Wells that he was approaching Grand Camp. He rode in with three of his spies that he had come upon, much to their chagrin, camped on a rise between the Mississinewa and the Salamonie.

Piney Thompson jested, "Do not stop and stare. They will draft you to sharpen axes and saws."

Buck MacIntire chimed in, "They had Piney chopping with an ax in each hand."

Piney countered, "You should have seen Buck fell a beech with his teeth, just like a big old beaver."

Daniel Peterson, "I swear Mad Anthony has his men working like beavers. I have never seen anything remotely like it."

"You would work, too, if you saw him hang those deserters," Piney shook his head. "Between soldiers getting hung and officers killing each other in duels, there may be no army left come spring."

Nothing prepared William for what he witnessed when they broke out of the timber. The forest had been cleared of trees over a stretch more than a half-mile wide and nearly a mile long. Stakes with ribbons outlined a fort site far to the left and right against Swift Creek, up to where it is joined by Muddy Creek. Row after row and column upon column of barracks were forming. Many were ready to be roofed. Breastworks housed cannon at strategic points.

"More like ants than beaver," he said half aloud.

"Fort Greene Ville, the general calls it," Peterson shared his wonderment. "He says that he fought the British with General Greene in the Carolinas. He says that General Greene was the best general in the war. He wants the soldiers under roof before the new moon. That done, they will start on the officers' quarters, then the blockhouses, then curtain walls. All of this before the heavy snows. He will have cribs for the smithy, the cooper, for all the artificers. It will be like a whole town inside the walls. Fort Washington could be put in there ten times and not fill it up!"

Buck confirmed, "Everything he needs he will place inside those walls. By the way, Swift Creek has been christened Greene Ville Creek."

"I think the walls are a waste of time," Piney mused, "no enemy is going to attack this concentrated army. The walls are probably just to make the soldiers feel safer."

"Lest we forget," Wells reminded the spies, "this is not Wayne's final destination. He will need to store up supplies before driving on to Kekionga. This is a mere way-station."

Buck exclaimed, "A wonder to behold, it is, all of this construction!"

"Agreed, it is a wonder, as is the denuding of so much forest," Wells lamented. "They cut and burn so readily what took generations to be created."

The band of spies rode in the direction of the General's marquee. Only Wells was permitted to approach the final stretch. The reception was brief. Wayne required no accounting of the militia's return to Kentucky or Wells's stopover at Louisville. The two men stood facing each other as the head of the Legion of the United States delved into the business at hand.

"I need you to pick six of your men to scour the country between here and the Maumee." Wayne waved as if drawing a map. "Put three more to the east and three to west. I do not want any surprise movements by the enemy while I fortify here. The remainder of the spies will be assigned to scout for the supply trains. You know that is where we are the most vulnerable."

Wells nodded.

"Keep your men continually in the field. Report to me every two weeks, even if there are no events." The general went on, "There are bound to be some wanderers or enemy scouts out there. Bring in two or three from time to time for me to interrogate. Warriors, chiefs, hunters, deserters, women, I do not care who. Each will have heard this or that, I will build the larger picture from the pieces."

The red-haired man clad in buckskin studied the stout man dressed in his immaculate uniform. Resoluteness shielded all emotion from his face. Here was a man totally engrossed in his endeavor. A student of military history, Wayne had undoubtedly studied every detail, every conceivable outcome of his options. A seasoned officer, he preferred strategy to clash of arms. However, when the clash of arms arose, he would strike tenaciously. Wells understood that the general wanted to personally interrogate captives. He would verify all that the spies had laid out. Plus, he would pick up any particular details that would help peg his plan together.

Wells questioned, "What will become of the captives?"

Wayne responded sharply, "What becomes of the captives taken by the tribes?" He let the question hang for a moment as he glared into the eyes of the frontiersman. "Beaten, enslaved, starved, mutilated, burned, boiled. Which of these have you seen?"

Perhaps the general asked rhetorically, but William answered factually, "I have seen each perpetrated by the tribes and the Virginians alike, except for the boiling and eating of flesh. Certainly there are stories of it, but not among the Shawnee nor the Miami. Not among the Wabash and the Illinois tribes. The stories are of the Canadian tribes. I have no faith in their telling. I believe it to be trickery to terrify the enemy." He did not share that his body had experienced beatings, hunger, and slavery. His mind refused to dwell on burning. "Some prisoners are ransomed to traders or to the British. Those who show courage in their time of trial are often adopted, becoming one of the tribe, even rising to power as Joseph did in your book of worship. It is the weak and cowardly who suffer." He looked around the tent and rested his eyes upon the neatly shelved books and manuscripts. "Your books of war tell of the generals and their movements. They do not tell you about the villagers who suffer when an army moves upon their homes. Lives are swept away without being recorded."

Wayne retrieved his worn copy of Julius Caesar's Commentaries on the Gallic War. He randomly thumbed through the pages as he rounded the table and found his seat. He plopped the book down, "Have a seat, Captain." He took a deep breath and released it. He stretched his arms and grunted. No other subordinates would have confronted him as did this frontiersman. Ample intrigue existed amongst the officers, but a dearth of honest criticism. "Do you have a problem with bringing in prisoners?"

"Anyone found out there has chosen to be on a battlefield between two armies. I have no problems taking captives on a battlefield. I trust that you will treat them as well as Wilkinson treated his captives." Wells saw that the use of the name "Wilkinson" had its effect.

Wayne spoke as if he were issuing a proclamation, "After their interrogation, all captives will be held in safety until after the hostilities have been concluded. They will be released if the chiefs sue for peace. They will be exchanged for captives held by the tribes."

Wayne poured wine for his guest and himself. He referred to Wilkinson's captives and Putnam's peace. "About Putnam's treaty at Vincennes, you were there, right?"

"I was the head interpreter for General Putnam."

"Well, that document was not ratified by Congress. There is no treaty. It seems the senators did not like the language about the Ohio River being a boundary."

William felt a sudden chill in his spine, as if he had spotted a panther out the corner of his eye. No treaty? Putnam had represented General Washington himself. How could his council not accept what he had promised to the Wabash tribes? Was Wayne indicating that he planned to invade the lower Wabash?

Wells's face was flushed even through his darkly tanned skin. "What do the chiefs know of ratification? Putnam has declared peace. Those tribes are in truce until General Washington returns the belts of wampum and the peace calumet. To attack them now would dishonor the American government not only among those tribes, but across the land. It would be a disaster. Neutral tribes would rally against you. They will never quit fighting if they cannot have an honorable peace with the Americans. It would be an endless war, ruthless in its consequences."

Wayne replied, "Vincennes is safe from my legion. President Washington wishes to honor the truce even in the absence of support by

258

the politicians. Only those tribes who stand against my army, those who continue deprivations against our citizens, are in harm's way." He stood and rested both arms upon the table. His voice raised a notch, "You can add to that those redcoat buzzards who keep the king's soldiers stationed on American soil. Talk about violating a treaty! Coercing the Indians to do their dirty-work, encouraging atrocities, as you, yourself, have testified. Talk about bringing dishonor to one's country. If my soldiers were all boys from my Pennsylvania line, I would not be crouching here. I would march straight through to Detroit and boot the scoundrels across the river! I would chase them all the way to Montreal if I had my way!"

* * *

Captain William Wells duly returned in two weeks with his captives. A Shawnee hunter with his squaw and child were turned over to the guard. Smelling of swamp, he decided to bathe and change into his uniform before addressing General Wayne. Infantrymen erecting the palisade along the Greene Ville Creek joked as they watched the spy strip naked and descend the steep bank.

"I have a watch, I would bet no more than half a minute."

"Ten seconds," called another.

"I say two minutes."

The wagering was on with cash in hand. The paymaster had arrived with a super-convoy, as it was called. Eight hundred packhorses had brought in food, clothing, and a hundred sundry items. Eight hundred head of cattle were herded along. Four hundred soldiers escorted the drovers safely to the grand fort.

Upon hearing the jeering from above, Wells determined to show the soldiers what a man of the woods could do. He secured a discarded stick and poked through the thin ice. Slowly he circled the hole, enlarging the opening as he went around. He plunged in feet-first to find the water reaching up to his third rib. He dunked and splashed. He scoured his skin with handfuls of sand. He lounged and floated. In his mind he pictured all the streams he had bathed in. Perhaps he should plot the locations on Clark's map. The calls turned to cheers of admiration. Once more he dunked. He clenched a handful of pebbles from the bottom and laid them upon the ice. Securing the stick, he cleared a path to the bank. Emerging, he went out to scoop up the pebbles, and then scurried up the bank.

"Eight minutes, men," the time observer stated.

The "two minute" man collected his prize. All were astonished to see the man had donned a captain's uniform. He was approaching from the bridge. They came to attention and held a long salute.

The captain returned the salute, "What a refreshing day it is!" He let out a laugh and handed each soldier a pebble. "I hope our general is in good spirits today," he shouted as he set out for Wayne's new headquarters.

The American stars and stripes fluttered on a huge flagpole that had been erected between the parade grounds and the rows of barracks. Nearby, a smaller pole marked the location of Wayne's headquarters. It bore a flag with five horizontal bands of blue, white, and red stripes. Fifteen stripes for fifteen states. The top corner held a white field with the lettering "A. Wayne, Commander in Chief."

The general was in a good mood as he received the report. Fewer than two hundred hostiles were in the area, generally to the east in bands of twenty or less. The north and west were empty.

"How do you celebrate Christmas?" the general inquired.

"Once I attended a Christmas feast in Detroit." Wells bit his lip; he should not have referred to Detroit. "But it is the French in Vincennes who really know how to celebrate Christmas. Many days they sing and eat. They have night parades. They forgive debts and give gifts to the church. There is wooing and courting by the youth, and many weddings. In Kentucky, my brother's wife spoke to me of how they will be having Christmas. It is quite different, as I understand it. I guess that there are many ways to do Christmas."

"So there are," the general laughed. "Do not be far away. Come here on the morning of the twenty-second. I will show you how I celebrate Christmas." This was said in the manner of one who has mischievous intent.

* * *

Wells the Spy bunked with Lieutenant William Henry Harrison on the night of the twenty-first of December, 1793. Harrison was in and out repeatedly attending to duties. Caught up in his business, there was little time for chatting, no time for storytelling. Harrison continued writing reports by the light of a lantern. Wells slumbered in his assigned berth.

Morning came early with Harrison banging on the bed of his guest.

"Breakfast is on the table. You are to report to the parade grounds in fifteen minutes."

"But, I am to see General Wayne today," Wells groggily protested, "we are having Christmas."

"These are Wayne's orders," Harrison chided. "You are to lead Major Burbeck and nine companies to the site of St. Clair's defeat. There they will build a fort. Wayne will follow shortly. You are to help recover the lost cannon."

Wells dressed and ate without replying. No one said to him directly, "We know you were there. We know you fought with the enemy. We know that you aided in bringing destruction to our army." Perhaps it would have been best to have stated his experiences in full. Keeping his past a mystery had led to exaggerated stories of his deeds and prowess.

The assembled force was quickly moving north. Pushing through the brush that had sprung up in St. Clair's trace, the mounted column would not be denied. Dawn of the twenty-fourth found them on the littered battlefield. Fog sprinkled with bits of ice crystals was reminiscent to William of the morning of the battle.

He dismounted and motioned to Major Burbeck, "This is where General St. Clair's marquee would have been." He pointed to the left, "There is the Wabash, it swings around in front of us and upstream to the right. Below it loops west, then back north."

The major quickly observed the lay of the land, "Then this is where we will build our fort."

Having served under Wayne in Georgia, Burbeck fully understood the intent of the general: inter the dead, recover the cannon, and build a fort to hold the ground on the exact spot of the battle. The location was as much symbolic as it was strategic.

He immediately issued commands to his aide, "Have the men dismount at a distance so as not to trample this ground any more than it already is. Captain Peters will secure the perimeter. Captain Eaton will gather bones for burial. Captain Jeffers will begin a search for the cannon; Captain Wells will assist. The remainder will be under Captain Gibson for the construction of the defenses."

His lieutenant whisked away to relay the orders. Burbeck looked about. How many? One hundred, two hundred skulls he beheld from this spot. He kicked at a rusted musket barrel with his boot. The mechanism was gone, the weapon was simply junk. Scrap metal, bones, broken trees, and charred wood marked the battle site. How could the

American army have been lead into such devastation? Wayne sent him here not only to recover the ground, to recover the remains of those who died, but recover the honor of the country and its army.

Gibson and Eaton came up to join the major. Burbeck pointed out the general outline of the fortress. Walking Eaton to a small opening in the trees, he instructed, "Clear this area first. Dig a hole to bury the bones. Stack them to the side for now. Wayne will be here to hold the ceremony."

Captain Edward Butler joined the group. "Major, if I may. I left my brother here mortally wounded. I leaned him against a spreading oak. As a child he had a broken left hip; his skeleton may be identified by it. If his bones have not been scattered, I would like to bury him properly. You may have heard the story from the Canadians as I have. The Indians cut out his still beating heart and chewed it as would a pack of wolves. What hatred they had of him!"

The officers gave voice and gesture to disgust.

Wells offered a correction, "Not hatred. It is a sign of highest respect to honor bravery. Those who eat of the brave heart are believed to gain possession of the courage of the one so honored."

Butler queried, "Do they really believe in these superstitions?"

Wells countered, "Do you partake of the ceremony where wine is changed into the blood of Jesus to cleanse your soul?"

Butler reached for his sword to strike the blasphemer. Eaton grabbed Butler's arm and pulled him back.

Wells offered apologetically, "I do not mean to offend. I only say that each man holds fast to his beliefs."

Eaton advised Wells, "You best go about your business now." To Butler he promised, "I will notify all my men to be on the lookout for the mended hip under the spreading oak."

Wells went in search of Captain Jeffers. He found that Jeffers had broken his company into squads of ten. Each squad was to have one man stand guard over their muskets and packs while the searching took place.

"Tell me, Wells, what you know about the cannon," Captain Jeffers asked diplomatically.

"The cannon would have been positioned on the little crest yonder. The stories say that after the battle, some of the big guns were dragged down the slope to the stream. Some were hidden under logs on the field. The English used the American horses to pull others into ravines where they were covered with soil and brush."

Four squads were assigned to the hillside and stream, two to the flat terrain above, others to prospect likely sites. Lines of uniformed men probed the soil with bayonets. Wells could not avoid peering across the stream at his battle position. He stood where he had lifted Metea while charging up this hill. The popping of muskets was now suggested by the whacking of axes. The cannon his warriors silenced had remained silent for two years.

Jeffers called to his men, "Close rank, no more than boot-length between probes." Seeing a man roll a skull from under a clump of twigs, he instructed, "Pick that up! Every bone you come across is to be collected."

A clank of steel to his left brought on a scurry of activity. Shovels and picks were advanced to the scene. But no, a large stone was the culprit. "There will surely be many stones. We must check them all."

Within an hour, the call came from men wading in knee-deep water, "Here! Down here!"

Wells splashed in to inspect. The unmistakable butt of a brass cylinder poked above the gravel under a small cut-bank.

The spy-captain called to Jeffers, "A big one it is! Mostly buried, but in loose gravel!"

A big smile swept across Jeffers' face. He personally had not given much credence to cannon stories; surely they had been taken north by the British. Now they had actually located one of the fabled guns. There was little time for contemplation. One cannon in this wilderness was worth two hundred men. He immediately sent word to Major Burbeck. He also sent for the artillerymen. If the gun could be recovered, cleaned, and pass inspection, it would be placed into service this day. Two squads manned the shovels with the remainder returned to prodding the earth.

"Two pints of brandy for the finder!" Jeffers announced, "and two pints for the next, and the next!"

Shovels dug, poles pried, horses pulled; out the cannon popped. It swooshed over the lip of the bank and was quickly towed up the hill. The six-pounder appeared to be in remarkably good shape. The artillery detachment began constructing a sled to haul it to the construction site. They checked the bore with a new six-pound ball, finding all in order. Copper brushes brought out the true luster of the brass. It had the makings of a serviceable piece.

The excavation had exposed the mouth of a three-pounder. It too was recovered before noon. Eating their cold pork and biscuits, the searchers watched the men of the artillery company care for the find. The cannoneers swarmed about the guns without thought of food. They concentrated on a thorough cleaning, reaming the firing hole, building a carriage. The heavy guns were treated as if they were treasures of gold. If all went well, they would test-fire with increasing loads.

The afternoon search produced a gulley filled with iron cannon balls. Many rocks were discovered, but no additional cannon. Captains Jeffers and Wells released the hungry men with enough daylight left for them to make their camp.

William Wells was startled to find four blockhouses marking the corners of the fort site. He found each twenty foot square to be already five logs high. Hewn and notched, the logs snugged tightly to one another forming a formidable barrier. The six-pounder pointed out from below the northwest block while the three-pounder was mounted on the wall of the one to the southeast. Soldiers were making their beds inside the squares by lantern light. A small fire lighted the mess area beside camps forming between the corners.

Stew and bread in hand, Wells roamed around to find a likely sleeping spot.

"Over here, Captain!" a private called out from the shadows.

The Miami warrior-turned-spy investigated the offer. He stepped up to the laughter of the lounging men. Here they had laid out a complete skeleton of collected bones. A rotted ensign's cap rested on its head. A musket barrel with broken stock was at its right side and a tomahawk was in its left hand. Relics of a cartridge bag and a canteen were draped around the shoulders and chest.

"My mistake, looks like it is already taken," the private said as he stood.

"So it is," Wells replied to the group. Addressing the bones, "Man, you look starved."

Bending down, Wells picked up the tomahawk, replacing it with his bowl and spoon. Standing, he let the tomahawk fly past the ear of the erect soldier. It lodged in the center of the wall's top timber three paces behind the wide-eyed private.

"Sorry, the handle was weak. I meant it to go past your other ear."

Being informed by the roar of laughter that he had been outdone, the soldier relented, "Ensign Bones here was just leaving to join his friends on yonder pile. You stay and I will assist him. Poor man is not well enough to make it by himself."

With that, he and a buddy began bundling the skeleton in a blanket.

"My regards to you and Mr. Bones. I will do just that. Spare me that blanket when you are finished." Taking a seat upon the bare ground, Wells scooped up his bowl. He spoke loud enough for all nearby to hear, "Years back, I saw four stag elk fighting on this very knoll. Two against two it was." He pointed to the northeast, "The harem was down in the valley, waiting for the victors."

Silence told him that he had an audience for his tale. This he followed with the escape from a panther by climbing out upon an overhanging tree and eventually plunging into the floodwaters of the Wabash. His horse falling under a buffalo during the hunt. Heckewelder and the bear.

Having little to offer for the search the next day, Burbeck released Wells to scout the region. He set out afoot to the west and circled around to the north. During the night the heavy clouds had given way. This day the sun warmed both earth and still air. The water level of the swamps was low which made travel easy. A few geese remained to feed in the coves before retreating from the coming winter's cold. No signs of habitation in the Miami hunting camps could be found. It was a peaceful day of wandering, reminiscent of his youth. He returned by midafternoon.

While wading the Wabash below the new fort, he heard the recovered cannon belch their boom. On the hill he found the ranks formed for ceremony. It was clear that Wayne had come up with more troops and materials. Wells drew closer as the last of the loose bones were placed in the pit. The skulls, each with a scalping mark and a hole, were next placed in rows atop the bones. A musket fired each time a skull was laid, six hundred and seven the count this day, plus Major Butler's bones buried separately.

Captain Wells could hear only part of Wayne's declaration. The general commended Major Burbeck and his officers. He named the defenses Fort Recovery. Captain Gibson was to be in charge of the garrison. He gave a final tribute to those who had fallen on the fourth of November, 1791. He ordered three more volleys from the recovered cannon. Thunder they did. So ended General Anthony Wayne's Christmas party of 1793. If there were any enemy scouts in the forest, they were now informed that there was a new American post at the Head of the Wabash.

CHAPTER 19
Auglaize

Metea focused on a log floating down the Maumee towards him. It passed by to be swirled about by the incoming waters of the Auglaize. Standing at the point, he spat into the merging rivers as if to spit out his disgust. His urging of a quick attack had gone unheeded. It had been well before the first snow of the winter that he had arrived with the news concerning Wild Carrot's scouting for the American army. The snows were now long gone; a warm breeze carried the fragrance of apple blossoms. Spring floods had subsided. Still, the chiefs sat in council.

He gazed across the waters to the north where long blue ribbons fluttered from a painted post. The marker designated where Pontiac had formed his confederacy to drive the English from the land. Could not the spirit of Pontiac return to move the chiefs to action? Would the chiefs allow General Wayne to hold the ground where the nations had their greatest of victories over the Americans? The chiefs began referring to Wayne as "The Man Who Never Sleeps." Others called him "Blacksnake" due to his steady plotting and stalking of his prey. Continual probing by the tribes' spies for American weaknesses proved fruitless.

Metea's frustration grew at Five Medals's continual counseling for peace over the objections of Pottawatomie village chiefs. Little Turtle and the Miami urged for peace unless the English produced their promised soldiers. Buckongahelas grew anxious to lead the Delaware against the invaders. Blue Jacket desired to lead an advance by the nations, but he was off to Detroit, some say assembling the Canadian tribes.

Metea cried out to the spirit of Pontiac, "Show me the way! I will lead the fight!"

Metea himself was ready to lead who would follow through the Black Swamp. Skirmishes with the supply convoys had not deterred the invaders. He would strike the enemy head-on. If the Americans were not pushed back, they would be drawn into the swamp where the rallying nations would surround them. In the swamps, their grand army would become fragmented, all efforts ending in chaos. Even if the Americans did prevail, an honorable defeat is preferable to inaction. Waiting in camp with the women and children for the enemy's banners to march in is incomprehensible.

Full sun turned to shadows, shadows which eventually reached the eastern bank of the Auglaize. Metea stood where he had invoked the spirit of the great chief of wars past. Still there was no answer. He resigned to once again go down to McKee's post where the new council fire burned. Once again he would implore Five Medals to hold forth the red belt of war. Launching solo into the river, he once again wailed, "Tell me if I am to lead the way! Must I sit with the squaws?"

Reaching Buffalo Rock under a waning moon, his paddle stabbed at the waves. He attacked the upper rapids as with a lance driving at a blue-uniformed soldier. His endeavor brought on an exceeding fatigue. Reaching the Pottawatomie camp, he slid his canoe up to some new grass, turned it over, and crept under to slumber until morn.

Aroused by sniffing dogs, Metea found the camp active with morning tasks. Ignoring breakfast, he made his way directly to the compound of Five Medals.

Stepping to the midst of the encircled wigwams he brought forth a shout, "I am Metea, chief of the Pottawatomie beyond the Tippecanoe! This day I am prepared to attack the blue coats! Prepare your weapons! Paint your bodies! Let us take battle to them!"

His exhortation brought heads popping out of the shelters.

Chief Sturgeon responded, "I will sport my paints!"

Chief White Pigeon stepped out and reprimanded his comrade, shushing Sturgeon back into his wigwam.

White Pigeon demanded of Metea, "How many warriors do you have to attack the three thousand blue coats? Do you have the king's cannon to break open their forts? Have our allies pledged to fight at your side? Have you brought provisions for all? Answer in truth and I will be at your right hand."

"All that is needed is a new leader. I am that leader! I will meet General Wayne and pluck out his heart!"

This brought out Five Medals, minus his usual regalia, "A man is not a leader until he has those who will follow. You claim to be a leader, but you have no followers. Bold speech alone does not signify a leader of the people."

"You lead us nowhere," Metea declared, "but to huddle beside the Maumee. Here you plead to the English for food and munitions. You plead for your own favors. You idle before the enemy waiting for the English soldiers to appear. They are but ghosts in the mist that never materialize on solid ground."

The leader elected by the Pottawatomie as war chief of the nation for the duration of this conflict was now flanked by White Pigeon and Sturgeon.

In a softer tone he offered, "Your impatience is understandable. You have served your nation well. You were betrayed by a friend who is now with the enemy. Sometimes a leader must have patience beyond patience. We will fight when our fist is full." Five Medals placed his hand on Metea's shoulder, "Come, make your camp among us. The corn is now planted; the rivers are now passable. Bring your warriors into our camp. I will seek your wisdom and we will fight together."

"The honor of our nation demands that we hold the ground where our warriors defeated General St. Clair!" Metea gave his last protest.

Five Medals nodded approvingly. He looked about, "Our meal is prepared. Join us, let us talk as men."

On a full stomach, Five Medals addressed six chiefs gathered round about, "The number of our warriors in this camp will grow quickly. When the leaves of these maples have grown full, we will be strong. The Miami, Shawnee, and Delaware camps will be full. Chief Black Hoof leads the Shawnee until Blue Jacket's return. Our friend Blue Jacket will make his return with five hundred warriors of the Chippewa. Hundreds of Canadian Militia in their green jackets will be with them."

"We have with us plenty of powder and lead. Our horses are strong. We are in need of more than one hundred muskets. To affront the forts we will need the king's cannon and red jacketed soldiers to fire them. I can tell you no more than that Little Turtle remains as Chief of All Nations. Blue Jacket and the English officers will be at his shoulders. We will attack the enemy in our strength. Know that the enemy is also strong, and the fighting will be terrible.

"You know that I counsel for peace. If peace will yield the same results as victory, then why not spare the lives of our warriors? When peace becomes a fleeting bird, then I stand with each of you to fight. We chiefs all know that if the Shawnee and Miami nations fall, the Americans will not stop short of the shores of the grand lake Michigan. It will then be the Pottawatomie villages that burn; our families will suffer the brutality of the Americans."

Grudgingly, Metea suffered to reawaken his patience, "The bird has long flown," he sighed. "I will be at your side in the coming battle. I must now go to the Tippecanoe to rally my force. I will bring them to this place prepared to fight."

* * *

The young chief from the edge of the plains delivered on his promise. Five chiefs and eighty-eight fully armed combatants entered the camp behind Metea. Announcing their presence with shouts and gunfire, they circled the Pottawatomie camp and made for the center. Return shouts arose from the warriors and women and children of the village. Dodging the melee to gain the dwelling of Five Medals, Metea found the chief awaiting his approach.

"I am Metea, chief of the Pottawatomie beyond the Tippecanoe! This day I am prepared to attack the blue coats! Look about and see my followers!"

Five Medals greeted him, "Your warriors are welcome in our camp. Bring your chiefs here and we will feast. When the sun sets you will address the war council."

* * *

Five Medals stood to address those in the council house. His gaze was not to Little Turtle, or any particular chief, but to a void above the gathering.

"Whenever you see me, you see that I wear this medal presented to me and my people by the French. The English officers chastise me, saying I should not wear it, I should wear the medal given by their king. I have little faith in their king. He asks much and provides little. He hears our pleas only when it is of interest to him. His ambassadors make promises that he does not fulfill. I would turn to the French king, but he is no more.

"It remains with us to decide how to face the Americans. We are told that General Washington prefers peace, but we see that General Wayne looks only to war. He is confident in his strength; he has not faltered. I have counseled for peace, but I see that bird has flown and will not return. Our warriors and our young chiefs demand that we fight. I must now hear their call and take up their chant. We cannot wait on English whims. We cannot wait for the ground to become firm under the enemy's feet. We must strike the enemy; we must strike swiftly; we must strike soon!

"Permit me to bring the voice of one of our young chiefs to this council. Metea has joined my camp with nearly one hundred warriors. He is known among our people as a strong and brave warrior. I will have him speak his own words."

Five Medals sat while Sturgeon darted out to signal Metea. The young chief took a deep breath, clenched his teeth firmly, and followed Sturgeon into the council house. Sturgeon indicated to Metea where he should stand. Metea had rehearsed his speech but found himself at a loss as to how to begin. Was he to wait for a signal, or words, from Five Medals or from Little Turtle? Should he address Little Turtle only or each of the chiefs individually or together as a whole? After an awkward moment, he decided there would be no cue, he should just begin.

Before he could get his first word out, a yelp screeched from beyond the entrance to the council house.

A voice rang forth, "Listen to my words! I am Tecumseh of the Shawnee! I have come to say that Blue Jacket returns! Blue Jacket will arrive with the morning sun! He brings five hundred Chippewa warriors! He is followed by hundreds of English soldiers!"

The outburst brought Chief Richardville dashing from the council house entrance. He shouted, "Hold your tongue! You shame yourself by disturbing this council. If you have a message, deliver it to your Chief Black Hoof when he is finished here."

Black Hoof was standing inside the council house. He offered an apology, "Our people the Shawnee have suffered much under the Americans. Our men become aroused and grow insolent."

The gathering was dismissed by Little Turtle. He said, "Let us each go to his village to prepare for the arrival of our friend. Let us properly welcome the warriors from the north. Let us greet the English soldiers in celebration."

The chiefs began to file out to go to their respective camps. Five Medals paused in front of Metea. The younger chief's clenched fists and clenched teeth bared his frustration at the missed opportunity.

The elder chief offered, "Patience is rewarded in stalking game or in stalking an enemy. It is the same in councils of men. The Great Spirit favors you. He will yet provide a fitting occasion for your voice. Perhaps you should meditate to see that your heart is pleasing to the Great Spirit. Only then will your words flow freely as if by a power other than your own."

* * *

The Chippewa contingent made a good show upon arrival. Their count was well under five hundred, well under four hundred. They were followed a day later by fourteen uniformed British officers and something over fifty green-coated Canadian militia. No cannon were seen. The tribes were once again deprived of the full portion promised by the British. Still, they had little option but to declare for battle.

On the third day, the army of the assembled nations trekked south. Each nation made its own way at a distance from the others. The march was slow, halted early each day to allow for hunting since few food provisions had been obtained. On the first day out a shaman of the Delaware died, said to be from snakebite. Buckongahelas halted his warriors, eventually falling behind the others by two days.

The objective was to first destroy the new fort at the Head of the Wabash. Using provisions from the Fort Recovery to sustain them, they would crush forts Jefferson and St. Clair to cut the American supply line. They would contain the Americans in their grand fort until the cannon from the smaller forts could be trained upon its walls. The bombardment would be designed to scatter the enemy forces and cut them down piecemeal. If the American army broke out, the nations would attempt to draw them into the swamps or chase them back to the river Ohio as the opportunity presented itself.

Little Turtle's Miami were beginning to position on the west side of Fort Recovery and Blue Jacket's Shawnee on the east. To the north, the left of the Chippewa line was bewildered by being fired upon by one of the other nations. Was it a mistake, or were they duped by supposed allies? Deciding that it was no mistake, they engaged the offenders with a wrath. Repulsing the attack, they learned that the foe was the hated Chickasaw from far south of the Ohio. Had these interlopers simply wandered into their position? Or, had Wayne invited them to probe beyond his perimeter? At the moment it made no difference. They were engaged in mortal combat with a despised enemy. They intended to deliver a crushing blow. Scalp trophies were to be had. The superior forces of the Chippewa drove the stubborn Chickasaw before them, unintentionally in the direction of the new American fort.

The planned surprise attack had been wasted and the Miami had not yet all come up. To his right, Little Turtle now heard an ascending intensity of gunfire. The Ottawa were having success against a supply train escort camped in the forest south of the fort. Soldiers fleeing from this ambush became visible in the clearing as they dashed for the fort. The Miami and Shawnee, still assembling, were forced by the events to initiate frontal attacks on the fort. Warriors bravely charged the palisade, some hacking at the walls and gates with axes. Musket balls were flying in all directions, whacking into fort timbers, trees, and men. The attack was sustained for an agonizingly long period, but the walls could not be breeched. A second wave, though better coordinated, was quickly repulsed by cannon fire. A consistent long-range fire from cover consumed the remainder of the day.

Under the cover of darkness, warriors claimed the bodies of their dead comrades. Of necessity they left a few beneath the fort walls. In battle-council the British officers disavowed ordering a frontal assault. They complained that the warriors knew nothing about military maneuvering. They ridiculed the chiefs for not being able to locate the hidden cannon.

Pointing to the fort walls, Little Turtle lamented, "There are your cannon. There is the fort that you should have built before the American army descended the Ohio."

The Chippewa had apparently learned what the other nations knew from years of raids in Kentucky: assaulting fortifications was a risky business. Realizing that easily won trophies and quick booty were illusions, the chiefs of the Chippewa declared that they had fulfilled their duty and were needed in their home country. The Ottawa would not remain without the Chippewa. At dawn, only the Miami and the Shawnee remained to fire upon the Americans. Cannon splintered the forest about them, eventually silencing the assaulting tribes' barrages. The arrival of the Delaware brought neither hope nor joy. A quick council decided that the Delaware would stay and harass Wayne's support lines while the remainder retreated to the Maumee.

By midafternoon, Wells the Spy stepped out of the gates of Fort Recovery at the head of a reconnaissance sortie. Captain Gibson had seen British and Canadian jackets amongst the enemy. He wanted to gather some proof that Wayne could relay back to Philadelphia. There were plenty of British musket balls in the fort timbers; something more substantial would be better. Wells concentrated his attention on the bodies in the clearing. At Wells's encouragement, Gibson had issued orders that none of the bodies be scalped or mutilated. After Wells's inspection, they were gathered. Burial was conducted a mile from the fort. When he deemed it safe, a rescue and burial detail was sent to the convoy camp.

One of the fallen enemy laid near the wall with an ax gripped in his hands. A large Miami wearing two feathers, he was soon recognized by the red-haired spy. It was Buffalo Man, his loyal companion of days past.

"You served your nation with your last breath. The Miami will be told of your greatness." Two soldiers came up to collect the body. "This is an important man among the Miami,"Wells told them. "He should not be buried with the others lest they find him. Bury him across the river, just over the crest of that ridge." He pointed to the place he had commanded his rifleman warriors seemingly a lifetime ago.

Captain Gibson began writing his report to his commander. "July 1, 1794, Fort Recovery. General A. Wayne, Fort GreeneVille. On the morning of June 30, Major McMahon's convoy was attacked by the combined forces of several nations of hostiles suffering _____ casualties." He did not yet have a number for the blank.

He considered it best to send off a quick report of the battle and request new munitions. Details and a list of casualties could follow later. He knew that Wayne would not want him sending out a contingent to chase the offenders. His duty was purely defensive. The fort had suffered no structural damage. He had plenty of food which had been delivered by the unfortunate convoy. The net result was perhaps as many as fifty officers and men dead and the loss of two hundred horses. Wayne would certainly consider the death of Major William McMahon a great loss. The general had respected the major's abilities to command. Gibson put down his pen and recounted the battle in his mind. Yes, his men had done well. And Wells had read the signs to alert them to be diligent in their guard. His command had fared as well as could possibly be expected at this advanced frontier post.

* * *

Four weeks to the day after the Battle of Fort Recovery, every available man of the garrison of the fort stood at the ramparts watching in disbelief. They had each predicted that Wayne's march would disintegrate into chaos upon passing through the forest. "The tail will not get started before the head is ready to make camp for the night." "The right hand will end up in Oswego and the left will fall into the Mississippi." "The only way to get an army through these woods is to pick up all the trees and carry them along." But there it was in front of them, a grand spectacle to behold. Four sub-legions, each eight columns wide, were proceeding forward in parallel formation. They were not denied by brush, muck, trees, or streams. Colonel Hamtramck commanded the two sub-legions that passed the western wall while General Wilkinson's two passed the eastern. It was only their second day of the march. The grand army would make camp north of here. Fort Recovery would no longer be the advance post.

The men watched General Wayne return the salute of their commandant. Fifteen times, for fifteen states, the fort's artillery pieces roared in unison. When the smoke cleared, Wayne had already disappeared. "At this pace," a private declared, "Wayne will be in Kekionga by Sunday."

Sunday, being five days hence, found the army encamped at the St. Marys headwaters. Sunday was also the day that a giant beech went crashing down upon Wayne's marquee, pinning him and his bed to the ground. Consternation ensued until the general was freed and pronounced fit other than a bruised hip. After noon the general called in his leading officers to dispel rumors of his death.

The general added, "Following this river will lead us straight to Kekionga where we are to build a fort as directed by President Washington and General Knox. But first, we will proceed that way." He pointed to the northeast. "That is where the enemy is located, and that is where we will go. We will leave enough men here to finish erecting a suitable fort. Captain Wells and his boys will guide us along the enemy's route of retreat from Fort Recovery to their stronghold on the Maumee. The going will be tough, but our men are hardened to the country. You will see to it that they press on relentlessly. You see, the enemy wishes to attack and disappear, attack and disappear. We must force their hand. We must take battle to their camp."

All knew that if Wayne said "the going will be tough," that the going would be nearly impossible. The officers gathered in groups to consider this revelation. Wilkinson stormed off, insulted at the idea of being kept uninformed like the junior officers.

Wayne called in Wells, Nicholas Miller, William May, and Robert McClellan. "The four of you will scout the front close by. Report daily at four in the morning. The remainder of the spies will be assigned to the sub-legions."

Wells inquired, "Before the final push, I wish to visit my brother to the rear."

The general knew that Captain Samuel Wells was under General Todd in Scott's Kentucky militia, "You had two weeks with your brother at Louisville in May. Did you not get enough of him then?"

"I had one week to visit my wife. Samuel spent much of that week in Frankfort. And, no, I did not get enough of her, either."

Wayne let out a bellowing laugh, bending over even though it hurt his bruised rump. "Go then. Be quick about it. We move out in the morning. Remember, four in the morning."

* * *

General Anthony Wayne was positively beaming despite the rain. Five days of ardent march through wet and dry marsh, forest and glade, heat and brackish water had brought him here without incident. Enemy resistance had dissolved ahead of him. Enemy camps had been abandoned upon his approach. He took a step forward and dipped the toe of his right boot into the Auglaize River. Then he put his left toe in the waters of the Maumee as if to confirm to himself the reality of it. Downriver from here stands the new British Fort Miamis. A bit farther on is Lake Erie. If only Congress had followed his plan, he could have been able to join with an eastern army on the shores of the great lake and march northward to possess Detroit. But now here he was, on his own.

The general climbed to the top of the bluff where Lieutenant William Henry Harrison and Lieutenant William Clark waited with their leather pouches. He stood beside them as all three gazed through the drizzle at the beautiful landscape.

The general broke the silence, "I must send Washington a dispatch telling that we camp on the Maumee this night. But first, let us pause a moment and take in this Garden of Eden."

Harrison was taken aback at his commander's sudden poetic demeanor. He gave it a moment, then commented, "It is as Captain Wells says. This point has perfect command of the joining rivers. The fort should go where we stand."

"Yes," Wayne thought to himself, "perfect in locale, perfect in strategy, perfect in undermining the morale of the enemy, and beautiful."

The soldiers did not need to be told that there would be a fort erected here. Trees began falling before Clark could summon the engineers. The men rotated in shifts with a half-day of either fort-building or patrol and a half-day off. Free time was devoted to scrounging for vegetables, bathing, cleaning weapons, and mending clothing.

Upon examining the half-completed fort, General Scott congratulated Major Burbeck, head of the engineers. "I defy the British and all their hired devils to take it!" He slapped the major on the back, winked at Wayne, and rode off. Scott kept his forces occupied slashing and trampling field after field of corn.

The morning of the third day saw the four lead spies return from a skirmish. Under a full moon they had encountered a camp of Delaware and Shawnee on the north side of the Maumee at Buffalo Rock, a landmark prominent among the tribes. In the process of capturing a Shawnee warrior for interrogation, they were recognized by a Delaware who called the alarm. May had a bad left ankle. Miller had a gash in his right side. Wells's right wrist and forearm were smashed by a musket ball. McClellan had escaped by diving into the turbulent rapids. A musket ball had found his right shoulder during the dive. The band of spies had struggled back to headquarters where they promptly delivered the captive.

Wells's wound seriously incapacitated him. His magical good fortune had run out. He was ordered to remove himself from the spy business. Wayne assigned him to headquarters.

Clark and Wells worked on a detailed map of the Maumee. They drew the terrain from the joining of the rivers at Kekionga to where it flowed into Lake Erie. They presented their product to Wayne. After quiet inspection, the general inquired about travel times between points by canoe, by foot, by horse, upriver by tow barge.

Wayne inquired, "Can you guarantee that no British sailing vessel can pass up beyond the rapids at their new post?"

"It cannot happen."

"Can the ships' guns cover the approaches to Fort Miamis?"

"Not even close. The cliff is too high. Their guns cannot elevate to half the height."

Philosophically, the seasoned general asked his spy, "How do I break the alliance between the several tribes and the British?"

Wells's answer came quickly, "The tribes will respect a power that shows strength and courage, above all courage. They make their alliance with individuals, not with nations. Show that the English officers are weak and cowardly, and you will win them over. Be magnanimous in victory. Treat the vanquished tribes with respect, and you will gain their trust. They will not continue to war with you. It is wise to know that you cannot sustain an extended war so far from your home. The lower Wabash tribes respect Hamtramck as a warrior, and also as a judge. When he arrived at Vincennes, he reined in the unruly Virginians. He treated the tribes with respect. Now those who signed the treaty at Vincennes do not rise in arms against you. Learn from Hamtramck's ways."

"If you were the major general of this army, what would be your next move?" He anticipated that the answer would be the same as the thinking of Little Turtle.

"We do not know that the English will not reinforce Fort Miamis with soldiers and guns. We cannot tell when the next ship or fleet of ships will arrive. They appear without notice. I would bypass the fort and station cannon downriver to prevent the passage of ships. The English must come out and fight or abandon the fort."

"Well said. You have the makings of a good general. But my president tells me that we are not at war with the British. To train guns upon their fleet would be an act of aggression that I am not authorized to take," he hesitatingly added, "even on soil ceded to the United States by treaty. However, if the British commander thinks that I will cut off his supply line, then he must come out and fight anyway. The only weapon he has besides a few of the king's men and militia is his force of Indians. This he will use to block my path. This force he will not hesitate to use to protect his position, and this force is a legitimate target. The tribes will have to stand and fight!"

In the heat of the afternoon that day, August 12, 1794, drums beat to form the entire army in the clearing in front of the fort's gate. Though far from complete, the walls were enclosed and the big guns were in place. Major General Anthony Wayne congratulated his officers and men on their conduct thus far. He christened the structure Fort Defiance. Amid the celebration, Wayne informed his officers to be ready in three days to march down the Maumee to the approaches to Fort Miamis.

Harrison summoned Christopher Miller the next morning. The younger brother of Nicholas had recently defected from the Shawnee and joined the spies. Wells vouched for his dependability, saying that the youth had proven his trustworthiness in daring reconnaissance.

"You are the only healthy man left who is fluent in the languages of the Shawnee, Miami, and Delaware. Here is a letter from General Wayne to the tribes. It is a last-chance peace offer. They are to send delegates to us promptly under a flag of truce if they wish to talk about a just and lasting peace. Take the Shawnee captive with you under a white flag. I am sure you will have no trouble finding the chiefs. It is a risky mission. The general says that you will be well compensated if you accept it."

"I am the man to carry the general's message," the spy assured, "but my horse is lame."

"I will see that you get a fine horse and one for the captive. I will have everything, including the flag, prepared in one hour. God go with you, Miller."

Harrison spent the following day dashing between thunderstorms relaying orders for the march; Wells tagged along. Lieutenant Clark was sent to lead his rifle company under Hamtramck's command. Harrison struggled to contain the growing excitement within him. Days, months, even years of preparation would culminate in tomorrow's assembly of the Legion of the United States. Officers, soldiers, Kentucky volunteers, horses, uniforms, field cannon, muskets, rifles, sabers, ammunition, food, drums, flags, canvas, pens and paper, on down to needles and thread, all gathered to be directed by one man. He searched a checklist in his mind for anything that may have been overlooked. Nothing. He imagined soaring above as an eagle and looking down upon the glorious marching formation.

The confused fording of the Maumee in the early dawn did not appear quite so glorious. However, once formed on the north bank and moving towards the risen sun, a warm breeze at their backs, the columns took the form of a juggernaut. What force dare stand in its way? Harrison and Wells were in position with Wayne's command at the head of the center.

Harrison leaned in his saddle and asked quietly of Wells, "I wish Little Turtle could see us now. Do you think he will fight?"

"Honor demands that they take a stand," Wells the Spy replied tartly. "There will be a fight. If the English bring up their cannon, it will be a mean fight."

Realizing that he had trespassed on private grounds of the spy, Harrison refrained from further inquiry.

A commotion on the river bank caught the attention of William Wells the afternoon of the second day of the march. A squad of Wilkinson's mounted riflemen encircled an intruder. Eventually, the interloper was escorted towards the center, sandwiched between four mounted officers.

"Christopher!" Wells waved his broad hat and shouted.

The contingent grew close.

"I am glad that you did not make me a liar!" the spy Wells addressed the spy Miller. "I was the only one in this company of two thousand uniforms that said you were still alive! Not that I thought that you were so tough, but I knew you could talk your way out of anything, in any language!"

"At first they thought I was you!" the young spy Miller reported. "Simon Girty wanted to dangle me from a sycamore and fill me full of arrows. Little Turtle and Black Hoof set him straight. Besides, they wanted to send this back with me." He produced an unsealed paper from his frock and waved it high in the air. "Written in fine English, it is, from the pen of a red coat captain. The words are those of Little Turtle, though all the head chiefs were there except Blue Jacket. Blue Jacket is now Chief of All Nations. He will lead them in battle."

The paper was surrendered to Harrison who handed it to the commander-in-chief. Wayne called in General Wilkinson, Lieutenant Colonel Hamtramck, and General Scott. The leaders of the legion and their aides held conference right there as the army passed about them. Essentially, the letter stated that the chiefs asked the army to halt where it was, the chiefs would parley in ten days. All of the officers rejected the letter as unresponsive to Wayne's proposal, likely just a delay tactic. The officers returned to their positions. The legion marched on.

Spy Miller reported his observations to General Wayne, "Colonel McKee and Captain Elliott wore the king's full uniforms. Fort Miamis is commanded by Major William Campbell, newly arrived from Detroit. He has two hundred fifty regulars in the garrison. He has four nine-pounders, as many six-pounders, and three smaller guns. There is plenty of ammunition for each. The guns have only recently been mounted. They work feverishly to finish the fort."

"And who holds the deed to the grounds?" Wayne asked with a wink.

"I guess that is yet to be determined, General."

"So it is. Well done scout." The general left to inspect the movement of the artillery.

Harrison commented to the two spies, "You have witnessed a historic event." After a pause, "Rejecting the letter from the chiefs is the first time all of these officers have agreed on anything."

* * *

The shade of the front porch of Wellsmont provided a touch of relief from the continuing dog days. The flowers and flowering bushes were well past their prime. Only the sweet smell of the smokehouse permeated the air. The corn to the east of the pasture was exchanging its green for golden brown. Mary and Sweet Breeze looked up from their needlework to see a wagon bumping towards them up the river lane. Mary speculated on what Gabriel would be bringing from town this week. The strong black man halted the wagon at the tool shed and unloaded an iron farm tool of some sort and what appeared to be a keg of nails. Mary set aside her project. She continued to chatter about glass and cloth and yeast. The mules jerked. Once again the wagon went into slow motion, eventually coming to a stop directly in front of the house. Mary tried to peer over the sideboard to see what Gabriel was moving to the open rear of the grain bed.

Mary called into the house, "Rachel, bring Gabriel some tea. If there are any cranberry muffins left, bring some of those, too."

Gabriel thumped down on the porch boards a heavy wooden crate simply marked "Sam'l Wells – Louisville Landing". On this he laid two bolts of cotton cloth and one of silk. Mary stroked the silk while Gabriel returned for a third armload of wares.

"The wallpaper!" Mary squealed.

A broad smile came across Gabriel, "More than that. I have letters."

"Two letters from Samuel!" she squealed in a higher pitch as she snatched the two identically folded and sealed papers and clutched them to her breast. She ignored the newspaper from Lexington that was with them. She did not observe the headline, "Reports on the Indian Attack on Fort Recovery." Gabriel laid it across the porch rail and sat upon the step, anticipating the tea and any bit of gossip he could pick up.

"Samuel says that the campaign is underway. This was sent from a place called Fort Adams on the St. Marys River, I believe ten or eleven days ago. He says that the river would lead them to Kekionga, but they are destined for another way, to the confluence of the Auglaize and the Maumee, where a fight is eminent at the stronghold of Little Turtle."

Sweet Breeze pictured in her mind the beautiful land of fields, orchards, and gardens. Another sensation flashed in her mind: the stench of Eel Town the night after the raid.

"Such beautiful country made waste," she softly uttered.

She thought of her delicate silver necklace made by Kinzie at his post on the Auglaize. She left promptly to retrieve it. She decided to wear it until William's return. The quick exit of her sister-in-law startled Mary.

"I have upset her at the mention of her father's name," she thought introspectively, "how insensitive of me."

Sweet Breeze was soon back upon the porch, "Go on, Mary, I only wanted to gather this." She leaned forward and brushed her hand under the silver.

"The other is for you from William."

A letter from her husband gone off to war. A letter to a loved one is not something that a Miami warrior would do. First a bag of pearls, now a letter.

She asked of Mary "Will you read it, please?"

"Our friend and protector, Buffalo Man, gallantly gave his life in an assault on Fort Recovery by the Miami and allies. I buried him privately on high ground. The army shall now thrust through the Black Swamp with destination being McKee's Post. The only question is how much aid will be offered to the nations by the English which I expect to be little. Wayne provides all my needs to the point that I eat too much." Mary lowered the letter, disappointed in its content. "That is all he writes. It is signed in his hand. There are two marks, symbols perhaps, below."

She handed the paper to Sweet Breeze.

"Yes, that is his signature. The first mark indicates 'I will be true to my duty.' That is, true to self being. The second means his heart and mine go together."

Mary turned to hide a tear she could not control.

Gabriel perceived: Miami, slave, master, deep inside there was little difference.

"Mary," Sweet Breeze took her by one hand, then the other. "Do you believe the legend that our husbands' father was killed by my father?"

"Yes, I do," Mary gushed in voice and tears.

"We must pray for them that they do not meet my father in battle!"

"I pray for it daily."

"I know the prayer 'The Lord is my Shepherd.' It speaks for me and for William. Will you say it with me?"

"I would be proud to say it with you, dear Sister."

Gabriel, too, knew the prayer. He recited to himself along with the daughter of the Virginia planter and the daughter of the Miami chief.

* * *

The legion camped at Buffalo Rock that night. The rock jutted into the river producing the first of a series of rapids, blocking easy passage on the river. Fort Miamis was just below the last rapids some seven miles distant. The arm of Wells the Spy had puffed with infection; fever was mounting throughout his body. He reviewed the map with Wayne, pointing out the lay of the land.

He pointed to a crevasse in the face of the rock cliff, "Down there is where I got this. The wound is turning sour; I will be of little use to you. May is your man; he is the only one familiar with the terrain."

The two could not know that at that moment William May had been bound by leather straps and thrown into a fire by Ottawa captors.

"You, Captain Wells, have one last assignment," Wayne ordered. Captain Zebulon Pike will remain here during the final push. Take him, find a defensible site to deposit our baggage. You and the Miller brothers will not go beyond the stockade that is to be erected here."

* * *

A sliver of moon provided enough light for Metea to make his way through a tangle of tree trunks to find his battle position. For the third day in a row, he crouched in a void between three twisted timbers stripped of their limbs by the past spring's tornado. At dawn he would again thank the Great Spirit for providing the nations with these defenses. The tangled mass ran from the high bank of the Maumee straight out to the prairie more than an English mile distant. Here the nations would form a line to fight English-style. To the front, an open meadow would expose the American soldiers to their fire.

As was the case the two days before, Metea and his band were among the first to take position. He was in his fourth day of fast and did not know if he could go another if the battle did not happen today. His comrades were accustomed to stalking prey for more than a day. But he knew that three days would test the patience of each.

He encouraged them, "Have patience this day. Wait for the blue coats to come near the blown timbers." It felt strange to him that now it was he who was urging patience.

Moonlight vanished; the air cooled. Lightning and thunder heralded a downpour. The Pottawatomie chief from the plains beyond the

283

Tippecanoe waited it out. He grew agitated that the others were slow to come to position. With the passing of the storm, he could see forms moving to his left. The Chippewa and Ottawa were on the bluff above the floodplain. Together with his Pottawatomie, the force numbered more than four hundred.

To his right, the Shawnee and Miami numbered five hundred men. The two tribes could be distinguished not only by their paint, but by the fact that the Miami were devoid of any clothing whatsoever. Beyond them was a force of more than four hundred Delaware, Mingo, and Wyandot. A hundred French-Canadians of the militia held the end of the line. Thus situated, Blue Jacket and Little Turtle had Buckongahelas and Tarhe to their right and Five Medals and Little Otter to their left.

The sun broke brightly free of the clouds. Metea chanted his prayer. Soon the entire earth seemed to be full of rumbling voices. Many languages rose to the Great Spirit in supplication and thanksgiving. Quiet followed. Waiting began. All eyes peered to the west for a sign, a hint, of the approaching enemy.

It was not long until two riders emerged, zigzagging across the meadow. Behind them came one, two, three long lines of mounted soldiers. Halfway across the meadow, the American scouts fell from their mounts. Metea heard the popping of muskets, first from his left, then from the far right. Fools! Wait for them to reach the timbers! The soldiers advanced and dismounted. The firing became general. Metea kept his men down, "Wait! Draw them closer!"

A band of bluecoats upon matching black horses came dashing across from the right, firing as they went. He saw a block of soldiers appear to the left near the bluff. They maneuvered and began a steady barrage of fire. The Chippewa began rushing forward, engaging them in close order. To the right the Delaware took up the charge. Soon, half of the Miami and Shawnee were engaged in front of the defenses. The Pottawatomie remained tight. Metea gave a whoop as the soldiers gave ground.

The retreating soldiers were replaced by two new advancing lines. These held for a moment, but then slowly began yielding ground. Metea placed his left foot on a notch of the tree in front of him. He anticipated the signal to charge forward. He saw the gleam of sunlight on brass cannon being positioned directly opposite the Delaware. The first blast dropped eleven warriors. While some cannon raked the field, others lobbed exploding shells into the tangle of trees.

The young chief was startled to see some warriors slip away to the direction of the fort in the rear. "Stay and fight, you dogs, or I will skin your hides and tan them!"

"Cowards!" "Women!" His men sang out to the deserters.

The bombardment ceased. The smoke slowly thinned. Metea beheld an astounding vision. Blocks of soldiers in straight formations were walking steadily, directly at him. They were not firing, but held their guns with gleaming cold steel bayonets pointing forward. Every one seemed to be pointing at him.

"Shoot!" Metia yelled. "Shoot and hold your place!"

Here and there bluecoats dropped from the line. Metea's warriors kept firing as rapidly as possible. Their muskets did not need to be aimed to send three balls at random into the approaching enemy. Metea used the rifle given to him by Wells. Wells had shown him how to reload quickly while selecting a target, sighting the target, one quick breath, then firing, repeating the motions over and over. He dropped a soldier with each shot. Still the lines were solid with men and bayonets, perhaps a thousand strong.

The warriors that were out front were now driven back into the timbers. When the soldiers reached the natural fortress, the warriors abandoned their guns and took up tomahawks. Still the soldiers did not fire, but continued forward, penetrating the defenses. The reach of the bayonets negated the effectiveness of the tomahawks. On and on the soldiers came, now climbing onto the logs. One by one the warriors turned to retreat. It was then that the soldiers fired into their backs before they could find new positions. Panic overcame the tribes. The retreat became a stampede. Metea grabbed a bayonet, pulled its handler forward, and buried his tomahawk in the back of the soldier's neck. Foregoing the scalp, he gave a whoop and retired from the battle.

Gathering three of his squad, Metea made for Fort Miamis where the tribes were certain to rally. But, at the fort, disorder reigned. Tarhe was shouting insults at the unseen officers cowering behind the walls with the gates closed. Warriors from all of the nations were streaming by. Metea stopped to stare in disbelief. The young Pottawatomie chief saw many run up and spit upon the walls under the silent cannon.

A trusted friend urged Metea, "Chief, come! We must go beyond and help protect our families! This way, let us go down the bluff and find a boat."

The shocked chief followed the direction of his warriors. They ran and slid down the steep bank to the wharf. They commandeered two canoes. Rippling of the waves quieted the hubbub above. Slipping through the waters to the camps downriver, Metea realized that he was totally unprepared for defeat. He thought back to the victory on the Wabash, to all the events that lead him to these waters of the lower Maumee.

He turned to his companions half-heartedly, "We will form a line between the fort and the camps." He pointed ahead to a low point on the left bank, "Put in there." He looked up. The sun had yet to reach its zenith.

The band joined others determined to make a stand beside a low ravine carrying a brook. The little force grew quickly into a strong line. Metea was able to assemble all the warriors with which he had begun the day. They were all intact without a single injury of note. They all had their tomahawks and most had their knives, but only two held muskets. Two men were sent to the camps for food.

The Pottawatomie returned with meager rations. "The camps are already moving out towards the lake and Detroit."

The skirmish line stayed in place until dawn. With food becoming the primary concern, the thin line disintegrated. Men wandered through the remains of the camps and drifted off to the north.

"There will be plenty of food at the lakes between the Eel and the Tippecanoe," his men urged. "Let the others beg at Detroit. We will move to the west, beyond the reach of the Americans."

"To the west, then," Metea agreed.

CHAPTER 20
Fort Wayne

Blowing trumpets and the cadence of drums rolled and echoed across the waters of the Maumee. The tramping of marching feet aroused William Wells from his slumber. Discarding his covers, he began looking for his boots, but failed the task. Throwing back the tent flap, gleaming sun caught him off guard. The sun was high and bright. How could he have slept so late? Feeling lightheaded, he edged to a bench in front of the tent. Here he watched flags lead a company through the fort gates. Something was different about those gates, but he could not detect what it was. The American flag was raised on a tall pole; cannons boomed, he could faintly hear speeches being made by the officers.

Samuel approached at a trot. He said to his brother, "I see that you are up. That is good!"

William groggily replied, "Sorry, I slept late. What is all the ceremony?"

"The naming of the fort. Now what do you think they are naming it?" Samuel paused, "Wayne! Fort Wayne! Hamtramck is to command it."

"I understood that they already named it Defiance."

Samuel stooped and looked William in the face. He said, "Little brother, you have been under a fever for near a month. Do you remember traveling from Fort Defiance after the battle?"

"I remember being thrown into the back of a wagon like a sack of meal."

"Well, that was some time ago. Your arm became infected. You had chills and fever. Look at yourself, you are skinny as a rail," he squeezed William's good arm to test the muscle. "What you are looking at is a new fort at the three rivers. Wayne has completed what Washington sent him out here to do."

"Kekionga?" William quizzed, his mind not yet clear. He looked to the left to see two log huts, all that remained of the French buildings. He rose shakily. He walked to the right around the fort wall, Samuel close

287

behind. William leaned on the corner of the blockhouse and looked around to see the confluence. The unmistakable sight of the joining of the rivers was an overwhelming sight to him. He slid his back down the timbers of the fort wall until he sat upon the tamped earth. He felt his chest and head fill with emotion. Tears began to flow freely.

"You are weak," Samuel consoled. "Return to your tent; I will help you. We will fill your belly."

"Elizabeth!" Samuel called to the one who had been attending his brother. "William is awake. Bring some broth." He informed William, "I have employed Elizabeth to attend to you only, and a handful you have been. She has been a saint."

Iron pot in hand, the round-faced, round-bodied lady appeared. She filled a bowl and held it before her. She spooned a bite and held it to William's mouth.

"I will do it," William whispered as he took the spoon.

Elizabeth broke into a broad smile as she watched him feed himself with his left hand. "Look at that," was all she could muster.

"I spent the battle at Camp Deposit with Captain Pike," William recalled aloud. "I heard some, but saw nary a bit of it. Were you engaged, brother?"

"I was in the rear guard. Some in our unit were called forward as the fighting was ending, but I remained at my station. The second day after the battle I was able to move up to Wayne's headquarters. From there I got a good look at Fort Miamis. The third day, I went out with my men to burn McKee's buildings and destroy the crops on the south side. Following that, it was a slow march back to Fort Defiance, then to here, slashing and burning fields as we went."

"Is it true that Wayne kicked the gate of Fort Miamis with his boot?" William queried.

"That would be somewhat of an exaggerated tale. He did approach within a stone's throw on two occasions. The commanders exchanged letters of insult more than once. After it was determined the tribes, having dispersed, would offer no more resistance, Wayne held a ceremony for the dead and withdrew upstream."

"How many dead?"

"Fifty officers and men killed, one hundred wounded."

"How many of the tribes?"

Samuel was a bit agitated at the question, "We counted sixty bodies. Of course, there is no account of those carried off by the tribes." Samuel recalled their conversation at the Grand Camp on the prairie nearly a year prior. "The battle was quick and decisive, just as you wished. The tribes broke and fled. The British withdrew their support upon the approach of our army. We all looked for Wayne to push on to Detroit, but I am sure he has orders from the president. So, there it is, President Washington's fort at the Miami stronghold, blocking the route to the Wabash."

Samuel refilled the bowl. He put some twigs under the pot, then got a bowl for himself. "The Kentuckians are dismissed. Scott will lead them out tomorrow. I will stay with you a day or two longer, then catch up. If you are well enough, I will inform Wayne that you can meet with him. Take it easy today. Wayne is busy anyway. I will tell him tomorrow after the militia is gone."

* * *

Major General Anthony Wayne received Captain William Wells in front of his marquee on a sunny afternoon, "I see that you are recovering from your wound. How goes it?"

"The hand is numb. It is not behaving properly."

"Look around. I am told that you know this ground well." The general vainly searched his spy for a response. "First I recovered the field of St. Clair's defeat. Now we stand where Harmar's men fell. Little Turtle's confederacy has been broken. My army is intact. What do you think of my fort?" Wayne spoke, though not in the manner of boasting, with more than a touch of pride.

"Big. Strong. Well in command of the rivers. It conveys,'I plan to be here a good long time.'"

"The garrison will be. I will be leaving soon with the remainder of the army." He waved his right hand around the encampment. "We will travel that way." He pointed in the direction of the St. Marys River. "I will remain at Greene Ville to treat with the tribes in the spring. It will be your job, and yours alone, to see that Little Turtle and the head chiefs come for council. I declare that we are now at truce. It is not my intent to punish the tribes further. Let Little Turtle know that anyone who continues hostilities will feel the full weight of my wrath."

Years spent interpreting in council houses directed Wells's response, "As you say, the confederacy is broken. Little Turtle cannot contain the nations other than his Miami. Even the war chiefs of the many nations will find it difficult to contain bands of warriors bent on mischief. If a chief declares for peace, do not treat him harshly for transgressions by renegade warriors."

Wayne was taken aback at what sounded like negotiations. He did not intend to initiate peace dialogue this day. A strange, haunting, thought crept over his mind. Could it be that Little Turtle planted this man at his right hand as a trump card, one to plead his cause in case of defeat? If that was the case, he had been outmaneuvered by the acclaimed chief. No matter, Wells was the ideal man to carry the word to the tribes. He knew each of the chiefs; he spoke their languages; he knew the terrain. The man had proven his loyalty to the cause of the American army time and again. Wayne also knew that he needed the advice of this frontiersman on how to conduct the council.

The general commanded, "Your commission as captain will expire in seven weeks. At that time you will assume the position of interpreter at this post at the same pay. You are to carry my message throughout the land. Direct the leaders of the tribes to gather at Fort Greene Ville commencing on June 15. Tell them that I do not intend to drive them from their lands. Tell them that the British are powerless to resist me and I will crush any who continue hostilities. Tell them that I will hold the truce and will personally guarantee their protection."

Wells again negotiated, "The nations will expect the council of peace to be held here in Kekionga. It is the traditional place since before the French ruled this land."

"The council will be at Greene Ville. I cannot continue to supply a full army at this distance. I cannot sit here surrounded by all of the tribes during the council. I will honor what traditions I can."

Wells offered, "At Vincennes, Putnam brought many gifts and much food. Entire villages attended for many months. Do not anticipate that only the leaders will attend, but also village chiefs, their warriors, and their families. Do not offer up a list of demands, but bring forth your desires one at a time in humility. Do not ask for immediate response, but let the chiefs discuss until they are ready to respond. Do not beg nor show any weakness. Be prepared for treachery. Yet, it is not a weakness to show mercy; it is the sign of a magnanimous victor."

Wayne liked hearing the word "victor" from the frontiersman, "Your advice is well taken. Will your arm allow you to carry my message?"

"I am ready. To approach the chiefs I will need sealed papers, silver bracelets, beef cows, and milk cows," Wells conveyed as he laid his plans in his mind.

"You and Hamtramck understand each other well enough, and the two of you know the tribes well enough. I will leave it in your hands under the direction of the colonel. He will see to your needs. Wait seven days after I leave before you go out."

* * *

Dressed in the manner of a Miami hunter, William Wells leaned into the cold wind. Snowflakes were flittering in the air despite the bright sun peering between dark clouds. He was not wearing the feathers of a chief. Those he had relinquished when he parted with Little Turtle. He was wearing his feather-fan, in addition to his medicine bag and stone amulet, about his neck. The symbol of a shaman may prove useful traveling about the unstable country.

He had not expected to come this far before being accosted by scouts from the tribes. He herded along three cows and three steers. He soon learned that it was easier to lead the largest cow, the rest would follow. Coming near the Eel River, he halted and looked about. The causeway ahead was where Hardin had been ambushed. Little Turtle and he had waited on the far bank until the column was well committed. Is this where the scouts would confront him? Surely they could see that he was alone and lightly armed. One man tromping through the forest with cows posed no threat; however, the sight was sure to arouse curiosity. Perhaps the hidden warriors thought it best to send a runner ahead to the Elk Heart villages for instructions.

He gave the rope a hard tug, "Up you go, Elizabeth." He spoke in Pottawatomie, not for the cow's benefit, but for any spy close enough to hear. Proceeding only a few steps farther up the trail, he looked upon the anticipated band of nine warriors stepping from the brush. "I am Wild Carrot of the Miami! I have gifts for Five Medals!" he proclaimed.

The silent warriors stood motionless for a moment. One small man stepped forward, "Your hair will make a gift." He flipped off the cowherder's cap and circled round about him, eying his scalp. Taking the rope from Wild Carrot's hand, he raised his knife to the cow's neck.

"Would you steal the gift of your chief?" Wild Carrot demanded. He produced a cloth from his belt and unrolled it showing silver trinkets. "These are tokens from the Americans at the fort. I am to deliver them to Five Medals. I have the protection of Little Turtle and Five Medals."

The warriors glanced at each other, leaning from one foot to another. Their leader simply said, "Come."

There were no other words spoken that day or in the camp that night.

In the morning's light, Wild Carrot observed that one of the Pottawatomie was gone and another had replaced him. Undoubtedly, the message had been carried to the Elk Heart villages and a message returned. "We know who you are. We would feed your flesh to the wolves and your bowels to the crows, but for Five Medals's protection."

"Actually, I am happy that you are here," Wild Carrot responded, "for I could not have kept the wolves from the cattle during the night without your assistance." He took a sip from his canteen, "Did I not tell you my name when you came across my path?"

An entourage from Five Medals's village met the travelers to the south of the Elk Heart River and escorted them to the higher bank on the north. The entry into the village was that reserved for an ambassador from another nation. Facing Wild Carrot, Five Medals silenced the drums and chanting. He raised a decorated lance and pronounced the words of welcome.

Wild Carrot raised his gift bundle high to the four compass directions. He addressed the chief, "These gifts I bring from the fort at Kekionga. I bring a message from the soldiers. It is a message of truce."

"Gifts of fine silver and cattle!" the chief pronounced to the attending villagers.

It was then that he noticed Wild Carrot's crippled hand.

Wells handed over the bundle. He took a paper with ribbons and seal from a leather pouch, "I bring words from General Wayne to the people of the Elk Heart lands."

"We will hear these words!" The great chief led the way into the council house.

The usual opening ceremony was attended by three village chiefs and two warriors. Five Medals made a point to carefully inspect Wild Carrot's bad hand to show that the notable warrior would present no danger. He showed no preference to their long-time acquaintance, nor malice towards the guest's service for the Americans.

In due time, Wild Carrot stood and read the scribed message. He elaborated, "I have spoken in council with General Wayne. He desires peace to spread across the land, not only to the Elk Heart villages, but to all the Pottawatomie and all the tribes. He will be generous to all who hold the truce." He drew a map in the dirt, "General Wayne retires to the Swift Creek of the Great Miami River, to the grand fort he calls Greene Ville. There he will spend the winter. When the trees begin to bud, he will hold council there with all tribes."

"The council should be at Kekionga!" Chief Wanatah declared.

"Wayne will accumulate gifts and food for the grand council. He wishes to be generous in providing for all of the nations. This he cannot do at such a great distance from the river Ohio as is Kekionga." The sagamore-turned-spy-turned-ambassador added, "He leaves only a portion of his soldiers at his Fort Wayne. Do you wish him to return with a great body of soldiers to be in your midst?"

"Let him tear down his forts at Kekionga and at the Auglaize and we will come!" another firmly pronounced.

"How can he tear down his forts while the English stab his country in the back by holding the posts Miamis and Detroit in violation of the treaty between the English King and the Council of Fifteen Fires? It is known by all that our grandfathers permitted the French to build their fort at Kekionga; our fathers permitted the same to the English. Do you now say that the Americans cannot do the same?"

Observing no other speakers coming forth, Five Medals began the closing ceremony. "We accept you as the ambassador from the Americans. You will sleep in my lodge tonight. We will have an answer in the morning. Go now. You have my protection in this village and on your return to Kekionga. Tomorrow I will provide horses and an escort."

The following evening William Wells returned to the point on the north of the confluence. He stood at the same place where he had departed from the Miami nation. A few steps to the west was the place where Little Turtle had given him the revered war club. He was alone in the twilight, but he felt the serenity of being at home. Now, to the south across the merging waters, stood a mighty fortress with big guns and a flag of blue and red and white. This night would be the full moon of the naked trees. He returned with a promise that Five Medals would appear here the day after the next full moon, the moon of the north wind. This the chief had demonstrated to his people by throwing his tomahawk to the ground, followed by breaking an arrow and tossing it over his shoulder. He promised to bring chiefs from many nations. The chief of the Elk Heart lands wished to spare Wild Carrot the hazards of travel to the unsettled roaming tribes.

During his little expedition he had learned that Little Turtle was well, though no one knew where the Miami were currently located. He learned that although the nations lost less than one hundred warriors and chiefs, the fighting spirit melted away when the red coats turned backs to them in their time of need. Survival had become the theme amongst the tribes. Five Medals was anguished that wandering bands raided his stores of food at night. The chief would share what he had if they would only ask.

Above the fort walls, a sentinel spied Wells and called below. Two boats filled with soldiers crossed to retrieve their frontier scout. Those who had wagered against his survival paid up.

* * *

The full moon came and went without the appearance of the promised chiefs. Occasionally small bands came to the fort asking for food. Each time they would declare that the chiefs were on their way. Finally, on the tenth day, a lone buckskin-clad warrior appeared on the point with a flag of truce. Colonel Hamtramck sent a white flag to the walls. He ordered the colors to be marched to the temporary floating wharf. The guard reached its place and the drums ceased their beat. Hamtramck peered into the trees to detect signs of an entourage.

Wells called from below, "Send me over in a boat, then follow with four more."

Hamtramck issued the orders. He visually inspected to see that the men of the garrison were at their stations. This could be the beginning of a full peace in the Northwest. If treachery was the intent, it could signal a continuation of a long war.

Wells faced the flag-bearing Pottawatomie. They exchanged words undetectable at the fort. Hamtramck strained to hear, certainly not to understand the phrases, but to detect some inflection to the positive or negative. Soon, the lone tribesman turned about and gave a great shout into the woods.

"Ready men!" the colonel ordered. "No firing without my command!"

Figures slowly emerged from the trees. They approached Wells in a haphazard manner. They formed a semicircle at a distance of ten yards. Eighteen chiefs in the regalia of several nations, dressed as if for a pageant, stood stiffly. Behind them formed a ring of seconds who were bristling with weapons. Wells stepped to each chief, beginning on the east.

He placed his right hand on the chief's left shoulder. Words and gestures were exchanged. After Wells completed the greetings, the chiefs handed their weapons to the seconds who promptly disappeared into the brush. The chiefs made for the boats.

Hamtramck gave the signal to stand down. Captains were called to confer on how to accommodate the visitors. Only two or three chiefs had been anticipated. Hamtramck ended up relying upon his own experience gained at Vincennes. There he had learned how to treat with the tribes. His continual correspondence with Wayne defined the limits of what he could say and what he could promise. For three days with Wells and Nicholas Miller interpreting, he conducted an amicable parley. Ample spreads of beef, vegetables, and bread were prepared for the visitors. Pomp and ceremony were the order of the day.

In addition to the Pottawatomie of the Lakes, there were Pottawatomie of the St. Josephs of the Lake, and Pottawatomie of the Prairie. Chiefs of the Ottawa, the Chippewa, and the Wyandot all spoke in favor of an extended truce. Simple terms were agreed upon. The Americans would make available food, blankets, and some powder which the tribes could obtain at Fort Wayne. The tribes were free to move about and hunt beyond a ten mile radius of any fort, military camp, or en route convoy. In return, the nations promised to appear at the assigned time at Greene Ville. At the conclusion, all the chiefs received a new musket and a silver armband engraved with clasping hands. A pint of brandy per man closed out the conference.

At dawn of the forth day after the closing of the parley with the several tribes, a lone man stood in the clearing at the point. With the spyglass, Wells quickly determined him to be a Miami chief. He went alone to greet the visitor. Landing his canoe through an icy crust, he recognized Chief Soldier of Eel Town. He knew the chief had honored his pledge made at Vincennes by not opposing the Americans.

Wells greeted him warmly, "My friend, I am glad you have come. It is an honor to be in the presence of a noble chief." It was good to be speaking the Miami tongue, to be speaking without intrigue. "It is good that you are here, though our town is not what it once was."

Chief Soldier responded, "Nor are we the men we once were."

"Come to the fort and we will eat. Hamtramck is there to greet you."

"I will not cross over. I have not come to speak with the Americans, but to see you."

"Tell me about the town of my childhood. Does it prosper?"

"First I will tell you that I am here to take you to Little Turtle. He is at the Seven Pillars of the Mississinewa; he awaits you there. You will come without soldiers; I will be your escort. From there I will take you to Eel Town. Your father Porcupine is gravely ill and asks for you."

Wild Carrot instructed, "I will return to the fort for provisions and for gifts. I will tell Hamtramck that I will be in the forest for ten days. Tomorrow, I will return here at the morning sun. Do you have horses to carry us and wares?"

"I have sufficient horses with me. I will wait here thinking about the Kekionga that I once knew."

* * *

Shortly after sunrise soldiers unloaded the boats at the north bank: two kegs of powder, four beef quarters, and four bales of blankets. Wild Carrot carried the proclamation from Wayne and eight silver arm bands. The goods were whisked into the woods by a trio of braves. Wild Carrot and The Soldier followed.

Every bit of the trail along the north bank of the Wabash was familiar to the former war chief who was now Wayne's ambassador. They passed by the Forks of the Wabash, Sugarloaf Rock, and the mouth of the Salamonie. Cliffs stretching above the river opposite Pudding Rock marked their passing. They moved along quickly. There was no stopping at the little camps and villages. At isolated way-stations they were given nourishment while men switched the packs to fresh horses. Fluffy flakes of snow drifted down, settling onto limb and ground. What was dark gray now became white. The tromping of their steps and the rippling of the river became ever more muffled by the piling snow. Eventually, they entered a wide floodplain, soon crossed to the south, and moved away from the river in the flat bottom-ground. They dismounted to lead the horses up steep hills. They cut across the neck between the two rivers, then steeply down. The snow was becoming deep when they gained the Mississinewa.

They rode their steeds across the limestone shelf that was the river bed. It was a beautiful place, Wild Carrot knew, but the darkness kept it secret. Shortly up the west bank, fires were visible flickering through the dancing flakes. The camp! Would the great chief be present? Would Little Turtle receive him warmly? How should he greet his father-in-law? Suddenly, he felt unprepared.

In the darkness, the camp was little more than a mirage. Heavy-falling snow obstructed the view of the wigwams, mere white mounds in a field of white. Sycamore and river birch held heaps of powder upon their limbs creating illusions in black and white. Surely this was the camp at the Seven Pillars. He could hear the rippling of the little rapids formed by many limestone shelves of the river bottom. If he could only detect the dark pockets between the columns on the cliff on the opposite side, he would know beyond doubt that he had reached the revered place of refuge. Wild Carrot was led to a small wigwam that held only orange embers of a fire, two blankets, and a basket with corncakes and apples. Grabbing an apple, he reached outside. He felt under the snow in search of firewood. With his body half extended outside, he pulled in enough for the night. A head peeped in.

"Little Turtle will be with you in the morning,"The Soldier informed him.

He knew that "morning" meant well before dawn. Embracing sleep was in order. He did not remember falling asleep when he was shaken awake. Little Turtle was crouched beside him in the bare wigwam.

"Arise. Come," the Chief of the Miami Nation, his father-in-law, his fellow sagamore, beckoned.

Wild Carrot sat and tried to quickly shake his slumber. Little Turtle swung a pouch to him and dashed out. The younger followed the steps of the elder through the deep, soft snow. Directly to the edge of the Mississinewa they went. The great chief led them upstream across exposed rocks slick with ice and snow. A leap across the current, then more rocks downstream led them to a miniature cave in the cliff-face directly opposite the camp. It was only a small climb to the cave, but Wild Carrot was having some difficulty mounting. Dripping seeps from above had coated the white limestone with smooth, clear ice. In the pre-dawn darkness, tuffs of snow obscured handhold pockets. He realized that this was the first climbing he had attempted since his hand became crippled. Its action was deficient. A strong arm clenched his jacket shoulder and lifted him to the ledge. He landed between two pillars formed long ago by swift currents of repeated floods. He turned and placed his back against the cliff.

He could see the silhouette of his companion, but not his features. He wanted to ask, "Are you well? Is your wife well?" However, the elder must speak first. He searched the pouch and opened a rabbit skin to find roasted turkey.

Breaking the extended silence, Little Turtle asked, "What do you think of my little village?"

Stating the obvious, Wild Carrot answered, "I arrived late. The camp was quiet. I went to my wigwam and went to sleep." He looked up. The morning sun would rise behind them. It would need to rise high above the cave and cliff and trees to light the meadow across the waters. Just now, beams were illuminating the tops of the barren maples and walnuts on the west hill behind the camp. "Now I can see only dimly. I cannot distinguish enough to count the lodges."

"So it is. I fear that Blue Jacket and Buckongahelas also only see dimly. I send messages, but they do not reply. I fear that they have not thrown off the shackles of the English as I have, and as the other nations have. In preparing for war, they held the hands of the English too tightly. I fear that they will continue to hold on to save honor among their chiefs and warriors. I fear that they will attack the Americans, perhaps one of the food convoys. Our confederation has been broken. If the American general leans his weight on any of the fractured tribes, he will annihilate them completely. The Miami nation will not be the aggressor, but will ally with any nation that is attacked. I will hold the truce as will my chiefs and warriors, but I cannot come to the fort at Kekionga to declare truce until I have words from the Shawnee and the Delaware. After the defeat, and the denial by the English, they see only dimly. One day they will see clearly. I hope that the veil will soon be lifted from their eyes."

Wild Carrot walked a line between being an ambassador for Wayne and a confidant to one with whom he was intimate. "Wayne does not wish to drive you from these lands. He will want reserves for his forts, and secure trails for his supplies. Be assured that he wants to sever all relations between the nations and the English. He will be restless until the English abandon Fort Miamis and Detroit. As for the many nations, he requires an end to hostilities with his army, and an end to the raids on the settlers."

Little Turtle rebuffed, "He will want land to give to his soldiers as the Americans have done before in the east, towards Marietta. On his maps he has marks for Clark's Grant. This he will want and more."

"I do not think that he will ask for the lands round about us on the Wabash, the Salamonie, the Eel, or this Mississinewa. The Miami will be free to hunt and make their villages. He has placed Hamtramck at his Fort Wayne; this is a man who understands the ways of the tribes.

Hamtramck will not recklessly instigate conflict, but will assure the peace."

The darkness had given way enough that Wild Carrot could now see the face of the man opposite. Little Turtle smiled knowingly that the younger of them had influenced Wayne's decision on the fort commander. "Let me examine your injury."

Wild Carrot held forth his right arm, "The healing has stopped. I have some ability with it. I cannot handle a bow or knife. I am trying new ways to load and fire a gun. I write my papers with the other hand, so I am spared learning that."

"When Wayne gives land to his soldiers, you will be awarded for your service and more for your injury. Ask for land at Kekionga that you can settle. There I may be assured an honorable burial where my grandfathers lie."

"I do not expect that land at Kekionga will be offered." Wild Carrot surprised himself at the vigor of his protest, for the first time speaking as an equal to the great chief. "If it is so, I could not own the sacred ground."

Little Turtle waved his hand from left to right in front of his face, essentially ending discussion on the point. He munched a handful of nuts and retrieved some water.

Little Turtle spoke softly, "Do not bring Sweet Breeze to our lands for a time. Famine lurks; marauders roam; treachery fills the air. When there is peace, you will build a fine home near the fort. You can live among the Americans and watch over the Miami. Her mother is worn to exhaustion by the war. Your father Porcupine is feeble. The Miami are weary as a nation. I, too, am weary. We cannot endure an extended war. If battles resume, we will fight, but eventually we will perish or seek refuge in the Spanish lands."

Wild Carrot sat quietly for a spell. He had not heard the great chief speak in this manner, nor with this voice. He slowly realized that no other person had heard it, either. The man's soul was yearning for peace, for the survival of his people.

Wild Carrot asked his mentor, "You have no injuries from the battles?"

"None."

"Were any chiefs lost at the battle at the fallen timbers?"

"The Miami were fortunate. The clash raged mainly on the wings, we were in the center. We lost nine warriors and no chiefs. In the prior battle at the new fort at the Head of the Wabash, our nation lost twenty-eight warriors and two war chiefs. Buffalo Man was left upon the field under the fort guns."

"Buffalo Man rests in a grave on the crest of the ridge opposite the fort," Wild Carrot solemnly stated. "I buried him with his bow. I sprinkled tobacco over his grave. That was all I could do for him."

The trumpeting of an elk rolled down from upstream. The sun made its presence known, sparkling tiny flashes of bright light on the snow-laden branches. A woodpecker began rattling the morning air.

Little Turtle pointed up, indicating the top of the cliff, "After our prayers, we will stroll about the camp together. All will see that our friendship endures unbroken. You will sleep in my lodge this day's night and tomorrow's night. The next day I will take you to Eel Town."

In an instant, the great chief led the way. He scampered up the notched log ladder and through the small hole in the cave ceiling.

* * *

The days on the rivers Mississinewa and Eel passed quickly. The two sagamores, accompanied by a trio of canoes, pushed out from Eel Town and paddled up to Turtle Town. From here, Wild Carrot was to traverse the portage to Kekionga alone.

At their parting, Wild Carrot asked, "What word do I take to General Wayne?"

Little Turtle stated, "I have no words for Wayne at the present. We have had no formal council, you and I. You have nothing to report other than your visit with your elderly Miami father. Return to the fort with your undelivered silver gifts, less the one given to Porcupine. Watch for my son Black Loon. When you see him appear at Kekionga, then you will know that the Miami declare for truce."

* * *

With severe cold and scarce game, the soldiers of Fort Wayne had a meager Christmas. No special rations, no relief from duty. Only a Biblical reading and a cannon salute marked the occasion. New Year's Day of 1795 was marked only as another day in the commander's log.

Two weeks into the new year, Chief Black Loon made his appearance. He was accompanied by chiefs Richardville, Pecan, and Crescent Moon. In parley with Hamtramck, interpreted by Wells, they pledged all Miami chiefs, including Little Turtle, would hold the truce. All would be present at the Greene Ville great council, though they protested that it should be conducted at Kekionga. They accepted the silver armbands and gifts of food and blankets. Hamtramck pledged that anyone who appeared at his fort and asked for food would be accommodated. Black Loon privately informed Wells that Blue Jacket and Buckongahelas would not come to this fort that Wayne built at the three rivers. Instead, they would visit Wayne directly at Fort Greene Ville.

So it was, within a month the great chiefs of the Shawnee and the Delaware made a spectacle of their entrance to the clearing before the gates of Fort Greene Ville. Overlooking the fact that they were vanquished, the two made great claims of power and prestige. Through interpreter Miller, they informed the general where they had made their camps, promised to hold the truce, pledged to attend the great council in the spring.

The two chiefs accepted gifts. They concluded by stating, "There may be warriors in the forests who will not hear our messages. We cannot be held accountable for the actions of those we cannot contact."

Despite this disclaimer, the Major General of the Legion of the United States was ecstatic. All of the tribes had ended hostilities. Only Little Turtle had sent surrogates, those being among the highest leaders of the Miami nation. If only the British would sail to the north of Lake Erie, all would be perfect. That was not likely to happen, so he would remain strong in defense and vigilant for treachery while preparing for the peace council. Wayne assessed his achievements. He had avenged the losses of Harmar and St. Clair. He had humiliated the British garrison on the Maumee. He had utterly destroyed the post of His Majesty's Indian Agent McKee, the base of instigation of the tribes by the British. The object of his mission as ordered by Washington and Knox, the fort at the three rivers in the heart of the Miami lands, proudly displayed the flag of the United States. He envisioned the president of the fledgling nation placing a square on his map and writing next to it "Fort Wayne".

Wayne quickly began organizing for the treaty palaver. He decided to rely on the knowledge of Hamtramck as well as his spies Miller and Wells. He resolved to remove General Wilkinson as far away as possible. He was astounded to learn from his advisors that the negotiations would take up to two months.

He learned from them that he should anticipate hosting well nigh a thousand men, women, and children of the tribes. Food and shelter would need to be provided for young and old. Fodder for many horses would need to be gathered. Each chief, whether greater or lesser, would need to be recognized and treated with respect. The finer the gifts that could be arranged, and the greater the banquets, the more the chiefs would be willing to negotiate. Pomp and ceremony would consume much time; they should be endured to the fullest. Liquor should be strictly controlled, yet available for special occasions. Upon signing the treaty, each chief would expect a silver peace medal with Washington's likeness engraved thereupon.

Though winter still held fast, there was little time to waste. Much was to be done leading up to the designated date of June 15. Anyway, it would be beneficial to keep the soldiers occupied in their labors. The general issued the necessary orders and made much correspondence. These things accomplished, he pondered the articles he wished to include in the treaty. If done properly and without incident, the accord could put to rest the problems of the frontier for years to come.

The general called in Wells the Spy to arrange for interpreters, "You are assigned to be lead interpreter as well as my personal agent. You will be present at all exchanges between me and the chiefs, whether formal or social. You will also interpret for the Miami, Piankashaw, and Wea nations plus any Illinois tribes in attendance." He added in a firm tone, "Just remember, you are working for me."

Wells stated the facts at hand, "The chiefs will speak freely knowing that their words will be spoken not as of children, but fully understood by you. Nicholas Miller, as you know, is the choice for Shawnee interpreter. Isaac Zane I recommend as interpreter for the Wyandot. He was raised in their villages and is called by them White Eagle. His wife is Walks On Water, the daughter of Chief Tarhe. Zane has interpreted for him at many council fires. Tarhe will undoubtedly lead the Wyandot at the peace council. It is said that the Wyandot lost many chiefs at the battle at the fallen timbers. Zane's English tongue is good. He has often traveled between the Wyandot and his kin in Wheeling."

Wayne was well aware that there were hundreds of captives living among the tribes, many remaining of their own accord. Yet he was amazed at the parallels between Zane and Wells. He had heard the full story of Isaac Zane directly from Colonel Ebenezer Zane of the Virginia militia. He had been visited by the eldest brother of Isaac during the winter at Legionville on the Ohio. The colonel was well versed in the ways of the tribes and frontier warfare.

Once again Wells's advice was on the mark. The general ordered,

"Make up a list of needed interpreters. After my review we will arrange to contact them."

His list nearly complete, William Wells pondered who should interpret for the feisty Chippewa.

Lieutenant William Henry Harrison interrupted, "A letter for you from Kentucky. Good tidings I hope."

It was from Mary. Scanning the wording, Wells let out a whoop, "I have a second daughter! My eyes and hair!"

"Virginian blood runs deep," Harrison quipped with a grin.

"Sweet Breeze hopes to join me here in the spring. Things have settled round about. How many soldiers have been killed since the truce?"

"Four here in these parts, to my knowledge," Harrison replied. "I am sure you have heard of the troubles in the Illinois country, and the few bands along the Ohio River."

"There will always be troubles of some measure. I will bring my family here. Do you have accommodations?"

"I will check with our supreme commander. I am certain that he would not deny you."

Wells left off with the list. Taking a new sheet of paper, he began a letter to Samuel. He asked his brother to personally escort Sweet Breeze and children to Fort Greene Ville. "Plan your arrival here at mid-May before the tribes are in motion to this place. Delay if the streams have not receded. I have much traveling to do. I hope to be present by then, certainly by early June. I do not anticipate Little Turtle to arrive until the appointed date of the fifteenth of June or soon thereafter. I will have need of my fine buckskins as I no longer wear the uniform of a legion captain though I am still well compensated. Ask Sweet Breeze to bring a pouch of her tea and some maple sugar if it can be obtained. All else can be obtained here."

* * *

Bags of grain provided a cushion beneath the baby, child, and mother as the wagon rattled and jolted slowly along. Sweet Breeze reached out and snapped off pink blossoms that were passing overhead. These she caressed against the cheeks of her children. She brushed them to their noses, allowing them to absorb the fragrance. Softly, she spoke the Miami word and again the English word for the bush. The scene was repeated time and again with a diverse assortment of sweet fragrances.

Captain Samuel Wells joined the game. His patience had been strained at the uneventful progress of the plodding caravan. He nudged his mount off the army road to a patch of purple flowers. In times past, he had ridden up and down this strip without taking notice of such things as this. He dismounted and plucked a handful of delicate stems.

He rode back to the wagon of precious cargo, "Sister, try these."

Sweet Breeze smiled gratefully. Delicate acts were not the nature of Samuel. His mind was always full of horses and guns, of farming and building, of soldiering and governing. A good and true man, he had interrupted tending to his business to trek again into the wilderness. He made all the arrangements to tend her to the peace council despite his personal objection to the concept. She knew that he had little faith in the truce and expected little from the impending parley. Yet it was her hope that he would remain at the treaty grounds long enough to meet her family. They, too, were leaders of their people. Her brother Black Loon would undoubtedly be present, perhaps Crescent Moon, also. The personality of her cousin Chief Richardville, who followed the Catholic doctrine, was so similar to Samuel. Though apprehensive of the initial meeting of Samuel and her father, she was certain that her husband's brother would grow to admire the great chief Little Turtle.

Her mind turned to her mother. How she yearned to present her children to their strong-willed, wise, yet tender grandmother. So many others she longed to see from her home country.

Perhaps there would be some present at the gathering who had long ago been imprisoned at Fort Hamilton. Five days earlier this convoy had set out from that post. She had sat against its walls and smelled the earth. She recreated the events of the release as had been told by her husband. She had walked to the bank of the Great Miami River where Primrose had first met Putnam. Before leaving, she had spat upon Wilkinson's house.

Day before last, they had passed the site of her father's raid on Fort St. Clair. Now men were shouting out orders as they approached another of the forts. Sweet Breeze balanced on her knees to peer ahead over the crest of the hill. The reddish glow of the late-afternoon sun highlighted Fort Jefferson. Herds of livestock grazed the hillsides. Rows of wagons obscured the outline of the palisade. The fort itself struck her as much smaller than she had expected. Canvas-covered piles of materials were stacked outside the walls. She searched intently; perhaps her husband would meet her here.

Samuel came galloping down the line from the hilltop. He directed the teamster to pull the wagon to the side and halt.

He addressed Sweet Breeze, "William is not here, nor will he be at Greene Ville. He is still amongst the tribes, cajoling all chiefs to present themselves at the council." Samuel saw the look of disappointment overtake the always sweet face. "We will not stay the night here. General Wayne sends an escort to bring us on to him."

He had no sooner spoken than eight legionnaires mounted upon matching black horses converged on them. The men were all in finely tailored uniforms. Their leader removed his plumed tricorn hat with a grand gesture.

He bowed slightly in his saddle, "It is my pleasure to meet you, Madam Wells. Allow me to introduce myself. I am Captain William Clark of the First Sub-Legion, sent by General Anthony Wayne to escort you to your station at Fort Greenville." Despite the general's continual protests, everyone substituted the common name for Wayne's "Greene Ville." Replacing his hat, he added with a nod, "I am acquainted with your husband."

Not accustomed to being addressed as "Madam Wells," Sweet Breeze took a brief moment to collect herself, "My husband has spoken of you." She thought about the lateness of the day, "Is it far?"

"I am told that you are an excellent rider. It will be only a pleasure outing. The way is well patrolled. A fire and bed await you."

"Then off we go!" she cheerily proclaimed.

An ensign came forward with a fine horse and saddle. Samuel gathered in Anne and placed her in front of him. Sweet Breeze knotted a blanket to cradle her unnamed infant and stepped from the sideboard into the vacant saddle. She rode forward and thanked the driver for her passage. He blushed and looked to the ground, waving in recognition of the compliment.

Thinking of the items she had carefully chosen and packed, she asked Samuel, "What about our things?"

Captain Clark provided the answer, "Allow me to present Ensign Meriwether Lewis of my rifle company. He will bring up your wares and deliver them to your door."

Ensign Lewis came into view, "My pleasure, Madam, I assure you."

A strange feeling began in her stomach and radiated throughout her body. What was it that brought this on? It was eerie, though not scary. An extraordinary peace enveloped her, giving her warmth and comfort.

They had trotted well past Fort Jefferson when it slowly dawned upon her mind. Lewis, Clark, Samuel, these men she placed her trust in were all Virginians by birth. She envisioned herself, not so long ago, standing at Eel Town wishing that every Virginian would die by the tomahawk. It was Virginians who were now taking her to be with her husband, taking her to soon greet her Miami kin.

It was Harrison, another Virginian, who greeted Clark's entourage. Even in the twilight, he was greatly taken aback at the appearance of Sweet Breeze. Her husband had not fully conveyed the extent of her beauty, her gracefulness and graciousness. Samuel gave Anne a lift, handing her to a soldier. When his feet met the ground, he went to assist Sweet Breeze. Ignoring his offer, she swung herself and infant free of the saddle and landed lightly. Samuel retrieved Anne while the horses were led away. Captain Clark exchanged formalities with Harrison and departed. The little group stood in a huddle outside the gate. Samuel viewed the foot and horse traffic that passed in and out of the entrance. Sweet Breeze took in the enormity of the structure. Her husband had described the grand scale of the compound, but she had certainly not imagined the scope of things she now witnessed.

Besides Samuel, Harrison and Wayne were the only ones of the entire population who knew with certainty that Sweet Breeze, wife of Wells the Spy, now Wells the Interpreter, was the daughter of Little Turtle.

Harrison was still assessing her attributes when Samuel spoke, "You have quarters for the lady?"

"Yes, yes indeed, let me show you the way."

Captain Harrison failed to introduce himself, but his guest had no doubt who it was leading the way. Her husband had described the man and his customs in detail. He was leading into the fort.

"No," she stopped and placed a hand on Samuel's arm. "Captain Wells, that is, my husband the interpreter should not reside inside the fort walls. If he is to stand between the Americans and the many nations, his family should dwell in one of the tents between the fort and the camps of the tribes."

Intrigued by her perception, Harrison needed to accomplish his assigned task. He said, "The general has issued orders that I cannot change. He is currently occupied. Besides, it would be of no use to ask. Our Commander-In-Chief has every detail laid out; there will be no changing orders already given by him. William Wells is to be quartered near the general's stoop-stone. He will be constantly in demand. The safety of you and your children is also paramount. There will be no changing him."

Samuel nodded agreement. With a motion he urged her forward. Once through the gate, they veered to the right across the parade grounds to a row of cabins attached to the east wall. Harrison opened the door to a well-appointed room. Samuel stepped in and inspected, stomping his boot on the floor planks and flapping the blankets. Finding all to his satisfaction, he escorted his brother's family inside.

Samuel said, "The general has provided well for you." Turning to Harrison, "You are providing an evening meal?"

"It is on its way: beef, vegetables, and some milk."

"Very well." Samuel next confided to Sweet Breeze, "I will stay three days. I must return whether William has shown his face or not."

She thanked him, "You have been most kind to me. What sacrifices you make!"

Samuel did not share that he wanted to see his brother with his own eyes to verify that he was still alive. He also wanted to learn the demeanor of the chiefs and the prospects for a meaningful treaty.

"I will visit you tomorrow. Now, if the kind captain will show me where I may rest these weary bones, I will be on my way."

* * *

Opening the door to catch the early morning air, Sweet Breeze was surprised to find a guard of two soldiers at her door. She was about to speak to the men when a cannon thundered, shaking not only her, but the door and seemingly the entire fort.

"Just your morning call," the shorter wiry fellow drawled, "you will get used to it. Morn and evening it is."

His stocky comrade gave a snort of laughter. Men came pouring out of row upon row of cabins located behind a string of larger buildings beyond the parade grounds. They were soon in formation and answering the roll. The short soldier explained the proceedings. He pointed out the main buildings: council house, Wayne's quarters, ovens-kitchen-offi-cers mess, powder laboratory, powder magazine, officers' quarters.

The soldier pointed, "Oh, yes, your assigned privy is there."

Sweet Breeze asked, "Am I free to walk about?"

"Yes, anytime. Inside the walls that is. You will need an officer's per-mission to venture beyond. Just know that wherever you go we will be two steps behind."

Another snort erupted from the silent one.

Private Wilhelm was surprisingly knowledgeable of happenings around the fort. Wells the Spy was not expected in for another week. Isolated bands of Pottawatomie had arrived several days ago followed by some Wea and "peace" Miami.

Wilhelm shared, "Chief Little Otter leads the Wea. Chief Soldier brought in a large contingent of the pacific Miami. He demanded to be recognized as an independent tribe separate from the Miami who waged war. Wayne calls them the Eel River Miami. Some Delaware and some Ottawa are said to be a day out. All are said to be on a friendly basis and eager for peace. It will not be long until the adjacent prairie is covered with their camps."

* * *

After five days Sweet Breeze had learned the routine of the fort. Since all of her needs were met, she had little to do but care for her children and socialize. She spoke freely with the officers and soldiers, learning many by name. Wayne had granted her a singular privilege. He provided a tent on the outer limits of the American camp. He supplied it with a banquet table, seating eight, at which she could invite peoples of the tribes to dine with her. In accepting, she had agreed to certain stipulations: she must be accompanied by her guard; she must not travel beyond the limit of the American camp; she could host no more than six guests from the tribes at one time; no spirituous drink was to be consumed; she need report any discovery of treachery.

She sat in her open door preparing the wording of the first invitation to her banquet. It would be to Chief Soldier and whoever he wished to bring. She noticed a lone rider with a tired horse sauntering towards headquarters. No one else seemed to notice the man in tattered buckskin and drooping felt hat. She watched him dismount and swing a pouch from the saddle to his shoulder. Surely it must be him! When he swaggered past the guards at headquarters, there was no doubt.

"Wild Carrot!" she called in her native Miami.

He did not hear. The Private Wilhelm, seated on a log by her door, looked at her in a quizzing manner.

"My husband, Captain Wells!" she stood and pointed.

The lad jumped up and shouted in the manner that a man calls his hunting dog, "Captain Wells! Captain Wells! Over here!"

The man looked over his shoulder in puzzlement. He raised his hat to shield the sun and peered towards the shouting. With a few words, he handed his hat and pouch to a sentry and trotted the width of the parade grounds.

With radiant smile, Sweet Breeze spoke as she had when caressing petals to the soft skin of her baby girl, "Come in, husband. See what I have brought you."

"Tell the general," the frontiersman instructed the private, "tell him I may be delayed a bit." The door shut.

Private Wilhelm wondered if he was really supposed to address the general. If so, how long would "a bit" be?

A guffaw erupted from his stout companion, "Better you than me! Ha! You and the general! What a sight! Too bad that I will miss it. I had better stay here at a safe distance to guard this door. We would not want our lady and her husband to be disturbed, now would we?"

CHAPTER 21
Philadelphia

Streams of rainwater poured down from the eve of the roof, splashing irregular patterns on the rock stoop. Sweet Breeze had placed her chair in the open doorway to catch cool whipping winds of the thunderstorm. The baby twitched at each nearby crack of lightning and the accompanying roll of thunder. Despite the annoyances, the infant continued her nursing unabated. Anne lined up cornhusk dolls, relating a story about a frog. The dolls listened to the words in Miami interspersed with occasional English, seemingly understanding both.

The parade grounds soaked up the rains as fast as they fell. Soldiers had scattered quickly after the morning formation. Chiefs were filing into the council house. She identified Pottawatomie, Ottawa, Chippewa, Wyandot, Delaware, Miami, Eel River Miami, Wea, Piankashaw, Kickapoo, and Kaskaskia. Only Blue Jacket and the Shawnee were not present.

All had been awaiting this day. The great council would formally begin. For weeks, Wayne had greeted arrivals and held banquets and informal councils. William Wells was always at his side interpreting, advising. Sweet Breeze's husband had frequently told her how proud he was of Wayne's display of patience and congeniality. He was overjoyed when the fort sheep flock was distributed to the chiefs.

The reunion with her father and mother was not what Sweet Breeze had hoped. She was present at Wayne's greeting of Little Turtle's arrival. Also, she sat at one of Wayne's banquets, her only invitation, with her father and seven chiefs of the Wabash tribes. Only in these public occasions had she been able to exchange a few words. Tulip Leaf had visited her banquet tent thrice. Her mother was uncharacteristically asocial. Sweet Breeze attributed this to constant preparation for war followed by sudden defeat. The woman's faith in her husband, who had been chosen the Chief of All Nations, had not allowed her to prepare herself for the possibility of American dominance. The presence of new grandchildren brought a brief expression of cheer, but that, too, faded.

The sun suddenly chased the dark clouds to the east. Officers and men scurried about setting up the parade grounds for an out-of-doors council. It was not long until the chiefs filed out and organized themselves by tribes geographically from east to west. Officers found their places. Wayne emerged from the council house followed by Wells the Interpreter carrying a carved black-walnut calumet. Wayne sat alone at a table facing the tribes, the row of officers seated at tables behind. Wells placed the calumet upon Wayne's table and stood to the left.

Sweet Breeze called to Anne, "Come, child, look upon your father."

The child trotted to the door, little dolls in each fist. She looked back and forth over the crowd.

"Across the way," the mother urged, "he is the only one standing. It is just as I imagined, standing between the Americans and all the tribes from the river Ohio to the grand lakes. He will see that there is peace in all the land."

"What is peace, mama?"

The question brought a burning sensation to the mother's throat. She tried to answer once, twice, but no words came out.

Finally she offered, "Peace is something everyone wants, but they just do not know how to find."

"Like a treasure?"

"Yes, like a treasure," she reassured. "Sit upon my lap awhile and we will watch."

The preliminary formalities had been dispensed inside, so the business began with the swearing in of the interpreters. Sweet Breeze was proud that William was by far the best dressed of the eight, the best dressed of the entire assembly in her mind, and the most handsome, too. Wayne lifted the calumet and said some words over it. What she could not hear clearly, she picked up in the translations.

"I, Major General Anthony Wayne, stand in place of General Washington and the Council of the Fifteen Fires. I have been granted powers as Commissioner of the United States to conduct these affairs with the many tribes gathered. You see that on the seal of my country, an eagle holds both arrows and a branch of peace. Now that our council fire has been kindled, let us throw our hatchets into a bottomless lake. Let us turn our eyes from the arrows of war towards the branch of peace."

The general then faced each tribe in turn and lifted the calumet overhead. This done, he laid the pipe upon the table and took up a paper.

"I will now read the text of the Treaty of the Muskingum, signed by many chiefs who are here present. This treaty was concluded six years ago between the many tribes and Governor St. Clair at Fort Harmar at Marietta. This text will lay plain the ground upon which we will build our treaty of this place."

Wayne read and commented on the articles of the treaty. Finally he read the names of the signers.

Chief Tarhe raised his tall frame and responded for the chiefs, "This treaty is not known to many of us here. Allow us some time to ponder these words." Tarhe turned to his fellow chiefs, "We are here to do great works. Let us not quarrel among ourselves. Let us put away small things and be united in our thinking."

In the evening, William was exhausted. He lay upon the floor and looked up at his wife, "I have seen you work your threads day by day to make a thing of beauty. I, too, have toiled each day since before Christmas to make a shawl of peace. Now it is pieced together. Whether it will hold or unravel I do not know. It is now up to the chiefs to make of it what they will. Certainly Wayne has done all in his power to ensure success."

"I sense tranquility among the chiefs that I have never encountered," his wife reassured. "The Great Spirit gave me a vision today. As you were interpreting the treaty paper, you became a mighty oak with roots reaching deep into the ground. Your arms sheltered many peoples from all nations. The flag of the Americans was draped over a branch. Acorns fell and covered the ground. Children played in the field of plenty."

"This oak would be a willow swaying in the winds without you," he sighed. He sat up, "Child's play it will be!"

He sprang over and picked up the naked baby. He ran his finger lightly on the back of her neck, "Have I ever told you the story of the lost woolly-worm?" The tiny girl smiled and cooed. "Your smile is just like little Rebecca's."

"She needs a name," the mother suggested. "Do you like Rebecca?"

"I will ask her. Do you like the name Rebecca?"

She cooed agreeably and gave an audible laugh.

* * *

The council resumed on the third day. The opening was interrupted by the long-awaited arrival of Blue Jacket, entering the fort with thirteen warriors. In his address he scathed the British and disavowed any association with them.

Later in the day, Little Turtle raised some ire by disclaiming the validity of the Muskingum Treaty. In his speech he claimed that ancestral Miami lands reached from the river Detroit to the river Chicago to the mouth of the river Wabash and up the Ohio to take in the length of the river Scioto. He insisted that the Delaware and the Shawnee tribes were merely interlopers, residing at the invitation of the Miami nation. The chiefs in attendance at the earlier treaty had no authority to form a boundary and sell off land.

By the end of the week, Wayne had conveyed the claim for the land he required for American settlement. From Fort Recovery the line stretched easterly to the Muskingum River. From Fort Recovery again, a boundary ran south and somewhat west to the Ohio River opposite the mouth of the Kentucky River. Also to be ceded were military reserves, most being six miles square, at forts Defiance and Wayne now in his possession, plus British occupied Miamis, Sandusky, Detroit, and Mackinac. The same was to be had at Ouiatenon, the mouth of the Chicago River, and Loramie's Post. Various other reserves were identified at strategic portages including the Wabash-St. Marys. Also to be included were Clark's Reserve north of the Falls of the Ohio, and the town of Vincennes, the French titles in that area to be honored.

In compensation the government would, at the signing of the treaty, distribute to the assembled tribes goods to the value of twenty thousand dollars. Henceforward, every year forever the government would distribute an annuity of one thousand dollars in goods each to the Wyandot, Delaware, Shawnee, Miami, Ottawa, Chippewa, and Pottawatomie. Also, the Kickapoo, Wea, Eel River, Piankashaw, and Kaskaskia tribes would each receive annually five hundred dollars in goods. The chiefs appeared to be delighted at the generous terms. The Chippewa, relinquishing very little, urged immediate acceptance so they could head north.

The fort wall and attached cabin provided convenient shade for Sweet Breeze to observe the proceedings each day. There, she heard Wayne read an astonishing paper. He called it "Jay's Treaty with the English." The words of the treaty told how the English king promised to withdraw his soldiers from the posts Miamis, Detroit, Mackinac, Sandusky, Niagara, and Oswego within ten moons. Everyone, other than Wayne and two officers, was completely flabbergasted at the hearing of this treaty.

She witnessed the Pottawatomie Chief Sun surrender a red war belt to Wayne. "This belt, presented to me by the English, has brought only misery." Blue Jacket publicly resigned as war chief of his nation. Buckongahelas promised to "be a steady friend as I have previously been an active enemy." Tarhe, given authority to speak for all nations, declared, "All the assembled nations do now acknowledge the fifteen fires to be our father."

Wayne once again read the articles of the treaty: the declaration of peace, the restoration of prisoners, the boundaries, the annuities, the affirmation that future land sales could be made only to the government of the United States, the punishment of trespassers on Indian lands, the rights to hunt, the licensing of traders, the policing of criminals, and the nullification of previous treaties with both the United States and Great Britain. The general polled each tribe individually, each answering the treaty adoption affirmatively. The signing ritual was scheduled for August 3, 1795.

* * *

The garrison band played briskly as the companies marched their drill. The colorful array of chiefs milled about jovially. In preparing to sign, Wayne raised a quill, waving it to and fro with great pomp. His eyes rested upon the figure in the bright yellow dress standing at the end of the table. The wife of his interpreter had invaded the space. Her dress was of cotton, patterned after the style of Philadelphia, but different. It was a cross between the eastern style and an Indian tunic. The arms were bare. The shortened length revealed delicately adorned moccasins. Tatted lace trimmed short sleeves and the neckline. River pearls dangled from the lace. A wide blue sash gathered the loose dress at the waist. Blue strips of ribbon were attached at seemingly random intervals. A delicate necklace of fine silver and large looping silver earrings complemented her dark skin. No bonnet covered her shining hair which was tied back with a yellow ribbon, then free flowing to her waist, not bunched in the back as was the general custom among the tribes. He noticed Wells observing him noticing her. Wells nodded towards the paper. Wayne winked at Sweet Breeze before signing with a flourish.

The quill was passed to Tarhe, first of the chiefs to sign. The tribes signed in their customary order of council. Each made his mark, gave and received wampum belts, then received the coveted silver medal before passing the plume. The large oblong medals, with an engraved likeness of Washington greeting a chief, the American seal on the back, were badges of distinction both for the wearer and his village. Twenty-four chiefs of the Wyandot and the Delaware made their marks the first day. It would be two more days until all of the ninety chiefs inked the treaty. Finally eighteen officers and dignitaries scribed their signatures, followed by Wells and the other interpreters. The treaty duly witnessed by all concerned, Wayne pronounced the council closed. He ordered a salute of fifteen cannon blasts.

Sweet Breeze embraced her husband. She whispered between the firings, "I do not wish to celebrate with the Americans. Let us have our own little celebration. Tell the general that you require the day off tomorrow. I should think that he would be glad to be rid of you for one day."

"We will have many days to celebrate this treaty, also to celebrate a new life for us. But now, we are free to move about the camps. Let us go to your father's fire this night."

"Would we be welcomed?" she wondered.

William gazed at her in wonderment. How could she question this? He had not yet responded when Richardville stepped up, separated them, and took each by the hand.

In the Miami language he invited, "You are to be guests of honor at the Miami feast, both of you." He placed their hands back together, then said in French to Sweet Breeze, "Your family will be reunited."

Blinking to clear her eyes of moisture, she replied, "Yes, we will be there."

William looked about quickly, "I must find Harrison to see where I may procure a fine knife or gun."

"No gun, no knife. I brought gifts. Samuel provided a large pouch of his secret tobacco. I have already given my mother a shawl in her favorite color. Our prime gifts will be Anne and Rebecca."

He kidded, "You do remember how to dance, I hope."

"I will show you dancing like you have never seen!"

* * *

The treaty concluded, the goods dispersed, the festivity waning, camps began to be struck. Little Turtle requested a last audience with the general. Major General Anthony Wayne waited by the large council house with Interpreter Wells, Major Henry DeButts, Captain William Henry Harrison, and a scribe. The great chief arrived accompanied by chiefs LeGris, Richardville, and Black Loon.

Omitting the formal opening, Little Turtle spoke directly. "Forgive my imprudence during the council talks. Early on, I did not fully comprehend the moderation and liberality with which terms were presented. I am now perfectly acquainted with every article of the treaty. I recognize that you presided in sincerity and justice. I am determined to adhere closely to all stipulations."

His lean muscular body, covered only by the usual breechcloth, showed not a hint of quivering. His voice conveyed his resoluteness. His eyes pierced the air. Richardville laid a string of wampum over the outstretched hands of the head chief. These were given to Wayne who in turn handed them to Harrison.

Little Turtle continued, "I was obligated to my nation to speak on my several objections. There was no intent to sew discord. I now come to ask certain considerations. The portage to the Wabash is a primary means of wealth to the Miami. We ask that this tradition be continued. The Wea ask that a fort be built at Ouiatanon, and that traders be sent to that place. We will be leaving soon. I will rekindle the fire at Kekionga. There we will rebuild our towns in the shadows of your Fort Wayne. We ask that the annuities be dispensed at Fort Wayne. I will regularly visit your commander at that fort in order to preserve harmony. It is our wish that Mr. Wells be placed there as resident interpreter, as he has our confidence as surely as he has yours."

Wayne, recognizing the posturing of a good statesman, made no immediate promises. "You have spoken well for your tribe and those of your confederation. Wait here one moment."

Proceeding to the pole in front of his headquarters, he hauled down his campaign flag, the one he had marched under since the formation of the legion at Legionville. He returned and handed it to his former adversary. The symbolism could not be mistaken. Up to this time he had treated all the tribes without favoring one above the other. The war was now over; the goals had been met. He revealed one more surprise by pulling a paper from his jacket.

Wayne said, "I have a letter from President Washington. He invites you to be his guest in Philadelphia. Respond by the next moon so that arrangements can be made."

317

He handed the letter to Wells. This Wells took as affirmation that he would continue to be the interpreter for the Miami. Little Turtle carefully tucked the flag-treasure under his arm and departed.

* * *

An unscheduled ceremony was conducted before Little Turtle left Greenville. The fort's military band led a funeral procession to the burial place for Tulip Leaf. She had taken ill and seemed to have surrendered herself to the illness. At the burial's conclusion, a cannon salute was given in her honor. Captain David Jones, Chaplain of Wayne's legion, entered a circle of mourners seated on blankets. He delivered a short sermon that was well received, Wells interpreting. Little Turtle and Sweet Breeze thanked the chaplain and sent their thanks to Wayne for rendered courtesies.

* * *

"We will be going home in two weeks," William announced upon entering the cabin.

"Home?" Sweet Breeze let the word rise to the rafters. She thought of Turtle Town, Eel Town, Vincennes, Wellsmont. "Just where might that be?"

"Kekionga! It is to be rebuilt. Perhaps not upon the identical village sites, maybe beyond the six mile reserve, but it will be rebuilt. It will once again become a great town of the Miami. I am to serve the fort as interpreter."

"Are we to live inside the fort?"

"We will build our own home. I will have land compensation for my services and injury to the cause. With my wages since Vincennes, we can build our own home and start a farm with orchards and horses and fields."

"Will you be required to travel the country and be away from me?"

"I will only accompany your father to visit General Washington. Afterwards we can settle with a farm on one of the three rivers."

"When you are there, wherever it is, it will be home."

* * *

William Wells sat stiffly in a high-backed chair. He inspected the front and sleeves of his fine buckskin jacket. He rubbed the toe of his left boot on the back of his right pant leg. Certainly his distinctive outfit had served well on all important occasions. But now, he questioned if he should not have obtained something from an eastern tailor. He wished to check the foyer mirror to see if his hair was tied back evenly. He tapped his fingernail on the chair arm. Not to worry, all eyes would be on the man to his right.

In equally adorned buckskin jacket, pants, and moccasins, Little Turtle additionally had red leggings with fringe and silver studs. He wore his usual bear-tooth necklace. To this he had attached his Greenville peace medal with the likeness of the man he was about to meet. Silver earrings with three loops hung from each ear. He displayed no apprehension, no discomfort, despite the need to lean forward to keep his headdress feathers from poking into the chair back.

Wells wondered how the great chief could remain so calm. They were about to meet the most famous man in the entire world! Actually, Wells had been surprised to find that Little Turtle, as well as himself, was a high celebrity in Philadelphia and the burghs along their route. Wherever they went, everyone seemed to know who they were. He heard myths repeated about their exploits. These were often mixed with tales of the hero Boone and the villain Girty. It was useless to attempt to straighten the twisted stories. The tellers were not interested in facts and details. To those who had not ventured beyond the metropolis, the Miami were ignorant naked heathens running about the woods.

Wells had been fascinated by the workings of a flour mill that was adjacent to the inn of two nights previous. Both buildings were of finished stone three stories high. He had watched the miller open the sluice, allowing water from the pond above the dam to cascade upon the giant wheel. He heard the mill creak and felt it shake to life. All around him gears turned and machinery moved. Grain flowed, dust rose, and flour poured from one spout, bran from another. How industrious are the Pennsylvanians. In every town they shaped wood, beat iron, dug coal.

Even with the senators and representatives away during the recess of Congress, Philadelphia was vigorous with activity. He wondered what his companion thought about their visit to the stores and warehouses, docks and shipyards. These questions would wait for their return trip. They were to remain here for the remainder of December and into the new year. They would take the army road to Pittsburgh. There he wished to have Little Turtle describe the battle in which the tribes and French defeated the British of Braddock. Then down the Ohio they would go. He could recall only fleeting moments of his family's flatboat trip to Limestone Landing, now Maysville. He recalled a hazy image of his father on the tiller and his eldest brother in the boat's bow pointing out obstacles.

The door to the parlor opened with a jerk. A well-groomed black servant emerged, his boots echoing sharply in the small waiting room. He bowed and motioned for them to stand, "Mister Washington will receive you now."

Close behind the servant was Timothy Pickering, Secretary of War, supplanting the resigned Secretary Knox. It was Pickering who had been their host and escort since the previous morn.

Pickering gestured, "We will have a brief gathering prior to the banquet. After you, if you please."

He motioned them in. Wells the Interpreter followed Little Turtle. Three dignitaries, handsomely dressed, plus a major in uniform, stood near the far wall. The President of the United States, also in uniform, was standing in the center of the room by a table. On the table, in addition to glass and silver accompaniments, were the Greenville calumet and the Miami peace belt. A long polished leather case lay behind.

The servant announced, "I present Chief Little Turtle of the Miami Tribe and William Wells." He stepped back and closed the door. Secretary Pickering came to their left.

Pickering introduced, "Gentlemen, Mister Washington."

Washington stepped close in front of them and bowed. His eyes were fixed intently upon the form of the chief. He had previously found it successful diplomacy to bring in leaders of the tribes. The idea was to impress the chiefs with the power of the American people. Besides, he could not be away the amount of time required to travel to the distant lands. He wished to personally meet people of influence in these lands and judge their character. The character in front of him was one that had frustrated his government since its inception.

Wells bowed, the chief remained erect.

Washington opened, "Welcome to Philadelphia. I trust that your accommodations have been agreeable. If you have been shorted in any way, let Mr. Pickering know and it will be provided."

Wells interpreted the greeting and the chief's response.

Little Turtle said, "My needs are simple. Your escorts have treated me well. I have long wished to visit Philadelphia. I find it pleases me greater than does Detroit or Montreal."

Washington recognized the mention to the towns founded by the French and occupied by the British as reference to the Miami's former alliances to those nations.

The president replied, "I am displeased that I have not been to the lands beyond the Scioto. As a young man I led expeditions to some of the Ohio country. I still marvel at the beauty and the fertility of the lands I witnessed."

Little Turtle gave a bit of a smile acknowledging the compliment as well as acknowledging the intent of Washington to engage in informal conversation.

The chief said, "When you are able to make the journey, I will be your host and guide. You will feast on all manner of game, also the finest white corn known only to the Miami."

Pickering chimed in, "Let us have a toast."

One of the dignitaries poured the wine. "To everlasting peace between the United States and the Miami Tribe. May all prosper in true friendship."

The major opened the case and produced its contents. He removed a gleaming engraved silver sword from its silver trimmed leather scabbard. This he delivered to Washington who wiped it with a cloth and examined it closely.

The president laid it across both hands and held it to his former foe, "I ask that you accept this from one warrior to another in honor of our mutual friendship."

The chief accepted it gracefully and admired it approvingly. He looked at Wells. The interpreter realized that he had left the gift for Washington by his chair in the hallway. He excused himself and scurried to retrieve it. Returning, he unwrapped a silk bundle and laid the painted leather belt over the outstretched arms of Little Turtle. The worked elk hide was painted with symbols for the three rivers, for longevity, for peace, for prosperity, and the seal of the United States. Silver fobs hung from thongs at each end.

"When you wear this belt you will know that Little Turtle is a true friend. It is given as a brother to General Washington."

Washington received it and tied it around his waist. The major gave the guest the scabbard, which the chief strapped to his waist. Washington invited Little Turtle to be seated, showing him how to position the sword in so doing. A general hubbub began with smoking and wine drinking.

Washington spoke of his early career surveying in the wilds of Virginia. Little Turtle used the opportunity to state his case for annuities to be distributed at Fort Wayne. He suggested that Wells be the representative for the United States at that place. Washington related that the service of Wells was well stated by Wayne. He would speak with Pickering about the appointment. Little Turtle remarked that every chief knew Washington to be a great warrior and an honorable man.

"It has been my good fortune," the president repaid the compliment to his guest, "to not meet you on the field of battle."

Wells cringed at the chief's response, "You are mistaken. When I was a youth, I traveled with my father and his warriors to the Forks of the Ohio, to Fort Duquesne. There we joined the French in the victory over Braddock."

He did not relay the part about holding horses, a necessary though secondary action. Washington searched the face of his former foe to detect if this was meant as an insult. There he saw the playful eyes of a mischievous child. After a moment he laughed and slapped his leg, "We took a whipping that day, for certain!"

Washington had fought in many battles since that day, and had directed many more. He had sat in camps and huts and buildings with many generals and politicians. He had learned to size up a man quickly, and to his judgment he was seldom wrong. Here he found a statesman who would use every advantage at his disposal, yet a man who stood on noble principles. The guest's integrity was paramount. A mutual trust and respect grew quickly.

"I have one favor to ask of you," Washington stated, "that you sit for a portrait by the artist Gilbert Stuart. Your likeness will remind us of your friendship when you depart. Both you and Mr. Wells, I would like."

The chief was familiar with portraits in Detroit. He had observed some on this trip. He perceived it to be an honor to the person whose likeness was painted. He looked at Wells who in turn nodded approvingly. "I will do as you request, and I thank you for the honor."

The servant proclaimed that the meal was prepared. Washington, Little Turtle, and Wells stood silently while the dignitaries filed out. The three stood waiting awhile until the two guests were ushered across the hallway to the dining parlor. Here the dignitaries, three more uniformed officers, and wives of most of the men, were in place. The opulent spread with china and silver was as overpowering to the two guests from the frontier as their appearance was to the women. The attendees could not know that Wells had tutored his father-in-law on the ways of fine dining. Finally, George and Martha Washington entered. The party began.

* * *

General Wayne placed his hand upon the shoulder of William Wells. He pointed to the American flag fluttering in the stiff October breeze over Fort Detroit. "Cast your eyes on the loveliest sight in the land."

Wells knew the satisfaction that filled Wayne. The general had raised that flag shortly after Independence Day, 1796. The general had returned to the frontier to supervise the British capitulation of the several forts.

"The scourge of the British has been removed," the Indian Agent replied tactfully, "The whole of America is indebted to you. These chiefs now live freely in peace due to your treaty that provided dignity among their nations."

Wells, as Indian Agent of the American government, was shepherding his charges into boats to be rowed out to a waiting schooner. Little Turtle, Blue Jacket, Buckongahelas, Black Hoof, and Five Medals, the premier names of the Northwest Territory, were eastward bound to visit Washington during his last days as president. The first distribution of the annuities had gone well enough during the previous month. All chiefs now looked to Wells, rather than the fort commanders, in matters of government affairs. The agent had been given little direction as how to conduct his business. He intended to obtain clarification from Pickering on jurisdiction and accounting matters.

For his part, Little Turtle was interested in bidding the retiring Washington farewell. He was eager to meet the elected President Adams and the elected Vice-President Jefferson. In these men he proved to be disappointed. Adams he did not find personable. Jefferson he simply did not like. He found Washington's new Secretary of War, James McHenry, well versed in terms of the Greenville Treaty. The secretary revealed that there would be no fort established at Ouiatenon, but rather on Lake Michigan at the Chicago River. In the secretary, Little Turtle found a statesman tempered by the metal of war.

After the speeches at Washington's banquet, during the meal, an army captain entered by the servant door. He awkwardly made his way to the president's chair. Washington read the note, wrung his hands, and rose.

"Forgive my interruption, but I must tell you the news that I have just now learned. General Anthony Wayne, my comrade-in-arms, hero of the revolution, recently celebrated for bringing peace to the northwest, has passed on to the great beyond. He took ill en route to this place from Detroit. He is buried at Post Erie on the shores of that great lake."

The president let the murmur subside. Knowing the penchant for the chiefs to assign loyalties to individuals, he felt it necessary to add, "My honored guests, I understand that you admired our departed general. Know that the government of the United States will remain strong despite the removal of Wayne by death, and myself by retirement. Abide by the treaty signed by General Wayne, and you will continue to live a life of abundance and liberty."

While the other chiefs concentrated on sightseeing and attention-getting, Little Turtle and Wells spent several days at the apartment residence of the philosopher and scientist Constantin Francois de Volney. The academic man was renown not only in his native France, but had his works published in many languages.

Greetings were exchanged. Volney explained, "My current work is on the understanding of the United States, its geography, its foliage, its people. To gain understanding, I traveled the length of the Ohio River. Of particular interest are the French settlements of Gallipolis and Vincennes. I was pleased to find that the French of Vincennes speak a very fine French and not vulgar dialects as I had supposed. They maintain peasantry customs of my country and seek close ties to the Catholic Church. Each of these things I find surprising to my mind."

The guests were pleased to know the man had journeyed to their lands in search of real knowledge of the area.

Volney continued, "In Vincennes I learned that the Miami language is rich in expression. I repeatedly heard of you, Mr. Wells, who was capable of translating the deepest meaning of the language. Of you, my chief, I was told that you speak good French and that you have traveled all the regions and know all the lands to a far extent. I endeavored to ascend the Wabash to meet you where you reside. I could not procure a passage, since all feared for my safety. Mr. Vigo suggested that I travel to Cincinnati, there to gain passage on Wayne's Trace. Upon reaching

Cincinnati and traveling north, a fever came upon me. I had to forgo my journey to your town, instead making on to Detroit, a place that was also on my itinerary.

"It is from there that I wrote you my letter. It is my pleasure to have you as my guests. As time permits, I wish to write down your descriptions of the waters, soils, rocks, trees, insects, animals, and climate. If you will permit, I wish to record your pronunciation of words of common usage. I wish to record daily customs of your people."

Since the Chief of the Miami had no intention of conversing in French, Wells translated whenever the Frenchman paused. Uncertain of the breadth of their commitment, the two agreed in general to the extended interview. Volney was specific in his questioning, making answering quite easy. Little Turtle felt it strange to talk about, and have recorded, things that could only be fully understood by experiencing them. How could marks on paper convey the taste of a spring, the texture of moss upon a rock, or a breath of the air after a thunderstorm? Still, as long as the man was genuinely interested, he would share his knowledge. Perhaps the man could help the Americans better understand the Miami ways.

The morning of the fifth interview day, Volney concentrated on language.

"How do you say: I eat." "Niouissini."

"How do you say: I have eaten." "Chaïani ouissiné"

"How do you say: I shall eat." "Nioussini kâté."

"How do you say: He eats." "Ouissinioua."

Three days the scientist took careful notes.

Little Turtle strode around the stuffy room plucking chin whiskers with his shell tweezers. Frequently he peered out upon the activities of Market Street. People of all shapes and sizes frequented hat shops and bakeries and furniture makers. The people of Kekionga would be helpless to make a living in this society, just as those below would be helpless in providing for themselves in his land. He, himself, wore a tailored blue suit purchased on that street. While he was proud of his native fashion, he did not wish to be seen only as a curiosity as had been the case on his first trip. By dressing as did the Americans, his words were heard more clearly when he was engaged in dialog with dignitaries.

On several occasions, the Chief of the Miami met with Quaker leaders at their invitation. The Friends were seeking ways to use the new-found peace to take the ways of civilization to the Indians. Little Turtle left an open invitation to any excursion to the three rivers.

Displaying his forearm he offered, "You see that I, myself, have been inoculated for the smallpox. Bring your medicines that the Miami may be spared of this scourge."

* * *

The morning cannon sent its rumble rolling across the confluence of the three rivers, shaking the double cabin to the north. Sweet Breeze heard another, then another. Each rattled dishes in the cupboard. For the first time she felt the baby kicking in her womb. A strong one this would be, she concluded.

Sweet Breeze asked, "What is the celebration this day?"

William was tossing his only son, William Wayne Wells, "A new year has arrived. The soldiers need an occasional celebration to break the drudgery."

She had never adapted to the American habit of marking time, "So, it is the month of January?"

"The month moves to January, the year to 1800, a new century."

Her mind could not comprehend who could have counted so many years since the birth of Jesus. Why was not Christmas the beginning of the year? Why was the changing of the calendar a cause for celebration? After all, the beginning day and month were arbitrary. Time, to her, was more like the flow of the St. Joseph passing through their fledgling farm. Events were as passing autumn leaves floating effortlessly upon its surface.

Her father made frequent visits to the fort. A day of celebration would guarantee his presence. He would spend the night in her home, leaving at noon the following day to walk to the council house a little farther up the St. Joseph. There he would spend a day, or a few, until returning to his town on the Eel. Grandfather's arrival was a special occasion for her children, especially in the winter when she did not take them on her visits to Turtle Town. Today, she would announce that Anne, Rebecca, William Wayne, and Juliana would have a new sibling. She always baked for her father when she knew that he was coming. The orchard had come into its own this year, flourishing with all varieties.

Sweet Breeze said, "Husband, go out and check the fruit cellar before you leave for the day. See what pie you would have me bake."

"One of each," was his quick reply.

* * *

The year proved to be one of peace and prosperity. The robust new-born Mary, called Polly, was the delight of all who beheld her. Fort Wayne remained a dusty frontier outpost with William settling only minor disputes. The government, now in Washington D.C., offered little notice of the fort that President Washington worked so long to establish. Crops grew high on the Wells farm and across the Northwest Territory. The federal government saw fit to form a separate Ohio Territory. St. Clair moved his capital from Marietta to the more populace Cincinnati. William Henry Harrison, former secretary of the Northwest Territory, was appointed governor of the newly named Indiana Territory with capital to be at Vincennes.

Wells, as both Fort Interpreter and Indian Agent, was mystified by the confusion over the jurisdiction between the agent, the fort commandant, the War Department, and the territorial governor. He filled the vacuum as an autonomous representative of the United States. The Greenville Treaty served as the law of the land. Outside the fort, there were no Americans within his reach. A handful of Canadian traders and occasional travelers required little in the way of governing.

Late in the year, Wells arranged to take fourteen head chiefs to the new capitol to meet with President-Elect Jefferson and the cabinet he was forming. Down the Maumee they went on their winter journey, across Lake Erie to Niagara, then overland to Albany. Once again by boat to New York. And on to the capitol city Washington. Henry Dearborn, appointed Secretary of War, assured that he would make no changes to the status quo. Jefferson spoke aloofly only on the need to involve the tribes in agronomy. On the side, Wells learned that Jefferson's objective was to free the Indians from the need to hunt so that the government could procure lands for settlement.

"The tribes in the east have been decimated, their villages surrounded by American settlements," Little Turtle lamented. "One day the same will be true of the Miami. It cannot be prevented; it can only be delayed."

The spring and summer being quiet at the three rivers, William and Sweet Breeze took their family for an extended visit to Samuel and Mary. The travel was leisurely and pleasurable with William pointing out significant landmarks to the children. It was just as Sweet Breeze remembered travels with her parents. The reunion at Wellsmont was sweet. The families blended smoothly into one. William constantly quizzed Samuel about agronomy procedures and animal husbandry. The younger brother recognized the elder as a master of these arts.

He urged Samuel, "If you would consent to three years, I am certain that Jefferson would support a demonstration farm at Fort Wayne."

"This is my home. Fort Wayne is yours. I will help you with the plans, but I have responsibilities here." Samuel was earnest. "Responsibilities to myself and my family, responsibilities to the town and state and the militia. With my advice you can do it."

William pleaded, "I, too, have equal responsibilities. My farm is only a fledgling. My skills are not of that vein."

"How many horses do you have?"

"Six," William replied sheepishly.

"That is enough to start. We will find two of Kentucky's finest studs for you to buy. Purchase four more locally, and you will have the start of a herd. Once established, they will multiply themselves."

In thus saying, Samuel conveniently forgot the many years it took himself to get established. He did not consider the constant demand for horses due to the past war, and the continually growing population. He did not factor in the harsh winters of the north, nor the quantities of panthers and wolves who still roamed the forests.

William had brought cash with him in hopes of obtaining horses for this very purpose. He wished to emulate all that his brother had accomplished. "I must trust your eye. You select them and I will purchase them."

Samuel crouched and cleared a patch of soil with his knife. With its point he made a map, beginning by tracing the Ohio River.

"Lexington will be our destination. Farms are sprouting up there by the day. No finer stock is to be found. We will make a holiday of it. On the way out, we can visit the Long Creek battlefield where our father fell. At Frankfort I can show you our government buildings. We will take our time in Lexington to assure that we have seen all the stock that is available. We can head north to visit the Big Blue Licks where the British and Shawnee sent Daniel Boone and his cohorts on the run. Finally, we can go to Limestone Landing where father made his first claim. We can retrace our trail, or we can hitch a ride back on a flatboat. What do you say, little brother, shall we make it a holiday? I wager we both would like to find where father's old lean-to stood."

William originally thought to purchase his studs from Samuel. The idea of sightseeing in Samuel's domain did sound appealing. After all, Samuel had traveled to Kekionga and all points between.

William nodded in agreement, "Throw in Big Bone Lick, and you have a deal."

Samuel's knife marked a large "X" on the spot. He stood and shook his brother's hand.

"Deal," he said. As in all his dealings, Samuel had a trump card that he did not expose. He was not a man to go gallivanting on a whim. He would reveal his full agenda at the appropriate time.

* * *

That time came in Duncan Tavern at Paris, north of Lexington.

Samuel asked, "You have seen all the families traveling on the roads?"

"I am aware," William replied. "According to the newspapers, the whole country is headed to Cane Ridge. Thousands are converging upon a covey of preachers. I surmise that we would not have a room tonight if you did not know the proprietor."

Samuel urged, "It is only a little off our road. I propose to investigate the curiosity. What say you?"

Feeling a bit entrapped, but indebted to his brother upon completing his business, and with a bit of curiosity himself, he consented, "I only follow your lead."

The trails to Cane Ridge Meeting House were choked with people. Farmsteads along the route hawked food and fodder at more than twice the typical market value. Every item the settlers possessed could be had for a price. The two travelers found the meeting grounds anything but orderly. The first preacher encountered stood in the rear of a wagon railing against the evils of drunkenness. No more than a youth, the young man held a spellbound audience numbering nearly fifty. Women were shaking, twitching. One woman jerked hard in a manner that made her bonnet fly into Samuel's face. Farther on, a second preacher perched precariously on a rock, arms waving, yet somehow clutching a Bible, was portraying Saul blinded on the road to Damascus. The third, atop a stump, spoke to a huddled few, and many passersby, on the steadfastness of Daniel.

Samuel Wells wound his way amidst the throng up the hill to the large wooden meeting house. The doorway was packed. He gained a window and looked about inside. Leading around the corner, he came to a crude bench. Balancing himself with a hand on William's shoulder, he looked over the crowd.

"This way."

He strode quickly to a clearing to the east. There he stopped to listen to a stout elderly preacher. William watched a swooning woman drop to the ground. No one, not even her family, paid the least bit of attention to her.

"I, too, was lost to salvation, wallowing in my own sin," the husky voice called. "My soul was dark as coal until I was washed in the blood of the Lamb. You, too, can be cleansed of the sins that shackle your heart. Do it today. Do it now! Confess your sins unto the Lord. Be baptized into the faith in the name of Jesus the Christ. Now is the time! Come near and be baptized."

Four souls stepped forward to be restored to the way of truth. Samuel calmly waited for the proceedings to transpire. When finished, the preacher instructed the converts and dismissed them with a blessing. As if on cue, the preacher extended a burly arm and pointed directly at William.

"And you, sir, are you right with God?"

William was well versed in scripture, having used the Bible extensively to improve his English. He had no qualms with the faith.

William replied, "Me and my house serve the Lord."

The preacher challenged, "Do you believe in the risen Christ, our Lord and Savior?"

"He is the way, the truth, and the light."

"Have you been baptized in the faith?"

"I have not."

"Do you choose to do so now?"

"I do."

Samuel was astonished and delighted.

The unnamed preacher instructed, "We will begin." Pointing to William's chest, he said, "You only need remove that medicine bag."

"If that is a requirement, I will decline."

The preacher turned abruptly to walk away.

Samuel caught him, "Wait!"

The two conferred. Samuel led his brother down the hill to where they had encountered the first preacher. The strong bushy-haired youth was now sitting in the wagon bed sans jacket, dousing himself with water.

Samuel inquired, "Are you Peter Cartwright?"

The young preacher wiped his brow with a bandanna. He looked over the two gentlemen in superior attire, "At your service."

"My name is Samuel Wells. This is my brother William. He wishes to be baptized this day."

The preacher recognized the names. Eager to add a lost soul to the kingdom, he donned his coat.

"You should know that I am not Presbyterian. I follow the Methodist way. In the Methodist faith we only ask that you confess your sins before man and God, and state your belief in the Living Christ. Are you prepared?"

William nodded in agreement. The minister conducted the sacrament and pronounced a blessing, "May the peace of Christ be with you all of your days."

"Thank you, Reverend," Samuel responded. He shook the man's hand and pressed forward folded money. He congratulated his brother.

Cartwright admonished, "Forgo the evils of whiskey and gambling. Read the Bible diligently. Pray always."

"Thank you," William extended his hand to the minister. With the other he removed his medicine bag. He let it drop to the dirt.

CHAPTER TWENTY-ONE

CHAPTER 22
Grouseland

The smell of Chesapeake Bay permeated the air. A stiff easterly breeze carried a slightly pungent odor, a mixture of smells that Little Turtle could not identify. The Miami chief bent over and cupped his hand into the lapping waves. He tongued a few drops to find its taste. He compared it to the mineral springs of his hunting trails. Ships sailed in and out of Baltimore harbor. Smaller skiffs and fishing boats dotted the bay. He lifted some shells and washed off the sand.

"Volney must have had an effect on you," John Conner joked. "Are you turning into a scientist?"

William Wells had recruited Conner to accompany the group as interpreter for Buckongahelas. The trader had established a relationship with the Delaware villages on the White River. He frequented Fort Wayne where Wells contracted him to assist in the annuity distribution and sundry services.

The chief simply stated, "If my path crosses a stream I can know its name and where I am on its length by observing the flow, tasting the waters, and feeling the shells. Volney would need to bring his entire library with him, looking at the pages instead of sensing the signs." He added his own quip, "He would measure the length of a panther's teeth while they were sinking into his flesh."

"I am told that Jefferson is a scientist," Five Medals stated as if questioning. "He makes books. I will ask him what book he is now making."

Wells scolded, "I fear that you enjoy your travels too much, seeing sights, meeting dignitaries, being doted upon."

The Chief of the Miami intervened, "I will earn my keep this day at the convention of Friends. Have no fear of that." He pointed to a fisherman down the beach, "Inquire if this sea ever freezes."

Hours later, they were in a packed meeting house. Little Turtle captivated the audience while speaking eloquently on only two items. His morning speech was dotted with pleas for agricultural assistance. "Not a single plow has been seen in the lands of the Miami." "Our crops are sparse, our game is dwindling." "Hunger is constant; starvation is a frequent visitor." "Send plows and hoes and seeds." "Send someone well versed in farming to teach our people." By the noon break the Quakers were all spellbound.

In the afternoon he gave an impassioned plea. "Traders come among us bringing whiskey. At first they offer it cheaply to a man. When he has had his taste, they increase the cost. The weakness of the man is such that he sells all that he possesses to procure more drink. The man is left to wallow in his own filth. A once noble man sinks into a pit of debauchery; he pulls his family into the pit." "Whiskey has brought more death to our nation than war." "Whiskey, more than pox and pestilence, is the scourge of our lands." "The president must enforce the trade laws. He must drive out the illicit traders."

The Quakers were fascinated by the speaker. They were mesmerized by his speeches. They were moved to fervent action, passing resolutions to send farm tools, to establish schools, and to see an end to the whiskey trade. These items became an abiding theme within their denomination.

These matters were also laid before Jefferson and Dearborn who endorsed them vehemently. To these Wells added, "Many of the annuity goods we receive are of inferior quality. As I have reported, some are stolen or damaged in transport. We require a storehouse where we can exchange goods for pelts, the storehouse at Detroit being too far distant. A blacksmith, a carpenter, and fence builders are needed. Lastly, a system for carrying letters at regular intervals should be established."

These items were duly noted by the Secretary of War as necessary steps to pacify the tribes.

* * *

The children were enjoying their ride. It was especially fun when their parents stepped out to wade, floating the canoe over the shallow bed.

"Let me help, Mama," Anne already had her left calf over the rail.

"Stay in the vessel," her mother directed, "you must be captain of the children. Next year, perhaps, you will be big enough to wade with your father."

They had just left Squirrel's Village where they remained only for a brief visit. It was good to see the town once again prospering. Instead of the usual trip up Squirrel Creek to their lake, the family planned to spend the later part of summer in Vincennes. Young Chief Squirrel, who had taken the name of his father upon succeeding him, accompanied them along with three warriors and their families. His village was now affiliated with the Eel River Tribe. All were bound for Vincennes where Governor William Henry Harrison was convening a council of the Wabash tribes.

Sweet Breeze wondered if her little ones would grow to cherish this river as she had. Once again in the canoe, paddling unconsciously in rhythm with her husband, she spoke a prayer aloud, "Thank you, Lord, for allowing peace to be restored to these lands. May our children know peace all of their days." Silently she added, "May we find sufficient water in the Wabash to provide easy passage."

Travel proved easy; fishing and game were good. The number of paddlers grew to more than fifty by the time they landed in the eddy of Fort Knox's dock. William trampled up the sandy slope to the fort accompanied by a lieutenant. His family mixed with those being guided northward to the camp set up by the army. Being among the first to arrive, they had choice of tents. Sweet Breeze selected a temporary location at the corner nearest the fort. She hoped her family would not be required to reside among the soldiers. Peering towards the town, she began to recognize familiar settings even though many new buildings had risen and older ones had changed.

Her husband soon approached, "We are to dine at the Vigo home this evening. Harrison and his bride will be there. The lieutenant seems to have done well for himself."

"Do you like this choice of tents?" she asked. "It is nearest the fort."

"Harrison would have us stay in a room in the town, but there is none to be had. He has a row of tents to the south of the fort for dignitaries. We are assigned Number Two."

"Of course the military would give our home a number instead of a name." She waved at the formation of closely spaced identical tents, "Have you ever witnessed a Miami camp such as this?"

The camp slowly took shape during the hot steamy summer days, overflowing to the number that had attended Putnam's conference. Harrison had learned well from Hamtramck and Wayne. Being generous with gifts, he continually expounded on friendship and peace. Wells learned that the Wea and Piankashaw, though often disappointed in

American justice, were pleased with the governor's efforts to limit aggressive settlers.

Harrison opened the council in mid-August, "The lands that your grandfathers granted to the Frenchman Vincennes, whose name continues at this place, have never been marked. These lands were inherited by the British, and now by the government of the United States as designated by the Treaty of Greenville. I witnessed that treaty myself as did many of you in attendance here." He held up a copy of the treaty. "To ensure complete understanding by all, both on the part of the government and the part of the tribes, I propose to survey and mark the boundaries of this grant. I have called you here to seek agreement on the demarcations prior to the survey. We should also agree on the mutual protection of the surveyors."

There was general agreement that it would be a good thing to do as it may eliminate future disputes. Terms of the original grant to the French was read by Harrison. Interpreter Wells looked at him in disbelief. He hesitated. The governor nodded to continue with what he had said. Wells spoke to the chiefs explaining the dimensions of a vast tract of land stretching a long length up and down the Wabash and east well beyond the forks of the White River to the salt springs. It extended nearly half the length of the Buffalo Trace. Though Harrison had not completed his opening speech, there was immediate reaction.

"We ceded only the limits of the town of Vincennes, the fort grounds, and the French farms! We have no knowledge of such an extensive grant!"

Protocol was shattered. The governor completely lost control of the proceedings. Some chiefs waved disapproval. Some shouted curses. Others stomped off.

Wells stated the obvious, "You have great trouble on your hands."

After weeks of negotiations, the chiefs affirmed that they were bound to honor the Vincennes Tract. A slightly reduced rectangle, thirty-seven miles wide and seventy-two miles long with one corner anchored at the mouth of the White River, was agreed to. The chiefs would sign on the condition that the Governor present it to the Pottawatomie and the Miami council at Kekionga the following year. The marks of Little Turtle, Richardville, Topenebee, and Winamac would need to be obtained to make it binding. Harrison promised to treat with those chiefs the following summer. In the meanwhile, the surveyors would be about their business.

After the last chief made his mark, Harrison addressed the chiefs, "I have words from President Jefferson that will make your hearts glad." The chiefs listened attentively. "The president declares that he will send tools for cultivation to your villages." He waited for the translation, no reaction. "The president promises to send men who will teach you the ways of farming." No reaction. "The president declares to restrict the whiskey trade that has been a cloud over your heads." Only somber looks. "The president wishes you to know that it is likely that soon the French will relieve the Spanish in the lands beyond the Mississippi."

At the last statement, stoicism turned to expressions of joy. Harrison suddenly understood the full meaning of it. The tribes would be eager to ally with the French. Once the French occupied St. Louis, the tribes would be empowered to resist American domination. That is why Jefferson had instructed him to acquire as much ground as possible despite offending the tribes.

* * *

Sweet Breeze accompanied her husband to the Forks of the Wabash trading post. She wanted to be present for the momentous occasion. "Harrison will be the first American official to ascend the length of the Wabash," she said.

"I believe that distinction is mine," her husband admonished.

"I mean real official," she put emphasis on "real."

"The real official we anticipate does not seem to have the sense to wait for all of the ice to clear," he chided.

Sweet Breeze continued her needlework. She had placed her chair where she could view the trail through the plate-glass window. William read and studied maps where he could see the river.

"A runner approaches from the west," she announced.

William opened the door to a chilly damp early spring breeze.

The runner remained outside, "The Americans approach. They have reached Skunk Island. I observed one large boat with two officers, twelve soldiers, and four long coats."

William acknowledged, "Well done. Continue to the fort with this message: 'Wells and the governor arrive yet this day.'" Wells turned to his wife, "Gather our things quickly. I will ready the horses. We must move quickly to make the fort tonight."

Rather than have the dignitaries ford the St. Marys, Wells had arranged for them to be ferried across from the point. The honor guard led them up to the gate of Fort Wayne. Captain John Whistler conducted a formal greeting ceremony completed by cannon barrage.

Upon settling in, Harrison called Wells to his assigned office, "I will be traveling on to Detroit. Call in the tribes for six weeks from today. I will return with everything needed for the council. In addition to ample gifts, I will bring the annuities for early distribution. That should entice the tribes to promptly assemble in good spirits. Just know that the annuities will not be paid until after the signing." In a softer, somber tone he added, "At Detroit I will be administering the estate of Hamtramck."

"Hamtramck was a friend and mentor," Wells implied to both of them. "He was a noble warrior."

"An officer of distinction," the governor added, "He should have been made general."

Governor Harrison returned to Fort Wayne ahead of his flotilla of supplies. He was eager to set about the business at hand and descend the Wabash as soon as possible. In this he was disappointed. The tribes slowly straggled in, each seeming to vie to be last. Buckongahelas did not wait for the convening of the council to express his repugnance against the Vincennes pact. A Shawnee contingent no sooner appeared than they threatened to leave.

Harrison used the leverage of the annuities, plus gifts, to press his points. Wells suggested that if one hundred fifty bushels of salt were added to the annuities to compensate for the loss of the springs, Little Turtle and Richardville would relinquish. This done the governor soon obtained agreement from Topenebee and Winamac. On June 3, 1803, the Treaty of Fort Wayne signing was conducted, including Shawnee and Delaware signers. That evening Governor William Henry Harrison dined at the table of Sweet Breeze, satisfied not only with the treaty itself, but also with the precedence it set for future purchases from the tribes.

* * *

Sweet Breeze placed two handfuls of sweet-grass on the fire and watched gray smoke waft in the still air. She lifted each of the drying fish and turned it carefully on the rack. The lake was still, the birds were quiet. The whole earth was taking a break until the passing of the hot sun. Not so her little daughters, scraping deer hides under the spreading walnut. They knelt at their task, their mother instructing them on tricks that created soft leather.

Six families had invaded the solitude of the once private camp. Smoke rose from two other camps on the east and the north of the lake. She glanced at the spring. She had stashed a copper box filled with Spanish gold coins. It rested under a flat rock in the bottom of the little pool. That was before the victory over St. Clair, before these children were born. She contemplated revealing the secret to her daughter. She placed a stick and a bit more grass on the smoke-fire. She cleaned her hands with the wet sand of the shore.

Sweet Breeze noticed movement on the crest of the hill above them. A rider appeared followed by a string of three packhorses. To Sweet Breeze it was reminiscent of the initial meeting of Metea. She missed that energetic man, but attempts of reconciliation by her husband continued to prove fruitless. Metea had not attended the treaties at Greenville, Vincennes, or Fort Wayne. He seemed to avoid the presence of William. The Pottawatomie chief had married a lovely Miami girl. He was friendly to Pecan and other Miami chiefs.

The man up the hillside dismounted and tied his animals. He walked towards the camp with an American swagger. She recognized the trader.

"Children, do you know Conner who resides among the Delaware?" She called motioning to the approaching figure, "John, come! I have tea and cakes."

The man did not refuse. But first he gave trinkets to the girls and maple candy to their mother.

Sweet Breeze broke off a bite, "If you seek William, he and our son, William Wayne, are off to the Elk Heart villages."

"I need his advice, and I extend an invitation." Conner proceeded with extraordinary news, "It seems that Jefferson intends to mount an expedition up the Missouri to the unknown parts of the western lands. The object is to cross the Snowy Mountains and reach the shore of the Ocean of the Setting Sun. I have a letter from William Clark inviting me to join him at the Falls of the Ohio one month hence."

Sweet Breeze was rapt with attention. She sent the children off to play.

Conner continued, "On the trip to Washington City, I had several occasions to dine and speak with Jefferson's secretary. His name is Meriwether Lewis; he says that he once met you."

Sweet Breeze searched her mind, but could not recall.

"I now understand his inquisitiveness," Conner's eyes seemed to be seeing a vision. "Lewis is to head the mission. He is now in Pittsburgh fitting supplies. Clark is to be his second. Some good men have already been recruited by Clark. There is one of the Floyd brothers, Charles, the falls pilot. He has John Colter, Nathaniel Pryor, and John Shields, the blacksmith. All of these William and I know to be good men fit for the job. Clark asks me to join."

"It will be a long and arduous trip for any man," Sweet Breeze wondered.

"Quite long, quite arduous," he affirmed. "I have not decided what I shall do. If I do go I would like William to go also."

Sweet Breeze's heart sank. How could her husband decline such an adventure? She knew that it would take men like her husband to succeed in such an undertaking; even with that, the risks would remain high.

"My husband knows William Clark well. He will speak highly of him. His reputation in Louisville is sound; he has not the temperament of his aging brother. Clark's acceptance of leadership is endorsement enough as to the chances of successful completion."

She refilled the wooden cups, "Go to Fort Wayne. Zebulon Pike has assumed command there. Seek his opinion and return, surely William will arrive by then."

When her husband and son did return, she only informed, "Conner seeks you. He has some news and some questions."

William Wells caught up with John Conner at Fort Wayne. The discussion between Conner and Wells was brief.

"What is the status of your post?" William inquired.

"I have recently laid in much inventory. Both my brother's store and mine are full of merchandise."

"The personal cost to you will be high. During your absence, surely other traders will infiltrate the territory. Your presence helps keep peace among the Delaware. You are also a great help to me. Our language skills will be of little value in the country of the Sioux and beyond." Wells resolved, "I will not go. Peace is fragile, I have my duties here." He added, "Besides, I do not trust Jefferson. He wishes to own the land of all the tribes. Five Medals tells me that Harrison is this day in council with the Kaskaskia, hoping to purchase the prairie beside the Illinois River. Jefferson's expedition is only intended to increase his power over the tribes."

Conner pondered, "Pike encourages me to go. He would go if he were in my position."

Wells advised, "Robert McClellan, one of my scouts with Wayne, is trading in the Illinois country. Recommend him to Clark. McClellan may already be on the Missouri by now."

Conner was in Clarksville at the appointed time. He inspected the impressive custom-designed boat. He congratulated his friends who would be journeying down the Ohio without him. He attended the send-off ceremonies. George Rodgers Clark's speech only increased his yearning to go. He stood upon the dock and watched the expedition head for its first obstacle, the Falls of the Ohio.

* * *

Harrison honed his skills in manipulating the tribes. In the summer of 1804, he purchased from the Delaware and Piankashaw lands along the Ohio from the mouth of the Wabash to Clark's Grant. Soon after, news broke about Jefferson's purchase of the vast lands beyond the Mississippi from the French. The reestablishment of the alliance between the French and the tribes was not to be. Upper Louisiana was temporarily added to Harrison's jurisdiction. Harrison whimsically compared his domain to Napoleon's empire.

He traipsed off to St. Louis to establish a government. There he won over the established Spanish population. He took advantage of the opportunity to counsel with the Sauk and Fox tribes; he purchased fifteen million acres.

The governor returned to his new brick mansion in Vincennes. He named it Grouseland, reflecting his most pleasurable pursuit of partridge hunting. The grand brick structure, the only such building between Louisville and St. Louis, was in the style of his boyhood Virginia home. Its presence conveyed stability. Stability was not what he found along the Wabash. Chiefs were threatening to break the peace. The people of Vincennes were preparing defenses. They demanded the governor call for more federal troops. Little Turtle was furious upon learning of the Delaware Treaty. The Pottawatomie would not honor the Illinois sales.

To calm the storm, Harrison announced a grand treaty to be held the following summer. All interested tribes should gather at Vincennes to voice their grievances. He sent dignitaries, including Vigo, who was well respected by the head chiefs, to appease Little Turtle.

* * *

Once again the Wells family was off to Vincennes. This time they were in the company of every chief of the Miami nation. A new Fort Knox had been built a few miles to the north of Vincennes on higher ground. The tribes camped on the old parade grounds, an easy walk to Grouseland. This time, the Wells family resided in the encampment. William was more comfortable having his wife and children surrounded by family and friends. Townsfolk were unfriendly, if not hostile. Defiantly, Sweet Breeze spent many days shopping in the town stores purchasing cloth and gifts.

Wells, along with John Conner, was constantly occupied with formal sessions, conferences with Harrison, and relaying details to both sides. He reported to the governor the dismal failure of the Quaker's meager effort to establish a demonstration farm along the upper Wabash. He lamented the inability of the government to control the liquor trade.

Harrison informed them that Wilkinson had been made governor of Upper Louisiana. Wilkinson had sent Lieutenant Zebulon Pike, the son of Zebulon Pike that they had served with during Wayne's campaign, to explore the upper reaches of the Mississippi River. All speculated on the fate of Captain Lewis and Captain Clark and their crew.

Harrison keenly discerned that the Delaware and Pottawatomie chiefs, and of course the Eel River and Wea, would not capitulate until Little Turtle was won over. He lavished gifts of clothing, saddles, and livestock upon the chiefs who accepted them on behalf of their villages. Little Turtle, he surmised, was put out at not being consulted on the Delaware Treaty more than he was opposed to the selling of lands. The village of the Chief of the Miami had been receiving an annual government subsidy of one hundred fifty dollars. To this amount he added fifty dollars. Harrison capitulated to a house and a slave for the revered chief. With increased annuities to each of the attending tribes, he not only eliminated the squabble over the ceded lands, but purchased more acreage south of the West Fork of the White River, stretching to the Greenville Treaty line.

The Pottawatomie were unduly cordial. Winamac lead a contingent of the nearby plains villages whose chiefs declared pacific intent. War had become a burden that they wished to throw off. Topenebee promoted his interests in trading at the new Fort Dearborn, recently completed at the mouth of the Chicago River. Harrison knew that Topenebee's villages in the forests east of Lake Michigan, up the St. Josephs of the Lake, frequently hosted British traders. The new American fort apparently was having the desired effect of promoting trade and negating British influence. The signing of the Treaty of Grouseland was conducted on August 21, 1805. The length of the Ohio was now deeded to the United States.

Each evening during their Vincennes stay, William described some detail of Harrison's house to his wife. She, in turn, told about her day, seeing family and friends, gathering herbs, working her crafts. Occasionally, an acquaintance from the town sought her out, bringing baked goods or a bracelet. One evening a man brought a bundle to their tent. He unwrapped a blanket and laid its contents out for them to admire. It was the finest rifle William had ever seen. He rubbed its sleek walnut stock. He examined brass and silver engravings. He felt its balance as he sighted down its long slender octagonal barrel. He worked its mechanism. He observed an inlaid silver plate, "Jn. Small Vincennes."

"Well, Mr. Small," William finally commented, "if it shoots as pretty as it appears, this is one fine rifle!"

"Captain William Clark thinks so. He took one exactly like it with him to the west," the man declared proudly.

"I ordered it to be made," Sweet Breeze beamed. "It is for you to give to Porcupine when we return."

"It is a fine weapon, but my father could not hit a tree with it, much less a squirrel."

"Never mind, he will admire and cherish it. It will give him joy that you think that he can still handle it."

He also had a surprise for her. He pulled a large heavy book from a cloth bag. He showed her the embossed title on the leather cover.

"This is Volney's discourse on the American continent. Very wordy and boring, I must say. Actually, Volney wrote it down in French. This is an English translation by a man in Philadelphia." He flipped the pages to near the back. "Look, your father's name. And there is mine." He showed all the references to Little Turtle and himself. Turning to the back he displayed words in columns. "Here is a listing of his spelling of Miami words. Beside, he has the French translation, and some in English." He gave a big laugh. "Harrison tells me that our fame has reached beyond cities of the east to the entire world."

Treaty affairs concluded, William and Sweet Breeze and brood launched their canoe along with those of relatives, including Little Turtle. Richardville and his wife, Natoequah, kept their canoe alongside because their three small children had grown close to the Wells children. William noticed Sweet Breeze move slowly. She winced when she sat in the canoe. She shifted position several times and moaned. He wondered if she may be pregnant.

"What is your condition?" he asked.

"I have a thorn in my hip. I found it when I returned from picking berries the day past. Natoequah pulled it out, but not all. It was large and long and stubborn. She had to make a cut to get it started."

"We should go to town for medicine. Or we could stop up at the fort."

"Not to worry. Natoequah applied her potion and a poultice. She added a smidgen of her secret pollen for me. However, I fear that I will not be much help with my paddle."

When the canoes reached the Wea villages, Sweet Breeze had given up any attempts at paddling. By the time they had steered into the Eel, she suffered chills and fever. At Eel Town, Natoequah inspected the wound. It had turned nasty. Sweet Breeze was sweating profusely.

Natoequah hurriedly made a brew. "Drink as much as you can. It will comfort you. Your wound is bad. We should remain here. I will care for you."

Sweet Breeze drank. She spoke softly, but in a straightforward manner. "No, we will go on. I will not die here where the ground is defiled by the Americans."

Natoequah did not answer. She would not deny that death was looming.

"Neither bury me at Kekionga where the American cannon shake the ground, where the Americans will surely one day build their brick homes over my grave."

"Not here. Not at Kekionga," Natoequah confirmed. Her mind saw the image of a small pond set deep in a bowl of surrounding hillsides. "Remember the meadow on the hillside south of the pond where our families had our secret camp during the Pottawatomie raids?"

"Yes, shortly west of the lake. It is a lovely place. So it shall be."

The little flotilla pushed on up the Eel River. At Squirrel Town, William sent the children ahead with Richardville. Sweet Breeze, her nurse, husband, and father remained. They did not raise her from the canoe, but rather lifted the canoe entirely and carried it into the village.

Learning that she was at Squirrel Town, she spoke to her father, "Bathe me and clothe me in my long doeskin dress. Take my silver necklace for yourself and give me the one that mother wore. Bury me with my prayer stick made with locks of my children's hair, and my silver cross."

During the night William nudged beside her to keep her warm. A feeling of helplessness such that he had never before experienced overcame him. So many times he had felt her to be close when they were physically apart. Now, with her next to him, somehow, he felt a gulf growing between their spirits. He wanted to recite all that she meant to him, but words would not come. "I will have no strength without you," he whispered to her soul.

She spoke a few words, "The Lord is my strength and song, and is become my salvation." *

Moonbeams cast their soft glow across the countryside. Moon shadows caressed the ground. Animals of the forest remained hushed this night. The creek and river rippled their poetic serenade.

* * *

Sunlight drenched the wildflowers on the isolated hillside. Only a beaver witnessed the father and husband performing the burial. The interment was followed by piling of fieldstones to cover the site, protecting it from animals. The stones in turn were covered by branches to disguise the little mound from the eyes of men. William would assume the task of returning in one year to scatter the stones, returning the earth to its natural form. Work and prayers finished, Little Turtle returned down Squirrel Creek to rejoin the mourners.

William, taking only his personal weapons, walked west to the Lake of the Manitou. He wandered north across the Tippecanoe and Yellow Rivers. He walked in sunshine and darkness. He came to the St. Josephs of the Lake and skirted the Kankakee Marsh. He mounted sand dunes and followed their declivity down to the lapping waters of Lake Michigan. Moonlight highlighted white caps of waves that repeatedly appeared and disappeared. He dropped to the wet sands. He wailed and mourned.

* [*King James Bible, Psalm 119, v14*]

CHAPTER TWENTY-TWO

CHAPTER 23
Tippecanoe

"I was splitting wood, as is my wont on many an evening, looking down into the curve of the river below after each whack." George Rogers Clark, white hair flowing over the collar of his uniform, pointed with his pipe stem to Judge Richards, "You have been to my home, you know how you can see any travelers from the foot of the falls on down for miles."

"A magnificent view it is from your Indiana point. Magnificent!" the judge concurred.

"Well, I recall that it was a beautiful evening, a bit cool, but all the better for chopping. I had returned from my mill that day, reviewing accounts with my miller. The sun had given the Ohio a purple hue. My glance lingered longer than normal, my mind misty with the forlorn hope of my long-lost brother." The tale-spinner had his listeners hooked. Audiences had grown weary of the old tales. In recent years the old general had supplanted his top story of the conquest of the Northwest Territory with this one.

"Another whack, then another. Then I heard a rustling coming from the direction of the Buffalo Trace, where it leads into the river for the crossing. Some still do cross, you know, but only in small groups. I had seen some sign of buffalo on the way back from the mill. I came to the corner of the porch where I could better see, expecting maybe a stray bull or a small harem. No, no animals, but the trapper Brouillette. He called out to me, 'My friend, my friend! It is I, Brouillette! I have news for you! I have come clear from St. Charles on the Missouri to see you!' Well, the man had traveled cross-country by his lonesome. He was tattered and worn to a frazzle. His horse had given out at the buffalo wallows. He did not come up to me; he simply sat down and motioned me to come near. That is the way I learned of it. Little brother William was alive! He had returned with his expedition a complete success! All of his men returned in good health except Floyd, whose demise we all knew about, rest his brave soul. A handful of men chose to stay in the wilds. He returned with his journals and specimens, exactly as the president had directed. A resounding success, all in all!"

General Clark drew deeply on his pipe, letting the accomplishment sink in. The circle of men slapped each other on the back in recognition of the accomplishment of one of their own. They had gathered at Locust Grove, the home of William and Lucy Croghan, a sister to George and William Clark. It was November 15, 1810, the fourth anniversary of the celebration held at Locust Grove in honor of Captain William Clark. Each year they gathered to celebrate anew that day. Each man would share a conversation he had with the explorer, revealing a personal tidbit of knowledge. This year the autumn had remained warm, so they gathered near the spit holding roasting ox.

Samuel and William Wells smiled approvingly at the story. Samuel continued to admire the elder officer of the Revolution whose influence had diminished over the years. Rumors of subterfuge with the French or the Spanish had tarnished relations with former loyal friends. Frequent losing bouts with his whiskey jug had chased away others. Yet Samuel had never heard a single one of those who had served with Clark utter anything but their leader's praises. The man's sisters and brother were above reproach. The Croghans were good neighbors. In their parlor John James Audubon, a local shopkeeper, had sought Samuel's help in preparing an expedition to the Miami lands to expand his collection of native birds. Samuel and George both advised Audubon that with hundreds of bands from the tribes flocking to visit a mystic medicine man, the area was too disturbed to ensure safe passage. It was George Rogers Clark who had advised Samuel to divorce himself from Aaron Burr's schemes. Samuel had hosted a meeting with Burr at his home at the request of the Floyd brothers. Heeding Clark's advice, he withdrew in time to save embarrassment. Burr, along with James Wilkinson, was suffering humiliation before the entire country. Even Andrew Jackson of Tennessee had narrowly escaped being caught in the web.

General Clark tapped the contents from his pipe, "I watched that river intently, unable to believe until I saw for myself. A month and a week I watched. Two keel boats of soldiers appeared. It had to be him! I crossed to Corn Island where I knew they would land to round the falls. There he was! A young brother, officer, trusted companion, returned as an ambassador, diplomat, scientist, explorer, leader of men! Before the crowd could descend upon him, I hurried him over to Clarksville. There we gave him a proper welcome at the place he had initiated the expedition three years prior. November fifth was the date. Remember that date. It should be set as a holiday in the Indiana Territory. That is the day we should be celebrating. The governor of Indiana should honor the Louisiana explorer, now Indian Agent for all of Louisiana, by proclaiming Clark's Day."

November fifteenth would do well enough for those on the Kentucky side of the Ohio River. Each man in turn shook the general's hand accompanied by words of congratulations. William Wells, being the last in line, gave the general an opening to delve into current events.

Clark asked the interpreter for the Miami and Pottawatomie in a voice loud enough for all to hear, "Did your trip to Washington City pacify Main Poc? And what of this Prophet, I hear he has relocated on the Wabash?"

William Wells was caught like a rabbit in a snare. The rising hubbub told him that he would have to expound on the troubles with the tribes.

He determined to make the most of it, "It will soon be two years since I took Main Poc and seven other chiefs to see Jefferson and to meet Madison's appointed cabinet. The Pottawatomie chief was insufferable, belligerent to no end. He made the entire trip miserable for me, the other chiefs, and all whom we met. To this day he remains unruly, marauding at will, unbound by Harrison's treaty lines. He pays no respect to the Treaty of Greenville. He intimidates village chiefs not only on the Illinois plains, but on the shores of Lake Michigan and north. He crosses the Mississippi to wage war on the Osage. The Miami and the greatest portion of the Delaware and Pottawatomie wish to remain peaceful, but he will not let it be. He continues to stir the pot of defiance. Turmoil is his natural state. Yes, it was Main Poc who brought the Prophet to the Wabash. He settled him above old Ouiatenon at the confluence with the Tippecanoe."

William Wells looked around the circle of men knowing that some of them surely had raided the region with Scott or Wilkinson. Samuel Wells hoped to turn the conversation to the Madison administration while trumping George Rogers Clark's tale.

Samuel urged, "Tell them, brother William, about your portrait hanging in the White House along with that of Little Turtle."

"It is true," Judge Richards nodded, "they hang prominently beside the main stairs."

A voice added, "I hear that the Prophet would like to see the two of you hang from a tree!"

William eyed the man, "I have steered hundreds of pilgrims away from the Prophet's camp, warning them that there are no provisions, that there is only hunger and disease. I tell them that the man is a faker, that they should honor their own village chiefs. I give them food and send them back home." He lowered his voice as if sharing a secret, "The Prophet came to Fort Wayne to see me and to hold audience with Little Turtle. The Great Chief of the Miami shunned him. I confronted him in front of his followers. I called him a coward and a woman. For this, Little Turtle and I are on his blacklist." He swept his eyes around to meet each man's in turn, "His threats are not to be taken lightly. He is responsible for the deaths of a Wyandot chief, a Delaware chief, and a number of Christian Delaware along the White River. These the deceitful liar accused of witchcraft. A few devoted followers saw to his wishes in the cruelest fashion."

"How many followers does this medicine man have?" asked Colonel Stewart of the Kentucky Militia.

"One day there are three hundred, another day two thousand, one-fourth of that number being warriors." He did not share that Metea, who follows the Prophet in principle, though not in method, keeps him informed of events at Prophet's Town. Metea had not reestablished friendship, but saw William as a means to achieve the desires of this reactionary faction. "I continually warn Governor Harrison that the Prophet's encampment should be dispersed. But, the governor turns a deaf ear to my advice." It would not hurt to have these men who carry political clout be aware of the strained relations between him and the governor. "As you know, Harrison came to Fort Wayne one year past to treat with the Miami, Delaware, and Pottawatomie. What you do not know is that he and John Johnston, who is the new Indian Agent at that place, handled the council badly. You do not know how close the three tribes came to warring against one another and against the United States. This would have unleashed not only those tribes, but the Chippewa and the Winnebago and others under the influence of the tempestuous Prophet. What you do not realize is the British are once again supplying all tribes with food and gifts. From Amherstburg, on the Canadian shore, they get arms and powder." Checking that he had the full attention of all, he concluded, "I tell you that the peace is now more fragile than any time since the armistice of fifteen years ago".

The men huddled in groups of three and four to share their knowledge of frontier matters.

"You have heard of the confrontation at Vincennes between Harrison and the brother of the Prophet," William again caught the attention of the assembly. "Tecumseh is not even a village chief; he has been elected by no council. Yet, he arrogantly claims to be the head chief of all tribes. He has circulated widely among the tribes. At each place he claims that those he has already visited follow his lead. But, after he is gone, those chiefs meet in council and find that none have vowed allegiance. Harrison called Tecumseh to Grouseland to explain himself, why he provokes violence. Tecumseh replied that his intent was only for peace and that he would come with twelve chiefs. He came, but he came with four hundred warriors. He would not meet in the Governor's house. He would not meet even within the fences of Grouseland, but demanded to parley in a walnut grove." William's tone had turned bitter. "At the first meeting, the imposter chief denounced that the president was not his 'father' and that Harrison was not his 'elder brother.' He proclaimed that the lands were held by all tribes in common and that no tribe had a right to sell any lands. At the second meeting, he grew more insolent and told that he was prepared to punish the chiefs who had signed the Treaty of Fort Wayne! His conduct was such that, had he been addressing General Wayne, he would have been placed in chains and imprisoned. On the third day, Tecumseh issued curses to Chief Winamac, a leader of the Pottawatomie who had greatly aided Harrison. Harrison was timid and did not defend his friend!" William's voice grew louder, attracting the attention of the ladies. "Tecumseh narrated a litany of injustices committed by the Americans, exaggerating and expounding upon each instance. When the governor initiated his reply, he was interrupted by the pretender."

Again William Wells assessed his audience, "You are all men of stature. You have heard it told of the confrontation. How Tecumseh stood and drew his tomahawk, how Harrison stood and drew his sword. How the soldiers stood to arms. How the militiamen came to position beside the buildings and atop Grouseland. You know how the council was disbanded, only to reconvene the third day. You have heard that Tecumseh apologized for his behavior, and stated that he had no desire for conflict. All of this you know. Now I will tell you what you do not know, what Harrison did not understand!"

He lowered his voice to be barely audible to the gathering; all leaned to listen intently. "Interpreter Barron refused to interpret the words that

Tecumseh uttered. Again the Shawnee demanded, 'Tell him he lies.' Barron would not do it. I tell you this. These words would have enraged Harrison. This was to be a signal to the warriors! Tecumseh was to first sink his tomahawk into the governor. This accomplished, other warriors were assigned to murder each of the gathered dignitaries. Mayhem would carry the day. War would spread across the frontier." He paused, "But, it did not happen. Cowardice prevented the Shawnee Tecumseh from performing his deeds!"

Two ladies approached. Mary nudged Samuel.

She asked, "May we interrupt long enough to claim our husbands for a stroll?"

Polly extended her bent elbow to William. It was Samuel who had encouraged the two to keep company. Polly Geiger was the daughter of his friend, comrade-in-arms and confidant, Captain Frederick Geiger of the Kentucky Militia. She would make a fine catch, in his opinion, and was well suited for his widower brother. After a summer of courting, the two had wed at Wellsmont in the spring of 1809 upon William's return from Washington City.

"May we?" Polly beamed her radiant smile to her man.

"A proper thing to do, and an impeccable time to do it," William whispered.

* * *

William and Polly returned to their farm opposite Fort Wayne for the winter. They took only their infant son Samuel with them, leaving his children in the care of Samuel and Mary. Samuel and William had established a school in which six families now took part.

Through Captain Nathan Heald, Commandant of Fort Wayne, William learned that Harrison, upon reflection, or perhaps from conversations with Kentucky dignitaries who had been present at the Locust Grove celebration, realized the threat to his life, his government, and his peace. He had implored Secretary of War Eustis to rush additional federal troops to the west. Wells's only official capacity currently was that of fort interpreter. In reality, he played a broader role of government liaison.

Heald, Wells, and others petitioned Eustis to remove Johnston as Indian Agent. In their opinion, Johnston was incapable of understanding the intricate relationships amongst the tribes. Harrison had grown to mistrust Wells, finding him to represent the Miami more than he did the government. However, to secure the peace Harrison needed the influence of Little Turtle. To secure the influence of Little Turtle, he needed Wells. Finally, Harrison relented to dividing the agency three ways: Wells became sub-agent for the Miami, John Conner for the Delaware, and a man named Shaw for the Pottawatomie. Johnston was sent to Black Hoof at Wapakoneta as agent for the dwindling Shawnee tribe.

In March of 1811, two riders approached the eastern bank of the Tippecanoe River. They chose to cross two miles above the ford at the old Pottawatomie town. Flood waters widened the river fourfold. It was necessary to swim the horses across.

The old town had never returned to the status it had before the raids of Scott and Wilkinson. Its population consisted of a few families huddled on the river bank. Across the way, shortly past the confluence with the Wabash, the new town, Prophet's Town, swarmed with activity. The riders made it to the western bank of the Tippecanoe and stopped atop a sandy hill covered with scrubby timber.

"Do you know the story of Daniel in the lions' den?" Conner asked.

"That I do," Wells affirmed.

"That is us." Conner dismounted and replaced the priming powder in his rifle and pistol. "What do we expect to learn for the governor that we do not already know? We know that the camp numbers nearly two thousand, increasing regularly. We know they have British arms and supplies. We know the terrain. We know that the Prophet refused the village's salt annuity and sent the Vincennes traders packing." Conner shook his head, "Exactly what does Harrison expect from us?" Conner remounted and kept watch while William Wells checked his weapons.

Wells replied, "For one thing, he knows that we will not be turned away. Your association with the Delaware chiefs and mine with Little Turtle will see us through. Our familiarity with the people will allow us to determine how much they will support open conflict." More solemnly he added, "You and I are to convey the message that the Americans have increased their strength. They will not cower. Governor Harrison has been given authority to punish anyone who threatens the peace." Wells removed his leggings and wrung them out, making a show of the water dripping to the ground. "We must wring all fear from our hearts and leave it at this place."

The two rode into the town on an open avenue that led west to the heart of Prophet's Town. No pickets or sentries were present to confront them. Only occasional glances questioned the presence of the riders. They encountered a nervous Pottawatomie standing at the entrance to the longhouse. The warrior was looking about for nonexistent support.

"We have a message for the one who calls himself the Prophet. Take us to him," Wells declared.

The warrior stammered, "He is not here. No one is in the longhouse. The Prophet is at his tent, meditating."

"Lead the way," Wells demanded. "Our business is urgent."

They were led across the street to an army tent fronted by a canopy. The trappings of a medicine man were strewn about. An odd effigy made of twigs and vines, clothed with vest and cap, was propped upon pillows near the tent entrance. Low moaning chants and an occasional rattle drifted from inside the tent. Their guide entered. The chanting stopped. A rustling of canvas followed.

The guide emerged declaring, "He is not here! He has gone to his place of prayer. You cannot follow."

Wells shouted with his loudest voice, "Is the Great Prophet such a coward that he cannot stand in front of the ambassadors from Governor Harrison."

Conner cringed. Bravery is one thing; inviting disaster is something else entirely. A crowd of women and children formed around them. A handful of warriors pressed through to the front brandishing war clubs and knives. A tall handsome Shawnee, his tomahawk still tucked in his belt, strutted to the center. He wore a large oval English silver medal around his neck. Silver crosses wiggled from a nose ring.

"What is your business here?"

Wells stated plainly. "Our business is with the one who calls himself the Prophet."

"Who is it that comes seeking the Prophet?" the Shawnee asked.

"I am Wild Carrot of the Miami, a warrior who has fought in battle at Little Turtle's side. I fought beside him in the Pottawatomie Battles. I earned two feathers in the Battle of the Pumpkinheads on the Eel and on the Maumee. I was made a war chief of the Miami. I led the riflemen who destroyed the American cannon at the great battle at the Head of the Wabash. For this I was given a third feather. In honor of my peace efforts I was made a sagamore of the Wabash Tribes. I stood with Tarhe and Little Turtle and Wayne to negotiate a just peace after the defeat at the Fallen Timbers." He gestured to those gathered about them, "All of these gathered know me as a just and honorable man." He turned his back to the challenger. "And who is it that questions my presence?"

Surely this Wild Carrot, this William Wells, knew who he was. The question had to be meant as an insult. "I am Tecumseh, brother of the Prophet. These are my followers. You are in my camp. Your business is with me."

"Are these your followers? I thought that they came to see the Prophet and hear him speak. Is this place not known as Prophet's Town?" Still, his back was to Tecumseh. "You wear a feather on your head. What is it that you are a chief of? Who made you a chief? One day I asked the Great Chief Little Turtle if in his many councils he had heard of a chief known as Tecumseh. He says that there is no Shawnee chief by that name. He has known no Tecumseh as a war chief in any battles."

Tecumseh was burning with rage. However, he could not allow himself to become outwardly disturbed by Wells's tricks. "I see that you do not wear your feathers. Did you lose them? Did you hand them to the Americans? Did you now come to speak for the Americans? Tell me, tell us all, on what errand Governor Harrison sent you?"

Wells turned and faced Tecumseh square-on, "Since the Prophet has gone off to pray, since he has sent you on the errand to hear the governor's message, I will relay what he says to you for delivery. The governor is disturbed that the Prophet continues to shout war cries to his neighbors. The Prophet invites tribes from the north and the west to come and wear war paint. The Governor will not stand idly by while threats are made to his surveyors and to those who have legally settled on their farms. The Council of Seventeen Fires delivered new soldiers to all the forts north of the Ohio River. The government of the United States has empowered Governor Harrison to punish all who go against existing treaties. His forces will fall upon transgressors like a swarm of mosquitoes. If the Prophet is a friend of the Unites States, he will send away those who hold the tomahawk high. He will return the distant tribes to their homes."

Tecumseh replied tersely,"Take this message to Harrison. I will come to Vincennes. There I will lay to rest all fears."

"If the Prophet comes, or if you come as his ambassador, do not come in more than four canoes. More than four will be an act of war."

With that said, Wells swiftly made his way through the onlookers, Conner at his side. The two mounted and rode east at a brisk trot. On a sandy hill, short of the Tippecanoe, Conner pulled up and took a swig from his canteen.

Conner said, "I surveyed what I could see while your words were trying to get us killed. From the count of abodes, I would say the Prophet could field a touch over one thousand warriors. It is hard to say for sure, so many are recently arrived while others are prepared to leave. The goods and packs show ample signs of English trade. I suspect that they have plenty of guns and such hidden away outside of town. I also suspect that we will be followed by a pack of renegades. Their intent will be killing us east of here, nearer Fort Wayne, where the Prophet can plead innocence."

"I concur with both observations," Wells agreed. "Instead of crossing the Tippecanoe, we could detour north then west to Fort Dearborn. There we could add to our report by knowledge gained from our friend Captain Whistler. Perhaps a visit to Chief Black Partridge would be in order. We could have the soldiers carry our message to Harrison, or go to Vincennes ourselves."

The two frontiersmen held Whistler in highest regard. The Irishman had first come to America as a British soldier in Burgoyne's brigade. He was held as a prisoner of war in the colonies after the surrender at Saratoga. He was exchanged and returned to England, only to elope to America with his bride. Eventually he accepted an ensign's commission in St. Clair's campaign. Receiving injuries at St. Clair's defeat, he could have opted out of the service. Instead, he remained to slowly move up the ladder of command. Pike had entrusted him to build the fort at the mouth of the Chicago River where Whistler continued in command. Much like Hamtramck had in Vincennes, Whistler acted somewhat like a governor at the isolated post. He had maintained a long-standing working relationship with the local tribes.

John Conner advised his companion, "Harrison already gets reports from Whistler. The chances of finding Black Partridge on the Chicago are slim. He is more likely out upon the Illinois plains, or who knows where. Besides, I suspect that some of the warriors in the town behind us are from his villages. I propose that we go north, but to the east side of Lake Michigan to Topenebee's villages. There we can learn how many British traders, or maybe even soldiers, there are at the site of their old Fort St. Joseph. I suspect that there we will find a way-station for supplies destined for the Prophet."

"Topenebee has been loyal to his Greenville mark, but, I know that he will trade wherever there is an advantage. North it is! Let us move with urgency before word of our visit here reaches the St. Josephs of the Lake."

* * *

John Conner and William Wells were warmly received by the Pottawatomie of the St. Josephs. They found the main town bristling with materials. The majority of materials, however, were American. The trader Kinzie had arranged delivery by the schooner Contractor. Captain Lee had delivered goods to the trading post on the Chicago along with government supplies to Fort Dearborn. Kinzie then accompanied the vessel Contractor across the lake to the mouth of the St. Josephs of the Lake. The ship was now carrying bales of pelts back to Detroit on the great lakes, saving the Pottawatomie much toil from the river and overland route.

The people of Topenebee's town could not tell enough tales about the sailing ship. The whole affair was cause for rejoicing among them. They claimed no knowledge of British goods. Lettering on packs and crates indicated otherwise. Conner and Wells decided not to wait on Topenebee who was transporting John Kinzie back to the west side of Lake Michigan. They reckoned for the Elk Heart lands and on to Fort Wayne.

* * *

William Wells remained at Fort Wayne tending to his farm and family. His daughters Anne and Rebecca, and Samuel's daughter Rebecca, joined them during the spring and summer months as they had the previous year. Despite the fort being locked tightly every night, Captain Heald found opportunities to resume courting niece Rebecca, the eldest of the girls. Niece Rebecca became a notable rider and marksman under his tutelage.

In August, all were in Louisville for the wedding of Rebecca Wells and Nathan Heald. Following a week of celebration, the newlyweds traveled up the Buffalo Trace to Vincennes. They continued overland to Fort Dearborn. Captain Heald relieved Captain Whistler as commandant of Fort Dearborn.

It seems that Captain John Whistler, long in command at the fort on the sands by the mouth of the Chicago River, had become embroiled in a feud with the trader John Kinzie. Major Zebulon Pike recalled Whistler to Detroit. Captain James Rhea, in turn, was given command of Fort Wayne. Nathan and Rebecca Heald relished the adventure of establishing their first home at the unique frontier post facing Lake Michigan.

It was while in Louisville that William learned of the second meeting of Governor Harrison and Tecumseh. While the Prophet remained in Prophet's Town, Tecumseh descended the Wabash with three hundred warriors dressed for battle. Scouts along the Wabash warned the town and the garrison at Fort Knox. The garrison had been strengthened by the Fourth Regiment. The Indiana Militia had been drilling regularly. Tecumseh was visibly shaken by the forces who constantly paraded about. The Shawnee self-appointed leader only made mild protests. He stated that he was leaving to gather up thousands of followers from the southern tribes, and that nothing should transpire until he returned the following spring. At the end of the second day, he headed downstream with ten warriors, sending the remainder back to their stronghold by the Tippecanoe.

Samuel Wells requested that William remain for two additional weeks to meet Harrison who was coming to Fort Steuben to greet Colonel John Boyd of the Fourth Infantry. William readily agreed. He had not met William Henry Harrison face to face since the treaty council at Fort Wayne two years previous. The governor had answered only a few of the many letters William had sent.

Samuel hosted the Governor of Indiana Territory in his home. Harrison met the Wells brothers as though they were long-lost relatives. He heaped praises of their services to the territory and the state of Kentucky, much to the delight of the ladies. In private, the governor laid out his plans. He had designs to lead an expedition up the Wabash to demonstrate against those assembled with the Prophet. Boyd, heading three hundred fifty regulars, would be Harrison's second-in-command. Samuel, with the rank of major, would lead two hundred Kentucky mounted rifle volunteers. Four hundred Indiana militia and two hundred dragoons would complete the force.

"The Kentuckians are ready to move," Samuel vowed. "I am ready! We are drilled and equipped. These scoundrels have carried on too long with their insults!"

The governor assured, "Either the vagabonds will disband and scatter, or they will suffer their punishment. What do you think of it, William?"

"They lack leadership," William suggested. "There is no cohesiveness among them. They will scatter at your approach." He then added, "Unless."

The two planners looked up from the pencil drawings on the table. "Unless what?" Harrison demanded.

"Unless the British send officers to Prophet's Town," he replied straightforwardly.

The two planners looked at each other, checking to see if the other thought it was a possibility.

Harrison declared, "They dare not do so!"

William pressed his point, "They have done all but that deed. The traffic between Fort Malden and Prophet's Town is incessant. Many warriors at the town wear red coats. Their training grounds are of English design. Their weapons and balls are of English make. Have you not seen the English medal that Tecumseh wears?" He picked up the newspaper from a side table. "All of your newspapers are full of talk of war with the British. I, with my own ears, have heard Henry Clay declare on the streets of Louisville that Congress is one step away from declaring war. If it is to be, who is to say that the spark that lights the flame cannot be struck where the Tippecanoe meets the Wabash?"

William let his comrades ponder these thoughts for a moment, then added, "I say go, and go quickly. Main Poc is known to be touring Canada. Chase away the Prophet before Main Poc can return and consolidate the two powers."

Harrison asked William directly, "Will the Miami move against an expedition up the Wabash?"

"Little Turtle wishes to be rid of this prophet as do the chiefs of the Shawnee and the Delaware. The Pottawatomie of Five Medals oppose the pretender. Young warriors from those nations that are already in the Prophet's camp will be with him. If allowed time, he will gather support from the west, and north beyond the Chicago River."

Samuel winced at this saying. His daughter at Fort Dearborn was directly on the path of warriors traveling to defend Prophet's Town.

* * *

Local Vincennes militia units paraded at the old fort grounds. Indiana Militia companies drilled on the north edge of the town, hemming in Grouseland. Samuel's mounted riflemen claimed the ground between there and Fort Knox. Samuel learned that the people of Vincennes had been living in fear of imminent attack. This had spurred the militia to take their maneuvers seriously. He judged that, though raw to battle, they were progressing nicely.

Colonel Boyd, though somewhat full of himself, had strong control of the regulars. All were anxious to fulfill the roles they had been assigned.

Matching the enthusiasm for duty were the fiery anti-slavery debates. The issue that divided the territorial legislature was brought to the front by the presence of the many New Englanders who had arrived with the regular troops, the presence of Kentucky volunteers, and the gathering of civilian-soldiers from the outreaches of the territory. Certainly, the Western Sun was at its highest period of circulation.

The column headed north on September 26, 1811. Harrison patterned his order of march after Wayne's. Samuel's men were positioned to protect the right flank during the march. For five days they trudged through soft low ground before reaching the old abandoned Piankashaw village of Terre Haute. Two miles north of the village, they stopped and set up their encampment. A crude fort stockade was thrown up in view of the Wabash. Here, in a smaller likeness of Legionville, Harrison drilled his army.

Week by week they trained. Supplies were ferried up by boat. Recruits who caved under the strain of war preparation were sent back to the home guard. Officers who had been strangers became companions. The motley crew began to resemble a fighting force. However, if their leader was expecting the enemy to capitulate at this demonstration of strength, he was disappointed.

Major Boyd became more than a little agitated at being second to what he considered a political appointee. His men favoring Lieutenant Colonel Zebulon Pike, son of Captain Zebulon Pike of Wayne's Legion, did not help his mood. The younger Pike had gained national stature because of his expeditions to the head of the Mississippi and to the head of the Arkansas. His near-death experience in a blizzard in the previously uncharted western mountains was a marvel. His subsequent capture by the Spanish bolstered his mystique to the young infantrymen. The fact that his ventures were underwritten by Wilkinson, rather than Jefferson, prevented him from leaping in rank.

Finally, on October 30, the army joyously received word that the march would resume in the morning. Only a few militiamen would remain to garrison the post which had been named Fort Harrison. Their camp after two days was at the mouth of Raccoon Creek. They had reached the demarcation of the northernmost treaty line. Samuel wondered if Harrison would cross the creek in the morning. This would be interpreted by the tribes as an invasion of their lands. Or, would the governor, now general, keep the position and send a party to invite the opposing leaders to council? The answer came quickly with the morning sun. It was the Wabash, not Raccoon Creek, that they crossed. The result was the same; it was a declaration of war against the Prophet and his allies.

In two days the force was across the Vermillion River. A blockhouse was erected to protect the boats that were left behind. The route taken was to the west and north of the Wabash. Though longer, it provided better travel. The ground was firmer and the forest was less dense. Samuel was pleased to find stretches of open prairie. Winamac and his scouts led the way. They circled several miles away from the river making creek crossings easier. Beyond Pine Creek, the direction was more east than north, through wide expanses of open prairie.

Spirits were high among the two companies of Kentucky volunteers. The terrain was much more appealing to their nature than had been the swampy grounds persistent throughout Wayne's campaign. Major Samuel Wells saw that the land held great potential for settlement. His troops, horses, and equipment were in better shape than he had hoped. He wondered at the total lack of resistance by the tribes; even sightings of enemy scouts were absent. Perhaps the army was moving faster than the enemy had anticipated; perhaps Harrison's choice of route had baffled them. He only knew that the army was fast closing in on its destination. Their advent would be from the west, not the south. The crossing of the Wabash, long behind them, would not hinder their approach.

The twelve hundred man army made camp on the night of November the fifth. It was informed by Winamac's scouts that Prophet's Town was twelve miles to their front. General Harrison called in his officers and drew up a plan of attack. The town was long and narrow, paralleling the river. A slow, steady frontal assault from the downriver end would drive the population upstream towards the Tippecanoe. At the far end of the town the army would halt, allowing the people to scatter to the north. The objective was to display the weakness of the Prophet's powers. Destroying the stores and crops would put an end to the medicine man's influence. Samuel's volunteers would have the left, furthest from the Wabash. Samuel's task was to sweep along the back side of the ridge which slopes down to a fen, preventing resisters from looping back behind the army.

Those that ate their lunch the following day only nibbled in small bites. The width of their line stretched a half-mile across a low crescent hill. The last of the autumn's wildflowers stood waist and chest high, swaying lazily in the gentle breeze. No clouds blocked the warming sunshine. No warriors had blocked their advance. The men watched and waited as the general and his lead officers gathered one hundred yards to their front. The huddle broke, the majors and captains swinging their mounts to the direction of their assigned positions. Only the general remained between the line and the village ahead.

* * *

A British captain emerged from the council house. He carried a white flag on a pole. He thrust it to Metea.

"Go quickly!" he shouted. "Meet their commander. Tell him that the Prophet will hold council with them on the field. Go!"

Metea sprang to his mount and galloped off, leaving a little whirlwind of dust. He dodged through the throng of women and children and old men who were running about, bundling their possessions, gathering their families, fleeing opposite his ride. He heard the beating of soldiers' drums signaling an advance. Clearing the last wigwam, Metea kicked and slapped his horse, urging it on. Once in the open meadow, he unfurled the makeshift flag and lifted the staff. He heard it snap overhead as he set his eyes on the general. Half-way across the distance he eased the reins. A little farther he slowed to a trot.

Finally, he saw the general turn about and shout orders. The drums signaled a halt. Two officers, six soldiers, and two scouts rode out to the general. Metea stopped his steed, then walked it ahead slowly, keeping the white flag aloft. The enemy contingent walked their horses towards him. An officer of the Kentuckians came galloping up from his right. Upon drawing closer, Metea recognized Harrison and Pike. Winamac was the lead scout; the others he did not know. The Kentuckian that joined them he had seen before. It was the man he had seen on the Muscatatuck with General Scott, Simon Kenton, and Wild Carrot.

"I am Metea of the Pottawatomie!" he called ahead.

Harrison did not wait for the interpreter. He gave no formal greeting, "Tell the people of this village that they are to disperse. They are to return to their homes and denounce the one who brings trouble upon them."

Winamac interpreted the essence of the message.

"I am not the chief of this town," Metea implored. "I carry a flag of truce with this message: 'The Prophet and his chiefs of council will follow to meet with you on this field. It is only required that your army turn back a ways.'"

"My line is formed. Here it will stay! I will meet the men of your village at those rocks. Go now and send them."

Metea turned his back and slowly, deliberately walked his horse towards the village. He did not know who was available to treat with the general. The two British officers with seven soldiers had only arrived at mid-morning of this day. Certainly, the British would not expose their presence in these lands. The war chiefs, and the vast majority of warriors, were across the river to the south, hunting and waiting to sight the enemy in that direction. The Prophet was at his place of prayer at the pudding rock, behind the invasion force.

Metea, upon reaching the town's edge, was relieved to find the Kickapoo war chief Stone Eater. Stone Eater had assumed the lead of not only his kinsmen, but also many of the Plains Pottawatomie who were loyal to Main Poc. Some of the Wea also followed his lead. The Kickapoo chief switched to a fresh horse. He was joined by the Ottawa chief Shabonee and a Wyandot unknown to Metea. The three rode out to meet Harrison. In a brief parley, they convinced the governor that their intentions were harmless. They agreed to hold a full council the following day with all chiefs present, including the Prophet, to hear the government's complaints.

Winamac selected a small ridge paralleling the fen and the town's ridge. The army made camp on the hill forested with huge oaks. They set up tight lines forming a tapered rectangle. Regular infantry and militia were set fronting the length of the ridge facing Prophet's Town, less than a mile distant. Infantry and militia also lined the back of the ridge overlooking a steeper drop to a swiftly flowing brook. Samuel Wells's Kentucky Mounted Riflemen were stationed at the head. At the narrower foot were the Harrison County Yellow Jackets, mounted riflemen under Captain Spencer.

Samuel had his men throw up light defenses of fallen logs and freshly cut limbs. A few shovels of earth filled the gaps. He set forward one row of skirmishers and two of sentries.

"Fire only if you mean business," he admonished his sentries, "or you will be answering to the entire army, not just to me." To his men he ordered, "Do not stack your arms this night. Keep them primed and within reach."

Samuel conferred with his officers, Captain Geiger to the left and Captain Robb to the right. He inspected his line. Satisfied, he lay on the ground with his back to a log. It would be a night of uneasy rest with the sound of distant drums drifting in from the front and the rear.

As was his habit, Major Wells awoke well before dawn. Heavy dew had soaked grass and leaves. His hat and jacket were damp. A private moved about fueling the fire from stacked logs. Long flickering shadows made eerie designs on tree trunks and overhead limbs. Samuel strode to the fire to feel the radiant heat on his hands and face.

"A fool thing to do," he thought to himself, "making a target in this light with the enemy camp within sight." He poured himself some coffee and fetched a biscuit from his pocket. "Better finish up quickly," he instructed the private, "and get out of this light."

Samuel returned to where he had made his bed. He sat down with his back against the log. He calculated that the morning trumpet would soon be sounding. He finished his biscuit and downed the warm coffee. He began rousting his men with the toe of his boot when he heard the pop of a rifle. It was to his front and somewhat to the left, near the creek upstream. He moved more quickly down the line, "Up boys, be alert!"

Two, then three more pops sounded, then shouting. The Kentucky officers began calling the alarm. The popping sounds increased in frequency. The scouts, followed closely by the skirmishers, came pouring in waving their hats and shouting. They had no sooner made the lines than a wave of musket fire rolled from the forest that they had evacuated. The private who had fueled the campfire dropped to his knees and began throwing sand into its flames. Others joined the effort, some with shovels, some throwing blankets.

The riflemen met the challenge with sharp rifle fire. They were soon supported on their left by a company of regulars. The engagement became heated. With the enemy still advancing, Samuel ordered a charge. The riflemen moved forward briskly. The stealthy opponents held their place as volleys were exchanged. With the volume of incoming balls steadily increasing, Samuel returned his force to their works. A second wave of the enemy attacked the Indiana volunteers near the corner to the right of Samuel's line.

Major Daviess rode up to Samuel, "Looks like your sentries caught them before the tribes were all in position. It appears that they are attempting to drive this end of our camp into the ravine to the rear."

"It will never happen, I assure you!" Wells replied.

"My dragoons are still in reserve, can you hold here?" Major Daviess questioned.

Major Wells knew that Daviess was anxious to commit his unit.

Samuel said, "Our boys know their business. They will hold. It looks as if the Indiana boys can use assistance."

Harrison rode up and conferred with Daviess. Daviess rode back to his men. Harrison shouted to Wells and his men, "Good show men! Give the savages their due!"

Harrison disappeared.

Wells saw Daviess' men charge the corner on foot. Trained primarily for fighting from horseback, they used the same tactic in close quarters on foot. Each man had a short musket in one hand, a sword in the other. In their belts each had two pistols and a knife. These men swept into the opposed position. Each fired his musket once at close range, then dropped it to the ground. Swinging and thrusting their swords, they hacked into enemy, using pistols to defend themselves and their comrades.

Daviess' charge had its effect. The resistance to Samuel's right slowly faded. Eventually, only intermittent firing came from his front. The Kentucky volleys did not diminish.

Battle sounds now shifted to the foot of the camp. Hazy early dawn changed the entire forest to a gray mass, making it impossible to distinguish enemy movements. Harrison came up and ordered half of Samuel's men to the opposite end to reinforce the Yellow Jackets where the battle still raged. In the first rays of the sun, a general charge by the front line drove the tribes into the scrub brush of the marsh. The warriors melted away in silence.

A council at the general's tent elected not to pursue. Their unfamiliarity with the terrain, plus the unknown strength of the enemy could result in a trap. They would increase their fortifications and tend to their injured, dying, and dead. An inventory of weapons, ammunition, and rations was in order. Thus ended the battle of November 7, 1811, along the Wabash below the confluence with the Tippecanoe.

Metea's forehead was bleeding, but it was only from scratches encountered in the brush. On the slope below the evacuated town, he tried in vain to rally bands of returning warriors. Many were occupied assisting their wounded and carrying the dead.

Metea called to them, "We are not defeated! There are enough warriors remaining to carry the fight! Let us rally in front of the town!"

They only snarled and cursed the Prophet's magic. At one instance he had rallied twenty warriors. But these, too, wandered away with passing bands of their compatriots.

At noon, Metea stood in disbelief at the corner of the council house. The town had been emptied of whatever a man could carry or load into his canoe. Footprints on the trails in all directions were all that was left of the dream of a united council of free men. Even the whereabouts of the Prophet were unknown.

CHAPTER 24
Chicago

Little Turtle reached into the gurgling water to grab a rock, but he could not lift it. He straightened and touched it with his walking stick, "This rock fell from the above pillar during the time of the great shaking earth, during the first one. It is said that during the last of the shakings this entire river went dry, then the waters came crashing back upon itself."

William Wells pulled the noble chief up to the ledge of the Seven Pillars of the Mississinewa.

"The last time we were here," the Chief of the Miami nation said, "it was I who pulled you up." He continued with his story, "See above, the opening is much larger now. I was in my cabin on the Eel during the first shaking. The walls danced, dust puffed up between the floor boards, all around items flew from their pegs. I expected the Great Spirit to carry me away. At the third shaking, one greater than those before, I was walking towards the Turtle Town trading post. I was knocked down and rolled down the bank where I landed against a stump that had lifted out of the ground. Trees fell all about. I saw the waters of the Eel rush upstream in a great wave. That day we filled baskets with fish that had been thrown upon the shore."

These stories he had heard before, but Wells let him finish. Strange tales indeed had circulated across the entire land. "Earthquake" was the English word for it. None had ever been recorded in the Miami legends. Even Volney's book said the land was free of them.

Little Turtle scattered some pinches of tobacco about the alcove and chanted a blessing. He stared into the passing waters and gravely stated, "If I had my strength, I would have stood at yesterday's council, walked to Tecumseh, and buried my tomahawk deep in his skull. But, I could not; he is physically stronger than my old bones."

William said, "At least you would have had the satisfaction of a warrior's death."

"Yes, but he would claim my power as his own and use it to his purposes. I could not present him with that opportunity."

"Tecumseh came with great hopes," Wells offered, "but went away disappointed. Though a few spoke for his cause, the council was unanimous in denouncing his violating the peace."

The old chief lamented, "The spirits of Buckongahelas and Blue Jacket have crossed beyond. Had their feet been upon the earth, they would not have tolerated the ways of the Prophet. Black Hoof, Tarhe, and Five Medals are true friends of mine. Unfortunately, they will not be able to contain their young warriors for long. I will soon be gone; the young chiefs of the Miami will not remain silent after my parting. The English and the Americans are once again bent on war and our people will have to choose where to stand. Tecumseh will invite the English to our lands. The defeat of the Prophet at the Tippecanoe did nothing to curb Main Poc. Governor Clark of Louisiana is already at war with the Plains Pottawatomie and the Winnebago. How can the valley of the Mississinewa be spared? How can the waters of the Eel avoid carrying the blood of our people? I fear that the endeavors you and I have put forth for eternal peace will vanish into nothingness."

William seethed, "The Shawnee pretender should have been humiliated to return from his journey to the southern tribes with only twelve warriors in allegiance. Yet, he stood in this council of many nations on the Mississinewa, continuing his boasting and arrogance."

Little Turtle surmised, "I suggest that those twelve were given gold coins by the Spanish or the English to come to this land. I should think that they sleep lightly in their beds in these forests."

The two sat quietly, gazing at the tumbling waters of the Mississinewa.

Little Turtle was compelled to add, "Tecumseh boasts that the shaking earth heralds his ascension as leader of all tribes. What insolence! All tribes say that I am a great leader. The British and the Americans say so. Even General Washington paid me homage. Yet I cannot lift one rock shaken loose by the Creator. The Creator displays his power to humble us. This Tecumseh does not understand. A great leader must be both strong and humble."

"The dogwood and redbud are in bloom," William Wells observed. "Seventeen times they had blossomed in tranquility after the Fallen Timbers Battle until the defeat of the Prophet's allies at the Tippecanoe

Battle. Seventeen times they brought their beauty to the Miami people, seventeen years of prosperity. The British once again agitate the peace. I fear Harrison's army will not be the last to visit the Wabash. These blossoms herald troubled times."

"You have been instrumental in promoting the tranquility. I am beholden to you, as is our nation. If American or English armies come again to this land, I feel that our people will perish. The Miami nation will disintegrate. The young warriors and chiefs want to fight. They want to take back the lands that have been sold." Little Turtle nodded towards the river, "Yes, once this river flowed backward, but only for a brief moment. Then it rolled back upon itself and came crashing forward, sweeping away all that was in its path. To think that our people will return to what we once were is folly. I have done my best to hold back the onslaught, but we are close to being swept away."

Both knew the words to be true. However, they were hard to say, and hard to hear.

"My father," the younger offered, "when we return to our homes you should make your bed in my house. Polly and I can better care for you. Our home is comfortable, we have good food, our servants will see to your needs."

The old chief drew some puffs on his pipe. He knew that his body was failing him. The trips from Turtle Town to the fort had become torturous. Only pride had kept him residing on the banks of the Eel. But, now, it was time to let pride pass.

"Apple blossoms will soon be appearing," he said, as if to someone far away, "Blossoms always brought joy to Tulip Leaf. Perhaps I will build a wigwam in your orchard. It is what she would have wanted."

* * *

Morning thunderstorms full of wild lightning poured soaking rains. The festivities for Independence Day, 1812, at Fort Wayne were temporarily postponed. By noon, low dark clouds raced across the sky chased by a strong wind whipping from the southwest. Suddenly, it was clear and calm. Birds took up their songs. William Wells took Little Turtle by the arm and led him from the house down to their favorite spot. They sat down upon the little ledge of flat rocks and surveyed the sweeping curves of the St. Marys River. Instinctively they gauged the height and flow of the waters. The low sluggish current told them that the upper reaches had not seen rain for some time during this exceedingly hot summer. They surmised that Wayne's Trace, the supply road from Fort Recovery, must be dry.

Likely too, the Black Swamp should be low providing hard-packed paths for crossing. This should allow Michigan Governor Hull, now general of a two thousand man army, quick passage. The government was bolstering the frontier forts. Hull's expedition of men from Ohio, Kentucky, and Pennsylvania would see to it that Detroit was secure. That would serve to block any pretense of invasion from Canada.

Little Turtle stared deeply into the river. "What is it that makes a man a sagamore?" he quizzed.

Wells thought. Integrity, honesty, bravery? Spirituality, decisive action, leadership of men? No, these are characteristics of great chiefs. What is it that sets a sagamore apart?

"I have never felt worthy of the title," was William's only response.

Little Turtle instructed, "If a man looks upon the water he sees sunlight or clouds, perhaps trees or the image of a man or even an eagle, reflected on the surface. If he looks closely from the correct position, he can see the stones of the bottom, a leaf rolling submerged in the current, a fish or even a turtle. When a heron stands in still water, it appears to a man that the leg of the bird is not straight, but broken. But, when the heron flies away, the man sees that the leg is straight. He wonders how his vision can be wrong. The Great Spirit has given the sagamore the gift to see deeply into a man's soul. He understands things about a man that the man himself does not know. Another man will see only the reflection that the man portrays, but the sagamore is not deceived. The sagamore seeks out those whose souls are filled with goodness to aid him in his quest."

The elder sagamore pointed to the little stream to their right. The brook bordered the west side of William's farm. Now known as Spy Run, it gushed with the new-fallen rain.

Little Turtle said, "When the waters are disturbed it is more difficult to see beyond the surface. These are disturbing times." In a moment he added, "Chief Richardville has this gift. When I am gone, Richardville will prove himself. He should be appropriately honored. The shaking earth has signaled the end of my days."

The Chief of the Miami used his walking stick to raise himself from the rock-bench. He hobbled to a sugar maple growing at the water's edge. He picked up a little bark sugaring bucket left from the spring season. He dipped it in the river and returned to his seat. There he dabbed some water on his forehead and cheeks. He pulled out his knife and dribbled river water over it, letting it run to the point were tiny drops sparkled in the sunlight.

"Where did this drop originate?" Little Turtle quizzed once again.

"No one can tell. In one drop may be waters from the marshes that form the St. Marys, some from the many creeks that feed into the river, even from rain that fell today and filled Spy Run."

Little Turtle expounded, "At the Great Falls of the Niagara I once dipped my hand into the roaring waters and drank. The Creator sends his rains to the lands of the Sioux, the Winnebago and Menominee, the Pottawatomie and Chippewa and Ottawa, the Miami, the Shawnee, and the Wyandot. Those who speak English and those who speak French get the same rains. The rains of all of these lands were mixed in that handful, indistinguishable one from another. The Great Spirit showed me the roaring falls in a dream last night. He revealed his plan to me. One day all peoples will be mixed. The Great Spirit will pour out his tears upon them; they will live in harmony with each other. No one will have a complaint against another. All will rejoice in peace and friendship. I will not live to see that day; nor you. But, in our days we are to continue our efforts to increase the peace."

A red-tail hawk swooped in low from upstream. With a little splash it plucked a shiny fish and flew overhead. Across the way the fort band struck up their martial music.

"Wait here," Wells said, "I will bring the family. We will cross over and have a merry day!"

Upon reaching the fort gates, Wells and Little Turtle were whisked away to Captain Rhea's headquarters. There the officers were huddled in the office. The junior officers gave the guests a look of bewilderment. Rhea was highly animated. He leaned towards Wells with both fists pressing hard on the table.

Rhea shouted, "War, Captain, War! Your Miami friends had best stay in check!"

"What is this about?" Wells demanded.

Lieutenant Curtis explained, "Word just arrived from Hull. It seems our politicians in the east saw fit to declare war on the British on the eighteenth of the month past."

Little Turtle promptly left the room.

"Your fort is well stocked," Wells assessed, "and your supply lines are secure. There is a two thousand man army between you and Canada. Detroit and Defiance block the invasion route." He took up the cause of the officers in calming their panicking commander. "The war may never get this far."

"I am no fool!"Rhea shouted,"I know the British have been cultivating the tribes all around me! Will the Miami stay with us?"

"Little Turtle has been loyal ever since Greenville. He did nothing to oppose Harrison's invasion to the Tippecanoe. Now you have insulted him to his face questioning his devotion. You insulted the same man that was presented a sword by Washington, the man to whom Wayne handed his own banner. You best make it right!" Wells turned more to the other officers, some new to the region. "In their councils the Miami chiefs denounce those who would rise up in arms. However, they will defend their villages and fields from all trespassers. As for myself, I am at your service when called."

He departed to let the officers lay out their plans.

* * *

Three officers, and the two soldiers with them, were all a bit nervous. Their stuffy uniforms did nothing to ease their discomfort at the heat of the sticky morning air. It had been nearly two weeks since the huff at the fort on Independence Day. There had not been a sighting of Little Turtle or William Wells at the fort since that day. The officers knew that Wells and his wife were home, but were unsure of the whereabouts of the Chief of the Miami. Captain Rhea was coerced by his subordinates into visiting the Wells home. He would make a formal apology and ask for advice dealing with the local villages. They bore gifts of wine for the men and worked silver bracelets for the lady of the house.

A black man greeted them at the door,"May I ask who is calling?" "Captain James Rhea, commander of the garrison, Lieutenant Ostrander and Lieutenant Curtis."

"I will announce you." He did not invite them inside.

Wells appeared at the door,"Captain Rhea, gentlemen."

Rhea took the initiative,"Good day to you, sir. I have come to seek an audience with the Great Chief Little Turtle.

Wells said,"I am sorry to inform you that you are too late."

The officers exchanged glances. "Has he gone to the British?"

"He has gone to the Lord."

The astonished men quickly huddled. "I offer you and the family of Little Turtle the condolences of the United States Army and those of us gathered here. The news will be a great shock to the nation. I offer, if you will accept it, a military burial with the highest honors."

"You may step inside and view the body if you need confirmation."

"We will not disrupt your family. Be assured that my proposal is offered with only the highest intentions. Accept these gifts and we shall depart. Lieutenant Curtis will return shortly for your reply and to make arrangements."

"My answer is yes, your proposal is accepted. The lieutenant may stay. Your gifts are graciously received with thanks."

Rhea questioned, "Who is Chief of the Miami now?"

"I have sent for my father, Porcupine of Eel Town. He is the eldest chief."

"Then I invite Chief Porcupine to counsel me after the burial."

"No," Wells explained. "His powers will be only to preside at council to oversee the election of the new chief. It may take a month, perhaps two. There will be pilgrims to the great chief's grave and a proper time of mourning. I think one month."

"Again, my condolences to you and yours. We will have a cannon salute at noon."

* * *

"Depart. I will speak with this man in private," Five Medals ordered.

The head of the guard protested, "We should stay. It is our duty to protect you from one such as this."

"Depart!" the chief of the Elk Heart lands repeated.

"Send his knives with us."

Five Medals stared at his protector. He said once again, more firmly, "Depart!"

The three warriors finally did depart.

"You ask what I know," the chief opened. "I know that many of my old friends have deceived me. Those who continue to be loyal find it difficult to remain neutral. Tell me what you have heard."

"The Council of Kekionga continues. Richardville will prevail, though the Owl and others use the opportunity to voice their desires. The council of the Miami will continue to declare for peace," William Wells reported. He turned to what brought him to the Elk Heart village,

"I have heard that Main Poc has gone to Detroit with three hundred war- riors to join the British. Tecumseh with forty warriors has passed through with the same destination. Others flock to the British call. It is said that the American General Hull has squandered his advantage; he is now surrounded. It is said that the American Fort Mackinac has been taken by the Chippewa and is now under British control. Many of that tribe are descending upon Detroit."

"All of this is true. Some warriors have departed from our villages to head for Detroit. It is beyond the power of our chiefs to hold them. It has always been the way of the Pottawatomie that a man should prove himself in battle. Our young warriors have been denied this tradition. They seize the opportunity to demonstrate their bravery. Some have gone to the Chicago River where a camp is established near the American fort at that place."

"From here I go to Fort Dearborn on the Chicago. My brother Samuel, who lives at the Falls of the Ohio, sent an express dispatch to me. He urges me to bring his daughter, my niece Rebecca, from Fort Dearborn to Fort Wayne and send her on to his home. She is the wife of Captain Heald who commands Dearborn. This is why I have come this way with ten Miami warriors and the lone officer of the soldiers. I ask your permission to pass through in peace. I ask you to send an emissary with me to Chief Topenebee and Chief Black Partridge requesting pas- sage and return."

"It is not easy, my friend, to say, 'Yes, you may pass.' To remain neu- tral one must walk a narrow and straight path." The Pottawatomie chief then spoke of his fellow loyal chiefs, "I tell you in confidence, Topenebee has gone to join the village of Black Partridge on the Chicago River. My friends will moderate those who are agitated."

"That is not all," Wells confessed, "when these ten Miami had gath- ered and I had secured the needed provisions, we were assembled at my home. I again was called to the fort due to a second dispatch. It came from the American General Hull. Fort Mackinac being held by the British severs support by ship to Fort Dearborn. Captain Rhea had received orders to be delivered to Captain Heald at Fort Dearborn. I tell you this for your ears only to hear. Hull instructs Heald to abandon Fort Dearborn. He is to carry only enough provisions from that fort to make a journey to Fort Wayne. The remainder of the fort possessions will be given to the local chiefs."

Five Medals simply nodded. He had known for many days about the capture of Fort Mackinac. The Chippewa spread the news rapidly across the land. Many of those warriors were now at Detroit, some were headed to the Chicago. He was aware that the Americans could not sustain Fort Dearborn with the shipping lane severed.

Wells continued, "I am sent to aid the removal of the garrison and their families, plus any citizens who wish to depart. I sent out a call for forty more Miami warriors to meet me here. I shall wait for them before continuing."

Wells thought to display the orders carried by Corporal Jordan, but chose not to do so.

Five Medals gave his considered response, "It is bad for me to have you stay within my village. It is also bad for your mission to delay going to the Chicago. I learn daily of more chiefs and warriors gathering near the fort. Menominee, Winnebago, prairie Pottawatomie, and Chippewa speak harsh words in council against the presence of the Americans. Black Partridge wishes the Americans to stay, as does Topenebee. The fort encourages traders. The trader Kinzie brings good wares. The villages are not required to carry their pelts to Detroit. I, too, wish the fort to stay."

Wells was aware that Kinzie was always on good terms with the local villages. From his post across the river to the north of Fort Dearborn, he would be a stabilizing influence. However, Five Medals' words and tone made William Wells uneasy. It sounded as if the immediate future of the fort was uncertain.

The chief continued, "You may stay here one night. Tomorrow you will leave. If the forty Miami arrive to travel with you, so be it. If they do not, so be it." He rose and headed for the opening, "Let us walk beside the river. We will speak of our friendship. We will speak of the deeds of Little Turtle."

During the walk, Five Medals confided, "I wish to remain your true friend. But, you must understand, General Wayne is long gone. The Americans forget our treaty with him which we continue to uphold. By the Treaty of Greenville, the Americans are to control the traders. You know that they have not done this. Whiskey ruins our people, young and old, men and women. The Americans promised to help us establish good farms. What farms do you see in my village? The Americans promised to keep their settlers from our lands. Although we sell more lands to Harrison, it is not enough for the settlers. They move across the boundaries marked on Harrison's maps. He does not send his soldiers to punish them, but to punish the tribes that have always resided on the grounds that have not been sold. How many seasons can I continue to honor a treaty that is ignored by the president?"

* * *

Black Partridge did not want war. However, his council house on the banks of the Chicago River held many who did. The American fort had been built nine years ago by Captain John Whistler. Whistler had encouraged the trade that Black Partridge conducted between the lake Peoria and the grand lake Michigan. Relations were not as cordial upon the arrival of the new fort commandant. Captain Heald displayed little understanding of the ways of the tribes.

The trade argument did not sway Blackbird who was heading the war faction. Chief Blackbird conducted his own trade farther north along the great lake. Even the brother of Black Partridge, Waubonsee of the Fox River, urged an attack on the fort. Chief Waubonsee's bitterness had not waned since Harrison's attack on Prophet's Town.

Metea intently followed the events, watching and listening to see which way the reed would sway in the wind. He too wished the tribes to avenge the defeat. But, he had seen lack of cooperation among chiefs lead to confusion and eventual humiliation.

Each day, more hostile warriors arrived; each night, more hostile chiefs sat at the council.

Four cannon on the fort walls were most persuasive. The fort was well stocked. Metea, in the company of Black Partridge, saw with his own eyes the guns and powder, the rations and salt. There were enough provisions to withstand a six-month siege. Local citizens huddled inside the fort may deplete the rations more quickly, but, he knew siege was not the Pottawatomie way.

Black Partridge let each of the chiefs have their say. Then he rose to deliver his surprise, "Some gathered here in my lodge speak of attacking the fort. Some speak of continued relations with the soldiers and the traders. I have news that should satisfy all. Captain Heald called me to visit with him this day. Chief Topenebee can verify what I have to say. Captain Heald received orders from General Hull at Detroit. These orders were brought to this place by Winamac, who is known to scout for the Americans. The orders say this to Captain Heald. He is to abandon his fort. He is to take his men and what he can carry to Fort Wayne. All of his provisions that he cannot carry, he is to distribute to us. These are his orders."

Pandemonium interrupted the protocol of the longhouse. Black Partridge let the hubbub die out, then spoke in a loud voice, "Tomorrow I will carry our response. We are to promise to escort the soldiers and the citizens who wish to depart to Fort Wayne. At that place we will be paid in silver for their safe conduct." He looked around at the approving nods. "In two days at the high sun, soldiers will fire a cannon. It will be a signal for all to assemble at the gates for the distribution. Those of us assembled here must decide this night how the materials will be divided."

"How do we know the truth of the message carried by Winamac?" Metea demanded.

The host responded, "The trader Kinzie attested to it. Those among us who know Kinzie know that he is a truthful man."

A Chippewa chief protested, "Kinzie plays his own game. He sides with the Americans or the English, which ever proves best for him. He feigns loyalty to the tribes to promote his trade."

Another proposed, "The chiefs can each take enough men and women to carry the materials. We will keep the remainder of our warriors beyond their sight so that they will not learn our strength."

Each chief stated his case for a share of the spoils.

* * *

An entourage of four moderate chiefs accompanied Black Partridge to the fort gates where they were met by Heald and Kinzie. Metea noticed that Kinzie was subdued in manner, not his usual self. He heard the head chief assure the trader and the captain that their families would be safe from harm. Soon, with Kinzie translating, the arrangements for distributing the fort equipment and supplies were made.

The chiefs were about to return to their camp when a shout came from a sentinel on the fort wall. Soldiers gathered. They were looking far south along the sweeping curve of the beach.

A man with a spyglass called out, "Fifty Indians headed this way!"

Captain Heald looked at the chiefs. The chiefs looked at one another. Metea had seen groups of warriors arriving each day. However, they never approached in the open in this manner, and there had not been fifty mounted riders at once.

Metea suggested to Topenebee, "Chippewa from Mackinac."

Kinzie requested that the chiefs stay close until the question of the approaching squad was answered.

Topenebee and Metea said it simultaneously, "Miami!" The markings on the nearly naked bodies were now evident.

"One soldier with them," the sentinel called below.

"Who is the chief?" Kinzie asked.

All stood watching, waiting. No chief could be distinguished.

Finally Metea recognized one of the men in front, "Wild Carrot leads them!"

Kinzie translated, "The one they call Wild Carrot. William Wells, the agent at Fort Wayne. He is the confidant of Little Turtle; I mean, was."

"I know Wells," Heald was irritated at being instructed by Kinzie. "My wife Rebecca is his niece."

Kinzie looked at Heald in wonderment. How could this be? Is the captain daft? Yet, he recalled, the captain had previously headed Fort Wayne.

The riders came square to the gate, stopping at thirty yards. The accompanying officer dismounted and hurried up to the Captain.

After saluting, he introduced himself, "Corporal Walter Jordan of Fort Wayne, I am a courier from Captain Rhea. I have a dispatch of utmost urgency from General Hull!"

He reached inside his shirt and pulled the paper from under his belt. Upon receiving the document, Heald inspected the seal. All was as it should be.

Heald walked inside the gate. In the tunnel of the guard house he opened the letter. Upon concluding the reading, he tapped it with the fingers of his left hand and waved it around.

Wells took the opportunity to greet Chief Black Partridge. He presented the chief with a gift of a knife sheath that Little Turtle had worn at the Greenville signing. He was greeting the other chiefs when Heald called him inside along with Kinzie and Jordan.

"The orders are a duplicate. Sorry, Captain Wells, but the orders are the same as I received by way of Winamac directly from Detroit. The vacating process is already begun. Tomorrow we distribute our materials to the chiefs in the neighborhood. We depart the morning after."

"Well then, Nathan," William used the familiar term rather than the military title, "direct me to my favorite niece. Her smile will be worth the trip."

* * *

Metea's band of eighteen warriors danced around their pile of booty. Most was useful, some they took simply because it was there to take. Part of the fun was watching the sour faces of the soldiers carrying stack upon stack of goods out the gates. Inside they could see the frenzy as some soldiers stacked stores while others packed for the evacuation. The Pottawatomie warriors kicked in the sand like children in a chase game. Tiosa lugged the final treasure, an unused saddle. They loaded their three packhorses, yet half the pile remained. The loaded merchandise was hauled to camp while Tiosa and Aubbeenaubbee stood guard over the remainder. The second trip was accomplished after a number of items were discarded as too cumbersome to take to camp, let alone to take home.

Late in the day, Metea stood in the midst of all the chiefs beside the gate. They silently waited there for a time.

Finally an ensign, accompanied by three soldiers, came out, "That is it. Be gone. There is no more. What little is left you can pick through when we are gone."

The ensign turned in a huff and left. The soldiers closed the gates. Conspicuously absent from the distribution were the many rifles and muskets known to be in the arsenal. Metea had seen no powder, no flints, no lead. The prized stores of whiskey were absent. The chiefs waited a little longer, then left single-file for the longhouse.

"Captain Heald mocks us by saying that he gives to us all that he does not need for his journey." "We gave our pledge for safe passage for his word of a full portion." "Outside his walls he lies and inside his walls he is deceitful." No chief was compelled to defend the actions of the commandant of the garrison. Metea thought of several explanations for the transgression, but remained silent.

Finally Topenebee offered, "It may yet be that the man is truthful. It may be that the soldiers will leave the guns and the whiskey in the fort as they depart. Can we not understand their fear? Our warriors with an abundance of whiskey along with guns and ammunition could cause great mischief. The Americans are correct to fear the waywardness of five hundred warriors." He looked around the lodge at the angry faces. "I will go to the fort. I will seek Kinzie, or if not him, Wild Carrot. I will ask if this is not the contention of Heald."

Blackbird arose, "They must allow our appointed guards to enter when the gates are opened. Our guards will inspect the stores. When they find that the promised materials are in place, it will be as you have spoken. The armistice will remain in effect." The war chief from the north placed a log on the fire. "Return with their reply before this log becomes ashes."

Topenebee approached the fort as he had many times past. In the darkness he could hear a commotion inside the walls. Beyond he could hear the calming swoosh of waves rushing upon the sands, wave upon wave. Oftentimes he had camped on the eastern shore of this lake at the mouth of the river St. Josephs. Three days camped on the shore would clear his troubled mind. But here, matters had only gotten worse. The waves seemed to bring turmoil instead of release.

As the chief neared the fort, he was startled by a voice behind him, "Topenebee! Wait!"

Metea had followed him, "Wait! You cannot walk directly to the fort this night. The sentries will be nervous. You may be shot. A battle would erupt here and now."

"You are correct. My thoughts were of another place. Do you have a truce flag?"

"No, but I will call to them. My English is better." Metea hailed, "Ahoy, the fort!"

"Stay back," a voice replied, "the gates are closed."

"I seek Kinzie for parley."

"The gates are closed. No one will come out."

"I seek the agent Wells."

"They are with the Captain. I have orders. Leave or I will fire."

"We must go," Metea told his comrade, "They will not parley tonight."

The pair retreated a few steps. Topenebee whispered, "I will creep near to the walls to discern their actions."

"I too will go."

Neither man wanted to return to the council without a report. Their stealthy mission did give them a report, but not what they wished. They heard the sound of busting of barrel tops. They smelled the odor of whiskey. The taste of the river waters turned to that of grog. They heard crashing of metal. Finally the smell of gunpowder permeated the river.

Metea placed his hand on the back of his fellow spy, "We have witnessed enough."

Topenebee nodded in agreement. He removed his silver medal presented by Wayne. This he hung on the side of the sally port. He motioned to his friend to head upstream.

* * *

Captain Heald walked the fort end to end and side to side. All was in order. He wrote in the fort log book, "August 15, 1812, Fort Dearborn vacated. March commenced at 9 AM." He signed his name to mark the occasion. He walked to the first of the three wagons. He handed the book to a private whose duty was to oversee the wagon's progress. He swallowed hard, then shouted the order, "Sergeant, strike the colors. Put the flag in this wagon!"

The commander strode to his wife. He reached up and held her hand for a moment. A magnificent sight she was, erect and fearless on her superb steed. He inspected his weapons and mounted his own Kentucky horse.

"Open the gates!" he ordered. "Lead on, Captain Wells."

Two days and two nights without sleep left Metea fighting to keep his senses. When the soldiers' drums beat the order and the gates of the fort opened, he was suddenly keen to the moment. He exchanged glances with his eight warriors who, along with himself, had been instructed on their assignment. They were to be the last of the Pottawatomie escort for the caravan. The Americans would follow the meander of the river to the beach. They would follow the lakeshore southward on the smooth wet hard-packed sand. The Pottawatomie escort would parallel their line through low dunes. Once across Calumet Creek, Metea's band would be relieved for the night.

Metea shielded his eyes from the bright morning sun to witness the procession. Through the open outer stockade gate he could see into the main gate tunnel that passed through the guardhouse. Two mounted officers emerged. Sunlight glistened on the buttons and medallions and swords of Captain Heald and Lieutenant Helm. The two were soon joined by a Miami warrior. It was Wild Carrot. His bare chest was painted in red and black diagonal stripes. His red hair was now blackened with soot and grease. His face, too, was completely black, the mask of a man who was prepared for death. He passed by near to Metea, but did not look to the side. In addition to his knives and tomahawk, he rode with a sleek rifle laid across his saddle. In front of the saddle was a pair of pistols in a dragoon-style holster.

Wells trotted ahead and was immediately joined by half of the painted Miami warriors. Behind them the two senior officers led forty-two uniformed troops. Next were three wagons, each with a soldier driver and an outrider. Atop the canvas-covered baggage of the first wagon were six infirmed soldiers. The second similarly carried lame and elderly civilians. In the third were twelve children. The civilians walked and rode in a mass behind the wagons followed by twelve men of the Chicago Militia. Metea nudged his horse into the long line of eighty fellow Pottawatomie that moved slowly in single file at a distance to the right. The remainder of the Miami trailed the rear.

Metea called across to the Miami in their own tongue, "My horse does not know how to move this slowly." His gesture was ignored.

The slow steady sway of the horse rocked Metea between the hot sun and the baking sand. The waves were silent today in the still air; no cooling breeze was to be found. Sunlight danced in patches over the water. The slightly curved line of the horizon made a sharp distinction between the bluish green waters and the azure sky. The sight always filled Metea's head with wonder. The long smooth curve of the lake shore continued unchanged as they moved forward.

Metea was contemplating a way to make a request of Black Partridge. He wished he and his men to be assigned to the escort all the way to Fort Wayne. Perhaps on the trail he and his old friend could reconcile their differences. He felt a poking in his ribs, the warrior Tiosa had jabbed him with the butt of his spear. "My chief, do not slumber. Look!"

The Miami warriors that had been behind them were prancing ahead on the left of the column. The hooves of their hoses were kicking up high splashes of water. Metea looked back to the fort, now a mere speck in the distance. The wagons stopped and the militia formed beside the civilians. Something was happening. Metea could not comprehend it.

Tiosa again spoke, "Ahead! Look! Blackbird leads our warriors."

A long narrow dune had split off the Pottawatomie escort from the military column. Metea's band was at the foot of the slope, only partially separated from the Americans. Hundreds of warriors were pouring into a miniature valley from the west.

Metea signaled his men to nudge into a cluster of small cottonwoods halfway up the dune. They concealed themselves while observing the developments. "We will hold fast here." He and his companions watched events quickly spiral out of control.

Along the shore, Wild Carrot came galloping back along the line, shouting. The soldiers formed a battle-line. The Miami, now in one group, continued to trot ahead, distancing themselves from the soldiers. The soldiers ran up the soft sands of the dune and took position on top. Blackbird's warriors had not yet taken their positions and were caught in the trough below. They began searching for cover as they fired haphazardly at the soldiers' position.

Metea yelled to his followers, "I was never told about this treachery! I will take no part in it!"

An effective volley from the soldiers drove the warriors back. The skirmish developed into a general engagement. Metea thought to block the militia from entering his end of the valley opening. He looked back to see that several warriors were already engaging the militia. Women were crouching behind scattering wagons. More warriors rushed past him and ahead to capture the soldiers' horses. Soon the entire scene was pandemonium with gunfire, shouting, and screaming.

The soldiers were in a hopeless position. Metea turned his attention to the rear. The militia had been riddled. Women and men of the Chicago settlement were being taken captive. Some were tomahawked and scalped. A chief was dragging a woman into the lake. Near the wagons, a warrior had the reins of Rebecca Heald's horse, apparently prizing the fine animal as a trophy more than he did her. She was whipping her attacker and shouting in broken Pottawatomie.

To his horror, Metea saw two young warriors climb aboard the wagon of panic-stricken children. They began hacking at the children, taking easy scalps for British payment. Metea immediately broke from the cover of the scrub trees and spurred his horse towards the wagon. Wild Carrot came galloping along beside him, apparently with the same intent, or perhaps heading to the rescue of Mrs. Heald. The two seasoned warriors briefly glanced at each other and urged their mounts ahead at full speed.

Metea lunged into the wagon where he quickly grabbed the nearest attacker of the children. He lifted the man and was about to throw him over when he saw a war club swinging directly at his own face. He deflected the blow with his elbow. A powerful force swept him into the air and over the side. His right foot became entangled in the ropes that secured the canvas. His body swung down sharply. His head banged against the wooden spokes of the wagon wheel. Dangling in this position, he viewed the world upside down through hazed vision.

Before him, Metea saw Wild Carrot twisting in the sands. The sagamore's crushed leg and hip were trapped solidly beneath his dead horse. The arm of his good hand was broken, leaving only his withered hand to aid himself. His weapons were all beyond reach. A circle of five Pottawatomie descended upon the one they knew as Wild Carrot, war chief of the Miami, Sagamore of the Wabash tribes, spy for the American Army, Indian Agent. Seeing his helplessness, they mocked and cursed him. They bragged upon the horrors that they had in store for him.

Metea fought to maintain consciousness. He twisted and turned to free himself. If only he could right himself, he would rescue the noble man. Yes, he had chosen to follow the Prophet and Tecumseh. Yet, he continued to admire Wild Carrot as a person and a leader.

A young blood-spattered chief hunched over Wild Carrot and declared, "Keep him for the fire post!"

Wild Carrot's mind flashed the sensation of roasting flesh. He spat on the bare foot of this assailant, "Not you! I know your kind. You are a woman!"

Rebecca Heald shouted, "No, Uncle William, take it back!"

In instant rage, the accused ran a knife through Wild Carrot's throat. A second man severed his head. Another hacked at his ribs. He pulled out the pulsing heart of the famed warrior and held it high. He sunk his teeth into the mass and tore off a bite.

"I eat of Wild Carrot's heart! I consume his bravery!"

The trophy was passed around the circle for each man to partake. The detached head was thrust on a spear driven into the ground to create a gruesome totem. Soon a multitude of warriors had joined the celebration.

Metea cried out, "I wanted to be your brother!"

* * *

Once more an army was forming in Cincinnati. William Henry Harrison was mustering troops for the relief of Detroit. Yet again Major Samuel Wells answered the call by leading the Louisville volunteers to the Newport landing. It was during the crossing of the Ohio River that he learned that Hull had surrendered Detroit to the British. Fort Dearborn had fallen to the Indians the day prior. Two forts lost in two days. Horrible stories circulated about the Fort Dearborn Massacre on the shores of Lake Michigan. The tale of the death of William Wells was told and retold. All were certain that Heald and his wife were dead.

News circulated that Fort Wayne was surrounded by hostiles. The tribes had also set siege to Fort Harrison on the Wabash above Vincennes. Captain Zachary Taylor was in command at Fort Harrison. Samuel knew Taylor well. As a lad, Taylor had worked summers on his farm making hay. He had confidence that Taylor was the man to best defend the post.

A family friend volunteered to carry the terrible news back to Wellsmont. Samuel would press on to join General Harrison's movement in the immediate relief of Fort Wayne, then on to Detroit. He hoped that it was not too late to rescue Polly. After all, it was he who had encouraged her courtship of his brother William.

CHAPTER TWENTY-FOUR

EPILOGUE

Samuel Wells, now a colonel in the United States Army, motioned to Captain Frederick Geiger. He pointed to a column of dark smoke ahead to the right. His advance column had been pressing hard since leaving Fort Greenville. They were now within a mile of Fort Wayne. What would they find? So far, the war had produced only bad news. The smoke did not promise cheer. He halted his riders for a weapons check and a brief respite. They were soon again moving, approaching the fort directly from the south.

They were surprised to find the fort intact with the American banner hanging limply on its post. The smoke proved to be from two outbuildings. The relief of the post was successful. They learned that the enemy had slipped away only hours before their arrival. A pregnant Polly Geiger Wells proudly greeted her father and brother-in-law. She and the other civilians had sought refuge within the fort walls at the earliest news of Detroit's surrender. Her home and farm buildings had been destroyed, but she and her toddling son had remained unharmed.

General William Henry Harrison and the full army arrived by evening. Having learned of Zachary Taylor's successful defense of Fort Harrison, the general was anxious to move down the Maumee to begin the task of recovering Detroit. But first, he needed to suppress any resistance in the immediate area. On the third day, he sent Colonel Wells on a punitive excursion to the north. Wells's men, including two of his sons, forded the Eel River at the site of Little Turtle's victory over Hardin. Orders were to destroy the Elk Heart villages. The warriors of Five Medals were not to be found, but the villages and crops were laid waste.

Before Wells's return from the north, Harrison sent out another foray. Colonel James Simrall's Kentucky mounted volunteers were directed against Turtle Town. Simrall found no resistance as he traversed the Eel River portage. He crossed the field of LaBalme's defeat to his destination. Here, too, the empty town was burned, crops were trampled, and stores were confiscated. Only the former residence of Little Turtle, built at government expense as directed by Governor Harrison, was spared.

Scouts reported to Simrall that they had discovered the trail of a retreating Miami band. He gave chase down the south bank of the Eel. At noon of the second day, they encountered a rear guard of the fleeing refugees determined to make a stand at the river crossing.   On September 21, 1812, Chief Black Loon, brother of Sweet Breeze, son of Little Turtle, laid down his life, along with those of over thirty of his comrades, in defense of his people. His blood mingled with the waters at the last clash of arms on the Eel River.

Harrison's dash to Detroit bogged down once beyond Fort Defiance. The hurried advance from Cincinnati had not allowed for proper organization of the army and the several militia units from Kentucky, Ohio, and Pennsylvania. What ammunition and supplies that were available had to be forwarded through the Black Swamp to positions reaching from Defiance to Sandusky. October turned to November with only sluggish movement.

* * *

It was November 16, 1813 that the citizens of Louisville witnessed the miraculous arrival of Captain Nathan Heald and his bride. Stories of their brutal deaths at the Fort Dearborn Massacre proved to be unfounded. They each had been badly wounded and captured by the assailants. With the help of Kinzie and the Pottawatomie chief Black Partridge, they were ransomed and smuggled the length of Lake Michigan to Fort Mackinac. Upon surrendering to the British at that post, they were transferred by ship to Detroit, and on to Erie where they were pardoned. Making their way to Pittsburgh, they gained passage down the Ohio River.

* * *

Bitterly cold air had lengthened the time of Blind Man's journey. Frigid weather gave him cause for concern for his grandson. The two had set out from Mississinewa Town at the juncture of that river with the Wabash. Chief Richardville had directed the Miami people to seek refuge along the Mississinewa for the duration of the war. Blind Man was taking fresh buffalo robes up the river to his two sons stationed with the rear guard. He expected to find them at the village of Chief Silver Heels. After a two-day journey traipsing through deep snow, he was told at that place that his sons were farther up the river at a cluster of Miami and Delaware camps. Others had offered to advance his pack when the weather broke, but he declined.

Leaving before daybreak they set out on the trail along the west bank. The rising sun brought no warmth. He found the snows growing deeper and the air growing colder.

"Grandfather, the trail descends the bluff here and crosses to the east bank. The river appears to be frozen solid. The bank is steep, perhaps we should slide down."

Blind Man cautioned, "Wait! I think that we should go back. Our skin is going to freeze."

"It cannot be far to the camps. I can smell the fires."

It was then that the youth detected strange movements in the forest beyond the far bank. A herd of elk? Buffalo?

He pulled Blind Man down behind the thickets, "Down. I see something."

Blind Man heard the clank of steel. The younger Miami saw an apparition appear not more than an arrow flight before him. He crouched lower and watched. In an instant there were ten mounted soldiers beside the first. All were peering in their direction.

"Soldiers," he stammered.

"I know," Blind Man replied, "remain still; remain quiet."

One of the soldiers raised a rifle and sighted at the dark lump in the snow. A commotion upriver drew his attention. Families from the camps on the east bank were streaming onto the ice, scampering for the opposite shore. The soldier turned his gun to his left and fired. The soldiers, now numbering nearly fifty, bolted towards the fleeing refugees.

Blind Man dropped his pack, "Quickly, back to the village!"

"No! We must help them!"

"Our duty is to raise the alarm. There are many warriors in the village. Chief Silver Heels and the son of Richardville can do more to help these people than can we. They will block the soldiers from coming farther down the river to the larger villages. We must get back to the village before the soldiers can turn that way. The warriors are not expecting an attack in this season. Now, lead the way!"

Chief Joseph Richardville directed half of his four hundred warriors to block the Mississinewa route. With the other half he attacked the camp of six hundred Americans at the next dawn. The Miami gave the Americans a hot engagement, then withdrew to the north.

Colonel Simrall gave his report to Colonel John Campbell, commander of the expedition from Fort Greenville. Eight soldiers were dead and nearly fifty wounded, six of those near death. The surgeon reported over three hundred were suffering from frostbite. Rations were low and much of the ammunition was damaged. They held seventy-six prisoners. He recommended an immediate return to Greenville. Though still some distance from the primary objective of Mississinewa Town, Campbell decided that he had met the essential part of his mission as directed by Harrison. The Miami would of necessity concentrate their forces to defend their population; they could not mount any offensive actions. With captives, four "enemy villages" plundered, and two-dozen warriors killed, he would return and report a great victory to General Harrison.

Seeing the Americans retreat was cause for great joy among the Miami warriors. With inferior numbers and weapons they had turned back a fully-mounted invasion force. Their stores of food for the winter remained intact. Though captives were lost and warriors had died, only four remote camps had suffered from a major campaign by the invaders. Thus ended the Battle of the Mississinewa on December 18, 1812. In the last armed resistance of the Miami nation, both sides were victorious.

* * *

Struggling through the winter, Harrison decided to build Fort Meigs on the south bank of the Maumee. Samuel Wells manned the defenses overlooking the ground where he and his militia had destroyed McKee's post during Wayne's campaign. Throughout the remainder of the winter, and well into spring, the new fort was bombarded by the British and harassed by warriors from several tribes directed by Tecumseh.

It was not until Commodore Perry struck a decisive defeat upon the British fleet on Lake Erie that the American army was able to make any significant progress. For the first time the advantage of armed ships and swift movement of troops and materials was denied the British. They quickly abandoned Detroit and retreated overland towards Lake Ontario. Colonel Samuel Wells accompanied General Harrison on the first ship to ferry American troops to Canada. They pressed hard upon the retreating British and, on October 5, 1813, soundly defeated them at the Battle of the Thames. Tecumseh's death in that battle punctuated the end of British influence in the former Northwest Territory of the United States of America.

The war in the east reached the nation's capitol. The British burned government buildings, including the White House. Dolly Madison hurriedly evacuated with treasured items, including a Gilbert Stuart portrait of George Washington. The portraits of Little Turtle and William Wells succumbed to pillaging and burning.

Samuel Wells remained in Detroit until resigning his commission in the spring of 1814. He returned to Wellsmont to organize anew his estate. Overseeing the education of his children and the children of the departed Sweet Breeze and William was paramount. Louisville was no longer the frontier, at least in his mind. Within three years, he loaded the entire clan onto flatboats and headed for St. Charles on the Missouri. The grown children of Sweet Breeze and William Wells all eventually settled on the banks of the Maumee. Their devotion to the remembrance of their parents would not fade away.

THE END

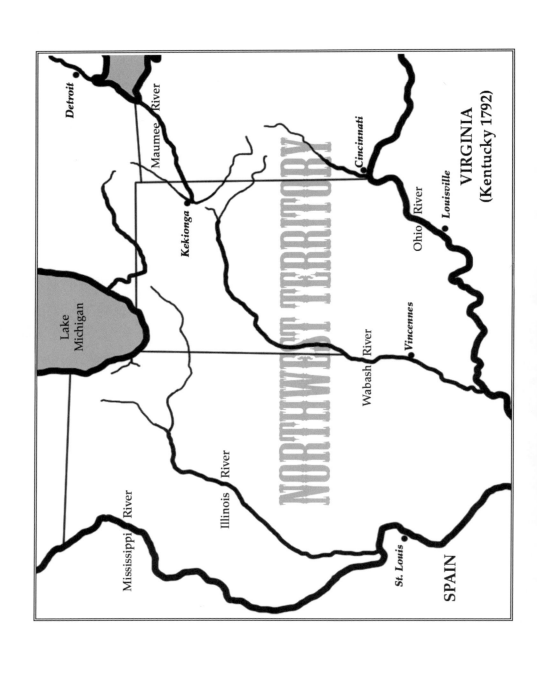

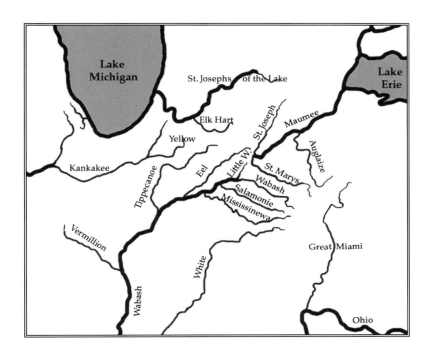

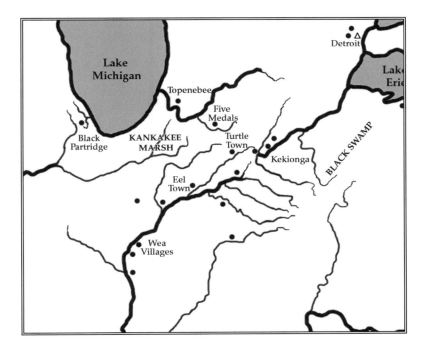

ACKNOWLEDGMENTS

My research for this book was enhanced immensely by persons staffing many libraries, historical society buildings, and museums. The courteous services they rendered are greatly appreciated. I benefited from their eagerness for sharing resources and personal knowledge. I encourage the reader to visit a local institution and delve into some research of personal interest.

I am grateful to my wife, Anita, for her devoted support in this endeavor. She traveled the highways and byways with me poking into tidbits of history. She kept notes and searched library racks. She read and reread my developing manuscript.

Nikki Fish, my daughter, worked with me during the developmental stages of the storyline. She offered encouragement and direction as she provided the reader's viewpoint.

April Paffrath and Doris Carpenter gave insights into writing style. They provided helpful coaching on readability. I am indebted to Dan Snider, John Krom, and Patricia Conrad for reading an early draft. Their comments led to greater clarity in later drafts.

Ryan Fish created the cover design, cover art, and maps. He served as technical advisor for text layout.

Finally, I wish to thank all the friends who directed me towards resources, loaned books, or provided overall support.

For additional information on this book browse to:

www.eelrivertraders.com

or e-mail to:

info@eelrivertraders.com